POSTCARDS FROM

Frommer's

Rome 2002

W9-BSK-947

The Vatican Museums are a giant repository of artistic treasures from antiquity and the Renaissance. See chapter 7. © Roberto Soncin Gerometta / Photo 20-20.

Vatican City is the world's second-smallest independent state. Here you can see its center-piece, St. Peter's Basilica, with Bernini's glorious St. Peter's Square stretching beyond. See chapter 7. © Guido Rossi / The Image Bank.

To enter the Vatican Museums, you ascend this impressive spiral ramp built in 1932 by Guiseppe Momo. See chapter 7. © Robert Frerck / Odyssey / Chicago.

On the Sistine Chapel's ceiling, Michelangelo frescoed nine main panels with scenes from Genesis and surrounded them with prophets and sibyls. The most famous panel is the Creation of Adam, in which God's outstretched hand imbues Adam with spirit. See chapter 7. © Marvin E. Newman / The Image Bank.

Though it's a mere shell, the Colosseum is the greatest legacy of ancient Rome. Titus inaugurated it in A.D. 80 with weeks of combat between gladiators and beasts. Centuries later, it was used as a quarry. See chapter 7. © Guido Rossi / The Image Bank.

The Colosseum could seat some 50,000 Romans for its bloody spectacles (it could even stage mock naval battles when it was flooded). On one side, part of the original four tiers remains; the first three levels were constructed in Doric, Ionic, and Corinthian styles to lend variety. See chapter 7. © Dave G. Houser / Houserstock, Inc.

The sculptures and paintings of the Capitoline Museum are housed in two Michelangelo palaces: the Palazza Nuovo and the Palazza dei Conservatori. The latter's courtyard contains fragments (the head, hands, a foot, and a kneecap) of an ancient colossal statue of Constantine the Great. See chapter 7. © Dave Bartruff Photography.

Browsing through Rome's food, flower, and flea markets is a great way to sample a slice of local life. See chapter 9 for our favorite markets and shopping finds.
© Kindra Clineff Photography.

Of all ancient Rome's great buildings, only the Pantheon remains intact. It stands on Piazza della Rotunda, which buzzes in the evening with a lively cafe and nightlife scene. See chapter 7. © John Lawrence / Tony Stone Images.

Michelangelo studied the Pantheon's dome before designing his masterpiece at St. Peter's. Raphael and monarchs Vittorio Emanuele II and Umberto I are interred here. See chapter 7. © RAGA / The Stock Market.

The Forum was the cradle of the Roman Republic and the epicenter of the ancient world. It takes a healthy imagination to turn what are now dusty chunks of stone, crumbling arches, and columns into the glory of ancient Rome, but this archeological zone is fun to explore anyway. See chapter 8 for a detailed walking tour. © RAGA / The Stock Market.

At Tivoli, 20 miles east of Rome, you'll find the ruins of Hadrian's Villa. He spent the last 3 years of his life in grand style here, enjoying acres of palaces, temples, gardens, and theaters built for a vast royal entourage. See chapter 11. © Sheila McKinnon / Houserstock, Inc.

When should I travel to get the best airfare?
Where do I go for answers to my travel questions?
What's the best and easiest way to plan and book my trip?

frommers.travelocity.com

Frommer's, the travel guide leader, has teamed up with **Travelocity.com**, the leader in online travel, to bring you an in-depth, easy-to-use resource designed to help you plan and book your trip online.

At **frommers.travelocity.com**, you'll find free online updates about your destination from the experts at Frommer's plus the outstanding travel planning and purchasing features of Travelocity.com. Travelocity.com provides reservations capabilities for 95 percent of all airline seats sold, more than 47,000 hotels, and over 50 car rental companies. In addition, Travelocity.com offers more than 2,000 exciting vacation and cruise packages. Travelocity.com puts you in complete control of your travel planning with these and other great features:

> **Expert travel guidance from Frommer's** - over 150 writers reporting from around the world!

> **Best Fare Finder** - an interactive calendar tells you when to travel to get the best airfare

> **Fare Watcher** - we'll track airfare changes to your favorite destinations

> **Dream Maps** - a mapping feature that suggests travel opportunities based on your budget

> **Shop Safe Guarantee** - 24 hours a day / 7 days a week live customer service, and more!

Whether traveling on a tight budget, looking for a quick weekend getaway, or planning the trip of a lifetime, Frommer's guides and Travelocity.com will make your travel dreams a reality. You've bought the book, now book the trip!

A New Star-Rating System & Other Exciting News from Frommer's!

In our continuing effort to publish the savviest, most up-to-date, and most appealing travel guides available, we've added some great new features.

Frommer's guides now include a new **star-rating system.** Every hotel, restaurant, and attraction is rated from 0 to 3 stars to help you set priorities and organize your time.

We've also added **seven brand-new features** that point you to the great deals, in-the-know advice, and unique experiences that separate travelers from tourists. Throughout the guide look for:

Finds	Special finds—those places only insiders know about
Fun Fact	Fun facts—details that make travelers more informed and their trips more fun
Kids	Best bets for kids—advice for the whole family
Moments	Special moments—those experiences that memories are made of
Overrated	Places or experiences not worth your time or money
Tips	Insider tips—some great ways to save time and money
Value	Great values—where to get the best deals

We've also added a **"What's New"** section in every guide—a timely crash course in what's hot and what's not in every destination we cover.

Other Great Guides for Your Trip:

Frommer's Italy

Frommer's Italy from $70 a Day

Frommer's Tuscany & Umbria

Frommer's Portable Rome

Frommer's Portable Venice

Frommer's®

Rome
15th Edition

by Darwin Porter & Danforth Prince

Here's what the critics say about Frommer's:

"Amazingly easy to use. Very portable, very complete."
—*Booklist*

"The only mainstream guide to list specific prices. The Walter Cronkite of guidebooks—with all that implies."
—*Travel & Leisure*

"Complete, concise, and filled with useful information."
—*New York Daily News*

"Detailed, accurate, and easy-to-read information for all price ranges."
—*Glamour Magazine*

Hungry Minds™

Best-Selling Books • Digital Downloads • e-Books • Answer Networks
e-Newsletters • Branded Web Sites • e-Learning

New York, NY • Cleveland, OH • Indianapolis, IN

About the Authors

A native of North Carolina, **Darwin Porter** was a bureau chief for the *Miami Herald* when he was 21 and later worked in television advertising. A veteran travel writer, he wrote Frommer's first-ever guide to Italy many years ago and has been a frequent visitor ever since. He is joined by **Danforth Prince,** formerly of the Paris bureau of the *New York Times,* who has lived in Italy and traveled there extensively. As a team, they've researched and written other best-selling Frommer guides, including *Frommer's Italy.*

Published by:

Hungry Minds, Inc.

909 Third Ave.
New York, NY 10022

ISBN 0-7645-6508-7
ISSN 1068-9338

Edited by Dog-Eared Pages, Inc.
Production Editor: Ian Skinnari
Cartographer: Roberta Stockwell
Photo Editor: Richard Fox
Chapter 2 Illustrations by Rashell Smith, Kelly Hardesty, and Karl Brandt
Production by Hungry Minds Indianapolis Production Services

Special Sales

For general information on Hungry Minds' products and services please contact our Customer Care department; within the U.S. at 800-762-2974, outside the U.S. at 317-572-3993 or fax 317-572-4002. For sales inquiries and reseller information, including discounts, bulk sales, customized editions, and premium sales, please contact our Customer Care department at 800-434-3422.

Manufactured in the United States of America

5 4 3 2 1

Contents

List of Maps

An Invitation to the Reader

In researching this book, we discovered many wonderful places—hotels, restaurants, shops, and more. We're sure you'll find others. Please tell us about them, so we can share the information with your fellow travelers in upcoming editions. If you were disappointed with a recommendation, we'd love to know that, too. Please write to:

Frommer's Rome, 15th Edition
Hungry Minds, Inc. • 909 Third Avenue • New York, NY 10022

An Additional Note

Please be advised that travel information is subject to change at any time—and this is especially true of prices. We therefore suggest that you write or call ahead for confirmation when making your travel plans. The authors, editors, and publisher cannot be held responsible for the experiences of readers while traveling. Your safety is important to us, however, so we encourage you to stay alert and be aware of your surroundings. Keep a close eye on cameras, purses, and wallets, all favorite targets of thieves and pickpockets.

New! Frommer's Star Ratings & Icons

Every hotel, restaurant, and attraction listing in this guide has been ranked for quality, value, service, amenities, and special features using a star-rating scale. In country, state, and regional guides, we also rate towns and regions to help you narrow down your choices and budget your time accordingly. Hotels and restaurants in the Very Expensive and Expensive categories are rated on a scale of one (highly recommended) to three stars (exceptional). Those in the Moderate and Inexpensive categories rate from zero (recommended) to two stars (very highly recommended). Attractions, towns, and regions are rated according to the following scale: zero stars (recommended), one star (highly recommended), two stars (very highly recommended), and three stars (must-see).

In addition to the rating system, we also use seven icons to highlight insider information, useful tips, special bargains, hidden gems, memorable experiences, kid-friendly venues, places to avoid, and other useful information:

(*Finds*   (*Fun Fact*   (*Kids*   (*Moments*   (*Overrated*   (*Tips*   (*Value*

The following abbreviations are used for credit cards:

AE	American Express	DISC	Discover	V	Visa
DC	Diners Club	MC	MasterCard		

FROMMERS.COM

Now that you have the best guidebook for a great trip to Rome, visit our website at **www.frommers.com** for travel information on nearly 2,000 destinations. With features updated regularly, we give you instant access to the most current trip-planning information available. At Frommers.com, you'll also find the best prices on airfares, accommodations, and car rentals—and you can even book travel online through our travel booking partners. At Frommers.com, you'll also find the following:

- Daily Newsletter highlighting the best travel deals
- Hot Spot of the Month/Vacation Sweepstakes & Travel Photo Contest
- More than 200 Travel Message Boards
- Outspoken Newsletters and Feature Articles on travel bargains, vacation ideas, tips & resources, and more!

What's New in Rome

A new and improved Rome awaits you in 2002. All that pre-millennium work that went into Jubilee-year renovations and restorations has paid off. The scaffolding has come down, facades are cleaner, ancient monuments have been shored up, deteriorating artworks have been restored, hotels have been spiffed up and modernized, and the museums and archaeological sites have been made more accessible and visitor-friendly than ever before. Now that the Jubilee is over, you'll find fewer crowds but you'll get the benefit of improved services, museums with better lighting and more reasonable hours, greater ground transportation, and restored monuments and archaeological areas.

The final result is being hailed as a second Renaissance for Rome. The city has more special exhibitions than ever before in its history; galleries are better lit; information centers and kiosks more plentiful; and the city's cultural life is more diverse than ever. But in spite of all the changes and the contemporary innovations, initiatives, and improvements, it is still the past that draws most pilgrims to Rome. After all, Rome is called the Eternal City.

New millennium or not, political chaos remains part of everyday life on the Roman landscape. At least until recently, it was sometimes assumed that anyone entering politics was doing so for personal gain. Some of that changed in the mid-1990s, when stringent penalties and far-reaching investigations were instituted by a controversial public magistrate, Antonio Di Pietro, who operated with a widespread public approval bordering on adoration. The "Clean Hands" (*Mani Pulite*) campaign he began mandated stiff penalties and led to reams of negative publicity for any politician accused of accepting bribes or campaign contributions that could be interpreted in any way as influence peddling.

Besides soccer (*calcio*), family, and affairs of the heart, the primal obsession of Rome as it moves deeper into the millennium is *il sorpasso*, a term that describes Italy's surpassing of its archrivals, France and Britain, in economic indicators. (Italy ranks fifth among world economic powers, third among European countries.) Economists disagree about whether or not *il sorpasso* has happened, and statistics vary widely from source to source. Italy's true economy is difficult to measure because of the vast Mafia-controlled underground economy (*economia sommersa*) that competes on a monumental scale with the official economy. Almost every Roman has some unreported income or expenditure, and people at all levels of Italian society are engaged to some degree in withholding funds from the government.

Another complicating factor is the surfeit of laws passed in Rome and their effect on the citizens. Before they get thrown out of office, politicians pass laws and more laws, adding to the seemingly infinite number already on the books. Italy not only has more laws on its books than any other nation of Western Europe but also suffers from a bloated bureaucracy. Something as simple as cashing a check or paying a bill can devour half a day. To escape red tape, Romans have become marvelous improvisers and corner-cutters. Whenever possible, they bypass the public sector and negotiate private deals *fra amici* (among friends).

A new millennium, a new currency, and Rome remains a city of contradictions. This simultaneously strident, romantic, and sensual city has forever altered the Western world's religion, art, and government. Despite the traffic, pollution, overcrowding, crime, and barely controlled chaos of modern Rome, the city endures and thrives. With a new millennium, a new currency, and a new billion-dollar media giant as premier, Rome is forging ahead into the 21st century.

In all the confusion of their city, Romans still manage to live a relatively relaxed way of life. Along with their southern cousins in Naples, they are specialists in *arte di arrangiarsi*, the ability to cope and survive with style. The Romans have humanity and humor, a 2,000-year-old sense of cynicism, and a strong feeling of belonging to a particular place. The city's attractions seem as old as time itself, and despite the frustrations of daily life, Rome will continue to lure new visitors every year, with or without a millennium celebration. Here are some late-breaking developments on the tourism scene.

ACCOMMODATIONS   The former home of Hans Christian Andersen has been converted into one of Rome's most charming upscale inns, **The Inn at the Spanish Steps,** Via dei Condotti 85 (© **06-699-25-657**). Each bedroom is furnished with stunning period decor.

The hottest hotel reservation in 2001 was the newly opened **Hotel de Russie,** 9 Via del Babuino (© **800/ 323-7500** in North America, or **06-328-881;** www.rfhotels.com), at the Piazza del Popolo. This opulently furnished luxury hotel has set a new standard in Rome. Amazing for a hotel in the overcrowded historic core, it boasts a garden with magnolias, orange trees, rose bushes, palms, a grotto, and a fountain. Service is excellent, and facilities are completely high-tech and up-to-date.

Longtime fans of Le Grand Hotel were a bit skeptical when news came out that it was now the **St. Regis Grand,** Via V.E. Orlando (© **06-47091;** www.stregis.com/grandrome). The St. Regis group poured $35 million into the decaying property, and all the rooms were richly restored in Empire, Louis XV, or Regency styles. Some 2,000 antiques in the suites alone were sent out for craftspeople to restore to their former luster.

At long last, Rome has a first-class airport hotel: the **Hotel Hilton Rome Airport,** Via Arturo Ferrarin 2, Fiumicino Airport (© **800/445-8667** in the U.S. and Canada, or **06-652-58;** www.hilton.com), which makes two Hiltons for Rome. Opening with 517 bedrooms, the first-class hotel is linked by a walkway with the Leonardo da Vinci International Airport at Fiumicino, 15 miles west of the center of Rome.

Westin's takeover of the landmark **Excelsior,** Via Vittorio Veneto 125 (© **800/325-3589** in the U.S., or **06-47-081;** www.luxurycollection.com), is a good sign that new life will be pumped into this grand but tired old palace.

DINING   At last there's a good place to eat in the former restaurant graveyard around the Forum and Palatine Hill. **Trattoria San Teodoro,** 49-51 Via dei Fienili (© **06-678-0933**), welcomes you to a shady terrace or else a dimly lit dining room resting under a vaulted brick ceiling with arched alcoves. The chef specializes in seafood (try his mini-sized baby squid with sautéed Roman artichokes, or his signature dish, seafood capriccio made with tuna, turbot, or sea bass). Pastas and succulent meats such as medallions of veal in a nutmeg-enhanced cream sauce round out the menu at this family-friendly place.

The current hot spot for dining is **Il Chicco d'Uva,** Corso Rinascimento 70 (**℗ 06-686-7983**), just off the Piazza Navona. In these two dining rooms, you'll spot a chic local crowd laughing, drinking, and eating in elegant surroundings softly lit by candles.

Near the U.S. Embassy, but away from the tourist traps of the Via Veneto, **Santo Padre Roman,** Via Collina 18 (**℗ 06-475-5405**), is being discovered by more discerning visitors. Run by three brothers, it offers delectable Roman food and family pictures. "Come here," say the owners, "and you'll be surrounded by friends." They mean it.

Near the Spanish Steps, **Di Fronte a...,** Via della Croce 38 (**℗ 06-678-0355**), is one of our favorite finds for lunch. Its tasty Italian cuisine is simple but good, and its salads are among the freshest in Rome, its half-pound burgers cooked to juicy perfection.

One of Rome's most acclaimed restaurants, **Il Convivio** (**℗ 06-686-9432**), is luring foodies to its new location at Vicolo dei Soldati 31. It was one of the few restaurants in Rome to earn a Michelin star in 2001.

Near Villa Borghese, **Testa Food & Wine,** Via Tirso 30 (**℗ 06-8530-0692**), has been recently renovated and its menu is even finer than before. It won a lot of new converts during 2001. The bar has become one of the places to be in Rome, as it now features live jazz on Tuesday nights.

EXPLORING   Good news for fans of the Oscar-winning smash *Gladiator.*

You can now get the same center-stage view of the **Colosseum** the fighters had before they met a bloody death or glory in the ring. Extensive renovations to this ancient structure have been underway for several years now, and visitors will soon be allowed to wander spaces under the Colosseum where elephants, lions, and wild animals from North America once waited to be hoisted up in cages to take on the gladiators.

City officials are converting unlikely venues, even industrial sites, into art galleries. The most noteworthy is **Le Scuderie Papali al Quirinale,** Piazza della Quirinale (**℗ 06-696-270**), the 18th-century papal stables across from the government palace, which have been transformed into an art gallery that hosts changing exhibitions (a project that was directed by architect Gae Aulenti, who transformed a Paris train station into the Musée d'Orsay). The first show featured 100 masterpieces on loan from Hermitage in St. Petersburg.

The area around **Castle Sant'Angelo,** Lungotevere Castello 50 (**℗ 06-6819-111**), the former residence of the Borgia popes, has been freed of cars and turned into a pedestrian zone. Visitors can walk through the landscaped section with a tree-lined avenue along the Tiber and a former garden.

SHOPPING   Specializing mainly in cosmetics and perfumes, **Antica Erboristeria Romana,** Via di Torre Argentina 15 (**℗ 06-687-9493**), is the Roman version of Charles Dickens's Old Curiosity Shop in London. From its tiny wooden drawers, various "wonders" are removed, some labeled with a skull & crossbones!

Officine Casa Matta, Via dei Latini 78–80 (**℗ 06-445-36580**), has emerged as a funky, offbeat shop run by an expert craftsperson who specializes in one-of-a-kind merchandise— great for unique gifts.

Visitors to Rome are flocking to **Underground,** Via Francesco Crispi 96 (℃ **06-3600-5345**), a vast underground car park near the Via Veneto, which bursts into a bustling flea market two days a month.

AFTER DARK A longtime landmark bar in the historic heart of Rome, Hemingway's Pub, has been recently transformed into the sleek, chic **Ricciolo Café,** Piazza delle Coppelle 10A (℃ **06-821-0313**), a popular new oyster and champagne bar. In elegant yet informal surroundings, you can order drinks, of course, but also oysters on the half shell. It's a scene, but the food actually lives up to the hype, with dishes like sea bass with mango and roast beef with green apples.

It looks like a bunker from the outside, but the San Lorenzo club of **Locanada Atlantide,** Via dei Lucani (℃ **06-4470-4540**), is heavily patronized when darkness falls across Rome. It's a nightclub, bar, concert hall, and theater, with some different program staged every night.

Near the train station, the century-old **Bar Marini,** Via dei Volsci 57 (℃ **06-490-016**), is enjoying a sudden vogue. Some people compare it to an old Fellini movie set. It attracts everybody from Japanese tourists to rock stars.

1

The Best of Rome

Rome is a city of vivid and unforgettable images: the view of the city's silhouette from Janiculum Hill at dawn; the array of broken marble columns and ruins of temples of the Roman Forum; St. Peter's Dome against a pink-and-red sunset, capping a gloriously decorated basilica.

Rome is also a city of sounds, beginning early in the morning with the peal of church bells calling the faithful to mass. As the city awakens and comes to life, the sounds multiply and merge into a kind of urban symphony. The streets fill with cars, taxis, and motor scooters, all blaring their horns as they weave in and out of traffic; the sidewalks become overrun with bleary-eyed office workers rushing to their desks after stealing into crowded cafes for the first cappuccino of the day. The shops lining the streets open for business by raising their protective metal grilles as loudly as possible, seeming to delight in their contribution to the general din. Before long, fruit-and-vegetable stands are abuzz with activity as homemakers, maids, cooks, and others arrive to purchase their day's supply of fresh produce, haggling over prices and clucking over quality.

By 10am the tourists are on the streets, battling crowds and traffic as they wind their way from Renaissance palaces and baroque buildings to the famous ruins of antiquity. Indeed, Rome often appears to have two populations: one of Romans and one of visitors. During the summer months especially, the city plays host to a horde of countless sightseers who converge on it with guidebooks and cameras in hand. To all of them—Americans, Europeans, Japanese—Rome extends a warm and friendly welcome, wining, dining, and entertaining them in its inimitable fashion. (Of course, if you visit in August, you may see only tourists, not Romans, as the locals flee the summer heat of the city. Or as one Roman woman once told us, "Even if we're too poor to go on vacation, we close the shutters and pretend we're away so neighbors won't find out we couldn't afford to leave the city.")

The traffic, unfortunately, is worse than ever, and, as the capital, Rome remains at the center of the major political scandals and corruption known as *Tangentopoli* (bribe city), which sends hundreds of government bureaucrats to jail each year.

Despite all this chaos, Romans still know how to live the good life. After you've done your duty to culture by wandering through the Colosseum and being awed by the Pantheon, after you've traipsed through St. Peter's Basilica and thrown a coin in the Trevi Fountain, you can pause to experience the charm of the Roman evening. Find a cafe at summer twilight and watch the shades of pink turn to gold and copper before night finally falls. That's when another Rome comes alive; restaurants and cafes grow more animated, especially if you've found one on an ancient hidden piazza or along a narrow alley deep in Trastevere. After dinner, you can stroll by the fountains or through Piazza Navona, have a gelato (or an espresso in winter), and the night is yours.

In chapter 7, we'll tell you all about the ancient monuments and basilicas. But monuments are only a piece of the whole. Below we've tried to capture a snapshot of the special experiences that might be the highlights of your visit.

1 Frommer's Favorite Rome Experiences

• **Walking Through Ancient Rome.** A vast, almost unified archaeological park cuts through the center of Rome. For those who want specific guidance, we have a walking tour in chapter 8 that will lead you through these haunting ruins. But it's fun to wander on your own and let yourself get lost on the very streets where Julius Caesar or Lucrezia Borgia once tread. A slice of history unfolds at every turn: an ancient fountain, a long-forgotten statue, a ruined temple dedicated to some long-faded cult. A narrow street suddenly opens, and you'll have a vista of a triumphal arch. The Roman Forum and the Palatine Hill are the highlights, but the glory of Rome is hardly confined to these dusty fields. If you wander long enough, you'll eventually emerge onto Piazza della Rotunda to stare in awe at one of Rome's most glorious sights, the Pantheon.

• **Hanging Out at the Pantheon.** The world's best-preserved ancient monument is now a hot spot—especially at night. Find a cafe table out on the square and take in the action, which all but awaits a young Fellini to record it. The Pantheon has become a symbol of Rome itself, and we owe our thanks to Hadrian for leaving it to the world. When you tire of people-watching and cappuccino, you can go inside to inspect the tomb of Raphael, who was buried here in 1520. (His mistress, La Fornarina, wasn't allowed to attend the services.) Nothing is more dramatic than being in the Pantheon during a rainstorm, watching the sheets of water splatter on the colorful marble floor. It enters through the oculus on top, which provides the only light for the interior.

• **Taking a Sunday Bike Ride.** Only a daredevil would try this on city streets on a weekday, but on a clear Sunday morning, while Romans are still asleep, you can rent a bike and discover Rome with your own two wheels. The Villa Borghese is the best place to bike. Its 4-mile borders contain a world unto itself, with museums and galleries, a riding school, an artificial lake, and a grassy amphitheater. Another choice place for Sunday biking is the Villa Doria Pamphilj, an extensive park lying above the Janiculum. Laid out in the mid-1600s, this is Rome's largest park, with numerous fountains and some summer houses.

• **Strolling at Sunset in the Pincio Gardens.** Above the landmark Piazza del Popolo, this terraced and lushly planted hillside is the most romantic place for a twilight walk. A dusty orange-rose glow often colors the sky, giving an otherworldly aura to the park's umbrella pines and broad avenues. The ancient Romans turned this hill into gardens, but today's look came from the design of Giuseppe Valadier in the 1800s. Pause at the main piazza, Napoleone I, for a spectacular view of the city stretching from the Janiculum to Monte Mario. The Egyptian-style obelisk here was erected by Emperor Hadrian on the tomb of his great love, Antinous, a beautiful male slave who died prematurely.

• **Enjoying Roma di Notte.** At night, ancient monuments like the Forum are bathed in a theatrical white light; it's thrilling to see the glow of the Colosseum with the moon rising behind its arches. Begin your evening with a Roman *passeggiata* (early-evening stroll) along Via del Corso or Piazza

Navona. There's plenty of action going on inside the clubs, too, from Via Veneto to Piazza Navona. Club kids flock to the colorful narrow streets of Trastevere, the area around the Pantheon, and the even more remote Testaccio. The jazz scene is especially good, and big names often pop in. A little English-language publication, *Info Rome,* will keep you abreast of what's happening, or check *Time Out*'s listings on the Web at www.timeout.co.uk.

• **Exploring Campo de' Fiori at Mid-Morning.** In an incomparable setting of medieval houses, this is the liveliest fruit and vegetable market in Rome, where peddlers offer their wares as they've done for centuries. The market is best viewed after 9am any day but Sunday. By 1pm the stalls begin to close. Once the major site for the medieval inns of Rome (many of which were owned by Vanozza Catanei, the 15th-century courtesan and lover of Pope Alexander VI Borgia), this square maintains some of its old bohemian atmosphere. We often come here when we're in Rome for a lively view of local life that no other place provides. Often, you'll spot your favorite *trattoria* chef bargaining for the best and freshest produce, everything from fresh cherries to the perfect vine-ripened tomato.

• **Attending the Opera.** The Milanese claim that Roman opera pales in comparison with La Scala, but Roman opera buffs, of course, beg to differ. At Rome's Teatro dell'Opera, the season runs between December and June and programs concentrate on the classics: Bellini, Donizetti, Puccini, and Rossini. No one seems to touch the Romans' operatic soul more than Giuseppe Verdi (1813–1901), who became a national icon in his support for Italian unification.

• **Climbing Janiculum Hill.** On the Trastevere side of the river, where Garibaldi held off the attacking French troops in 1849, the Janiculum Hill was always strategic in Rome's defense. Today a walk in this park at the top of the hill can provide an escape from the hot, congested streets of Trastevere. Filled with monuments to Garibaldi and his brave men, the hill is no longer peppered with monasteries, as it was in the Middle Ages. A stroll will reveal monuments and fountains, plus panoramic views over Rome. The best vista is from Villa Lante, a Renaissance summer residence. The most serene part of the park is the 1883 Botanical Gardens, with palm trees, orchids, bromeliads, and sequoias—more than 7,000 plant species from all over the world.

• **Strolling Along the Tiber.** Without the Tiber River, there might have been no Rome at all. A key player in the city's history for millennia, the river flooded the capital every winter until it was tamed in 1870. The massive *lungotevere* embankments on both sides of the Tiber keep it in check and make a perfect place for a memorable stroll. You not only get to walk along the river from which Cleopatra made her grand entrance into Rome, but you'll also see the riverside life of Trastevere and the Jewish Ghetto. Start at Piazza della Bocca della Verità in the early evening; from there, you can go for some 2 or more miles.

• **Picnicking on Isola Tiberina.** In ancient times this boat-shaped island stood across from the port of Rome and from 293 B.C. was home to a temple dedicated to

Aesculapius, the god of healing. A church was constructed in the 10th century on the ruins of this ancient temple. You can reach the island from the Jewish Ghetto by a footbridge, Ponte Fabricio, the oldest original bridge over the Tiber River, which dates from 62 B.C. Romans come here to sunbathe, sitting along the river's banks, and to escape the traffic and the crowds. Arrive with the makings of a picnic, and the day is yours.

• **Following in the Footsteps of Bernini.** One of the most enjoyable ways to see Rome is to follow the trail of Giovanni Lorenzo Bernini (1598–1680), who left a greater mark on the city than even Michelangelo. Under the patronage of three different popes, Bernini "baroqued" Rome. Start at Largo di Santa Susanna, north of the Stazione Termini, at the Church of Santa Maria della Vittoria, which houses one of Bernini's most controversial sculptures, the *Ecstasy of St. Teresa* from 1646. Walk from here along Via Barberini to Piazza Barberini, in the center of which stands Bernini's second most dramatic fountain, the Fontana del Tritone. From the piazza, go along Via delle Quattro Fontane, bypassing (on your left) the Palazzo Barberini designed by Bernini and others for Pope Urban VIII. At the famous crossroads of Rome, Le Quattro Fontane, take Via del Quirinale to see the facade of Sant'Andrea, one of the artist's greatest churches. Continue west, bypassing the Pantheon, to arrive eventually at Piazza Navona, which Bernini remodeled for Pope Innocent X. The central fountain, the Fontana dei Fiumi, is Bernini's masterpiece, though the figures representing the four rivers were sculpted by others following his plans.

• **Spending a Day on the Appian Way.** Dating from 312 B.C., the Appian Way (Via Appia) once traversed the whole peninsula of Italy and was the road on which Roman legions marched to Brindisi and their conquests in the East. One of its darkest moments was the crucifixion in 71 B.C. of the rebellious slave army of Spartacus, whose bodies lined the road from Rome to Capua. Fashionable Romans were buried here, and early Christians dug catacombs through which to flee their persecutors. Begin at the Tomb of Cecilia Metella and proceed up Via Appia Antica past a series of tombs and monuments (including a monument to Seneca, the great moralist who committed suicide on the orders of Nero, and one to Pope St. Urban, who reigned from A.D. 222–230). The sights along Via Appia Antica are among the most fascinating in Rome. You can go all the way to the Church of Domine Quo Vadis.

• **Enjoying a Taste of the Grape.** While in Rome, do as the Romans do and enjoy a carafe of dry white wine from the warm climate of Lazio. In restaurants and *trattorie* you'll find the most popular brand, Frascati, but try some of the other wines from the Castelli Romani, too, including Colli Albani, Velletri, and Marino. All these wines come from one grape: Trebbiano. Sometimes a dash of Malvasia is added for greater flavor and an aromatic bouquet. Of course, you don't have to wait until dinner to drink wine, but can sample it at any of hundreds of wine bars throughout the city, which offer a selection of all the great reds and whites of Italy.

- **Savoring Gelato on a Summer Afternoon.** Sampling gelato on a hot summer day is worth the wait through the long winter. Tubs of homemade ice cream await you in a dazzling array of flavors: everything from candied orange peels with chocolate to watermelon to rice. *Gelaterie* offer *semifreddi* concoctions (made with cream instead of milk) in such flavors as almond, *marengo* (a type of meringue), and *zabaglione* (eggnog). Seasonal fresh fruits are made into ice creams of blueberry, cherry, and peach. *Granite* (crushed ice) flavored with sweet fruit are another cool delight on a sultry night. Tre Scalini at Piazza Navona is the most fabled spot for enjoying *divino tartufo,* a chocolate concoction with a taste to match its name.

- **Dining on a Hidden Piazza.** If you're in Rome with that special someone, you'll appreciate the romance of discovering your own little neighborhood trattoria that opens onto some forgotten square deep in the heart of ancient Rome. And if your evening dinner extends for 3 or 4 hours, who's counting? The waiters won't rush you out the door even when you've overstayed your time at the table. This is a special experience, and Rome has dozens of these little restaurants. Two in particular come to mind: **Montevecchio,** Piazza Montevecchio 22A (© **06-686-1319**), on the square near Piazza Navona where both Raphael and Bramante had studios and Lucrezia Borgia was a frequent visitor. Try the pasta of the day or the roebuck with polenta. Or sample the menu at **Vecchia Roma,** Via della Tribuna di Campitella 18 (© **06-686-4604**), with a theatrical setting on a lovely square. Order spaghetti with double-horned clams and enjoy the old-fashioned ambience while you rub elbows with savvy local foodies.

- **Hearing Music in the Churches.** Artists like Plácido Domingo and Luciano Pavarotti have performed around Rome in halls ranging from churches to ancient ruins. Churches often host concerts, though by decree of Pope John Paul II, it must be sacred music—no hip-grinding, body-slamming stuff. When church concerts are performed, programs appear not only outside the church but also on various announcements posted throughout Rome. The top professionals play at the "big-name" churches, but don't overlook those smaller, hard-to-find churches on hidden squares. Some of the best music we've ever heard has been by up-and-coming musicians getting their start in these little-known churches. The biggest event is the RAI (national broadcasting company) concert on December 5 at St. Peter's—even the pope attends. Other favorite locations for church music include Sant'Ignazio di Loyola, on Piazza di Sant'Ignazio, and San Paolo Fuori le Mura, at Via Ostiense 186.

- **Walking from Fountain to Fountain.** Romans—especially those who live in crowded ghetto apartments without air-conditioning—are out on summer nights walking from fountain to cooling fountain. Every visitor makes at least one trip to Bernini's fountain on Piazza Navona, after stopping off at the Trevi Fountain to toss in a coin (thus ensuring their return to Rome), but there are hundreds more. One hidden gem is the Fontana delle Tararughe, in tiny Piazza Mattei. It has stood there since 1581, a jewel of Renaissance sculpture showing youths helping tortoises into a basin. Our favorite Bernini fountain is at Piazza

Barberini; his Fontana del Tritone is a magnificent work of art from 1642 showing the sea god blowing through a shell. If you think you can still jump into these fountains and paddle around as Anita Ekberg did in *La Dolce Vita,* forget it. That's now against the law.

- **Hanging Out in the Campidoglio at Night.** There is no more splendid place to be at night than Piazza del Campidoglio, where Michelangelo designed both the geometric paving and the facades of the buildings. A broad flight of steps, the Cordonata, takes you up to this panoramic site, a citadel of ancient Rome from which traitors to the empire were once tossed to their deaths. Home during the day to the Capitoline Museums, it takes on a different aura at night, when it's dramatically lit, the measured Renaissance facades glowing like jewel boxes. The views of the brilliantly lit Forum and Palatine at night are also worth the long trek up those stairs. There's no more stunning cityscape view at night than from this hill.

- **Shopping in the Flea Markets.** We've never discovered an original Raphael at Rome's Porta Portese flea market (which locals call *mercato delle pulci*). But we've picked up some interesting souvenirs over the years. The market, the largest in Europe, began after World War II when black marketers needed an outlet for illegal wares. Today the authentic art and antiques once sold here have given way to reproductions, but the selection remains enormous: World War II cameras, caviar from immigrant Russians, luggage (fake Gucci), spare parts, Mussolini busts, and so on. Near Porta Sublicio in Trastevere, the market has some 4,000 stalls, but it's estimated that only 10% of them have a license. Sunday from 5am to 2pm is the best time to visit, and beware of pickpockets at all times.

2 Best Hotel Bets

See chapter 5 for complete reviews of all these hotels.

- **Best Historic Hotel:** The truly grand **St. Regis Grand,** Via Vittorio Emanuele Orlando 3 (© 06-47-091; www.stregis.com/grand rome), was created by César Ritz in 1894, with the great chef Escoffier presiding over a lavish banquet. It was the first hotel in town to offer "a private bathroom and two electric lights in every room." Its roster of guests has included some of the greatest names in European history, including royalty, naturally, but also such New World moguls as Henry Ford and J. P. Morgan. This lavish hotel is within walking distance of many of Rome's major sights.

- **Best Newcomers:** A real discovery and a charmer, **The Inn at the Spanish Steps,** Via dei Condotti 85 (© **06-699-25-657**), is the former Roman residence of Hans Christian Andersen. It has been transformed into one of the most desirable little upscale inns of Rome, each bedroom furnished in gorgeous, authentic period decor. Not far away, the brilliantly restored **Hotel de Russie,** Via del Babuino 9 (© **800/323-7500** in the U.S., or 06/328-881; www.rfhotels.com), was a retreat for artists, including Picasso and Stravinsky. Reclaiming its 1890s style, it's been remade as a stunning little boutique hotel with a fabulous location right off the

Piazza del Popolo and excellent service.

- **Best for Business Travelers:** On the west side of the Tiber River, about 6 short blocks northeast of the Vatican, the **Hotel Atlante Star,** Via Vitelleschi 34 (© **06-687-3233;** www.atlantehotels. com), operates in conjunction with the **Atlante Garden,** a block away and under the same management. Together they share a conference room and a well-run business center. Many young executives check into these hotels and find a helpful staff composed of multilingual European interns eager to help visitors with their problems in the Eternal City. All the latest business equipment is available, and the reception desk is excellent at receiving messages.

- **Best for a Romantic Getaway:** A private villa in the exclusive Parioli residential area, the **Hotel Lord Byron,** Via G. de Notaris 5 (© 06-322-0404), is a chic hideaway. It has a clubby ambience, and everybody is oh-so-very-discreet here. You get personal attention in subdued opulence, and the staff definitely respects that DO NOT DISTURB sign on the door. You don't even have to leave the premises for dinner; the hotel's Relais Le Jardin is one of the finest and most romantic restaurants in Rome.

- **Best Classic Choice:** Ernest Hemingway and Ingrid Bergman don't hang out here anymore, but the **Hotel Eden,** Via Ludovisi 49 (© **800/225-5843** in the U.S., or 06-478-121; www.hotel-eden.it), remains grand and glamorous. Views over the city are stunning, the hotel restaurant (La Terraza) is one of the city's best, and everything looks as if it's waiting for photographers from *Architectural Digest* to arrive.

- **Best for Families:** Near the Stazione Termini (in one of the safer areas), the **Hotel Venezia,** Via Varese 18, near Via Marghera (© **06-445-7101;** www.hotel venezia.com), has rooms large enough to accommodate you and the kids. Some have balconies for checking out the action on the street below. The housekeeping is superb, and the management is caring. Extra beds for children can be brought into the room.

- **Best Moderately Priced Hotel:** So you're not on a bottomless expense account? We've still got a couple of wonderful values for you. Consider the **Hotel Columbia,** Via del Viminale 15 (© **06- 474-4289** or 06-488-3509; www. venere.it/ roma/columbia), one of the newest properties in the neighborhoods surrounding Stazione Termini; everything is well-maintained and comfortable. We also like **La Residenza,** Via Emilia 22–24 (© **06-488-0789;** www.italyhotel.com/ roma/la_residenza), with a convenient location near the Villa Borghese and Piazza Barberini. Here you'll get a good price on a homey, spacious guest room.

- **Best Friendly Pensione:** You can't get much simpler than the **Pensione Papà Germano,** Via Calatafimi 14A (© **06-486-919**), but it's a favorite budget choice, and warm and welcoming to boot. A high-turnover clientele of European and American students check in here, backpacks in hand, as the address is passed around by word of mouth. The energetic family owners may not speak the Queen's English, but they are receptive to your needs and happy to share their home.

- **Best Service:** Both management and staff at the **Hotel de la Ville Inter-Continental Roma,** Via

Sistina 67-69 (© **800/327-0200** in the U.S. and Canada, or 06-67-331; www.interconti.com), are highly professional and exceedingly hospitable. The staff is particularly adept at taking messages, giving you helpful hints about what to see and do in Rome, and fulfilling any special room service requests. Their general attentiveness to your needs, quick problem-solving, good manners, and friendly helpfulness make this place exceptional. Room service is available 24 hours daily.

- **Best Location:** Everybody knows about the astronomically expensive **The Hassler** (© **800/223-6800** in the U.S., or 06-699-340; www.hotelhasslerroma.com), a grand old hotel set right at the top of the Spanish Steps. But given its high prices and the fact that it's gotten a bit dowdy, we'll send you instead to the **Hotel Scalinata di Spagna,** Piazza Trinità dei Monti 17 (© **06-679-3006;** www.hotel scalinata.com), which is located right across the street and isn't so breathtakingly pricey. This intimate, upscale inn has a roof garden with its sweeping view of the dome of St. Peter's across the Tiber. When you step out your door, the heart of Rome is at your feet, including its best shopping streets.

- **Best Views:** From its perch atop Monte Mario, on 15 acres of landscaped grounds, the deluxe **Cavalieri Hilton,** Via Cadlolo 101 (© **800/445-8667** in the U.S. and Canada, or 06-3509-1224; www.hilton.com), opens onto panoramic views of the Eternal City's skyline. Many Romans themselves drive up here to linger over a drink at night just to take in the lights of the city. Another great place to book a room with a view is the **Albergo del Sole al**

Pantheon, Piazza della Rotonda 63 (© **06-678-0441;** www.italy hotel.com/roma/solealpantheon), where you can gaze out at the Pantheon from your bedroom window.

- **Best for Understated Elegance:** Of course, it's not as elegant or as grand as the Excelsior, Eden, or Hassler, but the **Hotel d'Inghilterra,** Via Bocca di Leone 14 (© **06-69-981;** www. charminghotels.it/inghilterra), has its own unique brand of low-key opulence. Two blocks west of the Spanish Steps, its public rooms feature black-and-white checkerboard marble floors and its upholstered lounges are filled with antiques. The fifth floor has some of the loveliest terraces in Rome, and the romantic restaurant below has trompe l'oeil clouds that give the impression of a courtyard terrace open to the sky.

- **Best in a Real Roman Neighborhood:** You can't get more Roman than the **Teatro di Pompeo,** Largo del Pallaro 8 (© **06-6830-0170**), which offers rooms with charming touches like hand-painted tiles and beamed ceilings. The hotel is actually built on top of the ruins of the Theater of Pompey, where Caesar met his fate. It's on a quiet piazzetta near the Palazzo Farnese and Campo de' Fiori, whose open-air market makes this one of Rome's most colorful neighborhoods. Shopping and nightlife abound in this fascinating section of Renaissance Rome, and restaurants and pizzerie keep the area lively at all hours.

- **Best Value:** Rated three stars by the government, the **Hotel delle Muse,** Via Tommaso Salvini 18 (© **06-808-8333**), lies half a mile north of the Villa Borghese. It's run by the efficient, English-speaking

Giorgio Lazar. The furnishings are modern and come in a wide range of splashy colors. In summer, Mr. Lazar operates a garden restaurant serving a reasonably priced fixed-price menu, and the bar is open 24 hours a day. This is one of Rome's best bargains, and you should consider checking in before he wises up and raises his rates.

3 Best Dining Bets

See chapter 6 for complete reviews of all these restaurants.

- **Best for Romance:** A great place to pop the question or just enjoy a romantic evening is **Relais Le Jardin,** in the Hotel Lord Byron, Via G. de Notaris 5 (𝄢 **06-361-3041**), a stunner of a place that also just happens to serve the best Italian cuisine in town. The decor is as romantic as the atmosphere; it's all white lattice and bold Italian colors highlighted by masses of fresh flowers. The setting is in a Relais & Châteaux-member hotel, an Art Deco villa set on a residential hilltop in Parioli, an area of embassies and exclusive town houses at the edge of the Villa Borghese.

- **Best for a Celebration:** Romans have been flocking to **Checchino dal 1887,** Via di Monte Testaccio 30 (𝄢 **06-574-6318**), since the early 19th century for fun and hearty food. With a bountiful array of wine and foodstuffs, every night seems like a party. The tables are packed nightly, and the place is a local legend. You'll have fun while still enjoying some of the best cuisine in town.

- **Best Decor:** By night, chic Romans and savvy foreign visitors alike show up at **El Toulà** (The Hayloft), Via della Lupa 29B (𝄢 **06-687-3498**), an elegant establishment set near the fabled Caffé Greco and some of the most upscale boutiques in Rome. It's no bargain, but once you see the sumptuous setting and, more important, enjoy the cuisine,

you'll think you've gotten your money's worth. Haute cuisine is served in a subdued, tasteful setting of antiques, paintings, ever-so-discreet lighting, and to-die-for flower arrangements.

- **Best View:** The stars really do come out at night at **Les Etoiles** (The Stars), in the Hotel Atlante Star, (𝄢 **06-689-9494**), which has been called "the most beautiful rooftop in Italy." This restaurant is a virtual garden in the sky, with a 360-degree view of Roman landmarks, including the floodlit dome of St. Peter's. Try for a table alfresco in summer, but even in winter the same incredible view can be seen through picture windows. Fortunately, the food—delicately prepared Mediterranean cuisine using the freshest of ingredients—lives up to the setting.

- **Best Pizzeria:** Even the hardest-to-please Roman pizza lovers head for **Pizzeria Baffetto,** Via del Governo Vecchio 114 (𝄢 **06-686-1617**). This is a popular and fun place, drawing a young crowd. The crusts are delightfully thin.

- **Best Wine List:** The food is only secondary at the **Trimani Wine Bar,** Via Cernaia 37B (𝄢 **06-446-9630**), but the wine list is fabulous, a deluxe tour through the vineyards of Italy. One of the best tasting centers in Rome for both French and Italian vintages, this elegant wine bar offers a dazzling array of wines at reasonable prices. The Trimani family has had a prestigious name in the wine business since 1821; simply sit down at one of their tables and let the pouring begin. If you like what you've tasted, you can buy bottles at the wine shop on the premises.

• **Best Value:** Less than $20 gets you one of the finest fixed-price menus in Rome at the **Ristorante del Pallaro,** Largo del Pallaro 15 (℗ **06-6880-1488**). Each dish is lovingly prepared by the chef-owner, Paola Fazi, who urges her diners to *Mangia! Mangia!* The moment you're seated at the table, the dishes start to arrive—first a selection of antipasto, then the homemade, succulent pastas of the day, which in turn are followed by such meat courses as tender roast veal. Everything's included, even a carafe of the house wine.

• **Best for the Kids:** After their tour of the Vatican or St. Peter's, many savvy Roman families head for the **Ristorante Il Matriciano,** Via dei Gracchi 55 (℗ 06-321-2327). It's not fancy, but the price is right, and in summer you can opt for a sidewalk table. Let your kids feast on good, reasonably priced, homemade fare that includes such crowd pleasers as ricotta-stuffed ravioli. At the next table you're likely to see some priests from the Vatican dining. And of course, after they've behaved themselves in all the churches and museums, you'll have to reward them with gelato from **Tre Scalini,** Piazza Navona 30 (℗ **06-687-9148**), or **Giolitti,** Via Uffici del Vicario 40 (℗ 06-699-1243).

• **Best Continental Cuisine:** The city's finest restaurant is now **La Terrazza,** in the Hotel Eden, Via Ludovisi 49 (℗ **06-478-121**), edging out a position long held by Sans Souci. In the newly and fabulously restored Hotel Eden, you can dine on continental cuisine that is both bold and innovative. The seasonal menu offers the most polished, sophisticated cuisine in Rome; perhaps you'll choose a "symphony" of seafood or a warm salad of grilled vegetables.

• **Best Pan-Italian Cuisine:** Italian food as you've (almost) never had it before is served at the **Relais Le Jardin,** in the Hotel Lord Byron, Via G. de Notaris 5 (℗ **06-361-3041**), a refined citadel of haute cuisine. In a luxurious setting, you'll feast on traditional fare prepared with a light, innovative touch, with specialties from such regions as Lazio and Abruzzi. The most demanding Roman palates wine and dine here and enjoy the freshest of seasonal produce, beginning with the bright zucchini blossoms of spring.

• **Best Emilia-Romagna Cuisine:** The area around Bologna has long been celebrated for serving the finest cuisine in Italy, and the little trattoria **Colline Emiliane,** Via Avignonesi 22 (℗ **06-481-7538**), maintains that stellar reputation among Romans. The pastas here are among the best in Rome, especially the handmade tortellini alla panna (with cream sauce) with truffles. You can order less expensive pastas as well, all of them good. Their prosciutto comes from a small town near Parma and is reputedly the best in the world.

• **Best Roman Cuisine:** The tempting selection of antipasti alone is enough to lure you to **Al Ceppo** (The Log), Via Panama 2 (℗ **06-841-9696**). Try such appetizers as stuffed yellow or red peppers or finely minced cold spinach blended with ricotta. Only 2 blocks from the Villa Borghese, this is a dining address jealously guarded by Romans, who often take their friends from out of town here. They feast on the succulent lamb chops, charcoal-grilled to perfection, or other grilled meats, such as quail, liver, and bacon.

- **Best Tuscan Cuisine:** For the most tender and delicious *bistecca alla fiorentina* (beefsteak Florentine style) in Rome, head for **Girarrosto Toscano,** off Via Veneto at Via Campania 29 (© **06-4201-3045**). The chefs grill the meats to perfection, using only virgin olive oil, salt, and pepper for seasoning. You get an array of other dishes as well, including one of the best selections of antipasti in town, everything from vine-ripened melon with prosciutto to a delectable Tuscan salami. Oysters and fresh fish from the Adriatic are also served.

- **Best Seafood:** Sure, it's expensive, but the fresh seafood is superb at **Quinzi & Gabrieli,** Via delle Coppelle 5–6 (© **06-687-9389**), where simple preparations let the flavor of the fish shine through. Nearby is another fantastic fish house, **La Rosetta,** Via della Rosetta 8 (© **06-686-1002**). The clear choice in Trastevere is **Alberto Ciarla,** Piazza San Cosimato 40 (© **06-581-8668**).

- **Best Nuova Cucina:** Near the Vittorio Emanuele monument, **Agata e Romeo,** Via Carlo Alberto 45 (© **06-446-6115**), serves one of Rome's most inventive and creative cuisines in a striking dining room done in Liberty style. If you'd like a sampling of the best selections of the day, you can order one of the fixed-price menus, available with or without wine. The menu reflects the agrarian bounty of Italy, with ample choices for everyone: meat eaters, fish fanciers, and vegetarians.

- **Best in the Jewish Ghetto:** For centuries, Romans have flocked to the Jewish Ghetto to sample

Jerusalem artichokes. No one prepares them better than **Piperno,** Via Monte de' Cenci 9 (© **06-6880-6629**), which serves savory (though nonkosher) Roman food. Of course, you can order more than these deep-fried artichokes here. A full array of delights includes everything from stuffed squash blossoms to succulent pastas.

- **Best Desserts:** It's a bit of an exaggeration to say that people fly to Rome just to sample the tartufo at **Tre Scalini,** Piazza Navona 30 (© **06-687-9148**), but we'd consider it, just to dig our spoons into a grated bitter chocolate-covered chocolate ice-cream ball swathed in whipped cream. On almost any night you'll find people lined up three deep at the ice-cream counter outside. If you can take your mind off the tartufo, you'll have a ringside seat at Rome's most beautiful square, Piazza Navona, facing Bernini's Fontana dei Fiumi.

- **Best Late-Night Pastry Shop:** Right on Piazza del Popolo, where the young and the restless drive up in their Maseratis and Porsches, the **Café Rosati,** Piazza del Popolo 5A (© **06-322-5859**), heats up as the night wears on. Although you can order whisky, many come for the delectable Italian pastries. A sidewalk table makes an ideal spot to enjoy an ice-cream dish.

- **Best Alfresco Dining:** In Trastevere, Piazza Santa Maria comes alive at night. If you reserve a sidewalk table at **Sabatini,** Piazza Santa Maria in Trastevere 13 (© **06-581-2026**), you'll have a view of all the action, including the floodlit golden mosaics of the church on the piazza, Santa Maria in Trastevere. At the next table you're likely to see . . . well, just about anybody (on our most recent visit, Roman Polanski). In addition to the view, you get some of the best grilled fish and Florentine steaks here.

- **Best for People-Watching:** Join the beautiful people—young actors, models, and artists from nearby Via Margutta—who descend at night on Piazza del Popolo. Young men with their silk shirts unbuttoned alight from sports cars to go on the prowl. At **Dal Bolognese,** Piazza del Popolo 1–2 (**℃ 06-361-1426**), you can not only take in this fascinating scene but also enjoy fine Bolognese cuisine as enticing as the people-watching. In the 1950s, Via Veneto was the place to be for Elizabeth Taylor, Frank Sinatra, and other Hollywood types. Today the celebs are long gone, and Via Veneto is more about overpriced tourist traps than genuine hip. But lots of folks like to stroll this strip anyway, and enjoy the passing parade from a table at the **Caffè de Paris,** Via Vittorio Veneto 90 (**℃ 06-488-5284**).
- **Best for a Cappuccino with a View:** Perhaps the best-located cafe in Rome is **Di Rienzo,** Piazza della Rotonda 8–9 (**℃ 06-686-9097**), which stands directly on Piazza della Rotonda, fronting the Pantheon. On a summer night there's no better place to be than "the living room" of Rome, as the square before you has been dubbed, as you sit and slowly sip your cappuccino. On the beautiful Piazza Navona, there's also **Tre Scalini,** Piazza Navona 30 (**℃ 06-687-9148**), for espresso, something sweet, or a more substantial bite to eat.
- **Best *Tavola Calda*:** One of the best *tavola caldas* (hot tables) in

Rome is at **Bar Cottini,** Via Merulana 286–287 (**℃ 06-474-0768**), which is convenient for those staying in hotels around the Stazione Termini. The food is artfully displayed, and the selection is bountiful—not only freshly made salads but also hot pastas and just-prepared main courses. Portions are mammoth, and tempting desserts such as a melt-in-your-mouth chocolate cake are prepared by the in-house bakery.

- **Best Picnic Fare:** When the weather is cool and the day is sunny, it's time for an alfresco meal, and there's no better place to purchase the makings of a picnic than the **Campo de' Fiori** open-air market, between Corso Vittorio Emanuele II and the Tiber. The luscious produce of Lazio is on display here right in the heart of the old city. If you wish, you can purchase vegetables already chopped and ready to be dropped into the minestrone pot. Romans are particular about their food— you'll see some people inspecting cherries or other items one by one by one. There are also several excellent delicatessen shops on the square. Visit one of the shops selling freshly baked Roman bread, pick up a bottle of wine, and a companion—and off you go.
- **Best Restaurant for Celebrity-Spotting:** Glitz and glamour reign supreme at **Sans Souci,** Via Sicilia 20 (**℃ 06-42-014-510**), Rome's flashiest dining room. You'll rarely find a Roman here, but those on the hipster international circuit show up. Another chic choice is **Café Riccioli,** Piazza delle Coppelle 10A (**℃ 06-6821-0313**), where you'll often spot models and other beautiful people having a light dinner of sashimi.

2

A Traveler's Guide to Roman Art & Architecture

By Reid Bramblett

The art of Rome ranges from Roman mosaics and Renaissance masterpieces by Michelangelo and Leonardo to baroque statues by Bernini and modern still lifes by Morandi, the architecture from Roman temples and Byzantine basilicas to Renaissance churches, baroque palaces, and postmodern stadiums that take their cues from the ancient Colosseum. This brief overview should help you make sense of it all.

1 Art 101

CLASSICAL: ETRUSCANS & ROMANS (6TH CENTURY B.C. TO A.D. 5TH CENTURY)

The **Etruscans,** who became Rome's pre-Republican Tarquin kings, arrived with their own styles from Asia Minor. However, by the 6th century B.C., they were borrowing heavily from the Greeks in their sculpture and importing thousands of Attic painted vases, which displayed the most popular and wide-spread painting style of ancient Greece.

Painting in ancient **Rome** was used primarily for decorative purposes. Bucolic *frescoes* (the technique of painting on wet plaster) adorned the walls of the wealthy. Rome's sculptures tended to glorify emperors and the perfect human form, often copying *ad nauseum* famous Greek originals.

Examples of classical art include:

- **Etruscan.** Etruscan artistic remains are confined to the Villa Giulia and Vatican Museums; the best is the Villa Giulia's terra cotta sarcofagi covers of reclining figures. Some tomb paintings also survive at Tarquinia in northern Lazio.
- **Roman.** Along with an army of also-ran statues and busts gracing most archaeological collections in Italy, you'll find a few standouts: the marble *bas-reliefs* (sculptures that project slightly from a flat surface) on the Arch of Constantine; the sculptures, mosaics, and remarkable fresco collections at the various branches of the Museo Nazionale Romano; and such sculptures as the gilded equestrian statue of Marcus Aurelius and *The Dying Gaul* at the Capitoline Museum. The reliefs on the Ara Pacis are a great example of A.D. 1st-century art-as-Imperial-propaganda.

BYZANTINE & ROMANESQUE (5TH TO 13TH CENTURY)

Artistic expression in the Dark Ages and early medieval Rome was largely church-related. Because Mass was recited in Latin, images were used to communicate the Bible's most important lessons to the illiterate masses. Bas reliefs around the churches' main doors, along with wall paintings and altarpieces inside, told key tales to inspire faith in God and fear of sin (*Last Judgments* were favorites). Otherwise, decoration was spare, and what little existed was often destroyed, replaced, or covered over the centuries as tastes changed and cathedrals were remodeled.

The **Byzantine** style of painting and mosaic was very stylized and static. The iconographic tradition was imported from the eastern half of the Roman Empire centered at Byzantium (the empire's major political outposts in Italy were Ravenna and Venice). Faces (and eyes) were almond-shaped with pointy little chins, noses long with a spoon-like depression at the top, and folds in robes (always blue over red) represented by stylized cross-hatching in gold leaf.

Romanesque sculpture was somewhat more fluid, but still far from naturalistic. Often wonderfully child-like in its narrative simplicity, the work frequently mixes Biblical scenes with the myths and motifs of local pagan traditions that were being slowly incorporated into early medieval Christianity. Romanesque art was seen as crude by most later periods and usually replaced or destroyed over the centuries; it survives mostly in scraps.

Good examples of this era include:

- **Byzantine mosaics.** The oldest, paleo-Christian mosaics (5th to 7th century) are in Santa Maria Maggiore, Santa Sabina (which also preserves remarkable 5th-century wood doors carved with Biblical reliefs), and San Giovanni in Laterano's San Venanzio and Santa Rufina chapels (the main church's apse mosaic is 13th century). Later Byzantine and Romanesque mosaics decorate Santa Maria d'Aracoeli, San Clemente Basilica, and San Paolo Fuori le Mura.

- **Romanesque painting.** San Clemente Basilica's lower church has some of the few remaining early medieval paintings in Rome.

- **National Museum of Palazzo Venezia.** Rome's best collection of medieval art, including the oldest painted wood statue (13th century), numerous Byzantine crosses, ivories, and an unusual enameled metal *Christ* (13th-century).

INTERNATIONAL GOTHIC (LATE 13TH TO EARLY 15TH CENTURY)

Late medieval Italian art continued to be largely ecclesiastical. In both Gothic painting and sculpture, figures tended to be more natural than in the Romanesque (and the colors in paintings more varied and rich), but remained highly stylized. The figures' features and gestures are exaggerated for symbolic or emotional emphasis. In painting especially, late Gothic artists such as Giotto started introducing greater realism, a sense of depth, and more realistic emotion into their art—characteristics that would later define the Renaissance. However, when the Pope fled Rome for Avignon, France, in 1308, the Eternal City became a provincial town and art languished.

The best Gothic artists with work in Rome include:

- **Giotto** (1266–1337). The greatest Gothic artist, Giotto lifted painting from its Byzantine funk and set it on the road to the realism and perspective of the Renaissance. His best works are fresco cycles in Assisi, Padua, and Florence, but in Rome you can see the *Stefaneschi Triptych* (1315) in the Vatican Pinacoteca.

- **Pietro Cavallini** (1250–1330). He designed the *Life of the Virgin* apse mosaics in Santa Maria in Trastevere, but his only painting to survive is the top half of a *Last Judgment* (1295–1300) on the entrance wall of Santa Cecilia in Trastevere (you have to make an appointment to see it).

- **Arnolfo di Cambio** (1245–1302). This Tuscan sculptor and architect left a venerated bronze *St. Peter* in St. Peter's Basilica.

RENAISSANCE (EARLY 15TH TO MID–17TH CENTURY)

From the 14th to 16th century, the popularity of the Humanist movement in philosophy prompted princes and powerful prelates to patronize a generation of innovative young artists. These painters, sculptors, and architects experimented with new modes in art and broke with static medieval traditions to pursue a greater degree of expressiveness and naturalism, using such techniques are linear perspective. The term *Renaissance,* or "rebirth," was only later applied to this period in Italy (from where it spread to the rest of Europe).

This list of Renaissance giants merely scratches the surface of the masters Italy gave rise to in the 15th and 16th centuries:

- **Fra Angelico** (1400–55). This Tuscan monk and early master was invited to Rome by the Pope to paint the Vatican's Nicholas V chapel (1448–50).
- **Leonardo da Vinci** (1452–1519). A true "Renaissance man," Leonardo dabbled his genius in a bit of everything from art to philosophy to science (on paper, he even designed machine guns and rudimentary helicopters). Little of his remarkable painting survives, however, as he often experimented with new pigment mixes that proved to lack the staying power of traditional materials. Leonardo invented such painterly effects as the fine haze of *sfumato,* which softens outlines and progressively blurs background landscapes and objects to create a sense of realism and vast distance within the painting. Unfortunately, nothing in Rome shows this, as the only major Leonardo here is an unfinished *St. Jerome* in the Vatican Pinacoteca.
- **Raphael** (1483–1520). Rightfully considered one of Western art's greatest draftsman, Raphael produced a body of work in his 37 short years that ignited European painters for generations to come. You'll find his ethereal *Transfiguration* (1520), almost finished when he died, in the Vatican Museums. Also in the Vatican are perhaps his greatest works, a series of frescoed rooms (1508–20) including the *School of Athens,* at once a celebration of Renaissance artistic precepts, the classical philosophers whose rediscovery spurred on the Renaissance, and Raphael's contemporaries (the various "philosophers" are actually portraits of Leonardo, Michelangelo, Raphael himself, and Bramante, an architect).
- **Michelangelo** (1475–1564). The heavyweight contender for the title of world's greatest artist, Michelangelo was a genius in sculpture, painting, architecture, and poetry. He marked the apogee of the Renaissance. A complex and difficult man—intensely jealous, probably manic-depressive, and certainly homosexual—Michelangelo enjoyed great fame in a life plagued by a series of never-ending projects commissioned by the Medici in Florence and Pope Julius II in Rome—the Sistine Chapel frescoes (ceiling 1508–12; *Last Judgment* 1535–41) and the tomb of Julius II, of which he only finished the powerful *Moses* (1513–15) in San Pietro in Vincoli and some *Slaves* in Florence. He sculpted the *Pietà* (1500) in St. Peter's Basilica at age 25.

  Michelangelo worshiped the male nude as the ultimate form and twisted the bodies of his figures (art historians call this *torsion*) in different, often contradictory directions (a positioning called *contraposto*) to bring out their musculature. When forced against his will to paint the Sistine Chapel, he broke almost all the rules and sent painting headlong in an entirely new direction—called mannerism—marked by nonprimary colors, impressionistic shapes of light, and twisting muscular figures.

BAROQUE & ROCOCO (LATE 16TH TO 18TH CENTURY)

The **baroque,** a more theatrical and decorative take on the Renaissance, mixes a kind of super-realism based on using peasants as models and an exaggerated use of light and dark, called *chiaroscuro,* with compositional complexity and explosions of dynamic fury, movement, color, and figures. **Rococo** is this later baroque art gone awry, frothy and chaotic.

The baroque period produced many fine artists, but only a few true geniuses, including:

- **Caravaggio** (1571–1610). Caravaggio started as a street urchin, rose to fame through the graces of a Borghese cardinal, became an honorary Knight of Malta, and ended his life on the run from murder charges in Rome. In between, he reinvented baroque painting, using peasants and commoners as models and including their earthy realism (dirty bare feet were a favorite) into his works. He added his chiaroscuro technique of playing areas of harsh light off deep, black shadows (which helps explain the deeply wrinkled faces he loved to paint). Among his masterpieces are the *St. Matthew* (1599) cycle in San Luigi dei Francesi, a series of paintings in the Galleria Borghese and Palazzo Corsini, and the *Deposition* (1604) in the Vatican Museums.

- **Pietro da Cortona** (1596–1669). This Tuscan painter moved to Rome and became the progenitor of a fluffy, pastel baroque style, which he used to decorate the ceilings of Palazzo Barberini with an allegorical *Glorification of the Reign of Urban VIII* (1635).

- **Bernini** (1598–1680). Bernini was the greatest baroque sculptor, a fantastic architect, and no mean painter. His finest sculptures include in the Galleria Borghese his youthful *Aeneas and Anchises* (1613), *Apollo and Daphne* (1624), *The Rape of Persephone* (1621), and *David* (1623–24)—the last a resounding baroque man of action rather than a Renaissance man of contemplation like Michelangelo's famous *David* in Florence. His other masterpiece is the *Fountain of the Four Rivers* (1651) in Piazza Navona.

LATE 18TH TO 20TH CENTURY

After carrying the banner of artistic innovation for over a millennium, Italy ran out of steam with the baroque. Nevertheless, the country did produce a few fine **neoclassical** sculptures in the late 18th century.

Italy did not play an important role in late 19th- or 20th-century art, although a few great artists did emerge. In 1909 Italian artists living in Paris made a spirited attempt to take the artistic initiative back into Italian hands, but what the **Futurist** movement's **Umberto Boccioni** (1882–1916) came up with was largely cubism—the "fractured" style, made famous by Picasso, in which objects are depicted from several perspectives at once—with an element of movement added in. **Gino Severini** (1883–1966) contributed a sophisticated take on color which rubbed of on the core cubists. You can see work by both artists in the National Gallery of Modern Art.

The greatest Italian artists of the modern era include:

- **Antonio Canova** (1757–1822). Italy's top neoclassical sculptor, Canova was popular for his mythological figures and Bonaparte portraits (he even sculpted both Napoléon and his sister Pauline as nudes). You'll find his work in the Galleria Borghese.

- **Amadeo Modigliani** (1884–1920). A sickly boy and only moderately successful in his short lifetime, Modigliani helped re-invent the portrait in painting and sculpture after he moved to Paris in 1906. He's known for his elongated, mysterious heads and rapidly painted nudes. Check them out at the National Gallery of Modern Art.
- **Giorgio de Chirico** (1888–1978). De Chirico founded freaky *pittura metafisica* (metaphysical painting), a forerunner of surrealism wherein figures and objects are stripped of their usual meaning though odd juxtapositions, warped perspective, unnatural shadows, and other bizarre effects and a general spatial emptiness. Look for them in the National Gallery of Modern Art and the Collection of Modern Religious Art in the Vatican Museums.
- **Giorgio Morandi** (1890–1964). In the painting of his eerily minimalist, highly modeled, quasi-monochrome still lifes, Morandi was influenced by *pittura metafisica*. His paintings decorate the National Gallery of Modern Art and the Collection of Modern Religious Art in the Vatican Museums.

2 Italian Architecture at a Glance

There are a couple of points to keep in mind when considering a building's style, particularly for structures built before the 20th century. First, very few buildings (especially churches) were actually built in only one style. Massive, expensive structures often took centuries to complete, during which time tastes would change and plans would be altered. Second, while each architectural era has its own distinctive features, some elements, general floor plans, and terms are common to many; features may appear near the end of one era and continue through several later ones.

From the Romanesque period on, most churches (see illustration, Church Floor Plan) consist either of a single wide **aisle,** or a wide central **nave** flanked by two narrow aisles. The aisles are separated from the nave by a row of **columns,** or by square stacks of masonry called **piers,** usually connected by **arches.**

This main nave/aisle assemblage is usually crossed by a perpendicular corridor called a **transept** near the far, east end of the church so that the floor plan looks like a **Latin cross** (shaped like a crucifix). The shorter, east arm of the nave is the holiest area, called the **chancel;** it often houses the stalls of the **choir** and the **altar.** If the far end of the chancel is rounded off, it's called an **apse.** An **ambulatory** is a curving corridor outside the altar and choir area, separating it from the ring of smaller chapels radiating off the chancel and apse.

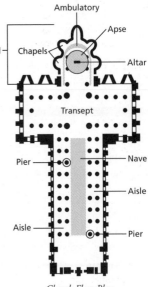

Church Floor Plan

Some churches, especially after the Renaissance when mathematical proportion became important, were built on a **Greek cross** plan, each axis the same length like a giant +. By the baroque, funky shapes became popular, with churches built in the round or as ellipses, for example.

CLASSICAL (6TH CENTURY B.C. TO A.D. 4TH CENTURY)

The **Romans** made use of certain **Greek** innovations, particularly architectural ideas. The first to be adopted was *post-and-lintel construction* (essentially, a weight-bearing frame, like a door). Inventive engineers, the Romans then added the load-bearing arch, and also developed hoisting mechanisms and a specially trained workforce.

Identifiable features of classical architecture include:

- **Classical orders** (see illustration). The orders are most easily recognized by their column capitals, with the least ornate capital used on a building's ground level and the most ornate used on the top: Doric (a plain capital), Ionic (a capital with a scroll), and Corinthian (a capital with flowering acanthus leaves).

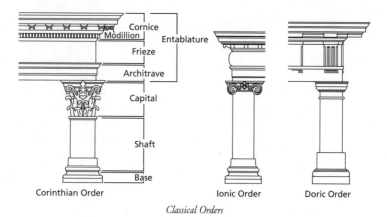

Corinthian Order   Ionic Order   Doric Order

Classical Orders

- **Brick and concrete.** Although marble is traditionally associated with Roman architecture, Roman engineers could also do wonders with bricks or even prosaic concrete—concrete seating made possible such enormous theaters as Rome's 6-acre, 45,000-seat Colosseum.

Roman architecture includes the sports stadium of the **Colosseum** (A.D. 1st century; see illustration), which perfectly displays the use of the classical orders; Hadrian's marvel of engineering, the temple of the **Pantheon** (A.D. 1st century); and the public brick **Baths of Caracalla** (A.D. 3rd century).

Another good example is the **Basilica of Constantine and Maxentius** in the Roman Forum (A.D. 4th century). Roman **basilica** served as law courts. They were rectangular in shape and contained a wide nave, two rows of columns supporting arches, and an apse at one or both ends; the style was adopted by early Christians for their first grand churches.

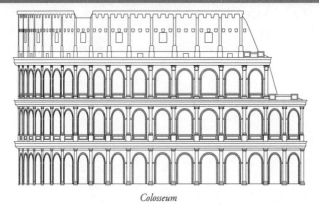

Colosseum

Rome's ancient seaport **Ostia Antica** has been preserved with its street plan, and even some virtually intact buildings.

ROMANESQUE & GOTHIC (7TH TO 15TH CENTURY)

The **Romanesque** took its inspiration and rounded arches from ancient Rome (hence the name). The first major churches in Rome were built on the basilica plan of Roman law courts. Architects constructed large churches with wide aisles to accommodate the masses who came to hear the priests say Mass, but mainly to worship at the altars of various saints. To support the weight of all that masonry, the walls had to be thick and solid (meaning they could be pierced by few and rather small windows) and supported by huge piers, giving Romanesque churches a dark, somber, mysterious, and often oppressive feeling.

By the late 12th century, the development of the pointed arch and exterior, *flying buttress* (see illustration, Cross Section of Gothic Church) freed architecture from the heavy, thick walls of Romanesque structures and allowed ceilings to soar, walls to thin, and windows to proliferate in the **Gothic** style, though there's only one surviving example in Rome.

Identifiable Romanesque features include:

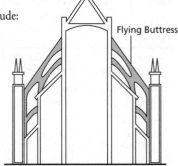

- **Rounded arches.** These load-bearing architectural devices allowed architects to open up wide naves and spaces, channeling all the weight of the stone walls and ceiling across the curve of the arch and down into the ground via the columns or pilasters.
- **Thick walls.**
- **Infrequent and small windows.**
- **Huge piers.**

Cross Section of Gothic Church

The great early basilicas, each at least partly altered in decor over the ages, include **Santa Maria Maggiore, San Giovanni in Laterano,** and **San Paolo Fuori le Mure.** Other less grand Romanesque churches include **Santa Maria in Cosmedin** (see illustration) and **Santa Sabina.**

Santa Maria in Cosmedin

Santa Maria Sopra Minerva is Rome's only **Gothic** church, all pointy arches and soaring ceilings. (Although, hemmed in by other buildings, it has an atypically dark Gothic interior.)

RENAISSANCE (15TH TO 17TH CENTURY)

As in painting, Renaissance architectural rules stressed proportion, order, classical inspiration, and mathematical precision to create unified, balanced structures.

Some identifiable Renaissance features include:

- **A sense of proportion.**
- **A reliance on symmetry.**
- **The use of classical orders.**

Bramante (1444–1514) was perhaps the most mathematical and classically precise of the early High Renaissance architects, evident in his (much altered) plans for **St. Peter's Basilica** (his spiral staircase in the Vatican has survived untouched) and his jewel of perfect Renaissance architecture, the textbook **Tempietto** (1502; see illustration) at San Pietro in Montorio on the slopes of Rome's Gianicolo Hill, where Christians once believed St. Peter had been crucified (as a plus, the little crypt inside is a riotous rococo grotto).

Renaissance man **Michelangelo** took up architecture later in life, designing the **dome atop St. Peter's Basilica;** and the sloping approach, 12-pointed star courtyard, and trio of palace facades that together make up **Piazza del Campidoglio** atop the Capitoline Hill; and the facade of the **Palazzo Farnese** (1566), which was otherwise built by **Antonio da Sangallo** (1483–1546).

Baldassare Peruzzi (1481–1537) designed the lovely **Villa Farnesina** (1508–11; he also painted a *trompe l'oeil* fresco in an upstairs room).

Vignola's (1507–73) monumental, barrel-vaulted **Chiesa del Gesù** (1568–75), with its graceful facade by Giacomo della Porta (1533–1602), became a Catholic Counter-Reformation model for churches throughout Europe.

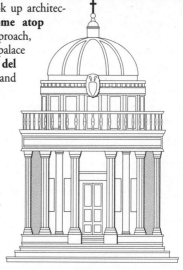

Tempietto

BAROQUE & ROCOCO (17TH TO 18TH CENTURY)

More than any other movement, the **baroque** aimed toward a seamless meshing of architecture and art. The stuccoes, sculptures, and paintings were all carefully designed to complement each other—and the space itself—to create a unified whole. This effect was both aesthetic and narrative, the various art forms all working together to tell a single Biblical story (or, often, to subtly relate the deeds of the commissioning patron to great historic or Biblical events). Excessively complex and dripping with decorative tidbits, **rococo** is the baroque gone awry.

Some identifiable baroque features include:

- **Classical architecture rewritten with curves.** The baroque is similar to the Renaissance, but many of the right angles and ruler-straight lines are exchanged for curves of complex geometry and an interplay of concave and convex surfaces. The overall effect is to lighten the appearance of structures and to add movement of line and vibrancy to the static look of the classical Renaissance.

- **Complex decoration.** Unlike the sometimes severe and austere designs of the Renaissance, the baroque was playful. Architects festooned structures and encrusted interiors with an excess of decorations intended to liven things up—lots of ornate stucco-work, pouty cherubs, airy frescoes, heavy gilding, twisting columns, multicolored marbles, and general frippery.

- **Multiplying forms.** The baroque asked, "Why make do with one column when you can stack a half dozen partial columns on top of each other, slightly offset?" The baroque loved to pile up its forms and elements to create a rich, busy effect, breaking a pediment curve into segments so each would protrude further out than the last, or building up an architectural feature by stacking short sections of concave walls, each one curving to a different arc.

The baroque flourished across Italy, but some of the best examples include **Sant'Ivo alla Sapienza** (1640s) by **Borromini** (1599–1667) with its interplay of concave and convex ovals, interlocking truncated triangles, and an elliptical ramp-like dome that looks like nothing so much as soft-serve ice cream (as scooped by a mathematician).

Though relatively sedate, **St. Peter's** facade by **Carlo Maderno** (ca. 1556–1629) and sweeping elliptical colonnade by **Bernini** make for one of Italy's most famous baroque assemblages. The two also collaborated (along with Borromini) on the **Palazzo Barberini** (1620–30s). The painter **Pietro da Cortona** designed the distinctive semi-circular portico on **Santa Maria della Pace** (1656–57).

For the rococo—more a decorative than architectural movement—look no further than the **Spanish Steps** (1726) by architect **Francesco de Sanctis** (1693–1740) or the **Trevi Fountain** (1762; see illustration) by **Nicola Salvi** (1697–1751).

Trevi Fountain

NEOCLASSICAL TO MODERN (18TH TO 20TH CENTURY)

As a backlash against the excesses of the baroque and rococo, by the middle of the 18th century, Italian architects began turning to the austere simplicity and grandeur of the Classical Age and inaugurated the **neoclassical** style. Their work was inspired by the rediscovery of Pompeii and other ancient sites.

From the 19th through the 20th century, Italian architects constructed buildings in a variety of styles. Italy's take on the early 20th-century Art-Nouveau movement was called **Liberty** style. Mussolini made a spirited attempt to bring back ancient Rome in what can only be called **Fascist** architecture. Since then, Italy has mostly erected concrete and glass skyscrapers like the rest of the world.

Some identifiable features for each of these movements include:

• **Neoclassical.** The classical ideals of mathematical proportion and symmetry, first rediscovered during the Renaissance, are the hallmark of every classically styled era. Neoclassicists reinterpreted ancient temples as buildings with massive colonnaded porticos.

- **Liberty.** Like Art Nouveau practitioners in other countries, Italian artists rebelled against the era of mass production and stressed the uniqueness of craft. They created asymmetrical, curvaceous designs based on organic inspiration (plants and flowers) and used such materials as wrought iron, stained glass, tile, and hand-painted wallpaper.
- **Fascist.** Deco meets Caesar. This period produced monumentally imposing and chillingly stark, white marble structures surrounded by classical statuary.

Of the **neoclassical,** the **Vittorio Emanuele Monument** (see illustration), which has been compared to a wedding cake or Victorian typewriter, was Italy's main monument to reaching its Risorgimento goal of a unified Italy.

Liberty style never produced any surpassingly important buildings, although you can glimpse it occasionally in period storefronts.

Fascist architecture still infests all corners of Rome (although most of the Right Wing reliefs and the repeated engravings of "DVCE"—Mussolini's nickname for himself—have long since been chipped out). You can see it at its, er, best in Rome's planned satellite community called **EUR** (including a multistory "square Colosseum" so funky it has been featured in many films and music videos) and the **Stadio Olimpico** complex.

The **mid–20th century** was dominated by **Pier Luigi Nervi** (1891–1979) and his reinforced concrete buildings, including the **Palazzeto dello Sport** stadium (1960).

Vittorio Emanuele Monument

3

Planning Your Trip to Rome

This chapter is devoted to the where, when, and how of your trip—the advance planning required to get it together and take it on the road. A little planning is in order to help you steer clear of disappointment and stay open to unanticipated pleasures.

1 Visitor Information

For information before you go, contact the Italian Government Tourist Board.

In the United States: 630 Fifth Ave., Suite 1565, New York, NY 10111 (© **212/245-4822;** fax 212/586-9249); 500 N. Michigan Ave., Suite 2240, Chicago, IL 60611 (© **312/644-0996;** fax 312/644-3019); and 12400 Wilshire Blvd., Suite 550, Los Angeles, CA 90025 (© **310/820-1898;** fax 310/820- 6367).

In Canada: 175 Bloor St. E., South Tower, Suite 907, Toronto, ON, M4W 3R8 (© **416/925-4882;** fax 416/925-4799).

In the United Kingdom: 1 Princes St., London W1R 8AY (© **020/7408-1254;** fax 020/7493-6695).

On the Web, the Italian National Tourist Board sponsors the sites **www.italiantourism.com** and **www.enit.it**.

For information on the **Vatican,** check out its website (**www.vatican.va**).

In Italy (**www.lainet.com/~initaly**) not only contains solid information on Italy and Rome presented in a very personal and friendly way, but also has one of the best sets of links to other Italy-related sites on the Web.

Another good site, **www.enjoyrome.com**, contains information about walking tours, accommodations, restaurants, side trips from Rome, useful links, and maps.

2 Entry Requirements & Customs

ENTRY REQUIREMENTS

U.S., Canadian, U.K., Irish, Australian, and New Zealand citizens with a **valid passport** don't need a visa to enter Italy if they don't expect to stay more than 90 days and don't expect to work there. If after entering Italy you want to stay more than 90 days, you can apply for a permit for an extra 90 days, which as a rule is granted immediately. Go to the nearest *questura* (police headquarters) or to your home country's consulate. If your passport is

lost or stolen, head to your consulate as soon as possible for a replacement.

CUSTOMS

WHAT YOU CAN BRING INTO ITALY Foreign visitors can bring along most items for personal use duty-free, including fishing tackle, a pair of skis, two tennis racquets, a baby carriage, two hand cameras with 10 rolls of film, and 200 cigarettes or a quantity of cigars or pipe tobacco not exceeding 250 grams (0.05 oz.).

There are strict limits on importing alcoholic beverages. However, for alcohol bought tax-paid, limits are much more liberal than in other countries of the European Union.

There are no restrictions on the amount of foreign currency you can bring into Italy, although you should declare the amount. Your declaration proves to the Italian Customs office that the currency came from outside the country, and therefore you can take out the same amount or less. Italian currency taken into or out of Italy may not exceed 200,000L (208€, $100) in denominations of 50,000L (52€, $25) or lower.

WHAT YOU CAN BRING HOME

Rules governing what you can bring back duty-free vary from country to country and are subject to change, but they're generally posted on the Web.

Returning **U.S. citizens** who have been away for 48 hours or more are allowed to bring back, once every 30 days, $400 worth of merchandise duty-free. You'll be charged a flat rate of 10% duty on the next $1,000 worth of purchases. Be sure to have your receipts handy. On gifts, the duty-free limit is $100. You cannot bring fresh foodstuffs into the United States; tinned foods are allowed. For more information, contact the **U.S. Customs Service** (② 202/927-6724), and request the free pamphlet *Know Before You Go.* It's also available on the Web at www.customs.ustreas. gov/travel/kbygo.htm.

Canadians should check the booklet *I Declare,* which you can download or order from Revenue Canada (② **613/993-0534;** www.ccra-adrc. gc.ca). **British** citizens should contact HM Customs & Excise (② **020 7202 4227;** www.hmce.gov.uk). **Australians** can contact the Australian Customs Service (② **1-300/363-263** within Australia, 61-2/6275-6666 from outside Australia; www.customs.gov.au/). **New Zealand** citizens should contact New Zealand Customs (② **09/359-6655;** www.customs.govt.nz/).

3 Money

CURRENCY

The basic unit of Italian currency is the **lira** (plural: **lire**), which you'll see abbreviated as **L.** Coins are issued in denominations of 10L, 20L, 50L, 100L, 200L, 500L, and 1,000L, and bills come in denominations of 1,000L, 2,000L, 5,000L, 10,000L, 50,000L, 100,000L, and 500,000L. Coins for 50L and 100L come in two sizes each. The most common coins are the 200L and 500L ones, and the most common bills are the 1,000L, 5,000L, and 10,000L.

With the arrival of the euro, things will change considerably. Until then, interbank exchange rates are established daily and listed in most international newspapers. To get a transaction as close to this rate as possible, pay for as much as possible with credit cards. ATMs and bank cards offer close to the same rate, plus an added fee for cash transaction.

THE EURO

The **euro,** the new single European currency, became the official currency of Italy and 10 other participating countries on January 1, 1999. You will run into prices quoted in both euros and lire.

Although the euro technically took effect in 1999—at which time the exchange rates of participating countries were locked together and are now fluctuating against the dollar in sync—this change has applied mostly to financial transactions between banks and businesses in Europe. The Italian lira remained the only currency in Italy for cash transactions throughout 2000 and 2001 (though the euro

The U.S. Dollar, the British Pound, the Italian Lira, and the Euro

The Euro   At this writing, 1€ equals approximately $1.07 and approximately 1,936L (or, 1L = 0.052 eurocents). During the lifetime of this edition, Italian businesses will begin accepting and making change in both lire and euros, a dual bookkeeping system that will probably cause some headaches and confusion, at least during the initial period of adjustment.

For American Readers   At this writing, $1 equals approximately 2,000L (or 100L = 0.05¢). This was the rate of exchange used to calculate the dollar values given throughout this book.

For British Readers   At this writing, £1 equals approximately 3,000L (or 100L = £0.03). This is the rate of exchange used to calculate the pound sterling values in the table below.

Note: The relative value of the lira to other world currencies fluctuates and might not be the same when you eventually travel to Italy. This table should be used only as an indication of approximate values. For daily updated rates, point your browser to **www.x-rates.com**.

Lira	U.S.$	U.K.£	Euro€	Lira	U.S.$	U.K.£	Euro€
50	0.03	0.02	0.03	10,000	5.00	3.00	5.20
100	0.05	0.03	0.05	20,000	10.00	6.00	10.40
250	0.13	0.08	0.13	25,000	12.50	7.50	13.00
500	0.25	0.15	0.26	30,000	15.00	9.00	15.60
750	0.38	0.23	0.39	35,000	17.50	10.50	18.20
1,000	0.50	0.30	0.52	40,000	20.00	12.00	20.80
1,500	0.75	0.45	0.78	45,000	22.50	13.50	23.40
2,000	1.00	0.60	1.04	50,000	25.00	15.00	26.00
3,000	1.50	0.90	1.56	100,000	50.00	30.00	52.00
4,000	2.00	1.20	2.08	150,000	75.00	45.00	78.00
5,000	2.50	1.50	2.60	250,000	125.00	75.00	130.00
7,500	3.75	2.25	3.90	500,000	250.00	150.00	260.00
9,000	4.50	2.70	4.68	1,000,000	500.00	300.00	520.00

was already used for noncash transactions, such as credit card purchases). But all that changed on **December 21, 2001,** when businesses began posting their prices in euros alongside those in Italian lire, which will continue to exist for a short time (many stores have started listing euro prices early).

On **January 1, 2002,** euro banknotes and coins will be introduced. Over a maximum 2-month transition period, Italian lire banknotes and coins will be withdrawn from circulation and the euro will become the official currency of Italy. The symbol of the euro is a stylized *E:* €. Its official abbreviation is EUR.

Exchange rates are more favorable at the point of arrival. Nevertheless, it's often helpful to exchange at least some money before going abroad (standing in line at the *cambio* [exchange bureau] in the Milan or Rome airport could make you miss the next bus leaving for downtown). Check with any of your local American Express or Thomas Cook offices or major banks. Or, order Italian lire in advance from the following: **American Express** (© 800/446-6234; www.americanexpress.com cardholders only), **Thomas Cook** (© 800/223-7373), or **Capital for Foreign Exchange** (© 888/842-0880).

It's best to exchange currency or traveler's checks at a bank, not a *cambio,* hotel, or shop. Currency and traveler's checks (for which you'll receive a better rate than cash) can be changed at all principal airports and at some travel agencies, such as American Express and Thomas Cook. Note the rates and ask about commission fees; it can sometimes pay to shop around and ask the right questions.

TRAVELER'S CHECKS

These days, traveler's checks seem less necessary because most larger cities have 24-hour ATMs, allowing you to withdraw small amounts of cash as needed. But if you prefer the security of the tried and true, you might want to stick with traveler's checks—provided that you don't mind showing an ID every time you want to cash a check.

You can purchase traveler's checks at any bank. In addition, **American Express** checks can be purchased by calling © 800/221-7282 or 800/721-9768; you can also purchase checks online at **www.americanexpress.com**. Amex gold or platinum cardholders can avoid paying the fee by ordering over the telephone; platinum cardholders can also purchase checks with no fee in person at Amex Travel Service locations (check the website for

the office nearest you). American Automobile Association members can obtain checks without a fee at most AAA offices.

ATMS

ATMs are linked to a national network that most likely includes your bank at home. Both the **Cirrus** (© 800/424-7787; www.mastercard. com) and the **Plus** (© 800/843-7587; www.visa.com) networks have automated ATM locators listing the banks in Italy that'll accept your card. Or, just search out any machine with your network's symbol emblazoned on it.

Important note: Make sure that the PINs on your bankcards and credit cards will work in Italy. You'll need a **four-digit code** (six digits won't work), so if you have a six-digit code you'll have to go into your bank and get a new PIN for your trip. If you're unsure about this, contact Cirrus or Plus (above). Be sure to check the daily withdrawal limit at the same time.

CREDIT CARDS

Credit cards are invaluable when traveling—they're a safe way to carry money and a convenient record of all your expenses. You can also withdraw cash advances from your cards at any bank (although this should be reserved for dire emergencies only because you'll start paying hefty interest the moment you receive the cash).

Note, however, that many banks, including Chase and Citibank, have begun to charge a 2% to 3% service fee for transactions in a foreign currency.

4 When to Go

April to June and **late September to October** are the best months for traveling in Italy—temperatures are usually mild and the crowds aren't quite so intense. Starting in mid-June, the

summer rush really picks up, and from **July to mid-September** the country teems with visitors. **August** is the worst month: Not only does it get uncomfortably hot, muggy, and crowded, but the entire country goes on vacation at least from August 15 to the end of the month—and many Italians take off the entire month. Many hotels, restaurants, and shops are closed (except at the spas, beaches, and islands, which are where 70% of the Italians head to). From **late October to Easter,** most attractions go on shorter winter hours or are closed for renovation. Many hotels and restaurants take a month or two off between **November and February,** spa and beach destinations become padlocked ghost towns, and it can get much colder than you'd expect (it might even snow).

High season on most airlines' routes to Rome usually stretches from June to the beginning of September. This is the most expensive and most crowded time to travel. **Shoulder season** is April and May, early September to October, and December 15 to 24. **Low season** is November 1 to December 14 and December 25 to March 31.

WEATHER

It's warm all over Italy in summer; it can be very hot in the south, especially inland. The high temperatures begin in Rome in May, often lasting until sometime in October. Winters in the north of Italy are cold, with rain and snow, but in the south the weather is warm all year, averaging 50°F in winter.

For the most part, it's drier in Italy than in North America, so high temperatures don't seem as bad because the humidity is lower. In Rome, Naples, and the south, temperatures can stay in the 90s for days, but nights are most often comfortably cooler.

The average high temperatures in central Italy and Rome are 82°F (27.8°C) in June, 87°F (30.5°C) in July, and 86°F (30°C) in August; the average lows are 63°F (17.2°C) in June and 67°F (19.4°C) in July and August.

HOLIDAYS

Offices and shops in Italy are closed on the following **national holidays:** January 1 (New Year's Day), Easter Monday, April 25 (Liberation Day), May 1 (Labor Day), August 15 (Assumption of the Virgin), November 1 (All Saints' Day), December 8 (Feast of the Immaculate Conception), December 25 (Christmas Day), and December 26 (Santo Stefano).

Many offices and business also close on June 29, for the feast day of Sts. Peter and Paul, the city's patron saints.

ROME CALENDAR OF EVENTS

For major events in which tickets should be procured well before arriving, check with **Global Edwards & Edwards** in the United States at ⓒ **800/223-6108.**

January

Carnevale, Piazza Navona, Rome. This festival marks the last day of the children's market and lasts until dawn of the following day. Usually January 4 to 5.

Epiphany celebrations, nationwide. All cities, towns, and villages in Italy stage Roman Catholic Epiphany observances. One of the most festive celebrations is the Epiphany Fair at Rome's Piazza Navona. Usually January 5 to 6.

Festa di Sant'Agnese, Sant'Agnese Fuori le Mura. During this ancient ceremony, two lambs are blessed and shorn, and their wool is used later for palliums (Roman Catholic vestments). Usually January 17.

March

Festa di Santa Francesca Romana, Piazzale del Colosseo near Santa Francesco Romana in the Roman Forum. A blessing of cars is performed at this festival. Usually March 9.

Festa di San Giuseppe, the Trionfale Quarter, north of the Vatican. The heavily decorated statue of the saint is brought out at a fair with food stalls, concerts, and sporting events. Usually March 19.

Holy Week observances. Processions and age-old ceremonies—some from pagan days, some from the Middle Ages—are staged throughout the country. The most notable procession is led by the pope, passing the Colosseum and the Roman Forum up to Palatine Hill; a torch-lit parade caps the observance. Beginning 4 days before Easter Sunday, which is March 31 in 2002.

Easter Sunday (Pasqua). In an event broadcast around the world, the pope gives his blessing from the balcony of St. Peter's.

April

Festa della Primavera, Rome. The Spanish Steps are decked out with banks of azaleas and other flowers; later, orchestral and choral concerts are presented in Trinità dei Monti. Dates vary.

May

Concorso Ippico Internazionale (International Horse Show), Piazza di Siena in the Villa Borghese. Usually May 1 to 10, but the dates can vary.

June

Son et Lumière. The Colosseum, the Roman Forum, and Tivoli areas are dramatically lit at night. Early June to end of September.

Festa di San Pietro, St. Peter's Basilica, Rome. This most significant Roman religious festival is observed with solemn rites. Usually around June 29.

July

Festa di Noantri. Trastevere, Rome's most colorful neighborhood, becomes a gigantic outdoor restaurant, with tables lining the streets and merrymakers and musicians providing the entertainment. After reaching the quarter, find the first empty table and try to get a waiter—but keep a close eye on your valuables. For details, contact the **Ente Provinciale per il Turismo,** Via Parigi 11, 00185 Roma (© **06/ 4889-9253** or 06/4889-9255). Mid-July.

August

Festa delle Catene, San Pietro in Vincoli. The relics of St. Peter's captivity go on display in this church. August 1.

Ferragosto. Beginning on August 15, most city residents not directly involved with the tourist trade take a 2-week vacation (many restaurants are closed as well). This is a good time *not* to be in Rome.

September

Sagra dell'Uva, Basilica of Maxentius, the Roman Forum. At this harvest festival, musicians in ancient costumes entertain and grapes are sold at reduced prices. Dates vary, usually early September.

December

Christmas Blessing of the Pope. Delivered at noon from the balcony of St. Peter's Basilica, the pope's words are broadcast around the world. December 25.

5 Health & Insurance

STAYING HEALTHY

If you worry about getting sick away from home and you're not confident that your existing health plan will provide the coverage you need, you might want to consider **medical travel insurance** (see "Insurance," below). Be sure to carry your identification card in your wallet.

If you suffer from a chronic illness, consult your doctor before your departure. For conditions such as epilepsy, diabetes, or heart problems, wear a **Medic Alert Identification Tag** (© 800/825-3785; www. medicalert.org), which will immediately alert doctors to your condition and give them access to your records through Medic Alert's 24-hour hot line.

Pack prescription medications in your carry-on luggage. Carry written prescriptions in generic, not brand-name form, and dispense all prescription medications from their original labeled vials. If you wear contact lenses, pack an extra pair in case you lose one.

Contact the **International Association for Medical Assistance to Travelers (IAMAT;** © 716/754-4883; www.sentex.net/~iamat). This organization offers tips on travel and health concerns in the countries you'll be visiting, and lists many local English-speaking doctors. In Canada, call **519/836-0102.**

INSURANCE

Check your existing policies before you buy, and don't buy more insurance than you really need.

Your existing health insurance should cover you if you get sick while on vacation—if you belong to an HMO, though, you should check to see whether you are fully covered when away from home. If you do need additional insurance, see the providers listed below.

Trip-cancellation insurance is a good idea if you have paid a large portion of your vacation expenses up front (say, by purchasing a package deal). Make sure you buy it from an outside vendor, though, not from your tour operator; you don't want to put all your eggs in one basket. There are two types of cancellation insurance—one that covers you if your packager or tour operator cancels your trip, and another type that will cover you in case of illness or the death of a family member. Trip-cancellation insurance costs approximately 6% to 8% of the total value of your vacation.

Your homeowner's or renter's insurance should cover stolen **luggage.** The airlines are responsible for only a very limited amount if they lose your luggage on an overseas flight, so if you plan to carry anything really valuable, keep it in your carry-on bag.

The differences between **travel assistance** and insurance are often blurred, but, in general, the former offers on-the-spot assistance and 24-hour hot lines (mostly oriented toward medical problems), whereas the latter reimburses you for travel problems (medical, travel, or otherwise) after you have filed the paperwork. The coverage you should consider will depend on how much protection is already contained in your existing health insurance or other policies.

Some credit-card and charge-card companies might insure you against travel accidents if you buy plane, train, or bus tickets with their cards. Before purchasing additional insurance, read your policies and agreements carefully. Call your insurers or credit-card companies if you have any questions.

Among the reputable issuers of travel insurance are Access America (© 800/ 284-8300; www.accessamerica.com) and Travel Guard International (© 800/826-1300; www.noelgroup. com). One company specializing in accident and medical care is Travel Assistance International (Worldwide Assistance Services, © 800/821-2828 or 202/828-5894; www.specialtyrisk. com/tai).

6 Tips for Travelers with Special Needs

FOR TRAVELERS WITH DISABILITIES

Laws in Italy have compelled rail stations, airports, hotels, and most restaurants to follow a stricter set of regulations about **wheelchair accessibility** to restrooms, ticket counters, and the like. Even museums and other attractions have conformed to the regulations, which mimic many of those presently in effect in the United States. Always call ahead to check on the accessibility in hotels, restaurants, and sights you want to visit.

Moss Rehab ResourceNet (www.mossresourcenet.org) is a great source for information, tips, and resources relating to accessible travel. You'll find links to a number of travel agents who specialize in planning trips for travelers with disabilities here and through **Access-Able Travel Source** (www.access-able.com), another excellent online source. You'll also find relay and voice numbers for hotels, airlines, and car-rental companies on Access-Able's user-friendly site, as well as links to accessible accommodations, attractions, transportation, tours, local medical resources and equipment repairers, and much more.

You can join the **Society for Accessible Travel & Hospitality** (SATH), 347 Fifth Ave., Suite 610, New York, NY 10016 (© 212/447-7284; www.sath.org), to gain access to its vast network of connections in the travel industry. The organization provides information sheets on destinations and referrals to tour operators who specialize in travelers with disabilities. Its quarterly magazine, *Open World,* is full of good information and resources.

You might also want to join a tour catering to travelers with disabilities. One of the best operators is **Flying Wheels Travel** (© 800/535-6790; www.flyingwheelstravel.com), offering various escorted tours and cruises with an emphasis on sports, as well as private tours in minivans with lifts. Other reputable operators are **Accessible Journeys** (© 800/TINGLES or 610/521-0339; www.disabilitytravel.com), for slow walkers and wheelchair travelers; **The Guided Tour** (© 215/782-1370); and **Directions Unlimited** (© 800/533-5343).

For British travelers, the **Royal Association for Disability and Rehabilitation (RADAR),** Unit 12, City Forum, 250 City Rd., London EC1V 8AF (© 020/7250-3222; www.radar.org.uk), publishes three holiday "fact packs" for £2 each or £5 for all three. The first provides general information, including tips for planning and booking a holiday, obtaining insurance, and handling finances; the second outlines transportation available when going abroad and equipment for rent; the third deals with specialized accommodations. Another good resource is **Holiday Care,** Imperial Building, 2nd Floor, Victoria Road, Horley, Surrey RH6 7PZ (© 01293/774-535; www.holidaycare.org.uk), a national charity advising on accessible accommodations for the elderly and persons with disabilities. Annual membership is £30.

FOR GAYS & LESBIANS

Since 1861, Italy has had liberal legislation regarding homosexuality, but that doesn't mean it has always been looked on favorably in a Catholic country. Homosexuality is much more accepted in the north than in the south, especially in Sicily, although Taormina has long been a gay mecca. However, all major towns and cities have an active gay life, especially Florence, Rome, and Milan, which considers itself the "gay capital" of Italy and is the headquarters of **ARCI Gay,** the country's leading gay organization with branches throughout Italy.

Capri is the gay resort of Italy, rivaled only by the gay beaches of Venice. (The World Pride celebrations in Rome in the summer of 2000 went off smoothly, but were preceded by months of denouncements by church officials and conservative politicians.)

As a companion to this guide, you might want to pick up *Frommer's Gay & Lesbian Europe,* with chapters on Rome, Florence, Venice, and Milan.

If you want help planning your trip, the **International Gay & Lesbian Travel Association** (IGLTA; ✆ **800/ 448-8550** or 954/776-2626; www. iglta.com) can link you with the appropriate gay-friendly service organization or tour specialist.

GayWired Travel Services (**www. gaywired.com**) is another great trip-planning resource; click on "Travel Services."

Out and About (✆ **800/929-2268** or 415/229-1793; www.outandabout. com) offers a monthly newsletter packed with good information on the global gay and lesbian scene, and its website features links to gay and lesbian tour operators and other gay-themed travel links. Out and About's guidebooks are available at most major bookstores and through **www.adlbooks.com**.

Other general-type U.S. gay and lesbian travel agencies include **Above and Beyond Tours** (✆ **800/397- 2681**). In the United Kingdom, try **Alternative Holidays** (✆ **020/7701- 7040;** info@alternativeholidays.com; www.alternativeholidays.com).

FOR SENIORS
One of the benefits of age is that travel often costs less. Always bring an ID card, especially if you've kept your youthful glow. Also mention the fact that you're a senior when you first make your travel reservations because many airlines and hotels offer discount programs for senior travelers.

Members of the **American Association of Retired Persons** (**AARP;** ✆ **800/424-3410** or 202/434-AARP; www.aarp.org) get discounts on hotels, airfares, and car rentals. If you're not already a member, do yourself a favor and join.

SAGA International Holidays, 222 Berkeley St., Boston, MA 02116 (✆ **800/343-0273**), offers inclusive tours and cruises for those 50 and older. SAGA also sponsors the more substantial **"Road Scholar Tours"** (✆ **800/621-2151**), which are fun-oriented but with an educational bent.

If you want something more than the average vacation or guided tour, try **Elderhostel** (✆ **877/426-8056;** www.elderhostel.org) or the University of New Hampshire's **Interhostel** (✆ **800/733-9753;** www.learn.unh. org), both variations on the same theme: educational travel for seniors. On these escorted tours, the days are packed with seminars, lectures, and field trips; the sightseeing is all led by academic experts. The courses in both programs are ungraded, involve no homework, and often focus on the liberal arts. They're not luxury vacations, but they are fun and fulfilling.

FOR STUDENTS
The best resource for students is the **Council on International Educational Exchange (CIEE).** This organization can set you up with an International Student ID card, and its travel branch, **Council Travel** (✆ **800/2-COUNCIL;** www. counciltravel.com), the world's biggest student travel agency, can get you discounts on plane tickets, rail passes, and the like. Council Travel has retail locations all around the United States; check the website for the location nearest you.

From CIEE, you can obtain the $20 **International Student Identity Card (ISIC),** the only officially acceptable form of student ID, good for cut rates on rail passes, plane tickets, and other discounts. It also provides you with basic health and life insurance and a 24-hour help line. If you're no longer a student but are still under 26, you can get a **GO 25 card** from the same people; it'll get you the insurance and some of the discounts (but not student admission prices in museums). CTS also sells **Eurailpasses** and **YHA (Youth Hostel Association)** passes, and can book hostel or hotel accommodations for you.

CTS's U.K. office is at 28A Poland St. (Oxford Circus), London WIV 3DB (☎ **020/7478-2000**); the Italy office is at Via Genova 16, 00184 Roma (☎ **06-844-0561**). In Canada, Travel CUTS, 200 Ronson St., Suite 320, Toronto, ON M9W 5Z9 (☎ **800/667-2887** or 416/614-2887; www.travelcuts.com), offers similar services. Usit Campus, 52 Grosvenor Gardens, London SW1W 0AG (☎ **0870/240-1010**; www.usitcampus. co.uk), opposite Victoria Station, is Britain's leading specialist in student and youth travel.

7 Getting There

BY PLANE

High season on most airlines' routes to Rome is usually June to the beginning of September. This is the most expensive and most crowded time to travel. **Shoulder season** is April and May, early September to October, and December 15 to 24. **Low season** is November 1 to December 14 and December 25 to March 31.

FROM NORTH AMERICA   Fares to Italy are constantly changing, but you can expect to pay somewhere in the range of $400 to $800 for a direct round-trip ticket from New York to Rome in coach class.

Flying time to Rome from New York, Newark, and Boston is 8 hours; from Chicago, 10 hours; and from Los Angeles, 12½ hours. Flying time to Milan from New York, Newark, and Boston is 8 hours; from Chicago, 9¼ hours; and from Los Angeles, 11½ hours.

American Airlines (☎ **800/433-7300**; www.aa.com) offers daily non-stop flights to Rome from Chicago's O'Hare, with flights from all parts of American's vast network making connections into Chicago. **TWA** (☎ **800/221-2000**; www.twa.com) offers daily nonstop flights from New York's JFK to Rome, Milan, and Venice. **Delta** (☎ **800/241-4141**; www.delta.com) also flies from New York's JFK to both Milan and Rome; separate flights depart every evening for both destinations. **United** (☎ **800/538-2929**; www.ual.com) has service to Milan only from Dulles in Washington, D.C. **US Airways** (☎ **800/428-4322**; www.usairways.com) offers one flight daily to Rome out of Philadelphia (you can connect through Philly from most major U.S. cities). And **Continental** (☎ **800/231-0856**; www. continental.com) flies twice daily to Rome from its hub in Newark.

Canadian Airlines International (☎ **888/247-2262**; www.cdnair.ca) flies daily from Toronto to Rome. Two of the flights are nonstop; the others touch down en route in Montréal, depending on the schedule.

British Airways (☎ **800/AIRWAYS**; www.british-airways.com), **Virgin Atlantic Airways** (☎ **800/862-8621**; www.fly.virgin.co.uk), **Air France** (☎ **800/237-2747**; www.airfrance. com), **Northwest/KLM** (☎ **800/374-7747**; www.klm.nl), and **Lufthansa** (☎ **800/645-3880**; www.lufthansa-usa. com) offer some attractive deals for anyone interested in combining a trip to Italy with a stopover in, say, Britain, Paris, Amsterdam, or Germany.

Alitalia (© **800/223-5730** in the United States, 514/842-8241 in Canada; www.alitalia.it/english/index. html) is the Italian national airline, with nonstop flights to Rome from different North American cities, including New York (JFK), Newark, Boston, Chicago, and Miami. Nonstop flights into Milan are from New York (JFK), Newark, and Los Angeles. From Milan or Rome, Alitalia can easily book connecting domestic flights if your final destination is elsewhere in Italy. Alitalia participates in the frequent-flier programs of other airlines, including Continental and US Airways.

FROM THE UNITED KINGDOM

Operated by the European Travel Network, **www.discount-tickets.com** is a great online source for regular and discounted airfares to destinations around the world. You can also use this site to compare rates and book accommodations, car rentals, and tours. Click on "Special Offers" for the latest package deals. Students should also try **USIT Campus** (© **0870/240-1010;** www. usitcampus.co.uk).

British newspapers are always full of classified ads touting slashed fares to Italy. One good source is *Time Out.* London's *Evening Standard* has a daily travel section, and the Sunday editions of almost any newspaper will run many ads. Although competition is fierce, one well-recommended company that consolidates bulk ticket purchases and then passes the savings on to its consumers is **Trailfinders** (© **020/7937-5400;** www.trailfinder. com). It offers access to tickets on such carriers as SAS, British Airways, and KLM.

Both **British Airways** (© **0345/ 222-111** in the U.K.; www.british airways.co.uk) and **Alitalia** (© **0870/ 5448-8249;** www.alitalia.it/english/ index.html) have frequent flights from

London's Heathrow to Rome. British Airways also has one direct flight a day from Manchester to Rome. **Virgin Atlantic** doesn't serve Italy at all at press time.

FLY FOR LESS: TIPS FOR GETTING THE BEST AIRFARES

- **Take advantage of APEX fares.** Advance-purchase booking, or APEX, fares are often the key to getting the lowest fare. You generally must be willing to make your plans and buy your tickets as far ahead as possible: The **21-day APEX** is seconded only by the **14-day APEX,** with a stay in Italy of 7 to 30 days. Because the number of seats allocated to APEX fares is sometimes less than 25% of plane capacity, the early bird gets the low-cost seat. There's often a surcharge for flying on a weekend, and cancellation and refund policies can be strict.
- **Watch for sales.** You'll almost never see sales during July and August or the Thanksgiving or Christmas seasons, but at other times you can get great deals. In the last couple of years, there have been amazing prices on winter flights to Rome. If you already hold a ticket when a sale breaks, it might pay to exchange it, even if you incur a $50 to $75 penalty charge. Note, however, that thelowest-priced fares are often nonrefundable, require advance purchase of 1 to 3 weeks and a certain length of stay, and carry penalties for changing dates of travel. Make sure you know exactly what the restrictions are before you commit.
- If your schedule is flexible, ask if you can secure a cheaper fare by **staying an extra day** or by **flying midweek.** (Many airlines won't volunteer this information.)

- **Consolidators,** also known as bucket shops, are a good place to find low fares, often below even the airlines' discounted rates. Basically, they're just big travel agents who get discounts for buying in bulk and pass some of the savings on to you. Before you pay, however, be aware that consolidator tickets are usually nonrefundable or come with stiff cancellation penalties.

  We've gotten great deals on many occasions from **Cheap Tickets** ☎ (✆ **800/377-1000;** www.cheaptickets.com). **Council Travel** (✆ **888/COUNCIL;** www.counciltravel.com) and **STA Travel** (✆ **800/781-4040;** www.sta.travel.com) cater especially to young travelers, but their bargain-basement prices are available to people of all ages. Other reliable consolidators include **Lowestfare.com** (✆ **888/278-8830;** www.lowestfare.com); **1-800/AIRFARE** (www.1800airfare.com); **Cheap Seats** (✆ **800/451-7200;** www.cheapseatstravel.com); and **1-800/FLY-CHEAP** (www.flycheap.com).
- Search the **Internet** for cheap fares—though it's still best to compare your findings with the research of a dedicated travel agent, if you're lucky enough to have one, especially when you're booking more than just a flight. Among the better-respected virtual travel agents are **Travelocity** (www.travelocity.com), **Expedia** (www.expedia.com), **Yahoo! Travel** (http://travel.yahoo.com), and **Orbitz** (www.orbitz.com).

BY TRAIN

If you plan to travel heavily on the European rails, you'll do well to get yourself a copy of the *Thomas Cook European Timetable of Railroads.* This 500-plus-page timetable accurately documents all of Europe's mainline passenger rail services. It's available from **Forsyth Travel Library,** 226 Westchester Ave., White Plains, NY 10604 (✆ **800/FORSYTH;** www.forsyth.com), for $27.95 (plus $4.95 shipping in the U.S. and $6.95 in Canada), or at travel specialty stores such as **Rand McNally,** 150 E. 52nd St., New York, NY 10022 (✆ **212/758-7488;** www.randmcnally.com).

New electric trains have made travel between France and Italy faster and more comfortable than ever. **France's TGVs** travel at speeds of up to 185 miles per hour and have cut travel time between Paris and Turin from 7 to 5½ hours and between Paris and Milan from 7½ to 6¾ hours. **Italy's ETRs** travel at speeds of up to 145 miles per hour and currently run between Milan and Lyon (5 hr.), with a stop in Turin.

RAIL PASSES
EURAILPASS Many travelers to Europe take advantage of one of the greatest travel bargains, the **Eurailpass,** which permits unlimited first-class rail travel in any country in western Europe (except the British Isles) and Hungary in eastern Europe. Oddly, it doesn't include travel on the rail lines of Sardinia, which are organized independently of the rail lines of the rest of Italy.

The advantages are tempting: There are no tickets; simply show the pass to the ticket collector and then settle back to enjoy the scenery. Seat reservations are required on some trains. Many of the trains have couchettes (sleeping cars), for which an extra fee is charged. Obviously, the 2- or 3-month traveler gets the greatest economic advantages. To obtain full advantage of a 15-day or 1-month pass, you'd have to spend a great deal of time on the train.

Eurailpass holders are entitled to considerable reductions on certain buses and ferries as well. You'll get a

20% reduction on second-class accommodations from certain companies operating ferries between Naples and Palermo or for crossings to Sardinia and Malta.

A **Eurailpass** is $554 for 15 days, $718 for 21 days, $890 for 1 month, $1,260 for 2 months, and $1,558 for 3 months. Children 3 and under travel free, provided that they don't occupy a seat (otherwise, they're charged half fare); children 4 to 11 are charged half fare. If you're under 26, you can buy a **Eurail Youthpass,** entitling you to unlimited second-class travel for $388 for 15 days, $499 for 21 days, $623 for 1 month, $882 for 2 months, and $1,089 for 3 months.

The **Eurail Saverpass,** valid all over Europe for first class only, offers discounted 15-day travel for groups of three or more people traveling together from April to September, or two people traveling together from October to March. The price is $470 for 15 days, $610 for 21 days, $756 for 1 month, $1,072 for 2 months, and $1,324 for 3 months.

The **Eurail Flexipass** allows you to visit Europe with more flexibility. It's valid in first class and offers the same privileges as the Eurailpass. However, it provides a number of individual travel days that you can use over a much longer period of consecutive days. That makes it possible to stay in one city and yet not lose a single day of travel. There are two passes: 10 days of travel in 2 months for $654, and 15 days of travel in 2 months for $862.

Having many of the same qualifications and restrictions as the previously described Flexipass is the **Eurail Youth Flexipass.** Sold only to travelers under 26, it allows 10 days of travel within 2 months for $458, and 15 days of travel within 2 months for $599.

The **Eurail Selectpass** is a flexipass, meaning that travel days need not be consecutive. Passes are available for 5, 6, 8, or 10 days within a 2-month period. Prices vary, of course, depending on the days selected, beginning at $328 for a 5-day pass.

EUROPASS The **Europass** is more limited than the Eurailpass, but it could offer better value for visitors traveling over a smaller area. It's good for 2 months and allows 5 days of rail travel within three to five European countries (Italy, France, Germany, Switzerland, and Spain) with contiguous borders. For individual travelers, 5 days of travel costs $348 in first class and $233 in second class; 6 days of travel, $368 in first class and $253 in second class; 8 days of travel, $448 in first class and $313 in second class; 10 days of travel, $528 in first class and $363 in second; and 15 days of travel, $728 in first class and $513 in second class.

For travelers under 26, a **Europass Youth** is available. The fares are 35% to 55% off those quoted above, and the pass is good only for second-class travel. Unlike the adult Europass, there's no discount for a companion.

ITALIAN RAIL PASSES If you'll be traveling beyond Rome by rail, you'll need to know a bit about the Italian train system. As a rule of thumb, second-class travel usually costs about two-thirds the price of an equivalent first-class trip. A couchette (a private fold-down bed in a communal cabin) requires a supplement above the price of first-class travel. Children ages 4 to 11 receive a discount of 50% off the adult fare and children 3 and under travel free with their parents.

If you don't buy the Eurailpass (see above), you might consider an **Italian Railpass** (known in Italy as a **BTLC Pass**), which allows non-Italian citizens to ride as much as they like on Italy's entire rail network. Buy the pass in the United States or at main train stations in Italy, have it validated the first time you use it at any rail station, and ride as frequently as you like within the time validity. An 8-day pass is $299 first class and $199 second, a 15-day pass $373 first class and $249 second, a 21-day pass $433 first class and $289 second, and a 30-day pass $522 first class and $348 second. All passes have a $15 issuing fee per class.

With the Italian Railpass and each of the other special passes, a supplement must be paid to ride on certain rapid trains, designated **ETR-450** or **Pendolino trains.** The rail systems of Sardinia are administered by a separate entity and aren't included in the Railpass or any of the other passes.

Another option is the **Italian Flexirail Card,** which entitles you to a predetermined number of days of travel on any rail line in a certain time period. It's ideal for passengers who plan in advance to spend several days sightseeing before boarding a train for another city. A pass giving 4 possible travel days out of a block of 1 month is $239 first class and $159 second, a pass for 8 travel days stretched over a 1-month period $334 first class and $223 second, and a pass for 12 travel days within 1 month $429 first class and $286 second.

You can buy these passes from any travel agent or by calling © **800/ 248-7245.** You can also call © **800/ 4-EURAIL** or **800/EUROSTAR.**

Where to Buy a Pass

In **North America,** you can buy these passes from travel agents or rail agents in major cities such as New York, Montréal, and Los Angeles. Eurailpasses are also available through **Rail Europe** (© **800/438-7245;** www. raileurope.com). No matter what everyone tells you, you can buy Eurailpasses in Europe as well as in America (at the major train stations), but

they're more expensive. Rail Europe can also give you information on the rail/drive versions of the passes.

For details on the rail passes available in the **United Kingdom,** stop in at or contact the **International Rail Centre,** Victoria Station, London SW1V 1JZ (© **0990/848-848**). The staff can help you find the best option for the trip you're planning. Some of the most popular are the **Inter-Rail** and **Under 26** passes, entitling you to unlimited second-class travel in 26 European countries.

Under 26 tickets are a worthwhile option for travelers under 26. They allow you to move leisurely from London to Rome, with as many stopovers en route as you want, using a different route southbound (through Belgium, Luxembourg, and Switzerland) from the return route northbound (exclusively through France). All travel must be completed within 1 month of the departure date. Under 26 tickets from London to Rome cost from £133 for the most direct route or from £209 for a roundabout route through the south of France.

BY CAR

If you're already on the Continent, particularly in a neighboring country such as France or Austria, you might want to drive to Italy. However, you should make sure that such travel is allowed by your car-rental company.

Most of the roads from western Europe leading into Italy are toll-free, with some notable exceptions. If you use the Swiss superhighway network, you'll have to buy a special tax sticker at the border. You'll also pay to go through the St. Gotthard Tunnel into Italy. Crossings from France can be through the Mont Blanc Tunnel, for which you'll pay, or you can leave the French Riviera at Menton and drive directly into Italy along the Italian Riviera toward San Remo.

8 Escorted Tours & Package Deals

The biggest operator of escorted tours is **Perillo Tours** (© **800/431-1515** or 201/307-1234 in the U.S.; www.perillotours.com), family operated for three generations—perhaps you've seen the TV commercials featuring the "King of Italy," Mario Perillo, and his son. Perillo's tours cost much less than you'd spend if you arranged a comparable trip yourself. Accommodations are in first-class hotels, and guides tend to be well qualified and well informed.

Another contender is **Italiatour,** a company of the Alitalia Group (© **800/845-3365** or 212/765-2183; www.italiatour.com), offering a wide variety of tours through all parts of Italy. It specializes in packages for independent travelers (not tour groups) who ride from one destination to another by train or rental car. In most cases, the company sells prereserved accommodations, which are usually less expensive than if you had reserved them yourself. Because of the company's close link with Alitalia, the prices quoted for air passage are sometimes among the most reasonable on the retail market.

Also working with volume and affiliated with Alitalia—and, therefore, promising discounts—is **Central Holidays Tours** (CHT; © **800/ 935-5000;** www.centralholidays.com), which offers package tours that are escorted, hosted, or independent. This outfitter is also a good choice if you want to mix and match your own arrangements; the company will help with air, hotel, and car rental according to your needs.

Trafalgar Tours (© **800/854-0103;** www.trafalgartours.com) is one of Europe's largest tour operators, offering affordable guided tours with lodgings in unpretentious hotels. Check with your travel agent for more information on these tours (Trafalgar takes calls only from agents).

One of Trafalgar's leading competitors is **Globus+Cosmos Tours** (© **800/ 221-0090;** www.globus.com). Globus has first-class escorted coach tours of various regions lasting from 8 to 16 days. Cosmos, a budget branch of Globus, sells escorted tours of about the same length. Tours must be booked through a travel agent, but you can call the 800 number for brochures. Another competitor is **Insight Vacations** (© **800/582- 8380**), which books superior first-class, fully escorted motor-coach tours lasting from 1 week to 36 days.

Abercrombie & Kent (© **800/ 323-7308** in the U.S., or **0845/ 0700-610** in the U.K.; www.abercrombiekent.com) offers a variety of luxurious premium packages. Your overnight stays will be in meticulously restored castles and exquisite Italian villas, most of which are four- and five-star accommodations.

SPECIAL-INTEREST TOURS

At the InfoHub Specialty Travel Guide (**www.infohub.com**), you can find tours in Italy (as well as other countries) centered on antiques, archaeology, art history, cooking, wineries, and much more.

Tennis fans who want to catch the mid-May Italian Open, held at the Foro Italica, near Mussolini's Olympic site, might contact California-based **Advantage Tennis Tours** (© **800/ 341-8687;** www.advantagetennistours. com). Their tours include 6 nights' accommodations in a deluxe Rome hotel, center court seats at three sessions of the tournament, city tours of ancient Rome, a farewell dinner, the services of a tour hostess, and the opportunity to play tennis.

VBT (formerly Vermont Bicycle Tours; © **800/BIKE-TOUR;** www. vbt.com) offers a variety of bike tours throughout Italy (current offerings include a 7-day trip through the relatively flat terrain of the Parma and Po Valley region, and a weeklong tour of Tuscany's hill towns). Accommodations, some meals, equipment, a support van, airport transfers, and activities are included in the price. **Backroads** (© **800-GO-ACTIVE** or 510/527-1555; www.backroads.com) also offers a wide variety of bike tours and other active vacations throughout Italy.

For hiking and walking tours and other adventures, try **Mountain Travel-Sobek** (© **6510/527-8100** or 888/687-6235; www.mtsobek.com) or **Above the Clouds Trekking** (© **800/233-4499** or 508/799-4499).

For both art and architecture and food and wine tours, **Amelia Tours International** (© **800/742-4591** or 516/433-0696) is the leader of the pack.

The oldest travel agency in Britain, **Cox & Kings** (© **020/7873-5000;** www.coxandkings.co.uk), specializes in unusual, if pricey, holidays. Its Italy offerings include organized tours through the country's gardens and sites of historic or aesthetic interest, opera tours, pilgrimage-style visits to sites of religious interest, and food-and wine-tasting tours.

4

Getting to Know Rome

In this chapter, you'll find all the details to help you settle into Rome, from arriving at the airport to how to get around. There's a quick breakdown of neighborhoods to help you figure out where you'll want to base yourself, and that will help organize yourself, and that will help organize and orient all the hotels, restaurants, and sights in the following chapters. We'll round it off with a list of "Fast Facts"—everything from cybercafes and embassies to where to find English-speaking doctors and how to make a phone call.

1 Essentials

ARRIVING

BY PLANE   Chances are, you'll arrive at Rome's **Leonardo da Vinci International Airport** (© **06-65-951** or 06-6595-3640), popularly known as **Fiumicino,** 18½ miles (30km) from the city center. (If you're flying by charter, you might land at Ciampino Airport, discussed shortly.)

After you leave Passport Control, you'll see two **information desks** (one for Rome, one for Italy; © **06-65-95-6074**). At the Rome desk, you can pick up a general map and some pamphlets from Monday to Saturday from 8:30am to 7pm; the staff can also help you find a hotel room if you haven't reserved ahead. A *cambio* (money exchange) operates daily from 7:30am to 11pm, offering surprisingly good rates. **Luggage storage** is available 24 hours daily in the main arrivals building, costing 5,000L (2.60€, $2.50) per bag.

There's a **train station** in the airport. To get into the city, follow the signs marked TRENI for the 30-minute shuttle to Rome's main station, **Stazione Termini** (arriving on Track 22). The shuttle runs from 7:30am to 10pm for 17,000L (8.85€, $8.50) one way. On the way you'll pass a machine dispensing tickets, or you can buy them in person near the tracks if you don't have small bills on you. When you arrive at Termini, get out of the train quickly and grab a baggage cart. (It's a long schlep from the track to the exit or to the other train connections, and baggage carts can be scarce.)

A **taxi** from Da Vinci airport to the city costs 90,000L (46.80€, $45) and up for the 1-hour trip, depending on traffic. The expense might be worth it if you have a lot of luggage or just don't want to be bothered with the train trip. Call © **06-6645,** 06-3570, or 06-4994 for information.

If you arrive on a charter flight at **Ciampino Airport** (© **06-794-941**), you can take a COTRAL bus, which departs every 30 minutes or so for the Anagnina stop of Metropolitana (subway) Line A. Take Line A to Stazione Termini, where you can make your final connections. Trip time is about 45 minutes and costs 1,500L (.80€, 75¢). A **taxi** from this airport to Rome costs the same as the one from the Da Vinci airport (above), but the trip is shorter (about 40 minutes).

BY TRAIN OR BUS   Trains and buses (including trains from the airport) arrive in the center of old Rome at the silver **Stazione Termini,** Piazza dei Cinquecento (© **1478/880-88**); this is the train, bus, and subway transportation hub for all Rome and is surrounded by many hotels (especially cheaper ones).

If you're taking the **Metropolitana** (subway), follow the illuminated red-and-white M signs. To catch a bus, go straight through the outer hall and enter the sprawling bus lot of Piazza dei Cinquecento. You'll also find **taxis** there.

The station is filled with services. At a branch of the **Banca San Paolo di Torino** (between Tracks 8–11 and Tracks 12–15), you can exchange money. **Informazioni Ferroviarie** (in the outer hall) dispenses information on rail travel to other parts of Italy. There's also a **tourist information booth** here, along with baggage services, newsstands, and snack bars.

BY CAR   From the north, the main access route is the **Autostrada del Sole (A1),** which cuts through Milan and Florence, or you can take the coastal route, **SSI Aurelia,** from Genoa. If you're driving north from Naples, you take the southern lap of the **Autostrada del Sole (A2).** All the autostrade join with the **Grande Raccordo Anulare,** a ring road encircling Rome, channeling traffic into the congested city. Long before you reach this road, you should study a map carefully to see what part of Rome you plan to enter and mark your route accordingly. Route markings along the ring road tend to be confusing.

Important Advice: Return your rental car immediately, or at least get yourself to a hotel, park your car, and leave it there until you leave Rome. Don't even try to drive in Rome—the traffic is just too nightmarish.

VISITOR INFORMATION

Information is available at three locations maintained by the Azienda Provinciale di Turismo (APT): a kiosk at **Leonardo da Vinci International Airport** (© **06-6595-6074**), a kiosk in **Stazione Termini** (© **06-360-04-399**), and a kiosk and administrative headquarters at **Via Parigi 5** (© **06-4889-9253**). The headquarters are open Monday to Friday from 8:15am to 7:15pm (Sat to 2pm).

Tips   A Few Train Station Warnings

In Stazione Termini, you'll almost certainly be approached by touts claiming to work for a tourist organization. They really work for individual hotels (not always the most recommendable) and will say almost anything to sell you a room. Unless you know something about Rome's layout and are savvy, it's best to ignore them.

Be aware of all your belongings at all times, and keep your wallet and purse away from professionally experienced fingers. Never ever leave your bags unattended for even a second, and while making phone calls or waiting in line, make sure that your attention doesn't wander from any bags you've set by your side or on the ground. Be aware if someone asks you for directions or information—it's likely meant to distract you and easily will.

Ignore the taxi drivers soliciting passengers right outside the terminal; they can charge as much as triple the normal amount. Instead, line up in the official taxi stand in Piazza dei Cinquecento.

The office at the airport and the one at the Stazione Termini are open daily from 8:15am to 7:15pm, but we've never found these locations to be great resources.

More helpful, and stocking maps and brochures, are the offices maintained by the **Comune di Roma** at various sites around the city, with red-and-orange or yellow-and-black signs saying COMUNE DI ROMA—PUNTI DI INFORMAZIONE TURISTICA. They're staffed daily from 9am to 6pm, except the one at Termini (daily 8am–9pm). Here are the addresses and phone numbers: in Stazione Termini (℗ **06-4890-6300**); in Piazza dei Cinquecento, outside Termini (℗ **06-4782-5194**); in Piazza Pia, near the Castel Sant'Angelo (℗ **06-6880-9707**); in Piazza San Giovanni, in Laterano (℗ **06-7720-3598**); along Largo Carlo Goldoni (℗ **06-6813-6061**), near the intersection of Via del Corso and Via Condotti; on Via Nazionale, near the Palazzo delle Esposizioni (℗ **06-4782-4525**); on Largo Corrado Ricci, near the Colosseum (℗ **06-6992-4307**); on Piazza Sonnino in Trastevere (℗ **06-5833-3457**); on Piazza Cinque Lune, near Piazza Navona (℗ **06-6880-9240**); and on Piazza Santa Maria Maggiore (℗ **06-4788-0294**).

Enjoy Rome, Via Varese 39, near the train station (℗ **06-445-1843;** www. enjoyrome.com), was begun by an English-speaking couple, Fulvia and Pierluigi. They dispense information about almost everything in Rome and are far more pleasant and organized than the Board of Tourism. They'll also help you find a hotel room, with no service charge (in anything from a hostel to a three-star hotel). Summer hours are Monday to Friday 8:30am to 7pm, and Saturday 8:30am to 1:30pm; winter hours are Monday to Friday 8:30am to 1:30pm and 3:30 to 6pm.

CITY LAYOUT

Arm yourself with a detailed street map, not the general overview handed out free at tourist offices. Most hotels hand out a pretty good version at their front desks.

The bulk of ancient, Renaissance, and baroque Rome (as well as the train station) lies on the east side of the **Tiber River (Fiume Tevere),** which meanders through town. However, several important landmarks are on the other side: **St. Peter's Basilica** and the **Vatican,** the **Castel Sant'Angelo,** and the colorful **Trastevere** neighborhood.

The city's various quarters are linked by large boulevards (large, at least, in some places) that have mostly been laid out since the late 19th century. Starting from the **Vittorio Emanuele Monument,** a controversial pile of snow-white Brescian marble that's often compared to a wedding cake, there's a street running practically due north to **Piazza del Popolo** and the city wall. This is **Via del Corso,** one of the main streets of Rome—noisy, congested, always crowded with buses and shoppers, and called simply "Il Corso." To its left (west) lie the Pantheon, Piazza Navona, Campo de' Fiori, and the Tiber. To its right (east) you'll find the Spanish Steps, the Trevi Fountain, the Borghese Gardens, and Via Veneto.

Back at the Vittorio Emanuele Monument, the major artery going west (and ultimately across the Tiber to St. Peter's) is **Corso Vittorio Emanuele.** Behind you to your right, heading toward the Colosseum, is **Via del Fori Imperiali,** laid out in the 1930s by Mussolini to show off the ruins of the imperial forums he had excavated, which line it on either side. Yet another central conduit is **Via Nazionale,** running from **Piazza Venezia** (just in front of the Vittorio Emanuele Monument) east to **Piazza della Repubblica** (near Stazione Termini). The final lap of Via Nazionale is called **Via Quattro Novembre.**

Finding an address in Rome can be a problem because of the narrow streets of old Rome and the little, sometimes hidden *piazze* (squares). Numbers usually run consecutively, with odd numbers on one side of the street and even numbers on the other. However, in the old districts the numbers will sometimes run consecutively up one side of the street to the end, then back in the opposite direction on the other side. Therefore, no. 50 could be opposite no. 308.

THE NEIGHBORHOODS IN BRIEF
This section will give you some idea of where you might want to stay and where the major attractions are located.

NEAR STAZIONE TERMINI
The main train station, **Stazione Termini,** adjoins **Piazza della Repubblica,** and most likely this will be your introduction to Rome. Much of the area is seedy and filled with gas fumes from all the buses and cars, but it has been improving. If you stay here, you might not get a lot of atmosphere, but you'll have a lot of affordable options and a very convenient location, near the transportation hub of the city and not too far from ancient Rome. There's a lot to see here, including the **Basilica di Santa Maria Maggiore** and the **Baths of Diocletian.** Some high-class hotels are sprinkled in the area, including the **Grand,** but many are long past their heyday.

The neighborhoods on either side of Termini have been improving greatly, and some streets are now attractive. The best-looking area is ahead and to your right as you exit the station on the Via Marsala side. Most budget hotels here occupy a floor or more of a palazzo; many of their entryways are drab, although upstairs they're often charming or at least clean and livable. In the area to the left of the station as you exit, the streets are wider, the traffic is heavier, and the noise level is higher. This area off Via Giolitti is being redeveloped, and now most streets are in good condition. A few still need improvement; take caution at night.

VIA VENETO & PIAZZA BARBERINI
In the 1950s and early 1960s, **Via Veneto** was the swinging place to be, as the likes of King Farouk, Frank Sinatra, and Swedish actress Anita Ekberg paraded up and down the boulevard to the delight of the paparazzi. The street is still here and is still the site of luxury hotels and elegant cafes and restaurants, though it's no longer the happening place to be. It's lined with restaurants catering to those visitors who've heard of this famous boulevard from decades past, but the restaurants are mostly overpriced and overcrowded tourist traps. Rome city authorities would like to restore this legendary street to some of its former glory by banning vehicular traffic on the top half. It makes for a pleasant stroll, in any case.

To the south, Via Veneto comes to an end at **Piazza Barberini,** dominated by the 1642 **Triton Fountain (Fontana del Tritone),** a baroque celebration with four dolphins holding up an open scallop shell in which a triton sits blowing into a conch. Overlooking the square is the **Palazzo Barberini.** In 1623, when Cardinal Maffeo Barberini became Pope Urban VIII, he ordered Carlo Maderno to build a palace here; it was later completed by Bernini and Borromini.

ANCIENT ROME
Most visitors explore this area first, taking in the

Rome Orientation

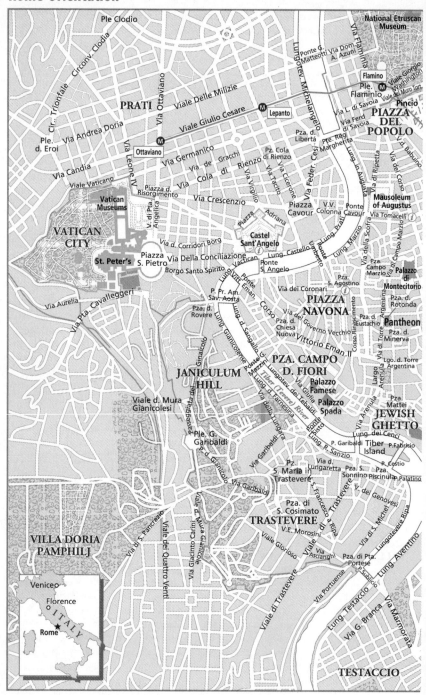

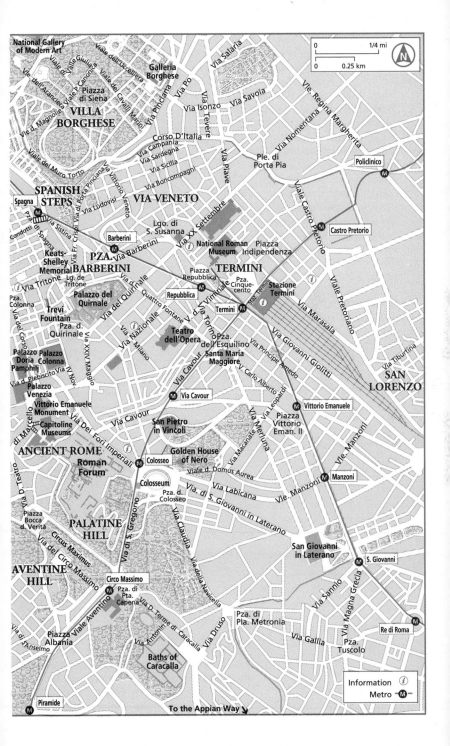

National Gallery
of Modern Art

Galleria
Borghese

Piazza
di Siena

VILLA
BORGHESE

Corso D'Italia

Ple. di
Porta Pia

Policlinico

SPANISH
STEPS

Spagna

VIA VENETO

Lgo. di
S. Susanna

Barberini

Castro Pretorio

National Roman
Museum

Piazza
Indipendenza

Keats-
Shelley
Memorial

PZA.
BARBERINI

Lg. de
Tritone

Piazza
Repubblica

TERMINI

Trevi
Fountain

Palazzo del
Quirinale

Repubblica

Pza.
Cinque-
cento

Stazione
Termini

Pza. d.
Quirinale

Termini

Palazzo
Doria
Pamphilj

Palazzo
Colonna

Teatro
dell'Opera

Pza.
dell'Esquilino

Santa Maria
Maggiore

SAN
LORENZO

Palazzo
Venezia

Vittorio Emanuele
Monument

Via Cavour

Vittorio Emanuele

Capitoline
Museums

San Pietro
in Vincoli

Piazza
Vittorio
Eman. II

ANCIENT ROME

Roman
Forum

Golden House
of Nero

Manzoni

Colosseo

Colosseum

Piazza
Bocca
d. Verità

Pza. d.
Colosseo

San Giovanni
in Laterano

PALATINE
HILL

S. Giovanni

AVENTINE
HILL

Circus Maximus

Circo Massimo

Pza. di
Pta.
Capena

Pza. di
Pla. Metronia

Re di Roma

Piazza
Albania

Pza.
Tuscolo

Baths of
Caracalla

Piramide

To the Appian Way

Information

Metro

0   1/4 mi

0   0.25 km

49

Colosseum, Palatine Hill, Roman Forum, Imperial Forums, and **Circus Maximus.** The area forms part of the *centro storico* (historic district)—along with **Campo de' Fiori** and **Piazza Navona** and the **Pantheon,** which are described below (we've considered them separately for the purposes of helping you locate hotels and restaurants). Because of its ancient streets, airy piazzas, classical atmosphere, and heartland location, this is a good place to stay. If you base yourself here, you can walk to the monuments and avoid the hassle of Rome's inadequate public transportation.

This area offers only a few hotels—most of them inexpensive to moderate in price—and not a lot of great restaurants. Many restaurant owners have their eyes on the cash register and the tour bus crowd, whose passengers are often hustled in and out of these restaurants so fast that they don't know whether the food is any good.

CAMPO DE' FIORI & THE JEWISH GHETTO South of Corso Vittorio Emanuele and centered on **Piazza Farnese** and the market square of **Campo de' Fiori,** many buildings in this area were constructed in Renaissance times as private homes. Stroll along **Via Giulia**—Rome's most fashionable street in the 16th century—with its antiques stores, interesting hotels, and modern art galleries.

West of Via Arenula lies one of the city's most intriguing districts, the old **Jewish Ghetto,** where the dining options far outnumber the hotel options. In 1556, Pope Paul IV ordered the Jews, about 8,000 at the time, to move into this area. The walls weren't torn down until 1849. Although ancient and medieval Rome has a lot more atmosphere, this working-class neighborhood is close to many attractions. You're more likely to want to dine here than to stay here.

PIAZZA NAVONA & THE PANTHEON One of the most desirable areas of Rome, this district is a maze of narrow streets and alleys dating from the Middle Ages and is filled with churches and palaces built during the Renaissance and baroque eras, often with rare marble and other materials stripped from ancient Rome. The only way to explore it is on foot. Its heart is **Piazza Navona,** built over Emperor Domitian's stadium and bustling with sidewalk cafes, palazzi, street artists, musicians, and pickpockets. There are several hotels in the area and plenty of trattorie.

Rivaling Piazza Navona—in general activity, the cafe scene, and nightlife—is the area around the **Pantheon,** which remains from ancient Roman times and is surrounded by a district built much later (this "pagan" temple was turned into a church and rescued, but the buildings that once surrounded it are long gone).

PIAZZA DEL POPOLO & THE SPANISH STEPS Piazza del Popolo was laid out by Giuseppe Valadier and is one of Rome's largest squares. It's characterized by an obelisk brought from Heliopolis in lower Egypt during the reign of Augustus. At the end of the square is the **Porta del Popolo,** the gateway in the 3rd-century Aurelian wall. In the mid–16th century, this was one of the major gateways into the old city. If you enter the piazza along Via del Corso from the south, you'll see twin churches, **Santa Maria del Miracoli** and **Santa Maria di Montesanto,** flanking the street. But the square's major church is **Santa Maria del Popolo** (1442–47), one of the best examples of a Renaissance church in Rome.

Tips **Handy Tip**

Rome has *four* daily rush hours: to work, to home for lunch (riposo), back to work, and to home in the evening.

Since the 17th century, the **Spanish Steps** (the former site of the Spanish ambassador's residence) have been a meeting place for visitors. Some of Rome's most upscale shopping streets fan out from it, including **Via Condotti.** The elegant **Hassler,** one of Rome's grandest hotels, lies at the top of the steps. This is the most upscale part of Rome, full of $500-a-night hotels, designer boutiques, and upscale restaurants.

AROUND VATICAN CITY Across the Tiber, **Vatican City** is a small city-state, but its influence extends around the world. The **Vatican Museums, St. Peter's,** and the **Vatican Gardens** take up most of the land area, and the popes have lived here for 6 centuries. The neighborhood around the Vatican—called the "Borgo"—contains some good hotels (and several bad ones), but it's removed from the more happening scene of ancient and Renaissance Rome, and getting to and from it can be time-consuming. And the area is rather dull at night and contains few, if any, of Rome's finest restaurants. For the average visitor, Vatican City and its surrounding area are best for exploring during the day. Nonetheless, the area is very popular for those whose sightseeing or even business interests center around the Vatican.

TRASTEVERE In Roman dialect, Trastevere means "Across the Tiber." For visitors arriving in Rome decades ago, it might as well have meant Siberia. All that has changed now, as this once medieval working-class district has been gentrified and overrun with visitors from all over the world. It started to change in the 1970s when expats and others discovered its rough charm. Since then Trastevere has been filling up with tour buses, dance clubs, offbeat shops, sidewalk vendors, pubs, and little trattorie with menus printed in English. There are even places to stay here, but as of yet it hasn't burgeoned into a major hotel district. There are some excellent restaurants here as well.

The original people of the district, and there are still some of them left, are of mixed ancestry—mainly Jewish, Roman, and Greek. For decades they were known for speaking their own dialect in a language rougher than that spoken in central Rome. Even their cuisine was spicier.

The area still centers on the ancient churches of **Santa Cecelia** and **Santa Maria** in Trastevere. Trastevere remains one of Rome's most colorful quarters, even if it is a bit overrun. Known as a "city within a city," it is at least a village within a city.

TESTACCIO & THE AVENTINE In A.D. 55, Nero ordered that Rome's thousands of broken amphoras and terra-cotta roof tiles be stacked in a carefully designated pile to the east of the Tiber, just west of Pyramide and today's Ostia Railway Station. Over the centuries, the mound grew to a height of around 200 feet and then was compacted to form the centerpiece for one of the city's most unusual working-class neighborhoods, **Testaccio.** Eventually, houses were built on the terra-cotta mound and caves were dug into its mass to store wine and foodstuffs. Once home to the slaughterhouses of Rome and its former port on the Tiber, Testaccio means "ugly head" in Roman dialect. Bordered by the Protestant cemetery, Testaccio is known for its authentic Roman restaurants. Chefs here still cook as they always did, satisfying local—not tourist—palates. Change is on the way, however, and this is a neighborhood on the rise. Nightclubs have sprung up in the old warehouses, although they come and go rather quickly.

Another offbeat section of Rome is **Aventine Hill,** south of the Palatine and close to the Tiber. In 186 B.C., thousands of residents of the area were executed for joining in "midnight rituals of Dionysos and Bacchus." These bloody orgies are a thing of the past today, and the Aventine area is now a leafy and rather posh residential quarter.

THE APPIAN WAY Via Appia Antica is a 2,300-year-old road that has witnessed much of the history of the ancient world. By 190 B.C., it extended from Rome to Brindisi on the southeast coast. Its most famous sights today are the **catacombs,** the graveyards of patrician families (despite what it says in *Quo Vadis?,* they weren't used as a place for Christians to hide out while fleeing persecution). This is one of the most historically rich areas of Rome to explore, but it's not a viable place to stay. It does contain some restaurants, however, where you can order lunch on your visit to the catacombs.

PRATI The little-known **Prati** district is a middle-class suburb north of the Vatican. It has been discovered by budget travelers because of its affordable *pensioni,* although it's not conveniently located for much of the sightseeing you'll want to do. The **Trionfale flower-and-food market** itself is worth the trip. The area also abounds in shopping streets less expensive than those found in central Rome, and street crime isn't much of a problem.

PARIOLI Rome's most elegant residential section, Parioli, is framed by the green spaces of the **Villa Borghese** to the south and the **Villa Glori** and **Villa Ada** to the north. It's a setting for some of the city's finest restaurants, hotels, and nightclubs. It's not exactly central, however, and it can be a hassle if you're dependent on public transportation. Parioli lies adjacent to Prati but across the Tiber to the east; like Prati, this is one of the safer districts. We'd call Parioli an area for connoisseurs, attracting those who shun the overrun Spanish Steps, the overly commercialized Via Veneto, and those who'd never admit to having been in the Termini area.

MONTE MARIO On the northwestern precincts of Rome, **Monte Mario** is the site of the deluxe Cavalieri Hilton, an excellent stop to take in a drink and the panorama of Rome. If you plan to spend a lot of time shopping and sightseeing in the heart of Rome, it's a difficult and often expensive commute. The area lies north of Prati, away from the hustle and bustle of central Rome. Bus no. 913 runs from Piazza Augusto Imperator near Piazza del Popolo to Monte Mario.

2 Getting Around

Rome is excellent for walking, with sites of interest often clustered together. Much of the inner core is traffic-free, so you'll need to walk whether you like it or not. However, in many parts of the city it's hazardous and uncomfortable because of the crowds, heavy traffic, and narrow sidewalks. Sometimes sidewalks don't exist at all, and it becomes a sort of free-for-all with pedestrians competing for space against vehicular traffic (the traffic always seems to win). Always be on your guard. The hectic crush of urban Rome is considerably less during August, when many Romans leave town for vacation.

BY SUBWAY

The **Metropolitana,** or **Metro,** for short, is the fastest means of transportation, operating daily from 5:30am to 11:30pm. A big red "M" indicates the entrance to the subway.

Tickets are 1,500L (.80€, 75¢) and are available from *tabacchi* (tobacco shops), many newsstands, and vending machines at all stations. These machines accept 50L, 100L, and 200L coins, and some will take 1,000L notes. Some stations have managers, but they won't make change. Booklets of tickets are available at tabacchi and in some terminals. You can also buy a **tourist pass** on either a daily or a weekly basis (see "By Bus & Tram," below).

Building a subway system for Rome hasn't been easy because every time workers start digging, they discover an old temple or other archaeological treasure, and heavy earth-moving has to cease for a while.

BY BUS & TRAM

Roman buses and trams are operated by an organization known as **ATAC (Azienda Tramvie e Autobus del Comune di Roma),** Via Volturno 65 (℃ **06-46-951** for information).

For 1,500L (.80€, 75¢) you can ride to most parts of Rome, although it can be slow-going in all that traffic and the buses are often very crowded. Your ticket is valid for 75 minutes, and you can get on many buses and trams during that time by using the same ticket. Ask where to buy bus tickets, or buy them in tabacchi or bus terminals. You must have your ticket before boarding because there are no ticket-issuing machines on the vehicles.

At Stazione Termini, you can buy a special **tourist pass,** which costs 6,000L (3.10€, $3) for a day or 24,000L (12.50€/$12) for a week. This pass allows you to ride on the ATAC network without bothering to buy individual tickets. The tourist pass is also valid on the subway—but never ride the trains when the Romans are going to or from work, or you'll be smashed flatter than fettuccine. On the first bus you board, you place your ticket in a small machine, which

---

⌂Tips **Two Bus Warnings**

Any map of the Roman bus system will likely be outdated before it's printed. Many buses listed on the "latest" map no longer exist; others are enjoying a much-needed rest, and new buses suddenly appear without warning. There's also talk of completely renumbering the whole system soon, so be aware that the route numbers we've listed might have changed by the time you travel.

Take extreme caution when riding Rome's overcrowded buses—pickpockets abound! This is particularly true on bus no. 64, a favorite of visitors because of its route through the historic districts and thus also a favorite of Rome's vast pickpocketing community. This bus has earned various nicknames, including the "Pickpocket Express" and "Wallet Eater."

Rome Metropolitana

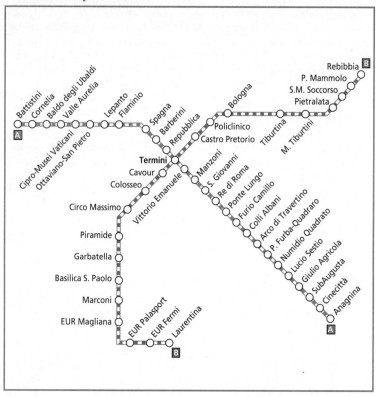

prints the day and hour you boarded, and then you withdraw it. You do the same on the last bus you take during the valid period of the ticket.

Buses and trams stop at areas marked FERMATA. At most of these, a yellow sign will display the numbers of the buses that stop there and a list of all the stops along each bus's route in order, so you can easily search out your destination. In general, they're in service daily from 6am to midnight. After that and until dawn, you can ride on special night buses (they have an "N" in front of their bus number), which run only on main routes. It's best to take a taxi in the wee hours—if you can find one.

At the **bus information booth** at Piazza dei Cinquecento, in front of the Stazione Termini, you can purchase a directory complete with maps summarizing the routes.

Although routes change often, a few old reliable routes have remained valid for years, such as **no. 27** from Stazione Termini to the Colosseum, **nos. 75** and **170** from Stazione Termini to Trastevere, and **no. 492** from Stazione Termini to the Vatican. But if you're going somewhere and are dependent on the bus, be sure to carefully check where the bus stop is and exactly which bus goes there—don't assume that it'll be the same bus the next day.

BY TAXI

If you're accustomed to hopping a cab in New York or London, then do so in Rome. If not, take less-expensive means of transport or walk. Avoid paying your fare with large bills—invariably, taxi drivers claim that they don't have change, hoping for a bigger tip (stick to your guns and give only about 10%). Don't count on hailing a taxi on the street or even getting one at a stand. If you're going out, have your hotel call one. At a restaurant, ask the waiter or cashier to dial for you. If you want to phone for yourself, try one of these numbers: ℂ **06-6645,** 06-3570, or 06-4994.

The meter begins at 4,500L (2.35€, $2.25) for the first 3 kilometers and then rises 1,300L (.70€, 65¢) per kilometer. Every suitcase costs 2,000L (1.05€, $1), and on Sunday a 2,000L (1.05€, $1) supplement is assessed. There's another 5,000L (2.60€, $2.50) supplement from 10pm to 7am.

BY CAR

All roads might lead to Rome, but you don't want to drive once you get here. Because the reception desks of most Roman hotels have at least one English-speaking person, call ahead to find out the best route into Rome from wherever you're starting out. You're usually allowed to park in front of the hotel long enough to unload your luggage. You'll want to get rid of your rental car as soon as possible or park in a garage.

You might want to rent a car to explore the countryside around Rome or drive on to another city. You'll save the most money if you reserve before leaving home. But if you want to book a car here, know that **Hertz** is at Via Vittorio del Gallopatoio 33, near the parking lot of the Villa Borghese (ℂ **06-321-6831;** Metro: Barberini); **Italy by Car** is at Via Ludovisi 60 (ℂ **06-482-0966;** Bus: 95 or 116); and **Avis** is at Stazione Termini (ℂ **06-481-4373;** Metro: Termini). **Maggiore,** an Italian company, has an office at Via di Tor Cervara 225 (ℂ **06- 229-351**). There are also branches of the major rental agencies at the airport.

 FAST FACTS: Rome

American Express   The Rome offices are at Piazza di Spagna 38 (ℂ **06-67-641;** Metro: Spagna). The travel service is open from Monday to Friday 9am to 5:30pm, and Saturday 9am to 12:30pm. Hours for the financial and mail services are from Monday to Friday 9am to 5pm. The tour desk is open during the same hours as those for travel services and also Saturday 2 to 2:30pm (May–Oct).

Baby-sitters   Most hotel desks in Rome will help you find a baby-sitter. Inquire as far in advance as possible, and be sure to ask for an English-speaking sitter. You won't always get one, but it pays to ask. A good choice is **Angels Baby Sitting Services,** at Via delle Quattro Fontane (ℂ **06-420-13-083** or 0338-667-9718), which offers British, American, or Australian baby-sitters. Rates range from 12,000 to 25,000 lire (6 to 12.50€, $6.25 to $13) per hour.

Banks   In general, banks are open from Monday to Friday from 8:30am to 1:30pm and 3 to 4pm. Some banks keep afternoon hours from 2:45 to 3:45pm. There's a branch of **Citibank** at Via Abruzzi 2 (ℂ **06-478-171;** Metro: Barberini). The bank office is open from Monday to Friday from 8:30am to 1:30pm.

Currency Exchange There are exchange offices throughout the city, and they're also at all major rail and air terminals, including Stazione Termini, where the cambio (exchange booth) beside the rail information booth is open daily from 8am to 8pm. At some cambi, you'll have to pay commissions, often 1½%. Likewise, banks often charge commissions.

Dentists To find a dentist who speaks English, call the **U.S. Embassy** in Rome at ✆ **06-46-741.** You might have to call around to get an appointment. There's also the 24-hour **G. Eastman Dental Hospital,** Viale Regina Elena 287 (✆ **06-844-831;** Metro: Policlinico).

Doctors Call the U.S. Embassy at ✆ **06-46-741** for a list of doctors who speak English. All big hospitals have a 24-hour first-aid service (go to the emergency room, *Pronto Soccorso*). You'll find English-speaking doctors at the privately run **Salvator Mundi International Hospital,** Viale delle Mura Gianicolensi 67 (✆ **06-588-961;** Bus: 41). For medical assistance, the **International Medical Center** is on 24-hour duty at Via Giovanni Amendola 7 (✆ **06-488-2371;** Metro: Termini). You could also contact the **Rome American Hospital,** Via Emilio Longoni 69 (✆ **06-22-551**), with English-speaking doctors on duty 24 hours. A more personalized service is provided 24 hours by **MEDI-CALL,** Studio Medico, Via Salaria 300, Palazzina C, interno 5 (✆ **06-884-0113;** Bus: 3, 4, or 57). It can arrange for qualified doctors to make a house call at your hotel or anywhere in Rome. In most cases, the doctor will be a general practitioner who can refer you to a specialist, if needed. Fees begin at around $100 per visit and can go higher if a specialist or specialized treatments are necessary.

Drugstores A reliable pharmacy is **Farmacia Internazionale,** Piazza Barberini 49 (✆ **06-487-1195;** Metro: Barberini), open day and night. Most pharmacies are open from 8:30am to 1pm and 4 to 7:30pm. In general, pharmacies follow a rotation system, so several are always open on Sunday.

Electricity It's generally 220 volts, 50 Hz AC, but you might find 125-volt outlets, with different plugs and sockets for each. Pick up a transformer either before leaving home or in any appliance shop in Rome if you plan to use electrical appliances. Check the exact local current at your hotel. You'll also need an adapter plug.

Embassies/Consulates In case of an emergency, embassies have a 24-hour referral service.

The **U.S. Embassy** is at Via Vittorio Veneto 119A (✆ **06/46-741;** fax 06/467-422-17).

The **Canadian Consulate** and passport service is at Via Zara 30 (✆ **06/445-981**). The **Canadian Embassy** is at Via G. B. de Rossi 27 (✆ **06/445-981;** fax 06/445-98754).

The **U.K. Embassy** is at Via XX Settembre 80A (✆ **06/482-5441;** fax 06/4890-3073).

The **Australian Embassy** is at Via Alessandria 215 (✆ **06/852-721;** fax 06/852-723-00). The **Australian Consulate** is in Rome at Corso Trieste 25 (✆ **06/852-721**).

The **New Zealand Embassy** is at Via Zara 28 (✆ **06/441-7171;** fax 06/440-2984).

The **Irish Embassy** is at Piazza di Campitelli 3 (✆ **06/697-912;** fax 06/679-2354). For consular queries, dial ✆ **06/697-91211.**

Emergencies   Dial **113** for an ambulance or to call the police; to report a fire, call **115.**

Internet Access   You can log onto the Web in central Rome at **Thenet-gate,** Piazza Firenze 25 (✆ **06-689-3445;** Bus: 116). Summer hours are Monday to Saturday 10:30am to noon and 3:30 to 10:30pm; winter hours are daily 10:40am to 8:30pm. A 20-minute visit costs 5,000L (2.60€, $2.50), and 1 hour (including mailbox) costs 10,000L (5.20€, $5). Access is free on Saturday from 10:30 to 11am and 2 to 2:30pm. You can kill two birds with one stone just north of Stazione Termini at **Splash,** Via Varese 33 (✆ **06-4938-2073;** Metro: Termini), a do-it-yourself laundromat (13,000L, 6.75€, $6.50 per load, including soap) with a satellite TV and four computers hooked up to the Internet (5,000L, 2.60€, $2.50 per half hour).

Legal Aid   The consulate of your country is the place to turn for legal aid, although offices can't interfere in the Italian legal process. They can, however, inform you of your rights and provide a list of attorneys. You'll have to pay for the attorney out of your pocket—there's no free legal assistance. If you're arrested for a drug offense, about all the consulate will do is notify a lawyer about your case and perhaps inform your family.

Liquor Laws   Wine with meals has been a normal part of family life for hundreds of years in Italy. Children are exposed to wine at an early age, and consumption of alcohol isn't anything out of the ordinary. There's no legal drinking age for buying or ordering alcohol, and almost no restriction on what kinds of stores or what days of the week wine or liquor can be sold, as in the United States.

Luggage Storage/Lockers   These are available at the Stazione Termini along Tracks 1 and 22 daily from 5am to 1am. The charge is 5,000L (2.50€, $2.60) per piece of luggage per 12-hour period.

Mail   Mail delivery in Italy is notoriously bad. Your family and friends back home might receive your postcards in 1 week, or it might take 2 weeks (sometimes longer). Postcards, aerogrammes, and letters weighing up to 20 grams sent to the United States and Canada cost 1,300L (.70€, 65¢); to the United Kingdom and Ireland, 800L (.40€, 40¢); and to Australia and New Zealand, 1,400L (.75€, 70¢). You can buy stamps at all post offices and at *tabacchi* (tobacco) stores, but it's easiest just to buy stamps and mail letters and postcards at your hotel's front desk. You can buy special stamps at the **Vatican City Post Office,** adjacent to the information office in St. Peter's Square; it's open Monday to Friday 8:30am to 7pm and Saturday 8:30am to 6pm. Letters mailed at Vatican City reach North America far more quickly than mail sent from within Rome for the same cost.

Newspapers/Magazines   You can get the *International Herald Tribune, USA Today, The New York Times,* and *Time* and *Newsweek* magazines at most newsstands. The expatriate magazine (in English) *Wanted in Rome* comes out monthly and lists current events and shows. If you want to try your hand at reading Italian, the Thursday edition of the newspaper *La Repubblica* contains "Trova Roma," a magazine supplement full of cultural and entertainment listings, and *Time Out* now has a Rome edition.

Police   Dial **113.**

Restrooms   Facilities are found near many of the major sights and often have attendants, as do those at bars, clubs, restaurants, cafes, and hotels, plus the airports and the rail station. (There are public restrooms near the Spanish Steps, or you can stop at the McDonald's there—it's one of the nicest branches of the Golden Arches you'll ever see!) You're expected to leave 200L to 500L (.10€ to .25€, 10¢ to 25¢) for the attendant. It's not a bad idea to carry some tissues in your pocket when you're out and about, either.

Safety   Pickpocketing is the most common problem. Men should keep their wallets in their front pocket or inside jacket pocket. Purse snatching is also commonplace, with young men on Vespas who ride past you and grab your purse. To avoid trouble, stay away from the curb and keep your purse on the wall side of your body and place the strap across your chest. Don't lay anything valuable on tables or chairs, where it can be grabbed up. Gypsy children have long been a particular menace, although the problem isn't as severe as in years past. If they completely surround you, you'll often virtually have to fight them off. They might approach you with pieces of cardboard hiding their stealing hands. Just keep repeating a firm *no!*

Taxes   As a member of the European Union, Italy imposes a **value-added tax** (called **IVA** in Italy) on most goods and services. The tax that most affects visitors is the one imposed on hotel rates, which ranges from 9% in first- and second-class hotels to 19% in deluxe hotels.

Non-EU (European Union) citizens are entitled to a **refund of the IVA** if they spend more than 300,000L (156€, $150) at any one store, before tax. To claim your refund, request an invoice from the cashier at the store and take it to the Customs office (*dogana*) at the airport to have it stamped before you leave. *Note:* If you're going to another EU country before flying home, have it stamped at the airport Customs office of the last EU country you'll be in (for example, if you're flying home via Britain, have your Italian invoices stamped in London). Once back home, mail the stamped invoice (keep a photocopy for your records) back to the original vendor within 90 days of the purchase. The vendor will, sooner or later, send you a refund of the tax that you paid at the time of your original purchase. Reputable stores view this as a matter of ordinary paperwork and are businesslike about it. Less-honorable stores might lose your dossier. It pays to deal with established vendors on large purchases. You can also request that the refund be credited to the credit card with which you made the purchase; this is usually a faster procedure.

Many shops are now part of the **"Tax Free for Tourists"** network (look for the sticker in the window). Stores participating in this network issue a check along with your invoice at the time of purchase. After you have the invoice stamped at Customs, you can redeem the check for cash directly at the Tax Free booth in the airport (in Rome, it's past Customs; in Milan's airports, the booth is inside the Duty Free shop) or mail it back in the envelope provided within 60 days.

Telephone   To call Italy from the United States, dial the **international prefix, 011**; then Italy's **country code, 39**; and then the city code (for example,

06 for Rome and **055** for Florence), which is now built into every number. Then dial the actual **phone number.**

A **local phone call** in Italy costs around 220L (.10€, 10¢). **Public phones** accept coins, precharged phone cards (*scheda* or *carta telefonica*), or both. You can buy a *carta telefonica* at any *tabacchi* (tobacconists; most display a sign with a white *T* on a brown background) in increments of 5,000L (2.60€, $2.50), 10,000L (5.20€, $5), and 15,000L (7.80€, $7.50). To make a call, pick up the receiver and insert 200L or your card (break off the corner first). Most phones have a digital display that'll tell you how much money you've inserted (or how much is left on the card). Dial the number, and don't forget to take the card with you after you hang up.

To **call from one city code to another,** dial the city code, complete with initial 0, and then dial the number. (Note that numbers in Italy range from four to eight digits in length. Even when you're calling within the same city, you must dial that city's area code—including the zero. A Roman calling another Rome number must dial 06 before the local number.)

To **dial direct internationally,** dial **00** and then the country code, the area code, and the number. **Country codes** are as follows: the United States and Canada, 1; the United Kingdom, 44; Ireland, 353; Australia, 61; New Zealand, 64. Make international calls from a public phone, if possible, because hotels almost invariably charge ridiculously inflated rates for direct dial—but bring plenty of *schede* to feed the phone. Calls dialed directly are billed on the basis of the call's duration only. A reduced rate is applied from 11pm to 8am on Monday to Saturday and all day Sunday. Direct-dial calls from the United States to Italy are much cheaper, so arrange for whomever to call you at your hotel.

Italy has recently introduced a series of **international phone cards** (*scheda telefonica internazionale*) for calling overseas. They come in increments of 50, 100, 200 and 400 *unita* (units), and they're usually available at tabacchi and bars. Each *unita* is worth 250L (.15€, 15¢) of phone time; it costs 5 *unita* (1,250L, .65€, 65¢) per minute to call within Europe or to the United States or Canada, and 12 *unita* (3,000L, 1.55€, $1.50) per minute to call Australia or New Zealand. You don't insert this card into the phone; merely dial ℂ **1740** and then *2 (star 2) for instructions in English, when prompted.

To call the free **national telephone information** (in Italian) in Italy, dial ℂ **12.** **International information** is available at ℂ **176** but costs 1,200L (.60€, 60¢) a shot.

To make **collect or calling card calls,** drop in 200L (.10€, 10¢) or insert your card and dial one of the numbers given below; an American operator will shortly come on to assist you (because Italy has yet to discover the joys of the touch-tone phone, you'll have to wait for the operator). The following calling-card numbers work all over Italy: **AT&T** ℂ 172-1011, **MCI** ℂ 172-1022, and **Sprint** ℂ 172-1877. To make collect calls to a country besides the United States, dial ℂ **170** (free), and practice your Italian counting in order to relay the number to the Italian operator. Tell him or her that you want it *a carico del destinatario.*

Don't count on all Italian phones having touch-tone service! You might not be able to access your voice mail or answering machine if you call home from Italy.

Time In terms of standard time zones, Italy is 6 hours ahead of Eastern Standard Time in the United States. Daylight saving time goes into effect in Italy each year from the end of March to the end of September.

Tipping This custom is practiced with flair in Italy—many people depend on tips for their livelihoods. In **hotels,** the service charge of 15% to 19% is already added to a bill. In addition, it's customary to tip the chambermaid 1,000L (.50€, 50¢) per day, the doorman (for calling a cab) 1,000L (.50€, 50¢), and the bellhop or porter 3,000L to 5,000L (1.55€ to 2.60€, $1.50 to $2.50) for carrying your bags to your room. A concierge expects about 15% of his or her bill, as well as tips for extra services performed, which could include help with long-distance calls. In expensive hotels, these lire amounts are often doubled.

In **restaurants and cafes,** 15% is usually added to your bill to cover most charges. If you're not sure whether this has been done, ask, *"È incluso il servizio?"* (ay een-*cloo*-soh eel sair-*vee*-tsoh?). An additional tip isn't expected, but it's nice to leave the equivalent of an extra couple of dollars if you've been pleased with the service. Checkroom attendants expect 1,500L (.80€, 75¢), and washroom attendants should get 700L (.35€, 35¢). Restaurants are required by law to give customers official receipts.

Taxi drivers expect at least 15% of the fare.

Water Most Italians take mineral water with their meals; however, tap water is safe everywhere, as are public drinking fountains. Unsafe sources will be marked ACQUA NON POTABILE. If tap water comes out cloudy, it's only the calcium or other minerals inherent in a water supply that often comes untreated from fresh springs.

Accommodations

The good news is that Rome's hotels are in better shape than they've been in years; dozens upon dozens of properties have undergone major renovations at the dawn of the millennium.

The bad news is that with the huge surge in tourism the city has experienced in the last couple of years, finding a hotel room at any time of the year is harder than ever. **Make your reservations as far ahead as possible.** If you like to gamble and arrive without a reservation, head quickly to the **airport information desk** or, once you get into town, to the offices of **Enjoy Rome** (see p. 46)—their staff can help reserve you a room, if any are available.

Rome's poshest hotels are among the most luxurious in Europe. In addition to reviewing the best of the upscale hotels, we've also tried to give you a good selection of moderately priced hotels, where you'll find comfortable, charming lodgings with private bathrooms. Even our inexpensive choices are clean and cheerful, and they offer more in services and facilities than you might expect from the prices. In the less expensive categories, you'll find a few *pensiones,* the Roman equivalent of a boardinghouse.

The Italian government controls the prices of its hotels, designating a minimum and a maximum rate. The difference between the two may depend on the season, the location of the room, and even its size. The government also classifies hotels with star ratings that indicate their category of comfort: five stars for deluxe, four for first class,

three for second class, two for third class, and one for fourth class. Most former *pensiones* are now rated as one- or two-star hotels. The distinction between a *pensione* hotel (where some degree of board was once required along with the room) and a regular hotel is no longer officially made, although many smaller, family-run establishments still call themselves *pensiones.* Government ratings don't depend on sensitivity of decoration or frescoed ceilings, but on facilities, such as elevators and the like. Many of the finest hotels in Rome have a lower rating because they serve only breakfast.

Almost all the hotels listed serve breakfast (often a buffet with coffee, fruit, rolls, and cheese), but you can't take for granted that it's included in the room rate. That used to be universal, but it's not anymore, so check the listing carefully and ask the hotel to confirm what's included.

Nearly all hotels are heated in the cooler months, but not all are air-conditioned in summer, which can be vitally important during a stifling July or August. The deluxe and first-class ones are, but after that it's a toss-up. Be sure to check the listing carefully before you book a stay in the dog days of summer!

All Italian hotels impose an **IVA (Imposta sul Valore Aggiunto),** or value-added tax. This tax is in effect throughout the European Union countries. It replaces some 20 other taxes and is an effort to streamline the tax structure. What does this mean for you? A higher hotel bill. Deluxe hotels will slap you with a whopping 13% tax, whereas first-class, second-class, and other hotels will impose a mere 9%. Most hotels will quote a rate inclusive of this tax, but others prefer to add it on when you go to pay the bill. To avoid unpleasant surprises, ask to be quoted an all-inclusive rate—that is, with service, even a continental breakfast (which is often obligatory)—when you check in.

See "Best Hotel Bets" on p. 10 for a quick-reference list of our favorite hotels in a variety of categories. See also "The Neighborhoods in Brief" on p. 47 for a quick summary of each area that will help you decide if you'd like to stay there.

1 Near Stazione Termini

Despite a handful of pricey choices, this area is most notable for its concentration of cheap hotels. It's not the most picturesque location, and parts of the neighborhood are still transitional and edgy, but it's certainly convenient in terms of transportation and easy access to many of Rome's top sights.

VERY EXPENSIVE

Empire Palace Hotel ★★   This hotel combines a historic core (in this case, a palazzo built around 1870) with modern luxuries; together these elements create a very comfortable and appealing ambience. The original builders, an aristocratic Venetian family, installed ceiling frescoes showing the heavens in azure blue on some of the ceilings. Some of the striking combinations of the original core with unusual modern paintings are show-stoppers. Opened as a hotel in 1999, the Empire Palace is classified four stars by the Italian government. Bedrooms have marble bathrooms and conservative cherrywood furnishings.

The building's courtyard is outfitted with a splashing fountain and a verdant garden. Immediately adjacent, with tables spilling into the courtyard during fine weather, is the Aureliano Restaurant, which is outfitted with Murano chandeliers.

Via Aureliana 39, 00187 Roma. ℂ **06-421-281.** Fax 06-4212-8400. www.empirepalacehotel.com. 115 units. 650,000L (325€, $338) double; 950,000L (475€,$494) suite. Rates include breakfast. AE, DC, MC, V. Metro: Repubblica or Termini. **Amenities:** Restaurant, bar; concierge; room service; babysitting; laundry/dry cleaning. *In room:* A/C, TV, minibar, hair dryer, safe.

Mecenate Palace Hotel ★★ *Finds*   A real gem, this little charmer lies 5 blocks south of the Termini. It's even more intimate and more professionally run than its closest competitor, the Artemide (although it's also pricier). Its downside is that its location might make it inconvenient for those wanting to pay many visits to the Vatican or classical Rome.

The hotel is composed of two adjacent buildings. One of them was designed by Rinaldi in 1887; the second one (on Via Carlo Alberto) was designed a few years later. The guest rooms, where traces of the original detailing mix with contemporary furnishings, overlook the city rooftops or Santa Maria Maggiore. They range from small to medium but boast high ceilings and extras such as luxury mattresses. The spacious marble bathrooms are sumptuous, with makeup mirrors and deluxe toiletries. Three suites offer superior comfort, authentic 19th-century antiques, and a fireplace. Except for these suites, the other rooms are fairly standardized in amenities and comfort.

Via Carlo Alberto 3, 00185 Roma. ℂ **06-4470-2024.** Fax 06-446-1354. www.mecenatepalace.com. 62 units. 680,000L (353.60€, $340) double; 1,200,000L (624€, $600) suite. Rates include buffet breakfast. AE, DC, MC, V. Parking 45,000L (23.40€, $22.50). Metro: Termini or Vittorio Emanuele. **Amenities:** Restaurant, bar; cafe; room service; babysitting; laundry/dry cleaning. *In room:* A/C, TV, minibar, hair dryer, safe.

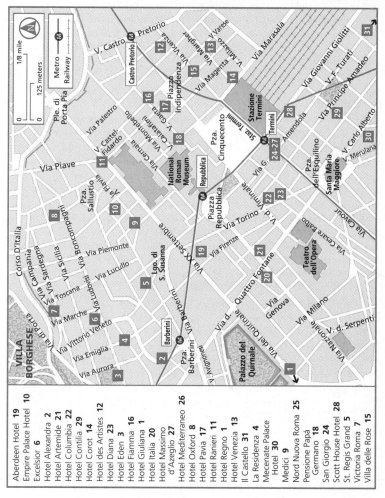

Aberdeen Hotel **19**
Empire Palace Hotel **10**
Excelsior **6**
Hotel Alexandra **2**
Hotel Artemide **21**
Hotel Columbia **22**
Hotel Contilia **29**
Hotel Corot **14**
Hotel des Artistes **12**
Hotel Diana **23**
Hotel Eden **3**
Hotel Fiamma **16**
Hotel Giuliana **1**
Hotel Italia **20**
Hotel Massimo
d'Azeglio **27**
Hotel Mediterraneo **26**
Hotel Oxford **8**
Hotel Pavia **17**
Hotel Ranieri **11**
Hotel Regno **1**
Hotel Venezia **13**
Il Castello **31**
La Residenza **4**
Mecenate Palace
Hotel **30**
Medici **9**
Nord Nuova Roma **25**
Pensione Papà
Germano **18**
San Giorgio **24**
Scott House Hotel **28**
St. Regis Grand **5**
Victoria Roma **7**
Villa delle Rose **15**

St. Regis Grand ★★★   This restored landmark is more plush and upscale than any hotel in the area—for comparable digs, you'll have to cross town to check into the Excelsior or Eden. And for sheer opulence, not even those hotels equal it. Its drawback is its location at the dreary Stazione Termini, but once you're inside its splendid shell, all thoughts of railway stations vanish.

When Ceásar Ritz founded this outrageously expensive hotel in 1894, it was the first to offer a private bathroom and two electric lights in every room. Today, a $35 million restoration has vastly improved it. Restored to its former glory, it is a magnificent Roman palazzo, combining Italian and French styles in decoration and furnishings. The lobby is decked out with Murano chandeliers, columns, and marble busts and cherubs. Guest rooms, most of which are exceedingly spacious, are luxuriously furnished with everything from sumptuous mattresses to Murano chandeliers. Hand-painted frescoes are installed above each headboard, and the large bathrooms are done in fabulous marble. For the best rooms and the finest service, ask to be booked on the St. Regis floor.

Via Vittorio Emanuele Orlando 3, 00185 Roma. ℂ **06-47-091.** Fax 06-474-7307. www.stregis.com/grand rome. 161 units. 1,100,000L–1,441,000L (572€–749.30€, $550–$720.50) double; from 3,520,000L (1,830.40€, $1,760) suite. AE, DC, MC, V. Parking 50,000L–60,000L (26€–31.20€, $25–$30). Metro: Republica. **Amenities:** 2 restaurants, bar; fitness center; massage; babysitting; laundry/dry cleaning. *In room:* A/C, TV, minibar, coffeemaker, hair dryer, iron, safe.

EXPENSIVE

Hotel Artemide ✦✦   While the Mediterraneo is a bustling business-oriented choice, the Artemide is a boutique hotel. Near the train station, it combines stylish simplicity with modern comforts against a backdrop of Art Nouveau motifs. The original stained-glass skylight dome was retained in the lobby. The midsize to spacious guest rooms are furnished in natural colors and have tasteful furnishings, including elegantly comfortable beds, and spacious marble bathrooms with a tub-and-shower combination. For those who want to pay more, a series of deluxe rooms are offered that have extra amenities such as VCRs, battery chargers for cellular phones, and more deluxe bedding.

Via Nazionale 22, 00184 Roma. ℂ **06-489-911.** Fax 06-4899-1700. www.venere.it/roma/artemide. 85 units. 580,000L–620,000L (301.60€–322.40€, $290–$310) double; 660,000L (343.20€, $330) suite. Rates include breakfast. AE, DC, MC, V. Parking 30,000L (15.60€, $15). Metro: Repubblica. **Amenities:** Unremarkable rooftop restaurant, bar; room service; laundry/dry cleaning. *In room:* A/C, TV, minibar, hair dryer, safe.

Hotel Massimo d'Azeglio ✦   This is a longtime favorite, an up-to-date hotel that was opened as a small restaurant by one of the founders of an Italian hotel dynasty more than a century ago. During World War II, it was a refuge for the king of Serbia and a favorite with Italian generals. Today, this centrally located hotel is the flagship of the Bettoja chain. Run by Angelo Bettoja and his charming wife, it offers a well-trained staff, and its rooms are brighter and better furnished than those at the Mediterraneo, its nearby sibling. Each is tasteful, with parquet floors, 18th-century reproductions, and generously sized beds. Extras include bedside controls, double-glazed windows, and marble bathrooms (more than half with tub-shower combinations, the rest with shower only). The hotel boasts one of the area's most elegant neoclassical facades.

For many decades, the hotel restaurant, Massimo d'Azeglio, was a neighborhood fixture. It's no longer *the* place to go around here, but if you're too tired to venture out, it's still a safe bet for good food with market-fresh ingredients.

Via Cavour 18, 00184 Roma. ℂ **800/783-6904** in the U.S., or 06-487-0270. Fax 06-482-7386. www.bettoja hotels.it. 198 units. 489,000L (244.50€, $254.30) double. Rates include breakfast. AE, DC, MC, V. Parking 35,000L–45,000L (17.50€–22.50€, $18.20–$23.40). Metro: Termini. **Amenities:** Restaurant; bar; concierge; room service; babysitting; laundry/dry cleaning. *In room:* A/C, TV, minibar, hair dryer, safe.

Hotel Mediterraneo ✦   This golden oldie sports vivid Italian Art Deco styling. A recent influx of cash has returned the hotel to some of its former glory, although it doesn't compare to the lavish, plush St. Regis Grand. Because it's located on the triumphant passageway through Rome along which Mussolini had planned to travel, local building codes were violated and approval was granted for the creation of this 10-floor hotel. Its height, coupled with its position on one of Rome's hills, provides panoramic views from the most expensive rooms on the highest floors (some with lovely terraces) and from its roof garden/ bar (open May–Oct), which is especially charming at night. Views from here are far superior to the rooftop restaurant at the Artemide.

Mario Loreti, one of Mussolini's favorite architects, designed the interior sheathing of gray marble, the richly allegorical murals of inlaid wood, and the Art Deco friezes ringing the ceilings of the enormous public rooms. The lobby is also decorated with antique busts of Roman emperors. Recent renovations have upgraded the guest rooms, most in Art Deco and all with comfortable mattresses, bedside controls, and the large marble bathrooms. The most luxurious accommodations are the seven top-floor suites (even the phones are antique).

Via Cavour 15, 00184 Roma. ℭ 800/223-9832 in the U.S., or 06-488-4051. Fax 06-474-4105. www.bettoja hotels.it. 274 units. 520,000L (270.40€, $260) double; from 580,000L (301.60€, $290) suite. Rates include buffet breakfast. AE, DC, MC, V. Parking 35,000L (18.20€, $17.50). Metro: Termini. **Amenities:** 2 restaurants, bar; car rental; room service; babysitting; laundry/dry cleaning. *In room:* A/C, TV, minibar, hair dryer, safe.

San Giorgio ⚡ *Kids*   This hotel is not as grand as its siblings, the Mediterraneo and Massimo d'Azeglio (see above), but still gets a four-star or first-class rating from the government. Built in 1940, San Giorgio is constantly being improved by its founders, the Bettoja family (it was the first air-conditioned hotel in Rome, and is now also soundproofed). The hotel is ideal for families, as many of its corner rooms can accommodate extra people. Behind wood-veneer doors, the bedrooms are middle of the road—clean, well maintained, and functional. All units are spacious except some on the upper floor, and contain bathrooms equipped with shower-tub combinations.

Via Giovanni Amendola 61, 00185 Roma. ℭ 800/783-6904 in the U.S., or 06-482-7341. Fax 06-488-3191. www.bettojahotels.it. 186 units. 412,000L (206€, $214.25) double; from 570,000L (285€, $296.40) suite. Rates include breakfast. AE, DC, MC, V. Parking 35,000L–45,000L (17.50€–22.50€, $18.20–$23.40). Metro: Termini. **Amenities:** Restaurant, bar; concierge; room service; babysitting; laundry/dry cleaning. *In room:* A/C, TV, minibar, hair dryer, safe.

MODERATE

Aberdeen Hotel   This completely renovated hotel near the opera and the train station stands in front of the Ministry of Defense. The guest rooms, ranging from small to medium, were renovated in 1998, with comfortable new mattresses added to all the beds, usually queens or twins. The marble bathrooms are rather small but nicely appointed (only eight have tub/shower combos). Many inexpensive trattorie lie nearby.

Via Firenze 48, 00184 Roma. ℭ 06-482-3920. Fax 06-482-1092. www.travel.it/roma/aberdeen. 26 units. 280,000L (145.60€, $140) double. Rates include buffet breakfast. AE, DC, MC, V. Parking 38,000L (19.75€, $19). Metro: Repubblica. Bus: 64 or 170. **Amenities:** Laundry/dry cleaning. *In room:* A/C, TV, minibar, hair dryer, safe.

Hotel Columbia ⚡⚡   This is one of the newest hotels in the neighborhood, with a hard-working multilingual staff. A government-rated three-star choice, originally built around 1900, it underwent a well-done radical renovation in 1997. The interior contains Murano chandeliers and conservatively modern furniture. The compact and cozy guest rooms compare well to the accommodations in the best hotels nearby. Each contains a comfortable bed with a quality mattress and fine linen, plus a medium-size tiled bathroom with adequate shelf space and a tub and shower. The appealing roof garden has a view over the surrounding rooftops.

Under the same management, on the opposite side of the rail station, is the Columbia's sibling, the **Hotel Venezia** (see below), which sometimes accommodates the Columbia's overflow in comparable digs.

Via del Viminale 15, 00184 Roma. ℭ 06-474-4289 or 06-488-3509. Fax 06-474-0209. www.venere.it/roma/ columbia. 45 units. 266,000L–503,000L (138.30€–261.55€, $133–$251.50) double. Rates include buffet breakfast. AE, DC, MC, V. Parking nearby 35,000L (18.20€, $17.50). Metro: Repubblica. **Amenities:** Breakfast room; laundry service. *In room:* A/C, TV, minibar, hair dryer.

Hotel Diana ☆   In the heart of 19th-century Rome, the Diana is totally renovated and has an inviting Art Deco style, recapturing its early 1900s heyday. It offers an elegant yet comfortable atmosphere, with a spacious lobby and welcoming lounges. The guest rooms are tastefully furnished in floral fabrics, with beds that boast luxury mattresses and first-rate linens. The bathrooms are tiled with attractive ceramics.

The hotel's restaurant offers a menu of classic Italian dishes and daily seasonal specialties. The American Bar in summer moves to the rooftop terrace, where lunch and dinner can be served; shaded by tents and surrounded by plants, you'll have sweeping views over the ancient roofs.

Via Principe Amedeo 4, 00185 Roma. ✆ **06-482-7541.** Fax 06-486-998. www.hoteldianaroma.com. 171 units. 400,000L (200€, $208) double; 600,000L (300€, $312) suite. Rates include breakfast. AE, DC, MC, V. Parking 40,000L (20€, $20.80). **Amenities:** Restaurant; bar; room service; babysitting; laundry/dry cleaning; no-smoking units available. *In room:* A/C, TV, minibar, hair dryer.

Hotel Ranieri ☆   The Ranieri is a winning government-rated three-star hotel in a restored old building. The guest rooms are a bit small but reasonably comfortable for two, with mattresses that are still firm. The bathrooms aren't very big but are newish. The public rooms, the lounge, and the dining room are attractively decorated, in part with contemporary art.

Via XX Settembre 43, 00187 Roma. ✆ **06-420-145-31.** Fax 06-420-145-43. www.hotelranieri.com. 47 units. 220,000L–350,000L (110€–175€, $114.40–$182) double. Rates include breakfast. AE, DC, MC, V. Parking 30,000L–45,000L (15€–22.50€, $15.60–$23.40). Metro: Repubblica. **Amenities:** Restaurant; bar; room service; babysitting; laundry/dry cleaning. *In room:* A/C, TV, minibar, hair dryer, safe.

Hotel Venezia ☆ *Kids* *Value*   Located 3 blocks from the rail station, in a bustling business/residential area with a few old villas, the Venezia offers charming public rooms. Some guest rooms are furnished in 17th-century style, although they are looking worn (the last renovation was in 1991); the rest are in modern style. All units are midsize to spacious, boasting Murano chandeliers and first-rate beds and mattresses; some have balconies for surveying the street action. You get either a full tub and shower or just a shower. The management really cares, and the helpful staff speaks English. This is the most family-friendly hotel in the neighborhood.

Via Varese 18 (near Via Marghera), 00185 Roma. ✆ **06-445-7101.** Fax 06-495-7687. www.hotelvenezia.com. 61 units. 353,000L–393,000L (183.55€–204.35€, $176.50–$196.50) double; 503,000L (261.55€, $251.50) triple. Rates include buffet breakfast. AE, DC, MC, V. Parking 35,000L (18.20€, $17.50). Metro: Termini. **Amenities:** Bar; room service; laundry/dry cleaning. *In room:* A/C, TV, minibar, hair dryer, safe.

Medici   Built in 1906, this hotel is near the rail station and the shops along Via XX Settembre. Many of its better guest rooms overlook an inner patio garden with Roman columns and benches. All rooms were renovated in 1997 in classic Roman style, with a generous use of antiques and first-class Italian mattresses. The cheapest are a good buy because they're only slightly smaller than the others (but they have older furnishings and no air-conditioning). The shower-only bathrooms are small but well organized. Breakfast is the only meal served.

Via Flavia 96, 00187 Roma. ✆ **06-482-7319.** Fax 06-474-0767. www.hotelmedici.com. 69 units. 350,000L (182€, $175) double. Rates include breakfast. AE, DC, MC, V. Parking 35,000L–40,000L (18.20€–20.80€, $17.50–$20). Metro: Piazza della Repubblica. **Amenities:** Bar; room service. *In room:* A/C, TV, minibar, hair dryer.

Nord Nuova Roma *(Value)*   Although rather plain, this is the best bargain in the Bettoja chain, and is often full of value-minded Italian families. This hotel was built in 1935; it's in a convenient position near Stazione Termini and the Baths of Diocletian. Rooms are quite spacious and bright. The standard rooms range from small to spacious and are well furnished, though some of the furniture is showing its age. Nonetheless, the beds are comfortable (twins or doubles) and bathrooms are fairly roomy.

Via Giovanni Amendola 3, 00185 Roma. ✆ **800/223-9832** in the U.S., or 06-488-5441. Fax 06-481-7163. www.bettojahotels.it. 158 units. 350,000L (175€, $182) double. Rates include breakfast. AE, DC, MC, V. Parking 35,000L–45,000L (17.50€–22.50€, $18.20–$23.40). Metro: Termini or Repubblica. **Amenities:** Restaurant, bar; babysitting;laundry/dry cleaning. *In room:* A/C, TV, minibar, hair dryer, safe.

Villa delle Rose *(Kids)*   Located less than 2 blocks north of the rail station, this hotel is an acceptable, if not exciting, choice. In the late 1800s, it was a villa with a dignified cut-stone facade inspired by the Renaissance. Despite many renovations, the ornate trappings of the original are still visible, including the lobby's Corinthian-capped marble columns and the flagstone-covered terrace that is part of the verdant back garden. The look is still one of faded grandeur. Much of the interior has been recently redecorated and upgraded with traditional wall coverings, new carpets, new mattresses, and tiled bathrooms, 80% of which have a shower only. Breakfasts in the garden do a lot to add country flavor to an otherwise very urban setting. Families often book here asking for one of the three rooms with lofts that can sleep up to five.

Via Vicenza 5, 00185 Roma. ✆ **06-445-1788.** Fax 06-445-1639. www.venere.it/roma/villadellerose. 37 units. 180,000L–300,000L (93.60€–156€, $90–$150) double. Rates include buffet breakfast. AE, DC, MC, V. Free parking (only 4 cars). Metro: Termini or Castro Pretorio. *In room:* A/C (23 rooms), TV, minibar, hair dryer.

INEXPENSIVE

Hotel Contilia *(Value)*   As the automatic doors part to reveal a stylish marble lobby with Persian rugs and antiques, you might step back to double-check the address. The popular old-fashioned Pensione Tony Contilia of yesteryear has taken over this building's other small hotels and upgraded itself to one of the best choices in the neighborhood. The guest rooms have been redone in modern midscale comfort, with perfectly firm beds and built-in units. Rooms overlooking the cobblestone courtyard are the most tranquil. The smallish contemporary bathrooms have a tub and shower.

Via Principe Amedeo 79d–81, 00185 Roma. ✆ **06-446-6942.** Fax 06-446-6904. www.hotelcontilia.com. 40 units. 150,000L–320,000L (78€–166.40€, $75–$160) double. Rates include buffet breakfast. AE, DC, MC, V. Parking 30,000L (15.60€, $15); free on street. Metro: Termini. **Amenities:** Breakfast room; room service; laundry/dry cleaning. *In room:* A/C, TV, hair dryer, safe.

Hotel Corot   This modernized hotel (last renovated in 1997) occupies the second and third floors of an early 1900s building that contains a handful of apartments and another inferior hotel. The Corot is a simple, safe haven north of the train station. You register in a small paneled street-level area and then take an elevator to your high-ceilinged guest room. Each room has simple but traditional furniture, including a good bed, and a modern shower-only bathroom.

Via Marghera 15–17, 00185 Roma. ✆ **06-4470-0900.** Fax 06-4470-0905. www.hotelcorot.it. 28 units. 190,000L–260,000L (98.80€–135.20€, $95–$130) double; 230,000L–290,000L (119.60€–150.80€, $115–$145) triple; 250,000L–360,000L (130€–187.20€, $125–$180) quad. Rates include breakfast. AE, DC, MC, V. Parking 30,000L (15.60€, $15) for first night; 19,000L (9.90€, $9.50) for the second. Metro: Termini. **Amenities:** Bar, lounge. *In room:* A/C, TV, minibar, hair dryer.

Hotel des Artistes *(Value)*   Completely renovated in 1997, this modest choice lies a few steps from Termini Station. It offers good-quality accommodations at a moderate price. One part of the hotel is a hostel with dormitory-style rooms, bathrooms in the corridors, and a TV in each room; rates for those accommodations range from 170,000L (88.40€, $85) for a triple, to 220,000L (114.40€, $110) for a quad. Regular rooms range from small to medium in size, some of them decorated with Oriental rugs. The furniture is simple but classic, and the maid service is excellent. The hotel's rooms have shower-only private bathrooms, small but neat and just renovated. Breakfast is the only meal served. The roof garden, open 24 hours, is an ideal place for socializing.

Via Villafranca 20, 00185 Roma. ℭ **06-445-4365.** Fax 06-446-2368. www.hoteldesartistes.com. 45 units. 270,000L (140.40€, $135) double; 305,000L (158.60€, $152.50) triple; 340,000L (176.80€, $170) quad. Rates include buffet breakfast. AE, DC, MC, V. Parking 25,000L–35,000L (13€–18.20€, $12.50–$17.50) nearby. Metro: Castro Pretorio. Bus: 310. **Amenities:** Breakfast room; babysitting. *In room:* A/C, TV, minibar, hair dryer, safe.

Hotel Fiamma   Near the Baths of Diocletian, the Fiamma is in a renovated building, with five floors of bedrooms and a ground floor faced with marble and plate-glass windows. It's an old favorite, if a bit past its prime. The lobby is long and bright, filled with a varied collection of furnishings, including overstuffed chairs and blue enamel railings. On the same floor is an austere marble breakfast room. The comfortably furnished guest rooms range from small to medium in size. The mattresses are a bit worn but still comfortable, and the small shower-only bathrooms are tiled, with adequate shelf space.

Via Gaeta 61, 00185 Roma. ℭ **06-481-8436.** Fax 06-488-3511. www.travel.it/roma/ianr. 78 units. 160,000L–320,000L (83.20€–166.40€, $80–$160) double. Rates include breakfast. AE, DC, MC, V. Parking 35,000L (18.20€, $17.50) nearby. Metro: Termini. **Amenities:** Breakfast room. *In room:* A/C, TV, minibar, hair dryer.

Hotel Italia   This is a turn-of-the-century building with an eight-room annex across the street. It's been a hotel for 20 years, but it's never been as well managed as it is now under the stewardship of the Valentini family. Both buildings employ a night porter/security guard, and both offer their guests a breakfast buffet that's one of the most appealing in the neighborhood. Mid-size bedrooms are well maintained and conservatively decorated with comfortable yet simple furniture. Most units have parquet floors, and 11 rooms are air-conditioned. All have private bathrooms, though the facilities for room no. 6 are across the hallway.

Via Venezia 18, 00184 Roma. ℭ **06-482-8355.** Fax 06-474-5550. www.hotelitaliaroma.com. 31 units. 200,000L (100€, $104) double. Rates include buffet breakfast. AE, DC, MC, V. Parking nearby 25,000L–40,000L (12.50€–20€, $13–$20.80). Metro: Repubblica. Bus: 64. **Amenities:** Bar; babysitting. *In room:* A/C, TV, minibar, hair dryer, safe.

Hotel Pavia *(★ Value)*   In a renovated 100-year-old villa, this hotel is a popular choice on this quiet street near the gardens of the Baths of Diocletian. You take a wisteria-covered passage to reach the recently modernized reception area and tasteful public rooms. All the rooms are comfortable and fairly attractive, and the maids keep everything beautifully maintained, including the medium-size bathrooms with new showers. The quality of the rooms makes this a bargain.

Via Gaeta 83, 00185 Roma. ℭ **06-483-801.** Fax 06-481-9090. www.hotelpavia.com. 20 units. 270,000L (140.40€, $135) double. Rates include breakfast. AE, DC, MC, V. Parking 25,000L (13€, $12.50). Metro: Termini. **Amenities:** Bar; room service. *In room:* A/C, TV, minibar, hair dryer, safe.

Il Castello   Simple, unassuming, and often filled with backpackers, this three-floor hotel was built in the 1950s. It has a small garden, and well-scrubbed, no-frills rooms. You don't get anything fancy—just low prices, a clean bed, and a bit more space, at least in some of the rooms, than you might have expected. Other than a phone, in-room amenities are scarce.

Via Vittorio Amedo II, no. 9, 00185 Roma. ℂ 06-7720-4036. Fax 06-7049-0068. www.ilcastello.com. 18 units (3 with private bathroom). 100,000L–130,000L (50€–65€, $52–$67.60) double without bathroom; 150,000L–180,000L (75€–90€, $78–$93.60) double with bathroom. MC, V. Metro: Manzoni. **Amenities:** Bar, lounge.

Pensione Papà Germano 🐸   This choice is about as basic as anything in this book, but it's clean and decent. This 1892 building, on a block-long street immediately east of the Baths of Diocletian, has undergone some recent renovations yet retains its modest ambience. The pensione offers clean accommodations with plain furniture, good mattresses, and well-maintained showers; it hosts a high-turnover crowd of European and North American students. The energetic English-speaking owner, Gino Germano, offers advice on sightseeing. No breakfast is served, but dozens of cafes nearby open early.

Via Calatafimi 14A, 00185 Roma. ℂ **06-486-919.** Fax 06-4782-5202. www.hotelpapagermano.it. 17 units, 7 with private bathroom. 90,000L (46.80€, $45) double without bathroom; 110,000L (57.20€, $55) double with bathroom; 100,000L (52€, $50) triple without bathroom; 160,000L (83.20€, $80) triple with bathroom. AE, DC, MC, V. Metro: Termini. *In room:* TV, hair dryer.

Scott House Hotel   Simple but adequate for low-maintenance travelers on tight budgets, this hotel occupies the fourth and fifth floors of a building originally constructed in the 18th century. Bedrooms are high-ceilinged, freshly painted, and compact; most have comfortable beds and at least one upholstered armchair. Each was completely renovated and freshened up in 1999.

Via Gioberti 30, 00185 Roma. ℂ **06-446-5379.** Fax 06-446-4986. www.scotthouse.com. 36 units (with shower only). 140,000L–180,000L (70€–90€, $72.80–$93.60) double. Rate includes breakfast. AE, DC, MC, V. Metro: Termini. **Amenities:** Bar, lounge. *In room:* A/C, TV, safe.

2 Near Via Veneto & Piazza Barberini

If you stay in this area, you definitely won't be on the wrong side of the tracks. Unlike the dreary rail station, this is a beautiful and upscale commercial area, near some of Rome's best shopping.

To locate the hotels in this section, see the "Accommodations near Stazione Termini, Via Veneto & Piazza Barberini" map on p. 63.

VERY EXPENSIVE

Hotel Eden 🐸🐸🐸   It's not as grand architecturally as the Westin Excelsior, nor does it have the views of the Hassler, and it's certainly not a summer resort like the Hilton, but the Eden is Rome's top choice for the certain discerning traveler who likes grand comfort but without all the ostentation.

For several generations after its 1889 opening, this hotel, about a 10-minute walk east of the Spanish Steps, reigned over one of the world's most stylish shopping neighborhoods. Hemingway, Callas, Ingrid Bergman, Fellini—all checked in during its heyday. It was bought by Trusthouse Forte in 1989 and reopened in 1994 after 2 years (and $20 million) of renovations that enhanced its grandeur and added the amenities that its government-rated five-star status calls for. The Eden's hilltop position guarantees a panoramic city view from most guest rooms; all are spacious and elegantly appointed with a decor harking back to the late 19th century, plus marble-sheathed bathrooms with deluxe toiletries and makeup mirrors. Try to get one of the front rooms with a balcony boasting views over Rome.

Via Ludovisi 49, 00187 Roma. 📞 **800/225-5843** in the U.S., or 06-478-121. Fax 06-482-1584. www. hotel-eden.it. 119 units. 1,100,000L–1,280,000L (572€–665.60€, $550–$640) double; from 1,600,000L (832€, $800) suite. AE, DC, DISC, MC, V. Parking 45,000L (23.40€, $22.50). Metro: Piazza Barberini. **Amenities:** One of Rome's best restaurants (La Terrazza, see the full review on p. 99; bar; health club; gym; room service; laundry/dry cleaning. *In room:* A/C, TV, minibar, hair dryer, safe.

Westin Excelsior ⭐ If money is no object, here's a good place to spend it. It's architecturally more grandiose than either the Eden or the Hassler, but it is not as up-to-date or as beautifully renovated as either the Eden or the St. Regis Grand. The Excelsior has never moved into the 21st century the way some other grand hotels have. For our money today, we prefer the newer Hotel de Russie, and we've always gotten better service at the Hassler, but the Excelsior remains a favorite, especially among older visitors, who remember it from decades past. The baroque corner tower of this limestone palace, overlooking the U.S. Embassy, is a landmark in Rome. A string of cavernous reception rooms is adorned with thick rugs, marble floors, gilded garlands decorating the walls, and Empire furniture. Everything looks just a tad dowdy today, but the Excelsior endures, in no small part because of the hospitable staff.

The guest rooms come in two varieties: new (the result of a major renovation) and traditional. The older ones are a bit worn, while the newer ones have more imaginative color schemes and plush carpeting. All are spacious and elegantly furnished, always with deluxe mattresses and often with antiques and silk curtains. Most rooms are unique; many have sumptuous Hollywood-style marble bathrooms with bidets. Ask for one of the larger doubles with spacious sitting areas; they're practically suites.

Via Vittorio Veneto 125, 00187 Roma. 📞 **800/325-3589** in the U.S., or 06-47-081. Fax 06-482-6205. www. luxurycollection.com. 321 units. 710,000L–1,193,500L (369.20€–620.60€, $355–$596.75) double; 2,035,000L–3,300,000L (1,058.20€–1,716€, $1,017.50–$1,650) suite. AE, DC, DISC, MC, V. Parking 70,000L (36.40€, $35). Metro: Piazza Barberini. **Amenities:** 3 restaurants; bar; salon; room service; babysitting; laundry/dry cleaning. *In room:* A/C, TV, minibar, hair dryer, safe.

EXPENSIVE

Hotel Alexandra ⭐ *(Finds)* This is one of your few chances to stay on Via Veneto without going broke (although it's not exactly cheap). Set behind the dignified stone facade of what was a 19th-century mansion, the Alexandra offers immaculate guest rooms. Those facing the front are exposed to roaring traffic and street noise; those in back are quieter but with less of a view. The rooms range from rather cramped to medium-size, but each has been recently redecorated, filled with antiques or tasteful contemporary pieces. They have extras such as swing-mirror vanities and brass or wood bedsteads with good mattresses. The full bathrooms are small to medium, and the largest doubles have tubs. The breakfast room is especially appealing: Inspired by an Italian garden, it was designed by noted architect Paolo Portoghesi.

Via Vittorio Veneto 18, 00187 Roma. 📞 **06-488-1943.** Fax 06-487-1804. www.venere.it/roma/alexandra. 64 units. 390,000L (202.80€, $195) double; 600,000L (312€, $300) suite. Rates include buffet breakfast. AE, DC, MC, V. Parking 30,000L (15.60€, $15). Metro: Piazza Barberini. **Amenities:** Laundry/dry cleaning. *In room:* A/C, TV, hair dryer.

Victoria Roma ⭐ The Victoria Roma's great location overlooking the Borghese Gardens remains one of its most desirable assets; you can sit in the roof garden drinking your cocktail amidst palm trees and potted plants, imagining you're in a country villa. The lounges and living rooms retain a country-house decor, with soft touches that include high-backed chairs, large oil paintings, bowls of freshly cut flowers, provincial tables, and Oriental rugs. You don't get opulence here, but you do get a sort of dowdy charm and good maintenance. Rooms range from standard to spacious; each is comfortably equipped with good beds, and most units were renovated during the late 1990s. Furnishings like Oriental carpets are common, and the bathrooms are generally spacious, with dual basins, phones, shower-tub combinations, and scales. Some of the tubs are extra-long. Floor number five has the best views of the Villa Borghese.

Via Campania 41, 00187 Roma. © **06-473-931.** Fax 06-487-1890. hotel.victoria@flashnet.it. 108 units. 500,000L (250€, $260) double. Rates include breakfast. AE, DC, MC, V. Parking 40,000L–50,000L (20€–25€, $20.80–$26). Metro: Barberini. Bus: 52, 53, 490, 495, or 910. **Amenities:** Elegant restaurant, bar; room service; babysitting; laundry/dry cleaning. *In room:* A/C, TV, minibar, hair dryer, safe.

MODERATE

Hotel Oxford   The Oxford is a solid if not spectacular choice adjacent to the Borghese Gardens. Recently renovated, it's now centrally heated and fully carpeted throughout. The guest rooms, which were recently freshened up, contain modern furnishings, including excellent mattresses on twin beds. Each bathroom is tiled, with adequate shelf space.

Via Boncompagni 89, 00187 Roma. © **06-4203-601.** Fax 06-4281-5349. www.hoteloxford.com. 59 units. 300,000L–370,000L (150€–185€, $156–$192.40) double; 370,000L–430,000L (185€–215€, $192.40–$223.60) triple; 400,000L–480,000L (200€–240€, 208–$249.60) suite. Rates include buffet breakfast. AE, DC, MC, V. Parking 40,000L–50,000L (20€–25€, $20.80–$26). Metro: Barberini. Bus: 53 or 63. **Amenities:** Restaurant, pleasant bar serving snacks; room service; babysitting; laundry/dry cleaning. *In room:* A/C, TV, minibar, hair dryer, safe.

Hotel Regno   Set in a great shopping area, this six-story hotel stands behind a severe stone facade. It was originally a library in the 1600s. In the 1960s, it was transformed into a simple hotel, and in 1999, it was upgraded into a well-managed, government-rated three-star hotel. Bedrooms are relatively small, but comfortably appointed with good mattresses and nondescript modern furniture. All units contain neatly kept bathrooms. The staff is friendly and hard-working. There's a simple breakfast room, and a sun deck on the building's roof.

Via del Corso 330, 00186 Roma. © **06-697-6361.** Fax 06-697-6361. www.hotelregno.com. 62 units. 340,000L–370,000L (170€–185€, $176.80–$192.40) double; 450,000L–500,000L (225€–250€, $234–$260) suite. AE, DC, MC, V. Metro: Spagna. **Amenities:** Simple breakfast room, bar; room service; babysitting; laundry/dry cleaning; rooftop sundeck. *In room:* A/C, TV, minibar, hair dryer, safe.

La Residenza ★★   In a superb but congested location, this little hotel successfully combines intimacy and elegance. A bit old-fashioned and homelike, the converted villa has an ivy-covered courtyard and a series of upholstered public rooms with Empire divans, oil portraits, and rattan chairs. Terraces are scattered throughout. The guest rooms are generally spacious, containing bentwood chairs and built-in furniture, including beds with quality mattresses. The dozen or so junior suites boast balconies. The bathrooms have robes and even come equipped with ice machines.

Via Emilia 22–24, 00187 Roma. © **06-488-0789.** Fax 06-485-721. www.italyhotel.com/roma/la_residenza. 29 units. 325,000L–360,000L (169€–187.20€, $162.50–$180) double; 375,000L–390,000L (195€–202.80€, $187.50–$195) suite. Rates include buffet breakfast. AE, MC, V. Parking (limited) 10,000L (5.20€, $5). Metro: Piazza Barberini. **Amenities:** Lounge; laundry. *In room:* A/C, TV, minibar, hair dryer, safe.

INEXPENSIVE

Hotel Giuliana   Close to the landmark Trevi Fountain deep in the heart of Rome, this is a well-maintained, neat little family-run hotel, facing the Basilica

Santa Maria Maggiore. Personal service is a hallmark. Although not grandly stylish, bedrooms are exceedingly comfortable and of good size, with up-to-date bathrooms. A generous breakfast is served every morning in a cozy room.

Via Agostino Depretis 70, 00184 Roma. ℂ 06-4880-795. Fax 06-482-4247. www.hotelgiuliana.com. 11 units. 150,000L–300,000L (75€–150€, $78–$156) double. Rates include breakfast. AE, DC, MC, V. Metro: Repubblica. **Amenities:** Breakfast room, bar; room service; babysitting. *In room:* A/C (some units), TV, hair dryer, safe.

3 Near Ancient Rome

To locate the hotels in this section, refer to the "Accommodations Near Piazza del Popolo & the Spanish Steps" map on p. 77.

EXPENSIVE

Hotel Forum ℛ   Once a former convent, this building of character and grace is a longtime favorite. Built around a medieval bell tower off the Fori Imperiali, the Hotel Forum offers old-fashioned elegance and accommodations that range from tasteful to opulent. The midsize rooms, which look out on the sights of the ancient city, are well appointed with antiques, mirrors, quality mattresses, and Oriental rugs. The hotel's lounges are conservative, with paneled walls and furnishings that combine Italian and French provincial styles. Dining is an event in the roof-garden restaurant. Reserve well in advance.

Via di Tor de Conti 25-30, 00184 Roma. ℂ **06-679-2446.** Fax 06-678-6479. www.hotelforum.com. 80 units. 420,000L–590,000L (210€–295€, $218.40–$306.80) double; 680,000L (340€, $353.60) triple; 800,000L (400€, $416) suite. Rates include breakfast. AE, DC, MC, V. Parking 40,000L (20€, $20.80). Bus: 75, 117, 85, 87, or 40. **Amenities:** Rooftop restaurant, bar; room service; babysitting; laundry/dry cleaning. *In room:* A/C, TV, hair dryer, safe.

MODERATE

Hotel Duca d'Alba ℛ   A bargain near the Roman Forum and the Colosseum, this hotel lies in the Suburra neighborhood, which was once pretty seedy but is being gentrified. Completely renovated, the Duca d'Alba yet retains an old-fashioned air (it was built in the 19th c.). The guest rooms have elegant Roman styling, with soothing colors, light wood pieces, luxurious beds and bedding, and bathrooms, mainly with showers. The most desirable rooms are the four with private balconies.

Via Leonina 14, 00184 Roma. ℂ **06-484-471.** Fax 06-488-4840. www.hotelducaalba.com. 27 units. 200,000L–390,000L (104€–202.80€, $100–$195) double; 350,000L–550,000L (182€–286€, $175–$275) suite. Rates include breakfast. AE, DC, MC, V. Parking 40,000L–55,000L (20.80€–28.60€, $20–$27.50). Metro: Cavour. **Amenities:** Dining area, bar; room service; babysitting; laundry/dry cleaning. *In room:* A/C, TV, minibar, hair dryer, safe.

Hotel Nerva   Some of the Nerva's walls and foundations date from the 1500s (others from a century later), but the modern amenities date only from 1997. The setting, above and a few steps from the Roman Forum, will appeal to any student of archaeology and literature, and the warm welcome from the Cirulli brothers will appeal to all. The decor is accented with wood panels and terracotta tiles; some guest rooms even retain the original ceiling beams. The furniture is contemporary and comfortable, with excellent beds and mattresses. The tiled bathrooms, mainly with showers, have adequate shelf space.

Via Tor di Conti 3, 00184 Roma. ℂ **06-678-1835.** Fax 06-699-22204. www.hotelnerva.com. 19 units. 230,000L–480,000L (119.60€–249.60€, $115–$240) double. Rates include breakfast. AE, MC, V. Metro: Colosseo. **Amenities:** Breakfast room; laundry. *In room:* A/C, TV, minibar, hair dryer, safe.

INEXPENSIVE

Casa Kolbe   Occupying an 1800 building, the Casa Kolbe (often full of bus tour groups from North America and Germany) has a great position between the Palatine and the Campidoglio. The guest rooms are simple and well kept, even if some are worn. The mattresses may be thin but still have comfort in them, and the shower-only bathrooms are small. Try to get a unit overlooking the small garden.

Via San Teodoro 44, 00186 Roma. © **06-679-4974.** Fax 06-699-41550. 65 units. 150,000L (78€, $75) double. AE, MC, V. Metro: Circo Massimo. **Amenities:** Restaurant, lounge. *In room:* Hair dryer.

Colosseum Hotel   Two short blocks southwest of Santa Maria Maggiore, this hotel offers affordable and small but comfortable rooms. Someone with flair and lots of lire designed the public areas and upper halls, which hint at baronial grandeur. The drawing room, with its long refectory table, white walls, red tiles, and provincial armchairs, invites lingering. The guest rooms are furnished with well-chosen antique reproductions (beds of heavy carved wood, dark-paneled wardrobes, and leatherwood chairs); all have stark white walls, and some have old-fashioned plumbing in the bathrooms.

Via Sforza 10, 00184 Roma. © **06-482-7228.** Fax 06-482-7285. www.italyhotel.com/roma/colosseum. 47 units. 190,000L–246,000L (98.80€–127.90€, $95–$123) double. Rates include breakfast. AE, DC, MC, V. Parking 35,000L (18.20€, $17.50). Metro: Cavour. **Amenities:** Breakfast room, lounge. *In room:* TV, hair dryer.

4 Near Campo de' Fiori
MODERATE

Hotel Teatro di Pompeo ★★ *(Finds)*   Built atop the ruins of the Theater of Pompey, this small charmer lies near the spot where Julius Caesar met his end on the Ides of March. Intimate and refined, it's on a quiet piazzetta near the Palazzo Farnese and Campo de' Fiori. The rooms are decorated in an old-fashioned Italian style with hand-painted tiles, and the beamed ceilings date from the days of Michelangelo. The guest rooms range from small to medium, each with a good mattress and a tidy but cramped shower-only bathroom.

Largo del Pallaro 8, 00186 Roma. © **06-6830-0170.** Fax 06-6880-5531. hotel.teatrodipompeo@tiscalinet. 13 units. 350,000L (182€, $175) double. Rates include breakfast. AE, DC, MC, V. Bus: 64. **Amenities:** Bar; room service; babysitting; laundry/dry cleaning. *In room:* A/C, TV, hair dryer.

INEXPENSIVE

Casa di Santa Brigida ★ *(Value)*   Across from the Michelangelo-designed Palazzo Farnese on a quiet square a block from Campo de' Fiori, Rome's best and most comfortable convent hotel is run by the friendly sisters of St. Bridget in the house where that Swedish saint died in 1373. Basically, there isn't much difference between this place and many other little pensiones, except that it's run by sisters (it's not a great place for carousing, obviously). Rooms where Santa Brigida lived and died are on the first floor. The library is quite large. This convent hotel accepts people of every age and creed. The rates are justified by the comfy and roomy old-world guest rooms with antiques or reproductions on parquet (lower level) or carpeted (upstairs) floors. The bathrooms are a little old but at least have shower curtains, and the beds are heavenly firm. There's a roof terrace, library, and church.

Via Monserato 54 (off Piazza Farnese). Postal address: Piazza Farnese 96, 00186 Roma. © **06-6889-2596.** Fax 06-6889-1573. www.brigidine.org. 20 units. 250,000L (130€, $125) double. Rates include breakfast. DC, MC, V. Bus: 46, 62, or 64. **Amenities:** Rooftop terrace; library. *In room:* No phone.

Accommodations Near Campo de' Fiori & Piazza Navona

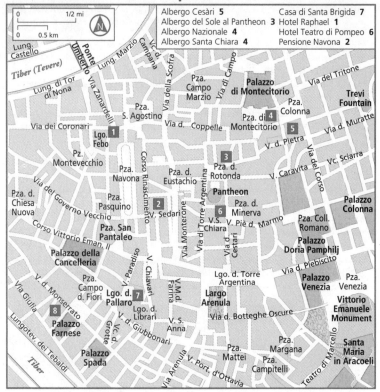

Albergo Cesàri **5**
Albergo del Sole al Pantheon **3**
Albergo Nazionale **4**
Albergo Santa Chiara **4**
Casa di Santa Brigida **7**
Hotel Raphael **1**
Hotel Teatro di Pompeo **6**
Pensione Navona **2**

5 Near Piazza Navona & the Pantheon

Travelers who want to immerse themselves in the atmosphere of ancient Rome, or those looking for romance, will prefer staying in this area over the more commercial Via Veneto area. Transportation isn't the greatest and you'll do a lot of walking, but that's the reason many visitors come here in the first place—to wander and discover the glory that was Rome. You're also within walking distance of the Vatican and the ruins of classical Rome. Many bars and cafes are within an easy walk of all the hotels located here.

VERY EXPENSIVE

Hotel Raphael ✸✸ With a glorious location adjacent to Piazza Navona, the Raphael is within easy walking distance of many sights. The ivy-covered facade invites you to enter the lobby, which is decorated with antiques that rival the cache in local museums (there's even a Picasso ceramics collection). The guest rooms (some quite small) were recently refurbished with a Florentine touch and contain quality mattresses on double or twin beds. Some of the suites have private terraces. The Raphael is often the top choice of Italian politicos in town for the opening of Parliament. We love its rooftop restaurant with views of all the major landmarks of Old Rome.

Largo Febo 2, 00186 Roma. ✆ **06-682-831**. Fax 06-687-8993. www.raphaelhotel.com. 65 units. 650,000L–750,000L (338€–390€, $325–$375) double; 980,000L–1,200,000L (509.60€–624€, $490–$600) suite. AE, DC, MC, V. Parking 45,000L (23.40€, $22.50). Bus: 70, 81, 87, or 115. **Amenities:** 2 restaurants, bar; fitness room; room service; babysitting; laundry; currency exchange. *In room:* A/C, TV, minibar, hair dryer, safe.

EXPENSIVE

Albergo Cesàri ★★   If you want to lose yourself on an ancient street in Old Rome, head here. Since 1787, this inn has stood in an offbeat location between the Pantheon and the Trevi Fountain, two of Rome's most enduring landmarks. Its well-preserved exterior harmonizes with the Temple of Neptune and many little antiques shops nearby. The guest rooms have mostly functional modern pieces, but there are a few traditional trappings to maintain character. The mattresses are fine and firm. Sixteen of the units come with tub-and-shower combinations. In 1998, all the accommodations and the breakfast room were completely renovated.

Via di Pietra 89A, 00186 Roma. ✆ **06-674-9701.** Fax 06-679-0882. www.venere.it/roma/cesari. 48 units. 440,000L (228.80€, $220) double; 520,000L (270.40€, $260) triple; 600,000L (312€, $300) quad. Rates include buffet breakfast. AE, DC, MC, V. Parking 50,000L (26€, $25). Bus: 492 from Stazione Termini. **Amenities:** Breakfast room; room service; babysitting. *In room:* A/C, TV, minibar, hair dryer, safe.

Albergo del Sole al Pantheon ★   You're obviously paying for the million-dollar view, but you might find that it's worth it to be across from the Pantheon. (Okay, so you're above a McDonald's, but one look at the Pantheon at sunrise, and you won't think about Big Macs.) This building was constructed in 1450 as a home, and the first records of it as a hostelry appeared in 1467, making it one of the world's oldest hotels. The layout is amazingly eccentric—prepare to walk up and down a lot of three- or four-step staircases. The guest rooms vary greatly in decor, much of it hit or miss, with compact, tiled full bathrooms. The rooms opening onto the piazza still tend to be noisy at all hours. The quieter rooms overlook the courtyard but are sans the view. We always opt to put up with the noise just to enjoy one of the world's greatest views from a hotel room. If you want the grandest view of the Pantheon, ask for rooms 106 or 108.

Piazza della Rotonda 63, 00186 Roma. ✆ **06-678-0441.** Fax 06-6994-0689. www.italyhotel.com/roma/solealpantheon. 25 units. 400,000L–600,000L (208€–312€, $200–$300) double; 450,000L–750,000L (234€–390€, $225–$375) junior suite. Rates include buffet breakfast. AE, DC, MC, V. Bus: 64. **Amenities:** Breakfast room; room service; babysitting; laundry/dry cleaning. *In room:* A/C, TV, minibar, hair dryer, safe.

Albergo Nazionale ★   The Albergo Nazionale faces the Piazza Colonna, with its Column of Marcus Aurelius, the Palazzo di Montecitorio, and the Palazzo Chigi. Because it's next to the parliament buildings, the Albergo is often full of government officials and diplomatic staff. The lobbies are wood-paneled, and there are many antiques throughout. The guest rooms are high-ceilinged, comfortably proportioned, and individually decorated in a late-19th-century style. They either have carpet or marble floors, and some offer interesting views over the ancient square outside. Beds and mattresses are luxurious.

Piazza Montecitorio 131, 00186 Roma. ✆ **06-69-5001.** Fax 06-678-6677. www.nazionaleroma.it. 560,000L (280€, $291.20) double; 1,410,000L (705€, $733.20) suite. Rates include breakfast. AE, DC, MC, V. Parking 45,000L (22.50€, $23.40). Bus: 52, 53, 58, 85, or 95. **Amenities:** Restaurant, bar; room service; babysitting; laundry/dry cleaning. *In room:* A/C, TV, minibar, hair dryer, safe.

MODERATE

Albergo Santa Chiara   This is a family-run hotel near the Pantheon in the very inner core of historic Rome. Since 1938, it has been welcoming sightseers to classic Rome. The Corteggiani family creates a welcoming atmosphere. Its white walls and marble columns speak of former elegance, although the rooms today are simply furnished, functional, yet comfortable. The size? They range from a broom closet to a suite large enough to be classified as a small Roman apartment. We go for those units facing the Piazza della Minerva, although you'll often have to listen to late-night revelers who don't know when to go home. Half the bedrooms come with complete tub-and-shower bathrooms.

Via Santa Chiara 21, 00186 Roma. ☎ **06-687-2979**. Fax 06-687-3144. www.albergosantachiara.com. 98 units. 300,000L–390,000L (156€–202.80€, $150–$195) double; 460,000L (239.20€, $230) junior suite. Rates include breakfast. Metro: Piazza di Spagna. **Amenities:** Room service; babysitting; laundry/dry cleaning. *In room:* A/C, TV, minibar, hair dryer, safe.

INEXPENSIVE

Pensione Navona   This pensione is on a small street radiating from Piazza Navona's southeastern tip. The rooms aren't as grand as the exterior, but the Navona offers decent accommodations, many of which have been renovated and some of which open to views of the central courtyard. Run by an Australian-born family of Italian descent, it boasts ceilings high enough to help relieve the midsummer heat and an array of architectural oddities (the legacy of the continual construction that this palace has undergone since 1360). The beds, most often twins or doubles, have fine linens and good mattresses. Each is equipped with a cramped, shower-only bathroom. You can get an air-conditioned room by request for 40,000L (20.80€, $20) extra per night (only in the doubles with bathrooms).

Via dei Sediari 8, 00186 Roma. ☎ **06-686-4203**. Fax 06-6880-3802. www.hotelnavona.com. 35 units, 30 with private bathroom. 130,000L (67.60€, $65) double without bathroom; 270,000L (140.40€, $135) double with bathroom; 320,000L (166.40€, $160) triple with bathroom. Rates include breakfast. No credit cards. Bus: 70, 81, 87, or 115. **Amenities:** Breakfast room. *In room:* A/C (some rooms), hair dryer.

6 Near Piazza del Popolo & the Spanish Steps

This is a great place to stay if you're a serious shopper, but expect to part with a lot of extra lire for the privilege. This is a more elegant area than the Via Veneto—think Fifth Avenue all the way.

VERY EXPENSIVE

Grand Hotel Plaza ⋆   This grand old favorite is experiencing a renaissance. Pietro Mascagni composed his *Nerone* in one of the guest rooms here and Vincent Price stayed here while making "all those bad movies." When you see the very grand decor, you'll understand why. Renovated in 1999 and 2000, this hotel's public rooms are vintage 19th century and contain stained-glass skylights, massive crystal chandeliers, potted palms, inlaid marble floors, and a life-size stone lion guarding the ornate stairway. The theatrical grandeur of the lobby carries over into the suites, where the furnishings mimic the gilded-age splendor of the public rooms on a smaller scale. But the standard guest rooms are just that—standard. They're contemporary, midsize, and streamlined, with efficient but comfortable furniture (including excellent mattresses).

Via del Corso 126, 00186 Roma. ☎ **06-6992-1111**. Fax 06-6994-1575. www.grandhotelplaza.com. 620,000L–800,000L (310€–400€, $322.40–$416) double; 1,100,000L–1,600,000L (550€–800€, $572–$832) suite. AE, DC, MC, V. Parking 45,000L (22.50€, $23.40). Metro: Piazza di Spagna. **Amenities:** Bar; concierge; room service; babysitting; laundry/dry cleaning. *In room:* A/C, TV, minibar, hair dryer, safe.

The Hassler ⋆⋆   The Westin Excelsior is a grander palace, and the Eden and the de Russie are more up-to-date, but the Hassler has something that no other hotel can boast—a coveted location at the top of the Spanish Steps, which ensures glorious views and easy access to upscale designer shopping. The Hassler, rebuilt

Accommodations Near Piazza del Popolo & the Spanish Steps

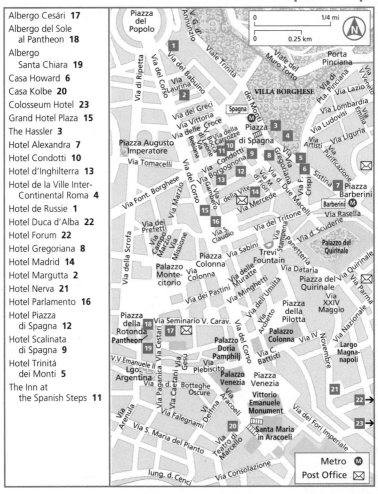

Albergo Cesári **17**

Albergo del Sole al Pantheon **18**

Albergo Santa Chiara **19**

Casa Howard **6**

Casa Kolbe **20**

Colosseum Hotel **23**

Grand Hotel Plaza **15**

The Hassler **3**

Hotel Alexandra **7**

Hotel Condotti **10**

Hotel d'Inghilterra **13**

Hotel de la Ville Inter-Continental Roma **4**

Hotel de Russie **1**

Hotel Duca d'Alba **22**

Hotel Forum **22**

Hotel Gregoriana **8**

Hotel Madrid **14**

Hotel Margutta **2**

Hotel Nerva **21**

Hotel Parlamento **16**

Hotel Piazza di Spagna **12**

Hotel Scalinata di Spagna **9**

Hotel Trinitá dei Monti **5**

The Inn at the Spanish Steps **11**

in 1944 to replace the 1885 original, is not quite what it used to be, but because it's such a classic, and because of that incredible location, it gets away with charging astronomical rates. The lounges and the guest rooms, with their "Italian Park Avenue" trappings, strike a faded, if still glamorous, 1930s note.

The guest rooms range from small singles to some of the most spacious suites in town. High ceilings make them appear larger than they are, and many of them open onto private balconies or terraces. The mattresses are deluxe and the beds are suitable for a president or king. Only medium in size, the bathrooms are classy, complete with a range of deluxe body and hair products. The front rooms, dramatically overlooking the Spanish Steps, are often noisy at night, but the views are worth it. For panoramas of the Roman rooftops, ask for a room on the top floor. Although some of the accommodations remain a bit dowdy, those on the fourth floor have been recently and elegantly renovated and are the most desirable. Most requested is the famous corner room 403. For Rome's most spectacular hotel room with a view, we nominate this one.

Piazza Trinità dei Monti 6, 00187 Roma. ✆ **800/223-6800** in the U.S., or 06-699-340. Fax 06-678-9991. www.hotelhasslerroma.com. 100 units. 960,000L–1,270,000L (499.20€–660.40€, $480–$635) double; from 2,860,000L (1,487.20€, $1,430) suite. AE, DC, MC, V. Parking 45,000L (23.40€, $22.50). Metro: Piazza di Spagna. **Amenities:** Restaurant; bar; tennis court; free use of bicycles; room service; massage; babysitting; laundry/dry cleaning. In room: A/C, TV, minibar, hair dryer, safe.

Hotel de la Ville Inter-Continental Roma ★★   We prefer this place, designed in 1924 by Hungarian architect Jozef Vago, to the overpriced glory of the Hassler next door. The hotel looks deluxe (although it's officially rated first class) from the minute you walk through the revolving door, where a smartly uniformed doorman greets you. Once inside this palace, built in the 19th century on the site of the ancient Gardens of Lucullus, you'll find Oriental rugs, marble tables, brocade furniture, and an English-speaking staff. Endless corridors lead to a maze of ornamental lounges. Some of the public rooms have a sort of 1930s elegance, and others are strictly baroque; in the middle of it all is an open courtyard.

The guest rooms and the public areas have been renovated in a beautifully classic and yet up-to-date way. The higher rooms with balconies have panoramic views of Rome, and you're free to use the roof terrace with the same view. Most units are small but boast chintz-covered fabrics and fine beds with quality mattresses. The spacious bathrooms have deluxe toiletries and generous shelf space.

Via Sistina 67–69, 00187 Roma. ✆ **800/327-0200** in the U.S. and Canada, or 06-67-331. Fax 06-678-4213. www.interconti.com. 192 units. 656,000L–880,000L (341.10€–457.60€, $328–$440) double; from 1,110,000L (577.20€, $555) suite. Rates include continental breakfast. AE, DC, MC, V. Parking 45,000L (23.40€, $22.50). Metro: Piazza di Spagna or Barberini. **Amenities:** Restaurant, 2 bars; salon; room service; babysitting; laundry/dry cleaning. In room: A/C, TV, minibar, hair dryer, safe.

Hotel de Russie ★★★   The new kid on the block is an old kid in new clothes, but this government-rated five-star hotel has raised the bar for every other hotel in the city. For service, style, and modern luxuries, it beats out the Eden, the Westin Excelsior, and the St. Regis Grand.

Just off the Piazza del Popolo, it opened in the spring of 2000 to rave reviews of its opulent furnishings and choice location. In its previous reincarnation, it was a favorite of Russian dignitaries (hence its name), and it also has hosted Jean Cocteau, Stravinsky, and Picasso. In World War II, it was used by the Italian government as a secret military center for spy secrets. The hardworking, multilingual staff works to make your stay memorable and comfortable.

Public areas are glossy and contemporary. About 30% of the bedrooms are conservative, with traditional furniture, while the remaining 70% are more minimalist, with a stark and striking style. Each is equipped with every conceivable high-tech amenity and offers lots of deeply upholstered comforts and views over a verdant garden.

The signature feature is the extensive terraced gardens, which can be seen from many of the bedrooms. Nothing is finer on a summer evening than sipping a cocktail in the Stravinskij Bar, which opens to the fragrant blooming gardens, and then enjoying an alfresco meal in Le Jardin du Russie.

Via del Babuino 9, 00187 Roma. ✆ **800/323-7500** in North America, or 06-328-881. Fax 06-328-8888. www.rfhotels.com. 129 units. 792,000L–1,100,000L (411.85€–572€, $396–$550) double; from 1,500,000L (780€, $750) suite. Rates include breakfast. AE, DC, MC, V. Metro: Flaminia. **Amenities:** Lovely restaurant and bar; gym; spa; salon. In room: A/C, TV, minibar, hair dryer, safe.

Hotel d'Inghilterra ★★   The Inghilterra holds on to its traditions and heritage, even though it has been renovated. Situated between Via Condotti and

Via Borgogna, this hotel in the 17th century was the guesthouse of the Torlonia princes. Rome's most fashionable small hotel is comparable to the Hassler and Inter-Continental. The rooms have mostly old pieces (gilt and lots of marble, mahogany chests, and glittery mirrors), complemented by modern conveniences. Some, however, are just too cramped, although all boast quality mattresses and fine linen. The preferred rooms are higher up, opening onto a tile terrace, with a balustrade and a railing covered with flowering vines and plants. The bathrooms have been refurbished and offer deluxe toiletries.

Via Bocca di Leone 14, 00187 Roma. © **06-69-981.** Fax 06-679-8601. www.charminghotels.it/inghilterra. 106 units. 490,000L–730,000L (254.80€–379.60€, $245–$365) double; from 1,870,000L (972.40€, $935) suite. AE, DC, MC, V. Parking 45,000L (23.40€, $22.50). Metro: Piazza di Spagna. **Amenities:** 2 restaurants, bar; gym; room service; babysitting; laundry/dry cleaning. *In room:* A/C, TV, minibar, hair dryer, safe.

The Inn at the Spanish Steps ★★★ *Finds*   This intimate, upscale inn is the first new hotel to open in this location in years. The people who run Rome's most famous cafe, Caffé Greco, created it where Hans Christian Andersen once lived. Andersen praised the balcony roses and violets, and so can you. Every room is furnished with an authentic period decor, featuring antiques, elegant draperies, and parquet floors. The superior units come with fireplace, a frescoed or beamed ceiling, and a balcony. The hotel is completely modern, from its anti-allergic mattresses to its generous wardrobe space. Each marble-paneled bathroom comes with a full tub, and others also offer a Jacuzzi as well. Designer boutiques galore lie nearby.

Via dei Condotti 85, 00187 Roma. © **06-699-25-657.** Fax 06-678-6470. 18 units. 600,000L–1,200,000L (312€–624€, $300–$600) double; from 1,200,000L (624€, $600) suite. Rates include breakfast. Metro: Piazza di Spagna. **Amenities:** Bar; room service; babysitting; laundry/dry cleaning. *In room:* A/C, TV, minibar, hair dryer, safe.

EXPENSIVE

Hotel Scalinata di Spagna ★★★   This is Rome's most famous little boutique hotel. The deluxe Hassler is across the street but far removed in price and grandeur from this intimate, upscale B&B at the top of the Spanish Steps. Its delightful little building—only two floors are visible from the outside—is nestled between much larger structures, with four relief columns across the facade and window boxes with bright blossoms. The recently redecorated interior features small public rooms with bright print slipcovers, old clocks, and low ceilings.

The decor varies radically from one guest room to the next. Some have low beamed ceilings and ancient-looking wood furniture; others have loftier ceilings and more run-of-the-mill furniture. The tiled bathrooms range from small to medium but offer state-of-the-art plumbing, each with a tub. The best units are any overlooking the steps, but the best of the best are room nos. 10 and 12.

Piazza Trinità dei Monti 17, 00187 Roma. © **06-679-3006.** Fax 06-6994-0598. www.hotelscalinata.com. 16 units. 400,000L–600,000L (208€–312€, $200–$300) double; 500,000L–650,000L (260€–338€, $250–$325) triple. Rates include breakfast. AE, MC, V. Parking 45,000L (23.40€, $22.50). Metro: Spagna. **Amenities:** Breakfast room; babysitting; laundry/dry cleaning. *In room:* A/C, TV, minibar, hair dryer, safe.

MODERATE

Casa Howard ★ *Finds*   It's rare to make a new discovery in the tourist-trodden Piazza di Spagna area. That's why Casa Howard comes as a pleasant surprise. The little B&B occupies about two-thirds of the second floor of a historic structure. The welcoming family owners maintain beautifully furnished guest rooms, each with its own private bathroom with tub and shower (although some baths lie outside the bedrooms in the hallway). The Pink Room is the most spacious, with its own en suite bathroom. Cristy at reception can "arrange anything" in Rome for you and will also invite you to use the house's private Turkish hummam.

Via Capa le Case 18, 00187 Roma. ℂ **06-6992-4555**. Fax 06-679-4644. www.casahoward.com. 5 units. 290,000L–360,000L (150.80€–187.20€, $145–$180) double. MC, V. Metro: Piazza di Spagna. **Amenities:** Babysitting; laundry/dry cleaning. *In room:* A/C, TV, hair dryer.

Hotel Condotti   The Condotti is small, choice, and terrific for shoppers intent on being near the tony boutiques. The born-to-shop crowd often thinks that the hotel is on Via Condotti because of its name—actually it lies 2 blocks to the north. The staff, nearly all of whom speak English, is cooperative and hardworking. The mostly modern rooms might not have much historic charm (they're furnished like nice motel units), but they're comfortable and soothing, each with a shower-only bathroom. Renovated in 1991, each is decorated with traditional furnishings, including excellent beds (usually twins). Room 414 is often requested because it has a geranium-filled terrace. Book here for the affordable price in a platinum-card neighborhood and the great location.

Via Mario de' Fiori 37, 00187 Roma. ℂ **06-679-4661**. Fax 06-679-0457. www.venere.it/roma/condotti. 16 units. 320,000L–490,000L (166.40€–254.80€, $160–$245) double; 410,000L–570,000L (213.20€–296.40€, $205–$285) minisuite. Rates include buffet breakfast. AE, DC, MC, V. Metro: Piazza di Spagna. **Amenities:** Breakfast room; car rental; laundry/dry cleaning. *In room:* A/C, TV, minibar, hair dryer, safe.

Hotel Gregoriana ⭐ *(Finds*   The intimate Gregoriana has many fans, including many fashion-industry types. It's comparable to the Hotel Condotti. The matriarch of an aristocratic family left the building to an order of nuns in the 19th century, but they eventually retreated to other quarters. (There might be a heavenly vibe in Room C because it used to be a chapel.) The elevator cage is a black-and-gold Art Deco fantasy. The smallish guest rooms provide comfort and fine Italian design, and the door to each bears a reproduction of a fanciful Erté print. Each has a queen or double bed, with a firm mattress. The bathrooms are a bit small but always spotless.

Via Gregoriana 18, 00187 Roma. ℂ **06-679-4269**. Fax 06-678-4258. 20 units. 320,000L–380,000L (166.40€–197.60€, $160–$190) double. Rates include breakfast. AE, DC, V. Parking 30,000L–40,000L (15.60€–20.80€, $15–$20). Metro: Spagna. *In room:* A/C, TV, hair dryer.

Hotel Madrid   Despite modern touches in the comfortable, if minimalist, guest rooms, the interior of the Madrid manages to evoke late-19th-century Rome. Guests often take their breakfast amid ivy and blossoming plants on the roof terrace with a panoramic view of rooftops and the distant dome of St. Peter's. Some of the doubles are large, with scatter rugs, veneer armoires, and shuttered windows. But other units are quite small, so make sure you know what you're getting before you check in. Each bed (usually double or twin) is fitted with a good mattress. The small, shower-only bathrooms were last renovated in 1998.

Via Mario de' Fiori 93–95, 00187 Roma. ℂ **06-699-1511**. Fax 06-679-1653. www.hotelmadridroma.com. 26 units. 270,000L–380,000L (140.40€–197.60€, $135–$190) double; 450,000L–550,000L (234€–286€, $225–$275) suite. Rates include breakfast. AE, DC, MC, V. Parking 40,000L–45,000L (20.80€–23.40€, $20–$22.50) nearby. Metro: Piazza di Spagna. **Amenities:** Breakfast room, lounge; babysitting; laundry. *In room:* A/C, TV, minibar, hair dryer, safe.

Hotel Piazza di Spagna   About a block from the downhill side of the Spanish Steps, this hotel is small but classic, with an inviting atmosphere made more gracious by the helpful manager, Elisabetta Giocondi. The guest rooms boast a functional streamlined decor; some even have Jacuzzis in the tiled bathrooms. Only eight units come with complete tub-and-shower combination.

Accommodations are spread across three floors, with very tidy bedrooms with high ceilings and cool terrazzo floors.

Via Mario de' Fiori 61, 00187 Roma. ℂ **06-679-6412.** Fax 06-679-0654. www.hotelpiazzadispagna.tt. 17 units. 320,000L–460,000L (166.40€–239.20€, $160–$230) double. Rates include breakfast. AE, MC, V. Parking 28,000L (14.55€, $14) nearby. Metro: Piazza di Spagna. Bus: 590. **Amenities:** Breakfast room; room service; laundry/dry cleaning. *In room:* A/C, TV, minibar, hair dryer.

Hotel Trinità dei Monti   Between two of the most bustling piazzas in Rome (Barberini and Spagna), this is a friendly and well-maintained place. The hotel occupies the second and third floors of an antique building. Its guest rooms come with herringbone-pattern parquet floors and big windows, and are comfortable, if not flashy. Each has a good mattress and a tidy tiled, shower-only bathroom. The hotel's social center is a simple coffee bar near the reception desk. Don't expect anything terribly fancy, but the welcome is warm and the location is ultraconvenient.

Via Sistina 91, 00187 Roma. ℂ **06-679-7206.** Fax 06-699-0111. www.trinitadeimonti. 25 units. 290,000L–370,000L (150.80€–192.40€, $145–$185) double. Rates include breakfast. AE, DC, MC, V. Metro: Barberini or Piazza di Spagna. **Amenities:** Bar; laundry. *In room:* A/C, TV, minibar, hair dryer, safe.

INEXPENSIVE

Hotel Margutta   The Margutta, on a cobblestone street near Piazza del Popolo, offers attractively decorated but tiny guest rooms, a helpful staff, and a simple breakfast room. You'll sacrifice space, but you'll get an affordable price and a chic location. The best rooms are the three on the top floor, offering a great view. Two of these three (nos. 50 and 51) share a terrace, and the larger room has a private terrace. (There's usually a 20% to 35% supplement for these.) Each room comes with a comfortable bed containing a good mattress, plus a small but tidy shower-only bathroom.

Via Laurina 34, 00187 Roma. ℂ **06-322-3674.** Fax 06-320-0395. 24 units. 190,000L–260,000L (98.80€–135.20€, $95–$130) double; 250,000L–290,000L (130€–150.80€, $125–$145) triple. Rates include breakfast. AE, DC, MC, V. Metro: Flaminio. **Amenities:** Breakfast room. *In room:* Hair dryer, no phone.

Hotel Parlamento   The Parlamento has a four-star government rating at two-star prices. Expect a friendly pensione-style reception. The furnishings are antiques or reproduction, and the firm beds are backed by carved wood or wrought-iron headboards. Fifteen rooms are air-conditioned, and the bathrooms were recently redone with heated towel racks, phones, and (in a few) even marble sinks. Only three come with a complete tub and shower. It's a three-story hotel with a recently added elevator. Rooms are different in style; the best are no. 82, with its original 1800s furniture, and nos. 104, 106, and 107, which open onto the roof garden. You can enjoy the chandeliered and tromp l'oeil breakfast room, or carry your cappuccino up to the small roof terrace with its view of San Silvestro's bell tower.

Via delle Convertite 5 (at the intersection with Via del Corso), 00187 Roma. ℂ **06-679-2082.** Fax 06-6992-1000. www.hotelparlamento@libero.tt. 23 units. 180,000L–220,000L (93.60€–114.40€, $90–$110) double. Rates include breakfast. AE, DC, MC, V. Parking 28,000L–30,000L (14.55€–15.60€, $14–$15). Metro: Spagna. **Amenities:** Restaurant, 2 bars; salon; room service; babysitting; laundry/dry cleaning; rooftop terrace.

7 Near the Vatican

For most visitors, this is a rather dull area in which to base yourself—it's well removed from the ancient sites, and it's not a great restaurant neighborhood. But if the main purpose of your visit centers on the Vatican, you'll be fine here, and you'll be joined by thousands of other pilgrims, nuns, and priests.

VERY EXPENSIVE

Hotel Columbus ⭐   This is an impressive 15th-century palace. The Columbus was once the home of the cardinal who became Pope Julius II, the man who tormented Michelangelo into painting the Sistine Chapel. It looks much as it must have centuries ago: a severe time-stained facade, small windows, and heavy wooden doors leading from the street to the colonnades and arches of the inner courtyard. The cobbled entranceway leads to a reception hall and a series of baronial public rooms. Note the main salon with its walk-in fireplace, oil portraits, battle scenes, and Oriental rugs.

The guest rooms are considerably simpler than the salons, furnished with comfortable modern pieces. All are spacious, but a few are enormous and still have such original details as decorated wood ceilings and frescoed walls. The best and quietest rooms front the garden. The bathrooms are medium in size and offer all the standards, like up-to-date plumbing and fine toiletries.

Via della Conciliazione 33, 00193 Roma. ℭ **06-686-5435.** Fax 06-686-4874. 92 units. 570,000L (285€, $296.40) double; 750,000L (375€, $390) suite. Rates include buffet breakfast. AE, DC, MC, V. Free parking for a few cars. Bus: 62 or 64. Metro: Ottaviano. **Amenities:** Excellent restaurant, bar; concierge; room service; babysitting; laundry/dry cleaning. *In room:* A/C, TV, minibar, hair dryer, safe.

Hotel dei Mellini ⭐   Only slightly less desirable than Atlante Star, this neoclassical hotel is a choice place for Vatican pilgrims. It dates from the early 1900s, when it was a town house. In 1995, after years of neglect, it was turned into a first-class hotel with a certain charm and luxury. It consists of two interconnected buildings, one with four floors and one with six; the top is graced with a terrace overlooking the baroque cupolas of at least three churches. A small staff maintains the lovely guest rooms, whose decor includes Art Deco touches, Italian marble, mahogany furniture, and beds with fine linen and quality mattresses. Accommodations with room numbers ending in "16" come with large sitting areas. The tiled full bathrooms have adequate shelf space.

Via Muzio Clementi 81, 00193 Roma. ℭ **06-324-771.** Fax 06-3247-7801. www.hotelmellini.com. 80 units. 580,000L–630,000L (301.60€–327.60€, $290–$315) double; from 700,000L (364€, $350) suite. Rates include breakfast. AE, DC, MC, V. Parking 45,000L (23.40€, $22.50). Metro: Lepanto or Flaminio. **Amenities:** Restaurant, room service; massage; laundry/dry cleaning. *In room:* A/C, TV, minibar, hair dryer, safe.

EXPENSIVE

Hotel Atlante Garden ⭐   The Atlante Garden stands on a tree-lined street near the Vatican. Although not as attractive or well appointed as its sibling, the Atlante Star (see below), you can often get a better rate here. The entrance takes you through a garden tunnel lined with potted palms, which eventually leads into a series of handsomely decorated public rooms. More classical in its decor than the Atlante Star, the Garden offers freshly papered and painted 19th-century–style midsize rooms that contain tastefully conservative furniture and all the modern accessories, such as quality mattresses and comfortable beds. Each was renovated in 1999. The renovated baths are tiled, each equipped with a shower and Jacuzzi.

Via Crescenzio 78, 00193 Roma. ℭ **06-687-2361.** Fax 06-687-2315. www.atlantehotels.com. 60 units. 395,000L–450,000L (197.50€–225€, $205.40–$234) double. Rates include breakfast. AE, DC, MC, V. Parking 50,000L (25€, $26). Metro: Ottaviano. Bus: 23, 32, 49, 51, or 492. **Amenities:** Lounge; babysitting; laundry/dry cleaning. *In room:* A/C, TV, minibar, hair dryer, safe.

Hotel Atlante Star ⭐⭐   This is the finest choice for those who'd like to lodge near the Vatican, with much more style and flair than its chief rival, the dei Mellini (see above), though its rates are lower. The Atlante Star is a first-class hotel with striking views of St. Peter's. The tastefully renovated lobby is covered

Accommodations & Dining Near the Vatican

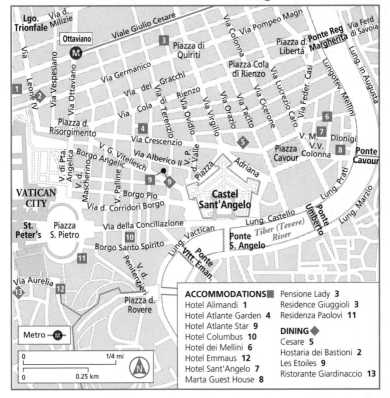

ACCOMMODATIONS ■
Hotel Alimandi **1**
Hotel Atlante Garden **4**
Hotel Atlante Star **9**
Hotel Columbus **10**
Hotel dei Mellini **6**
Hotel Emmaus **12**
Hotel Sant'Angelo **7**
Marta Guest House **8**
Pensione Lady **3**
Residence Giuggioli **3**
Residenza Paolovi **11**

DINING ◆
Cesare **5**
Hostaria dei Bastioni **2**
Les Etoiles **9**
Ristorante Giardinaccio **13**

with dark marble, chrome trim, and exposed wood; the upper floors will make you feel as if you're on a luxury ocean liner (no icebergs in sight). This stems partly from the lavish use of curved and lacquered surfaces, walls upholstered in printed fabrics, and wall-to-wall carpeting. Even the door handles are deco. The guest rooms are small but posh, with all the modern comforts, such as elegant beds with quality mattresses and modern, full bathrooms. The royal suite has a Jacuzzi. If there's no room here, the owner will try to accommodate you in his **Atlante Garden** nearby (see above).

Les Etoiles (see the complete review on p. 117) is an elegant roof-garden choice at night, with a 360-degree view of Rome and an illuminated St. Peter's in the background. The flavorful cuisine gives a nod to Venice. There's also a less formal restaurant, Terrazza Paradiso, serving international cuisine.

Via Vitelleschi 34, 00193 Roma. ☎ **06-687-3233.** Fax 06-687-2300. www.atlantehotels.com. 90 units. 410,000L–580,000L (213.20€–301.60€, $205–$290) double; from 750,000L (390€, $375) suite. Rates include buffet breakfast. AE, DC, MC, V. Parking 40,000L (20.80€, $20). Metro: Ottaviano. Bus: 23, 64, or 492. **Amenities:** Superb formal restaurant, more informal cafe, rooftop bar with a glorious view; concierge; business center; room service; babysitting; laundry/dry cleaning. *In room:* A/C, TV, minibar, hair dryer, safe.

Residenza Paolovi ★★ (Finds) Established on the premises of a former monastery, this hotel opened in 2000. With its marvelous views of St. Peter's Square, it offers one of the great views in Rome. One reader wrote, "I felt I was at the gates of heaven sitting on the most beautiful square in the Western world." In addition to its incomparable location, the hotel is filled with beautifully decorated and comfortable bedrooms, with modern bathrooms. In spite of its reasonable prices, the inn is like a small luxury hotel.

Via Paolo VI 29, 00193 Roma. ℭ **06-68-13-41-08.** Fax 06-68-67-74-28. www.residenzapaolovi.com. 28 units. 290,000L–450,000L (145€–225€, $150.80–$234) double. AE, DC, MC, V. Metro: Ottaviano. Bus: 64, 46, or J5. **Amenities:** Bar; babysitting; laundry/dry cleaning. *In room:* A/C, TV, minibar, hair dryer, safe.

MODERATE/INEXPENSIVE

Hotel Emmaus   Because of its relatively low prices and location near the Vatican, you might share this hotel with Catholic pilgrims from all over the world. Occupying an older building that was renovated in 1992, it offers unpretentious and basic but comfortable accommodations. The guest rooms have more recently been renovated but are still quite small, fitted with good mattresses on twin or double beds. Each comes with a small but efficiently organized shower-only bathroom.

Via delle Fornaci 25, 00165 Roma. ℭ and fax **06-635-658.** www.emmaus.it/roma/emmaus. 31 units. 300,000L (156€, $150) double. Rates include breakfast. AE, DC, MC, V. Parking 30,000L (15.60€, $15) nearby. Metro: Ottaviano. Bus: 65. **Amenities:** Breakfast room, lounge. *In room:* A/C, TV, minibar, hair dryer.

Hotel Pension Alimandi   Named after the three brothers who run it (Luigi, Enrico, and Paolo), this friendly guesthouse was built as an apartment house in 1908 in a bland residential neighborhood. The guest rooms are comfortable, albeit a bit small, with unremarkable contemporary furniture and cramped but modern-looking bathrooms. All have been upgraded and fitted with fine mattresses on the beds, which are mostly doubles. Each of the three upper floors is serviced by two elevators leading down to a simple lobby. The social center and most appealing spot is the roof garden, with potted plants and views of St. Peter's dome.

Via Tunisi 8, 00192 Roma. ℭ **06-3972-3948.** Fax 06-3972-3943. www.alimandi.org. 30 units. 270,000L (140.40€, $135) double. AE, MC, V. Parking 30,000L (15.60€, $15). Metro: Ottaviano. **Amenities:** Rooftop garden; laundry. *In room:* A/C, TV, hair dryer, safe.

Hotel Sant'Angelo   This hotel, right off Piazza Cavour (northeast of the Castel Sant'Angelo) and a 10-minute walk from St. Peter's, is in a relatively untouristy area. Maintained and operated by the Torre family, it occupies the second and third floors of an imposing 200-year-old building. The rooms are simple, modern, and clean, with wooden furniture and views of either the street or a rather bleak but quiet courtyard. Rooms are small but not cramped, each with a good mattress resting on a comfortable bed, plus a tiled, shower-only bathroom.

Via Mariana Dionigi 16, 00193 Roma. ℭ **06-32-42-000.** Fax 06-320-4451. www.novaera.it/hsa. 31 units. 160,000L–340,000L (83.20€–176.80€, $80–$170) double; 180,000L–380,000L (93.60€–197.60€, $90–$190) triple. Rates include breakfast. MC, V. Parking 40,000L (20.80€, $20). Metro: Piazza di Spagna. **Amenities:** Breakfast room, lounge. *In room:* A/C, TV, hair dryer.

Marta Guest House   Named after one of its owners, Marta Balbi, this is a friendly and well-scrubbed but simple pensione with a good location near Piazza Cavour. It fills the entire second floor of a 10-story apartment house built around 1900. Take an elevator upstairs to the unassuming reception area, where a staff member will lead you to one of the airy and high-ceilinged but utterly plain and unassuming rooms. Bedrooms are small but comfortable, with small bathrooms with showers and fine mattresses on the double beds. No breakfast is served, but the neighborhood is filled with cafes where you can get your morning cappuccino.

In 2000, the owners here invested heavily in an annex guesthouse on the nearby Piazza Cavour. Each of its 10 rooms has a private bathroom and is decorated in the same style, with the same price structure as the original guesthouse described above. Overflow from the main house is usually directed toward the annex.

Via Marianna Dionigi 17, 00193 Roma. © **06-324-0428**. Fax 06-323-0184. 9 units (2 with private bathroom). 120,000L (60€, $62.40) double without bathroom; 150,000L (75€, $78) double with bathroom. Bus: 492 to Piazza Cavour. Metro: Piazza Di Spagna. **Amenities:** Lounge. *In room:* No phone.

Residence Giuggioli ⭐   The force behind this place is Sra. Gasparina Giuggioli, whose family founded this guesthouse in the 1940s. It occupies most of the second floor of a five-story 1870s apartment house, with high-ceilinged rooms that were originally much grander but whose noble proportions are still obvious. Three of the five rooms have balconies overlooking the street; the one with the private bathroom is no. 6. The Giuggioli is always crowded, partly because the owner is so convivial and partly because the rooms are larger than expected and have a scattering of antiques and reproductions (though the mattresses could use replacing). No breakfast is served, but there are cafes nearby.

If this place is full, walk a few flights to the similar **Pensione Lady** (© **06-324-2112**), where up to seven rooms might be available at about the same rates.

Via Germanico 198, 00192 Roma. © **06-324-2113**. 5 units, 2 with private bathroom. 160,000L–180,000L (83.20€–93.60€, $80–$90) double without bathroom; 180,000L–200,000L (93.60€–104€, $90–$100) double with bathroom. No credit cards. Parking 25,000L–40,000L (13€–20.80€, $12.50–$20) in nearby garage. Metro: Ottaviano. **Amenities:** Lounge. *In room:* No phone.

8 In Trastevere

Once upon a time, tourists used to avoid Trastevere, but today, though it's off the beaten track, it's becoming more popular as an up-and-coming neighborhood where you can experience a true slice of Roman life.

INEXPENSIVE

Trastevere Manara ⭐ *Value*   Manara opened its newly restored doors in 1998 to meet the new demand for accommodations in Trastevere. This little gem has freshly decorated rooms, all gleaming with new tiles and fresh paint. All of the bathrooms have also been renovated and contain showers, though they're small. The price is hard to beat for those who want to stay in one of the most atmospheric sections of Rome. Most of the rooms open onto the lively Piazza San Cisimato, and all of them have comfortable, albeit functional, furnishings. Breakfast is the only meal served, but many good restaurants lie just minutes outside the door.

Via L. Manara 24–25, 00153 Roma. © **06-581-4713**. Fax 06-588-1016. hoteltrastevere@tiscalinet.it. 9 units. 190,000L (95€, $98.80) double. AE, DC, MC, V. Free parking on the street. Bus: H. Tram: 8. **Amenities:** Breakfast room, lounge. *In room:* TV, hair dryer.

9 In Prati

EXPENSIVE

Giulio Cesare ⭐   The tasteful Giulio Cesare, an elegant villa that was the former house of Countess Paterno Solari, lies in a sedate part of Rome across the Tiber from Piazza del Popolo. The guest salon, where the countess once entertained diplomats from all over the globe, is mostly furnished with antiques and Oriental carpets. Tapestries, Persian rugs, mirrors, ornate gilt pieces, and crystal chandeliers grace the public rooms; guests gather for drinks in a smaller salon with fruitwood paneling and 18th-century furniture. The carpeted guest rooms look like part of a lovely private home; some contain needlepoint-covered chairs. As befits a building of this age, rooms come in various dimensions, ranging from small to spacious, but each is comfortably furnished with excellent mattresses and well-maintained tiled bathrooms. Breakfast is served in a garden.

Via degli Scipioni 287, 00192 Roma. ✆ 06-321-0751. Fax 06-321-1736. www.travel.it/roma/giulioce/ giulioce.html. 86 units. 540,000L (270€, $280.80) double. Rates include breakfast. AE, DC, MC, V. Free parking. Metro: Lepanto. Bus: 280. **Amenities:** Bar, lounge; room service; babysitting. *In room:* A/C, TV, minibar, hair dryer, safe.

10 In Parioli

VERY EXPENSIVE

Hotel Lord Byron ✦✦✦   Lots of sophisticated travelers with hefty wallets are forgetting about the old landmarks such as the St. Regis Grand and choosing this chic boutique hotel. The Lord Byron exemplifies modern Rome—an Art Deco villa set on a residential hilltop in Parioli, an area of embassies and exclusive town houses at the edge of the Villa Borghese. From the curving entrance steps off the staffed parking lot in front, you'll notice striking design touches. Flowers are everywhere, the lighting is discreet, and everything is on an intimate scale. Each guest room is unique, but most have lots of mirrors, upholstered walls, sumptuous beds, spacious bathrooms with gray marble accessories, and big dressing room/closets. Ask for room nos. 503, 602, or 603 for great views. The hotel's restaurant, **Relais Le Jardin,** is one of Rome's top restaurants; see the full review on p. 122.

Via G. de Notaris 5, 00197 Roma. ✆ 06-322-0404. Fax 06-322-0405. www.lordbyronhotel.com. 37 units. 450,000L–705,000L (234€–366.60€, $225–$352.50) double; from 960,000L–1,660,000L (499.20€– 863.20€, $480–$830) suite. Rates include breakfast. AE, DC, MC, V. Parking 45,000L (23.40€, $22.50). Metro: Flaminio. Bus: 52. **Amenities:** One of the city's best restaurants, bar; room service; concierge; laundry/dry cleaning; currency exchange. *In room:* A/C, TV, minibar, hair dryer, iron, safe.

MODERATE/INEXPENSIVE

Hotel degli Aranci   This former villa is on a tree-lined street, surrounded by similar villas that are homes of consulates and diplomats. Most of the accommodations have tall windows opening onto city views and are filled with provincial furnishings or English-style reproductions, including good beds (fitted with fine mattresses and linen) and tiled, shower-only bathrooms with adequate shelf space. Scattered about the public rooms are medallions of soldiers in profile, old engravings of ruins, and classical vases. From the glass-walled breakfast room, you can see the tops of orange trees.

Via Barnaba Oriani 11, 00197 Roma. ✆ 06-808-5250. Fax 06-807-0704. 55 units. 150,000L–350,000L (78€–182€, $75–$175) double; from 450,000L (234€, $225) suite. Rates include breakfast. AE, DC, MC, V. Free parking. Bus: 3 or 53. **Amenities:** Breakfast room, bar; laundry. *In room:* A/C, TV, minibar, hair dryer, safe.

Hotel delle Muse ✦ *Value*   This little hotel, half a mile north of the Villa Borghese, is a winning but undiscovered choice run by the efficient English-speaking Giorgio Lazar. Most rooms have been renovated but remain rather minimalist, with modern furnishings. Nonetheless, there's reasonable comfort here, with good mattresses and tidy, shower-only bathrooms.

Via Tommaso Salvini 18, 00197 Roma. ✆ 06-808-8333. Fax 06-808-5749. www.hoteldellemuse.com. 61 units. 160,000L–260,000L (83.20€–135.20€, $80–$130) double; 200,000L–290,000L (104€–150.80€, $100–$145) triple. Rates include buffet breakfast. AE, DC, MC, V. Parking 30,000L (15.60€, $15). Bus: 360. **Amenities:** Garden restaurant, bar; room service; writing room. *In room:* TV, hair dryer.

11 In Monte Mario

VERY EXPENSIVE

Cavalieri Hilton ★★ *Kids*   This is not the place for you if you want to be in the heart of Rome, near attractions, shopping, and nightlife. But if you want resort-style accommodations and don't mind staying a 15-minute drive from the center of Rome (the hotel offers frequent, free shuttle service), consider the Hilton. Because of its pools and array of facilities, it attracts a lot of well-heeled families from all over the globe. The Cavalieri Hilton overlooks Rome and the Alban Hills from atop Monte Mario. It's set among 15 acres of trees, flowering shrubs, and stonework, in the cooler hills above Rome.

The entrance leads into a lavish red-and-gold lobby, with sculptures, winding staircases, and massive windows. The guest rooms and suites, many with panoramic views, are contemporary and stylish. Soft furnishings in pastels are paired with Italian furniture in warm-toned woods, including beds with deluxe mattresses and linen. Each unit has in-house movies, bedside controls for all the gadgets, and a spacious balcony. The bathrooms, sheathed in Italian marble, come with large mirrors, international electric sockets, vanity mirrors, piped-in music, and phones. There are facilities for travelers with disabilities.

Via Cadlolo 101, 00136 Roma. © **800/445-8667** in the U.S. and Canada, or 06-35091. Fax 06-3509-2241. www.hilton.com. 371 units. 900,000L–1,130,000L (468€–587.60€, $450–$565) double; from 2,000,000L (1,040€, $1,000) suite. AE, DC, DISC, MC, V. Parking 40,000L (20.80€, $20). Free shuttle bus to and from city center. **Amenities:** 2 restaurants, bar; 2 pools; 6 tennis courts; fitness center; free shuttle to the center of Rome; room service; laundry/dry cleaning. *In room:* A/C, TV, minibar, hair dryer, safe.

12 At the Airport

EXPENSIVE

Hotel Hilton Rome Airport   At long last, Rome has a first-class airport hotel for late-night arrivals and early-morning departures. Only 200 meters from the air terminal, this hotel is approached via a skywalk. The Hilton doesn't pretend to be more than it is—a bedroom factory at the airport. Follow the broad hallways to one of the midsize to spacious "crash pads," each with deep carpeting, generous storage space, and large, full bathrooms. The best units are the executive suites with extra amenities such as separate check-in, trouser press, data ports, and voice mail.

Via Arturo Ferrarin 2, 00050 Fiumicino. © **800/445-8667** in the U.S. and Canada, or 06-652-58. Fax 06-6525-6525. www.hilton.com. 517 units. 465,000L (241.80€, $232.50) double; from 770,000L (400.40€, $385) suite. AE, DC, MC, V. Free parking. Metro: Fiumicino Aeroporto. **Amenities:** 2 restaurants, bar; coffee shop; gym; sauna; room service; babysitting; laundry/dry cleaning. *In room:* A/C, TV, minibar, hair dryer, safe.

INEXPENSIVE

Cancelli Rossi   If you're nervous about making your flight, you could book into this very simple motel-style place, located 1½ miles from the airport. The hotel was built in 1994, and a full renovation was completed in 1999. Two floors are served with an elevator, and the decor is minimal. Rooms range in size from small to medium and are functionally furnished but reasonably comfortable, with good beds, along with perfectly clean, tiled bathrooms with shower stalls. The atmosphere is a bit antiseptic, but this place is geared more for business travelers than vacationers. A restaurant in an annex nearby serves Italian and international food.

Via R. La Valle 54, 00054 Fiumicino. © **06-650-7221.** Fax 06-6504-9168. 50 units. 198,000L (102.95€, $99) double. Rates include breakfast. Free parking. Free bus shuttle from/to the Leonardo Da Vinci airport every

Staying in J. Paul Getty's Former Villa

La Posta Vecchia, in Palo Laziale, just south of Ladispoli (© **06-994-9501;** fax 06-994-9507; www.lapostavecchia.com), lies 22 miles northwest of Rome and about 14 miles up the coast from Leonardo da Vinci airport. Set on foundations of villas possibly built by Tiberius, this palatial villa was owned between 1960 and 1976 by one of the world's richest men, J. Paul Getty. Set behind iron gates, the stucco-sided building stands amid formal gardens in an 8-acre park.

The villa contains many antiques collected by Getty, as well as many carefully disguised steel doors, escape routes, and security devices installed to protect him from intruders. Following the tragic kidnapping of his son in the early 1970s, Getty declared that the building's access to the sea was an unacceptable security risk. The house was sold and became a private home until 1990, when it was transformed into an exceptionally elegant hotel.

Guests stay in 17 sumptuously decorated suites, which range in price from 2,200,000L to 2,400,000L (1,100€–1,200€, $1,144–$1,248) a night. With discretion and politeness, staff members serve international cuisine at dinner and lunch in a richly formal dining room. The villa is closed from November 15 to April 6. The restaurant is open to non-residents if they phone in advance, but only if there are fewer than 11 guests in the dining room.

Extensive renovations initiated during Getty's ownership revealed hundreds of ancient Roman artifacts, many of which are on display in a mini-museum. There's an indoor pool, plus a staff (some of whom used to work for Getty) adept at maintaining the illusion that you've just arrived as a guest of the long-departed billionaire.

day 7–9:45am and 5–8:45pm every 20 min. **Amenities:** Room service; babysitting; laundry/dry cleaning. *In room:* A/C, TV, minibar, hair dryer.

13 On the Outskirts

EXPENSIVE

Borgo Paraelios ✦   This 19th-century villa, a 45-minute drive from the city center, is surrounded by olive groves and farmlands. It combines the formality and grace of a Relais & Châteaux with a down-home informality and friendliness. Guests are welcomed in a charming lobby decorated with Oriental rugs and Italian paintings, some of them by Canaletto. Rooms are tastefully furnished with Florentine-style antiques and they include all the modern comforts. The large marbled bathrooms have robes, hair dryers, and body care products. The 173-acre park offers the bucolic atmosphere of Roman hills. You can also sip a drink on the edges of the outside pool, framed by Mediterranean flowers.

Valle Collicchia, 02040 Poggio Cantino, Rieti. © **0765-26-267.** Fax 0765-26-268. www.relaischateaux. fr/borgo. 18 units. 450,000L (225€, $234) double; 550,000L (275€, $286) junior suite. Rates include continental breakfast. AE, DC, MC, V. Free parking. About 20 miles north of Rome, take autostrada A1, exit at Fiano Romano and follow signs for Passo Corese, take SS313 (on the left) to Terni. **Amenities:** Excellent restaurant; 2 pools; fitness center; sauna; Turkish bath; room service; babysitting; laundry/dry cleaning. *In room:* Hair dryer, safe.

6

Dining

Rome remains one of the world's great capitals for dining, with even more diversity today than ever. Most of its trattorie haven't changed their menus in a quarter of a century (except to raise the prices, of course), but there's an increasing number of chic, upscale spots with chefs willing to experiment, as well as a growing handful of ethnic spots for those days when you just can't face another plate of pasta. The great thing about Rome is that you don't have to spend a fortune to eat really well.

Most Italian restaurants are either called a *trattoria* or a *ristorante*. In theory there's a difference, but in reality it's difficult to discern. Traditionally, trattorie are smaller and less formal, but sometimes in a kind of reverse snobbism the management will call an elegant place a trattoria. A ristorante is supposed to be more substantial, but often the opposite is true.

It's difficult to compile a list of the best restaurants in a city like Rome. Everybody—locals, expatriates, even those who have chalked up only one visit—has their own finds. What follows is not a comprehensive list of all the best restaurants of Rome, but simply a personal running commentary on a number of our favorites. For the most part, we've chosen not to review every deluxe spot known to all big spenders. We've chosen the handful of splurge restaurants where you'll really get what you pay for, and then we've reviewed a large selection of moderately priced and affordable restaurants that will give you a wonderful meal, authentic cuisine, and a lovely experience without breaking the bank.

Roman meals customarily include at least three separate courses: pasta, a main course (usually a meat dish with vegetables or salad), and dessert. Meats, though tasty, are definitely secondary to the pasta dishes, which are generous and filling. The wine is so excellent (especially the white Frascati wine from the nearby Castelli Romani) and affordable that you may want to do as the Romans do and have it with both lunch and dinner.

PRACTICAL TIPS

For a quick bite, go to a **bar.** Although bars in Italy do serve alcohol, they function mainly as cafes. Prices have a split personality: *al banco* is standing at the bar, while *à tavola* means sitting at a table where you'll be waited on and charged two to four times as much. In bars you can find *panini* sandwiches on various rolls and *tramezzini* (giant triangles of white-bread sandwiches with the crusts cut off). These both run 2,000L to 6,000L (1.05€–3.10€, $1–$3) and are traditionally put in a kind of tiny press to flatten and toast them so the crust is crispy and the filling is hot and gooey; microwaves have unfortunately invaded and are everywhere, turning panini into something resembling a soggy hot tissue.

Pizza a taglio or *pizza rustica* indicates a place where you can order pizza by the slice. *Pizzerie* are casual sit-down restaurants that cook large, round pizzas with very thin crusts in wood-burning ovens. A *tavola calda* (literally "hot table") serves ready-made hot foods you can take away or eat at one of the few small tables often available. The food is usually very good. A *rosticceria* is the same type of place, and you'll see chickens roasting on a spit in the window.

A full-fledged restaurant will go by the name *osteria, trattoria,* or *ristorante.* Once upon a time, these terms meant something—*osterie* were basic places where you could get a plate of spaghetti and a glass of wine; *trattorie* were casual places serving full meals of filling peasant fare; and *ristoranti* were fancier places, with waiters in bow ties, printed menus, wine lists, and hefty prices. Nowadays, fancy restaurants often go by the name of *trattoria* to cash in on the associated charm factor; trendy spots use *osteria* to show they're hip; and simple, inexpensive places sometimes tack on *ristorante* to ennoble themselves.

The *pane e coperto* (bread and cover) is a 1,500L to 10,000L (.830€–5.20€, 75¢–$5) cover charge that you must pay at most restaurants for the mere privilege of sitting at the table. Most Italians eat a leisurely full meal—appetizer and first and second courses—at lunch and dinner and will expect you to do the same, or at least a first and second course. To request the bill, ask *"Il conto, per favore"* (eel *con*-toh, pehr fah-*vohr*-ay). A tip of 15% is usually included in the bill these days, but if you're unsure, ask *"È incluso il servizio?"* (ay een-*cloo*-soh eel sair-*vee*-tsoh?).

You'll find at many restaurants, especially larger ones and in cities, a *menu turistico* (tourist's menu), sometimes called *menu del giorno* (menu of the day). This set-price menu usually covers all meal incidentals—including table wine, cover charge, and 15% service charge—along with a first course (*primo*) and second course (*secondo*), but it almost always offers an abbreviated selection of pretty bland dishes: spaghetti in tomato sauce and slices of pork. Sometimes a better choice is a *menu à prezzo fisso* (fixed-price menu). It usually doesn't include wine but sometimes covers the service and *coperto,* and often offers a wider selection of better dishes, occasionally house specialties and local foods. Ordering a la carte, however, offers you the best chance for a memorable meal. Even better, forego the menu entirely and put yourself in the capable hands of your waiter.

The *enoteca* wine bar is a growing, popular marriage of a wine bar and an *osteria,* where you can sit and order from a host of local and regional wines by the glass (usually 3,000L–8,000L [1.55€–4.15€, $1.50–$4]) while snacking on finger foods (and usually a number of simple first-course possibilities) that reflect the region's fare. Relaxed and full of ambience and good wine, these are great spots for light and inexpensive lunches—perfect to educate your palate and recharge your batteries.

Restaurants generally serve lunch between 1 and 3pm, and dinner between about 8 and 10:30pm; at all other times, restaurants are closed. Dinner is taken late in Rome, so although a restaurant might open at 7:30, even if you get there at 8pm, you'll often be the only one in the place. A heavier meal is typically eaten at midday, and a lighter one is eaten in the evening. We recommend that you leave a few hours free for dinner and go to a restaurant in a different part of town each night. It's a great way to get a real taste of Rome. Romans think of meals as leisurely affairs, so allow yourself enough time and relax—do as the Romans do.

ROMAN CUISINE

Many visitors from North America erroneously think of Italian cuisine as one-dimensional. Of course, everybody's heard of minestrone, spaghetti, chicken cacciatore, and spumoni ice cream. But chefs hardly confine themselves to such a limited repertoire.

Rome's cooking isn't subtle, but its kitchens rival anything that the chefs of Florence or Venice can turn out. The city's chefs borrow—and sometimes improve on—the cuisine of other regions. Throughout your Roman holiday you'll encounter such savory treats as *zuppa di pesce* (a soup or stew of various fish, cooked in white wine and herbs), *cannelloni* (tube-shaped pasta baked with any number of stuffings), *riso col gamberi* (rice with shrimp, peas, and mushrooms, flavored with white wine and garlic), *scampi alla griglia* (grilled prawns, one of the best-tasting, and most expensive, dishes in the city), *quaglie con risotto e tartufi* (quail with rice and truffles), *lepre alla cacciatore* (hare flavored with tomato sauce and herbs), *zabaglione* (a cream made with sugar, egg yolks, and Marsala), *gnocchi alla romana* (potato-flour dumplings with a sauce made with meat and covered with grated cheese), *stracciatella* (chicken broth with eggs and grated cheese), *abbacchio* (baby spring lamb, often roasted over an open fire), *saltimbocca alla romana* (literally "jump-in-your-mouth"—thin slices of veal with cheese, ham, and sage), *fritta alla romana* (a mixed fry that's likely to include everything from brains to artichokes), *carciofi alla romana* (tender artichokes cooked with mint and garlic, and flavored with white wine), *fettuccine all'uovo* (egg noodles served with butter and cheese), *zuppa di cozze o vongole* (a hearty bowl of mussels or clams cooked in broth), *fritta di scampi e calamaretti* (baby squid and prawns fast-fried), *fragoline* (wild strawberries, in this case from the Alban Hills), and *finocchio* (or fennel, a celerylike raw vegetable, the flavor of anisette, often eaten as a dessert and in salads).

Incidentally, except in the south, Italians don't use as much garlic in their food as most visitors seem to believe. Most northern Italian dishes are butter based. Virgin olive oil is preferred in the south. Spaghetti and meatballs is not an Italian dish, although certain restaurants throughout the country have taken to serving it for homesick Americans.

WINES & OTHER DRINKS

Italy is the largest wine-producing country in the world; as far back as 800 B.C. the Etruscans were vintners. It's said that more soil is used in Italy for the cultivation of grapes than for growing food. Many Italian farmers produce wine just for their own consumption or for their relatives. It wasn't until 1965, however, that laws were enacted to guarantee regular consistency in wine making. Wines regulated by the government are labeled "DOC" (*Denominazione di Origine Controllata*). If you see "DOCG" on a label (the "G" means *garantita*), that means even better quality control.

Lazio (Rome's region) is a major wine-producing region of Italy. Many of the local wines come from the Castelli Romani, the hill towns around Rome. Horace and Juvenal sang the praises of Latium wines even in imperial times. These wines, experts agree, are best drunk when young, and they are most often white, mellow, and dry (or else demi-sec). There are seven different types, including **Falerno** (yellowish straw in color) and **Cecubo** (often served with roast meat). Try also **Colli Albani** (straw-yellow with amber tints and served with both fish and meat). The golden-yellow wines of **Frascati** are famous, produced in both a demi-sec and a sweet variety, the latter served with dessert.

Romans drink other libations as well. Their most famous drink is **Campari,** bright red in color and herb flavored, with a quinine bitterness to it. It's customary to serve it with ice cubes and soda.

Beer is also made in Italy and, in general, is lighter than German beer. If you order beer in a Roman bar or restaurant, chances are it will be imported unless you specify otherwise, and you'll be charged accordingly. Some famous names in

European beer-making now operate plants in Italy, where the brew has been "adjusted" to Italian taste.

High-proof **grappa** is made from the leftovers after the grapes have been pressed. Many Romans drink this before or after dinner (some put it into their coffee). To an untrained foreign palate, it often seems rough and harsh; some say it's an acquired taste.

Other popular drinks include several **liqueurs.** Try herb-flavored Strega, or perhaps an almond-flavored Amaretto. One of the best known is Maraschino, taking its name from a type of cherry used in its preparation. Galliano is also herb flavored, and Sambuca (anisette) is made of aniseed and is often served with a "fly" (coffee bean) in it. On a hot day the true Roman orders a vermouth, Cinzano, with a twist of lemon, ice cubes, and a squirt of soda water.

1 Restaurants by Cuisine

ABRUZZESE
Abruzzi (Near Ancient Rome, $, p. 102)

Ristorante al Cardello (Near Ancient Rome, $, p. 103)

BOLOGNESE/EMILIA-ROMAGNOLA
Césarina (Near Via Veneto & Piazza Barberini, $$, p. 100)

Colline Emiliane ★★ (Near Via Veneto & Piazza Barberini, $$$, p. 99)

Dal Bolognese ★ (Near the Spanish Steps & Piazza del Popolo, $$, p. 115)

CALABRESE
Le Maschere ★★ (Near Campo de' Fiori & the Jewish Ghetto, $, p. 106)

CONTINENTAL
Trimani Wine Bar ★ (Near Stazione Termini, $, p. 96)

ENGLISH
Babington's Tea Rooms (Near the Spanish Steps & Piazza del Popolo, $$, p. 114)

FLORENTINE
Da Mario (Near the Spanish Steps & Piazza del Popolo, $$, p. 114)

FRENCH
L'Eau Vive ★ (Near Piazza Navona & the Pantheon, $$, p. 109)

Sans Souci ★★★ (Near Via Veneto & Piazza Barberini, $$$$, p. 99)

GREEK
Antica Hostaria l'Archeologia (On the Appian Way, $$, p. 122)

INTERNATIONAL
Alfredo alla Scrofa (Near Piazza Navona & the Pantheon, $$, p. 107)

Il Chicco d' Uva ★ (Near Piazza Navona & the Pantheon, $$, p. 109)

Il Convivio ★ (Near Piazza Navona & the Pantheon, $$$, p. 107)

La Terrazza ★★★ (Near Via Veneto & Piazza Barberini, $$$$, p. 99)

L'Eau Vive ★ (Near Piazza Navona & the Pantheon, $$, p. 109)

Osteria dell'Antiquario ★ (near Piazza Navona & the Pantheon, $$, p. 110)

Taverna Flavia (Near Stazione Termini, $$, p. 96)

ITALIAN (PAN-ITALIAN)
Al Bric (Near Piazza Navona & the Pantheon, $, p. 111)

Al Moro ★ (Near the Spanish Steps & Piazza del Popolo, $$, p. 114)

Antico Arco ★ (In Trastevere, $$, p. 119)

Key to Abbreviations: $$$$ = Very Expensive $$$ = Expensive $$ = Moderate $ = Inexpensive

Arancia Blu ✿✿ (In San Lorenzo,
$, p. 98)

Asinocotto (In Trastevere, $$,
p. 119)

Aurora 10 da Pino il Sommelier
(Near Via Veneto & Piazza
Barberini, $$, p. 100)

Boccondivino ✿ (Near Piazza
Navona & the Pantheon, $$$,
p. 107)

Café Riccioli ✿ (Near Piazza
Navona & the Pantheon, $$,
p. 108)

Di Fronte a . . . (Near the Spanish
Steps & Piazza del Popolo, $$,
p. 115)

Gusto ✿ (Near the Spanish Steps
& Piazza del Popolo, $$, p. 115)

Hostaria Nerone ✿ (Near Ancient
Rome, $, p. 103)

Il Bacaro ✿ (Near Piazza Navona
& the Pantheon, $$, p. 108)

Il Chicco d'Uva ✿ (Near Piazza
Navona & the Pantheon, $$,
p. 109)

Il Dito e La Luna ✿ (In San
Lorenzo, $, p. 98)

Il Ristorante 34 ✿ (Near the Span-
ish Steps & Ancient Rome, $$$,
p. 114)

Insalata Ricca 2 (Near Piazza
Navona & the Pantheon, $,
p. 112)

La Dolce Vita (The Aventine &
the South, $$, p. 121)

La Terrazza ✿✿✿ (Near Via
Veneto & Piazza Barberini,
$$$$, p. 99)

Montevecchio (Near Piazza
Navona & the Pantheon, $$,
p. 109)

Myosotis ✿ (Near Piazza Navona
& the Pantheon, $$, p. 110)

Passetto ✿ (Near Piazza Navona &
the Pantheon, $$, p. 110)

Quirino (Near Piazza Navona &
the Pantheon, $$, p. 110)

Relais Le Jardin ✿✿✿ (In Parioli,
$$$$, p. 122)

Ristorante Giardinaccio (Near the
Vatican, $$, p. 118)

Sans Souci ✿✿✿ (Near Via Veneto
& Piazza Barberini, $$$$, p. 99)

Santo Padre Roman (Near Via
Veneto & Piazza Barberini, $$,
p. 101)

Testa Food & Wine ✿ (Near Via
Veneto & Piazza Barberini, $$,
p. 101)

Tre Scalini ✿ (Near Piazza Navona
& the Pantheon, $$, p. 111)

Vecchia Roma (Near Campo de'
Fiori & the Jewish Ghetto, $$,
p. 106)

JAPANESE

Café Riccioli ✿ (Near Piazza
Navona & the Pantheon, $$,
p. 108)

JEWISH

Da Giggetto (Near Campo de'
Fiori & the Jewish Ghetto, $$,
p. 104)

Piperno ✿ (Near Campo de' Fiori
& the Jewish Ghetto, $$$,
p. 104)

MEDITERRANEAN

Babington's Tea Rooms (Near the
Spanish Steps & Piazza del
Popolo, $$, p. 114)

Les Etoiles ✿✿ (Near the Vatican,
$$$$, p. 117)

MOLISIAN

Ristorante Giardinaccio (Near the
Vatican, $$, p. 118)

NEAPOLITAN

Il Quadrifoglio (Near Stazione
Termini, $$, p. 95)

Scoglio di Frisio (Near Ancient
Rome, $$, p. 101)

PACIFIC RIM

Gusto ✿ (Near the Spanish Steps
& Piazza del Popolo, $$, p. 115)

PIZZA

Pizzeria Baffetto ✿ (Near Piazza
Navona & the Pantheon, $,
p. 112)

Scoglio di Frisio (Near Ancient
Rome, $$, p. 101)

ROMAN

SARDINIAN

Il Miraggio (Near Piazza Navona
& the Pantheon, $, p. 111)

Monte Arci (Near Stazione
Termini, $, p. 96)

Trattoria San Teodoro ✸ (Near
Ancient Rome, $$$, p. 100)

SEAFOOD

Alberto Ciarla ✸✸ (In Trastevere,
$$$, p. 119)

Café Riccioli ✸ (Near Piazza
Navona & the Pantheon, $$,
p. 108)

Il Miraggio (Near Piazza Navona
& the Pantheon, $, p. 111)

La Rosetta ✸✸ (Near Piazza
Navona & the Pantheon, $$$$,
p. 106)

Quinzi & Gabrieli ✸✸✸ (Near
Piazza Navona & the Pantheon,
$$$$, p. 107)

Sabatini ✸ (In Trastevere, $$$,
p. 119)

SICILIAN

Il Dito e la Luna ✸ (In San
Lorenzo, $, p. 98)

Quirino (Near Piazza Navona &
the Pantheon, $$, p. 110)

TUSCAN

Cesare (Near the Vatican, $$,
p. 117)

Girarrosto Toscano ✸ (Near Via
Veneto & Piazza Barberini, $$,
p. 100)

Ristorante Nino (Near the Spanish
Steps & Piazza del Popolo, $$,
p. 116)

VEGETARIAN

Arancia Blu ✸✸ (In San Lorenzo,
$, p. 98)

Insalata Ricca 2 (Near Piazza
Navona & the Pantheon, $,
p. 112)

VENETIAN

El Toulà ✸✸ (Near the Spanish
Steps & Piazza del Popolo,
$$$$, p. 112)

---

2 Near Stazione Termini

VERY EXPENSIVE

Agata e Romeo ✸✸ NEW ROMAN   One of the most charming places near
the Vittorio Emanuele Monument is this striking duplex restaurant in turn-of-
the-century Liberty style. You'll enjoy the creative cuisine of Romeo Caraccio
(who manages the dining room) and his wife, Agata Parisella (who prepares her
own version of sophisticated Roman food). Look for pasta garnished with broccoli and cauliflower and served in skate broth, as well as a crisp *sformato* loaded
with eggplant, parmigiano, mozzarella, and fresh Italian herbs. Sweet-tasting
swordfish might be served thinly sliced as roulade and loaded with capers and
olives; beans will probably be studded with savory mussels, clams, and pasta. For
dessert, consider Agata's *millefoglie,* puff pastry stuffed with almonds and sweetened cream. There's a charming wine cellar with a wide choice of international
and domestic wines.

Via Carlo Alberto 45. ✆ **06-446-6115.** Reservations recommended. Main courses 45,000L–60,000L
(23.40€–31.20€, $22.50–$30). AE, DC, MC, V. Mon–Sat 1–3pm and 8–11:30pm. Metro: Vittorio Emanuele.

MODERATE

Il Quadrifoglio NEAPOLITAN   In a grandiose palace, this well-managed
restaurant lets you sample the flavors and herbs of Naples and southern Italy.
You'll find a tempting selection of antipasti, such as anchovies, peppers, capers,
onions, and breaded and fried eggplant, all garnished with fresh herbs and virgin olive oil. The pastas are made daily, usually with tomato- or oil-based sauces
and always with herbs and aged cheeses. Try a zesty rice dish (one of the best is

sartù di riso, studded with vegetables, herbs, and meats), followed by a hard-to-resist grilled octopus or a simple but savory *granatine* (meatballs, usually of veal, bound together with mozzarella). Dessert anyone? A longtime favorite is *torta caprese,* with hazelnuts and chocolate.

Via del Boschetto 19. *©* **06-482-6096.** Reservations recommended. Main courses 20,000L–30,000L (10.40€–15.60€, $10–$15). AE, DC, MC, V. Mon–Sat 7pm–midnight. Closed Aug. Metro: Cavour.

Taverna Flavia ROMAN/INTERNATIONAL   This tavern is a robustly Roman restaurant, still serving the same food that once delighted the late Frank Sinatra and the "Hollywood on the Tiber" crowd in the 1950s. It's not chic anymore, but you can still enjoy the hearty classics here. Specialties are risotto with scampi, spaghetti with champagne, *osso buco* (veal shank) with peas, a delectable seafood salad, and a to-die-for fondue with truffles. There's a daily regional dish (it might be Roman-style tripe, much better than you might expect). A chef always prepares our favorite salad in Rome: Veruska, made with five kinds of lettuce and mushrooms, including fresh truffles.

Via Flavia 9 (a block from Via XX Settembre). *©* **06-474-5214.** Reservations recommended. Main courses 20,000L–35,000L (10.40€–18.20€, $10–$17.50). AE, DC, MC, V. Mon–Fri 12:30–3pm and 7:30–11pm; Sat–Sun 7:30–11:30pm. Metro: Repubblica.

INEXPENSIVE

Bar Cottini ⟨Value⟩ ROMAN   Large and bustling, this is the most popular *tavola calda* in this congested neighborhood, feeding hundreds of hungry office workers and shopkeepers every day. At lunch, it's self-service, sort of like an American cafeteria but without the tuna casserole. Separate areas are devoted to hot pastas—most priced at 5,000L (2.50€, $2.60) per heaping portion—meats, and, to a lesser extent, fish. High turnover ensures a relatively fresh, if not particularly innovative, array of mass-produced, pan-Italian cuisine. For such a bustling food factory, the flavors and seasonings are pretty good. It's a great way to fill up on good, hearty food at a relatively modest price. Even when it's not serving food, it's a fine choice to visit as a bar, as it has a relaxed pub atmosphere until 9pm each evening.

Via Merulana 286–287. *©* **06-474-0768.** Reservations not accepted. Main courses 7,500L–9,500L (3.75€–4.75€, $3.90–$4.95) at lunch. No credit cards. Restaurant daily noon–3pm; bar daily noon–9pm. Metro: Termini.

Monte Arci ROMAN/SARDINIAN   On a cobblestone street near Piazza Indipendenza, this restaurant is set behind a sienna-colored facade. It features cheap Roman and Sardinian specialties (you'll spend even less for pizza) such as *nialoreddus* (a regional form of gnocchetti); pasta with clams, lobster, or the musky-earthy notes of porcini mushrooms; green and white spaghetti with bacon, spinach, cream, and cheese; and delicious lamb sausage flavored with herbs and pecorino cheese. It's all home-cooking, hearty but not that creative.

Via Castelfirdardo 33. *©* **06-494-1220.** Reservations recommended. Main courses 15,000L–20,000L (7.80€–10.40€, $7.50–$10); fixed-price menu 50,000L (26€, $25). AE, DC, V. Mon–Fri 12:30–3pm and 7–11:30pm; Sat 7–11:30pm. Closed Aug. Metro: Stazione Termini.

Trimani Wine Bar ⟨★⟩ CONTINENTAL   Opened as a tasting center for French and Italian wines, spumantis, and liqueurs, this is an elegant wine bar with a lovely decor (stylish but informal) and comfortable seating. More than 30 wines are available by the glass. To accompany them, you can choose from a bistro-style menu, with dishes such as salad niçoise, vegetarian pastas, herb-laden bean soups (*fagiole*), quiche, and Hungarian goulash. Also available is a wider

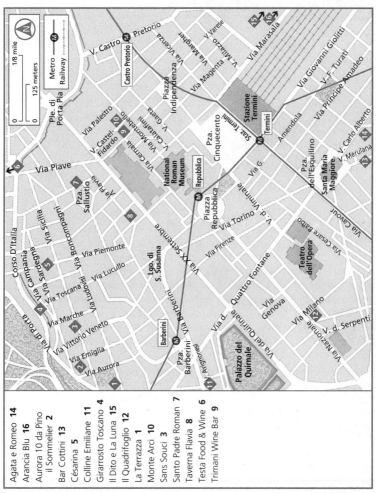

Agata e Romeo **14**
Arancia Blu **16**
Aurora 10 da Pino
il Sommelier **2**
Bar Cottini **13**
Césarina **5**
Colline Emiliane **11**
Girarrosto Toscano **4**
Il Dito e La Luna **15**
Il Quadrifoglio **12**
La Terrazza **1**
Monte Arci **10**
Sans Souci **3**
Santo Padre Roman **7**
Taverna Flavia **8**
Testa Food & Wine **6**
Trimani Wine Bar **9**

menu, including meat and fish courses. The specialty is the large choice of little "bruschette" with cheese and prosciutto—the chef orders every kind of prosciuti and cheese, from all over Italy. The dishes are matched with the appropriate wines. The dessert specialty is chestnut mousse served with a sauce of white wine (*Verduzzo di Ronco di Viere*), covered by whipped cream and meringue.

Trimani maintains a well-stocked shop about 40 yards from its wine bar, at V. Goito 20 (✆ **06-446-9661**), where an astonishing array of Italian wines is for sale.

Via Cernaia 37B. ✆ **06-446-9630**. Reservations recommended. Main courses 12,000L–26,000L (6.25€–13.50€, $6–$13); glass of wine (depending on vintage) 3,500L–20,000L (1.80€–10.40€, $1.75–$10). AE, DC, MC, V. Mon–Sat 11:30am–3:30pm and 6pm–12:30am (in Dec open also on Sun). Closed 2 weeks in Aug. Metro: Repubblica or Castro Pretorio.

Take a Gelato Break

If you're craving luscious gelato, our top choice is **Giolitti** ★★, Via Uffici del Vicario 40 (✆ **06-699-1243**), the city's oldest ice-cream shop, open daily from 7am to 2am. You'll find the usual vanilla (*vaniglia*), chocolate (*cioccolato*), strawberry (*fragola*), and coffee (*caffé*), but you'll also find flavors that you might not have heard of, such as *gianduia* (*chocolate hazelnut*), plus such treats as *cassata alla siciliana, zabaglione, mascarpone,* and *maron glacé.* The preposterously oversize showpiece sundaes have names such as Coppa Olimpico di Roma. Prices here and at each of the places below range from 3,000L to 16,000L (1.55€ to 8.30€, $1.50 to $8).

A close second is **Tre Scalini** ★, Piazza Navona 30 (✆ **06-687-9148**; see p. 111), which is celebrated for its *tartufo.* Gelato connoisseurs say that you haven't really experienced Rome until you've enjoyed a tartufo here. Another favorite is the **Palazzo del Freddo Giovanni Fassi**, Via Principe Eugenio 65–67 (✆ **06-446-4740**). More than 100 years old, this ice-cream outlet (part of a gelato factory) turns out yummy concoctions and specializes in rice ice cream. It's open from Tuesday to Sunday, from noon to 12:30am.

If you're fond of frothy *frullati* frappes, head to **Pascucci**, Via Torre Argentina 20 (✆ **06-686-4816**), where blenders work all day grinding fresh fruit into delectable drinks. It's open from Monday to Saturday, from noon to 1am.

3 In San Lorenzo

To locate the restaurants reviewed below, see the "Dining Near Stazione Termini, Via Veneto & Piazza Barberini" map earlier in this chapter.

INEXPENSIVE

Arancia Blu ★★ *Finds* VEGETARIAN/ITALIAN   Fabio Bassan and Enrico Bartolucci offer Rome's best vegetarian cuisine. Under soft lighting and wood ceilings, surrounded by wine racks and university intellectuals, the friendly waiters will help you compile a menu to fit any dietary need. The dishes at this trendy spot are inspired by peasant cuisines from across Italy and beyond. The appetizers range from hummus and tabbouleh to zucchini-and-saffron quiche or salad with apples, gorgonzola, and balsamic vinegar. The main courses change seasonally and may be lasagna with red onions, mushrooms, zucchini, and ginger; couscous *con verdure* (vegetable couscous); or *ravioli ripieni di patate e menta* (ravioli stuffed with potatoes and mint served under fresh tomatoes and Sardinian sheep's cheese). They offer 250 wines and inventive desserts, such as darkchocolate cake with warm orange sauce.

Via dei Latini 55–65 (at Via Arunci). ✆ **06-445-4105.** Reservations highly recommended. Main courses 14,000L–18,000L (7.30€–9.35€, $7–$9). No credit cards. Daily 8pm–midnight. Bus: 71.

Il Dito e La Luna ★ SICILIAN/ITALIAN   This charming, unpretentious bistro has counters and service areas accented with lovely displays of fresh fruits and vegetables. The menu—divided between traditional Sicilian and creative contemporary dishes—includes orange-infused anchovies served on orange segments, a creamy flan of mild onions and mountain cheese, and seafood couscous loaded with shellfish. The pastas are excellent, particularly the square-cut spaghetti (*tonnarelli*) with mussels, bacon, tomatoes, and exotic mushrooms. The specialty of the house is *caponata di melanzane,* chopped eggplant stewed in tomato sauce with onions and potatoes.

Via dei Sabelli 49–51, San Lorenzo. (C) **06-494-0726.** Reservations recommended. Main courses 22,000L–25,000L (11.45€–13€, $11–$12.50). No credit cards. Mon–Sat 8pm–midnight. Metro: Piazza Vittorio.

4 Near Via Veneto & Piazza Barberini

To locate the restaurants in this section, refer to the "Dining Near Stazione Termini, Via Veneto & Piazza Barberini" map on p. 97.

VERY EXPENSIVE

La Terrazza ★★★ ITALIAN/INTERNATIONAL   La Terrazza and Relais Le Jardin (see p. 122) serve the city's finest cuisine; here, you get the added bonus of a sweeping view over St. Peter's. The service is formal and flawless, yet not intimidating. Chef Enrico Derfligher, the wizard behind about a dozen top-notch Italian restaurants around Europe, prepares a seasonally changing menu that's among the most polished in Rome. You might start with zucchini blossoms stuffed with ricotta and black olives, or lobster medallions with apple purée and black truffles. Main courses may include red tortelli (whose coloring comes from tomato mousse) stuffed with mascarpone cheese and drizzled with lemon, or a sea bass baked in a crust of black olives and salt with oregano and potatoes.

In the Hotel Eden, Via Ludovisi 49. (C) **06-478-121.** Reservations recommended. Main courses 42,000L–78,000L (21.85€–40.55€, $21–$39); fixed-price menu 150,000L (78€, $75). AE, DC, MC, V. Daily 12:30–2:30pm and 7:30–10:30pm. Metro: Barberini.

Sans Souci ★★★ FRENCH/ITALIAN   Not long ago, Sans Souci was getting a little tired, but now it has bounced back, and Michelin has restored its coveted star. As you step into the dimly lit lounge, the maître d' will present you with the menu, which you can peruse while sipping a drink amid tapestries and glittering mirrors. The menu is ever changing, although the classics never disappear. A great beginning is the goose-liver terrine with truffles, one of the chef's signatures. The fish soup, according to one Roman restaurant critic, is "a legend to experience." The soufflés are popular (in varieties such as artichoke, asparagus, and spinach), as are the succulent truffle-filled ravioli, homemade foie gras, and tender Normandy lamb. Save room for a special dessert soufflé (prepared for two), in flavors such as chocolate and Grand Marnier.

Via Sicilia 20. (C) **06-482-1814.** Reservations recommended. Main courses 40,000L–70,000L (20.80€–36.40€, $20–$35). AE, DC, DISC, MC, V. Tues–Sun 8pm–1am. Closed Aug 10–30. Metro: Barberini.

EXPENSIVE

Colline Emiliane ★★ (Finds) EMILIANA-ROMAGNOLA   Serving the *classica cucina bolognese,* Colline Emiliane is a small, family-run place—the owner is the cook and his wife makes the pasta (about the best you'll find in Rome). The house specialty is an inspired *tortellini alla panna* (with cream sauce and truffles), but the less-expensive pastas, including *maccheroni al funghetto* and tagliatelle alla bolognese, are excellent, too. As an opener, we suggest *culatello di*

Zibello, a delicacy from a small town near Parma that's known for having the world's finest prosciutto. Main courses include *braciola di maiale* (boneless rolled pork cutlets stuffed with ham and cheese, breaded, and sautéed) and an impressive *giambonnetto* (roast veal Emilian style with roast potatoes).

Via Avignonesi 22 (off Piazza Barberini). ✆ 06-481-7538. Reservations highly recommended. Main courses 30,000L–60,000L (15.60€–31.20€, $15–$30). MC, V. Sat–Thurs 12:45–2:45pm and 7:45–10:45pm. Closed Aug. Metro: Barberini.

MODERATE

Aurora 10 da Pino il Sommelier ITALIAN Skip the tourist traps along Via Veneto and walk another block or two for the much better food and lovely service here. The wait staff is welcoming to foreigners, though you'll also dine with regulars from the chic neighborhood. The place is noted for its array of more than 250 wines, representing every province. The linguine with chunky lobster and the *rigatoni alla siciliana* with eggplant, black olives, and tomato sauce is better than anything Carmela Soprano could whip up. The fish is fresh every day, and the chefs grill it to perfection. The exquisite meat dishes include grilled strips of filet with seasonal vegetables. Among the more delectable desserts are crème brûlée and Neapolitan babba, filled with liqueur.

Via Aurora 10. ✆ 06-474-2779. Reservations recommended. Main courses 22,000L–35,000L (11.45€–18.20€, $11–$17.50). AE, DC, MC, V. Tues–Sun noon–3pm and 7–11pm. Metro: Barberini.

Césarina *Kids* EMILIANA-ROMAGNOLA/ROMAN Specializing in the cuisines of Rome and the region around Bologna, this place is named for Césarina Masi, who opened it in 1960 (many old-timers fondly remember her strict supervision of the kitchen and how she lectured regulars who didn't finish their tagliatelle). Although Césarina died in the mid-1980s, her traditions are kept going by her family. This has long been a favorite of Roman families. The polite staff rolls a trolley from table to table laden with an excellent *bollito misto* (an array of well-seasoned boiled meats) and often follows with misto Césarina— four kinds of creamy, handmade pasta, each with a different sauce. Equally appealing are the *saltimbocca* (veal with ham) and the *cotoletta alla bolognese* (tender veal cutlet baked with ham and cheese). A dessert specialty is *semifreddo* Césarina with hot chocolate, so meltingly good that it's worth the 5 pounds you'll gain.

Via Piemonte 109. ✆ 06-488-0828. Reservations recommended. Main courses 18,000L–30,000L (9.35€–15.60€, $9–$15). AE, DC, MC, V. Mon–Sat 12:30–3pm and 7:30–11pm. Metro: Barberini. Bus: 52, 53, 63, or 80.

Girarrosto Toscano *Value* TUSCAN Girarrosto Toscano, facing the walls of the Borghese Gardens, draws large crowds, so you might have to wait for a table. Under a vaulted cellar ceiling, it serves some of Rome's finest Tuscan fare. Begin by trying the enormous selection of fresh antipasti, from little meatballs and melon with savory prosciutto to *frittate* (omelets) and delectable Tuscan salami. You're then given a choice of pasta, such as creamy fettuccine. Although expensive, the delicately flavored *bistecca alla fiorentina* (grilled steak seasoned with oil, salt, and pepper) is worth every lira if you're in the mood to splurge. Fresh fish from the Adriatic is served daily. Order with care if you're on a budget; both meat and fish are priced according to weight and can run considerably higher than the prices given below.

Via Campania 29. ✆ 06-4201-3045. Reservations required. Main courses 25,000L–45,000L (13€–23.40€, $12.50–$22.50). AE, DC, MC, V. Thurs–Tues 12:30–2:30pm and 7:30–11pm. Bus: 95 or 116. Metro: Barberini.

Santo Padre Roman *(Finds* Away from the tourist traps around the U.S. Embassy, this is a little gem managed by three brothers who have a great passion for good food and sports (one of them was a professional soccer player). Once you enter the modest dining room, you'll be surrounded by family pictures and you'll feel as if you're among friends. As soon as you're seated, the owners proudly present their fare of the day—perhaps grilled zucchini (one of our all-time favorites); slices from a whole, fresh mozzarella ball; or tender, sweet prosciutto. For a savory dish, ask for their small meatballs (*polpette*) served with an herb-flavored tomato sauce. Their pastas are worth a return visit, especially the linguine with shrimp, saffron, and *pachino* (a variety of cherry tomatoes from the Naples area). Count yourself lucky if you're there the day the cooks are preparing *maialino*, which translates as "little pig." The meat is crispy yet tender, and it's served with the freshest of seasonal vegetables.

Via Collina 18. © **06-475-5405.** Reservations required. Main courses 18,000L–35,000L (9.35€–18.20€, $9–$17.50). AE, DC, MC, V. Mon–Sat 7:30–10:30pm. Metro: Barberini.

Testa Food & Wine ⋆ *(Finds* ITALIAN Near Villa Borghese, this recently renovated restaurant draws discerning palates seeking food and wine at a reasonable price. It's a sophisticated setting for masterfully crafted dishes composed of fresh ingredients. The *orecchiette* (ear-shaped pasta) gratinée with broccoli and sautéed clams is one of the city's finest pasta dishes. If you're not on a diet, opt for strozza Preti with creamy cheese and bacon. Another excellent homemade pasta dish, *cacio e pepe*, is made with crunchy artichokes. The tuna steak with sun-dried tomatoes is a delight, as is the duck breast stuffed with foie gras and sprinkled with roasted almonds and served with plums marinated in port. The bar is one of the hottest places in Rome on Tuesday nights, when it features live jazz.

Via Tirso 30. © **06-8530-0692.** Main courses 25,000L–35,000L (13€–18.20€, $12.50–$17.50). Mon–Sat noon–3pm and 8pm–midnight (bar open until 3am). Closed Aug. Bus: 19.

5 Near Ancient Rome

To locate the restaurants in this section, refer to the "Dining Near the Spanish Steps & Ancient Rome" map on p. 113.

EXPENSIVE

Trattoria San Teodoro ⋆ *(Finds* SARDINIAN At last there's a good place to eat in the former gastronomic wasteland near the Roman Forum and Palatine Hill. The helpful staff welcomes you to a shady terrace or a dimly lit dining room resting under a vaulted brick ceiling and arched alcoves. The chef handles seafood exceedingly well (try the mini baby squid sautéed with Roman artichokes). His signature dish is seafood carpaccio made with tuna, turbot, or sea bass. Succulent meats such as medallions of veal in a nutmeg-enhanced cream sauce round out the menu at this family-friendly place. All the pastas are homemade.

Via dei Fienili 49–51. © **06-678-0933.** Reservations recommended. Main courses 35,000L–50,000L (18.20€–26€, $17.50–$25). MC, V. Mon–Sat 1–3:30pm and 7:45pm–midnight. Closed Jan 15–Feb 7. Metro: Circo Massimo.

MODERATE

See also the listing for Il Quadrifoglio on p. 95; it's located about midway between Stazione Termini and Ancient Rome.

Scoglio di Frisio NEAPOLITAN/PIZZA This trattoria, a longtime favorite, offers a great introduction to the Neapolitan kitchen. Here you can taste a

Quick Bites

At **Dar Filettaro a Santa Barbara**, just off the southeast corner of Campo de' Fiori at Largo dei Librari 88 (*©* **06-686-4018**), you can join the line of people threading their way to the back of the bare room to order a filet of *baccalà* (salt cod), fried golden brown and served *da portar via* (wrapped in paper to eat as you take a *passeggiata,* or stroll). It costs 5,000L to 18,000L (2.60€–9.35€, $2.50–$9); it's closed Sunday.

Lunchtime offers you the perfect opportunity to savor Roman fast food: **pizza rustica,** by the slice (often called *pizza à taglio*), half-wrapped in waxed paper for easy carrying. Just point to the bubbling, steaming sheet with your preferred toppings behind the counter and hand over a few thousand lire; 4,000L (2.10€, $2) buys a healthy portion of "plain" tomato sauce: basil-and-cheese pizza *margherita. Pizza rossa* (just sauce) and *pizza con patate* (with cheese and potatoes) cost even less, as does the exquisitely simple *pizza bianca* (plain dough brushed with olive oil and sprinkled with salt and sometimes rosemary).

A **rosticceria** is a *pizza à taglio* with spits of chickens roasting in the window and a few pasta dishes kept warm in long trays. You can also sit down for a quick pasta or prepared meat dish steaming behind the glass counters at a **tavola calda** (literally "hot table") for about half the price of a *trattoria.* A Roman **bar,** though it does indeed serve liquor, is what we'd call a cafe, a place to grab a cheap *panino* (flat roll stuffed with meat, cheese, or vegetables) or *tramezzino* (large, triangular sandwiches on white bread with the crusts cut off, like giant tea sandwiches).

genuine plate-size Neapolitan pizza (crunchy, oozy, and excellent) with clams and mussels. Or perhaps you can start with a medley of savory stuffed vegetables and antipasti before moving on to chicken cacciatore or well-flavored tender veal scaloppini. Scoglio di Frisio also makes for an inexpensive night of hokey but still charming entertainment, as cornball "O Sole Mio" renditions and other Neapolitan songs spring forth from a guitar, mandolin, and strolling tenor. The nautical decor (in honor of the top-notch fish dishes) is complete with a high-ceiling grotto of fishing nets, crustaceans, and a miniature three-masted schooner.

Via Merulana 256. *©* **06-487-2765.** Reservations recommended. Main courses 12,000L–32,000L (6.25€–16.65€, $6–$16). AE, DC, MC, V. Mon–Fri 12:30–3pm; daily 7:30–11pm. Metro: Manzoni. Bus: 714.

INEXPENSIVE

Abruzzi *(Value* ABRUZZESE/ROMAN   Abruzzi, which takes its name from the region east of Rome, is at one side of Piazza S.S. Apostoli, just a short walk from Piazza Venezia. The good food and reasonable prices make it a big draw for students. The chef offers a satisfying assortment of cold antipasti. With your starter, we suggest a liter of garnet-red wine; we once had one whose bouquet was suggestive of Abruzzi's wildflowers. If you'd like soup as well, you'll find a good *stracciatella* (egg-and-Parmesan soup). A typical main dish is *vitella tonnata con capperi* (veal in tuna sauce with capers). But the menu ranges far wider than that; it's a virtual textbook of classical Italian dishes, everything from a creamy baked eggplant with mozzarella to meltingly tender veal cutlets in the Milanese style (fried with potatoes). No one in Italy does roast lamb better than the Romans, and the selection here is good—tender, grilled to perfection, seasoned with virgin olive oil and fresh herbs, and dished up with roast potatoes.

Via del Vaccaro 1. ℂ 06-679-3897. Reservations recommended. Main courses 14,000L–28,000L (7.30€–14.55€, $7–$14). AE, DC, MC, V. Sun–Fri 12:30–3pm and 7–11pm. Closed 3 weeks in Aug. Bus: 44, 46.

Hostaria Nerone ⊛ ROMAN/ITALIAN   Built atop the ruins of the Golden House of Nero, this trattoria is run by the energetic de Santis family, who cook, serve, and handle the large crowds of hungry locals and visitors. Opened in 1929 at the edge of the Colle Oppio Park, it contains two compact dining rooms, plus a terrace lined with flowering shrubs that offers a view over the Colosseum and the Bath of Trajan. The copious antipasti buffet represents the bounty of Italy's fields and seas. The pastas include savory spaghetti with clams and, our favorite, *pasta fagioli* (with beans). There's also grilled crayfish and swordfish and Italian sausages with polenta. Roman-style tripe is a local favorite, but maybe you'll skip it for the osso buco (braised veal shanks) with mashed potatoes and seasonal mushrooms. The wide list of some of the best Italian wines is reasonably priced.

Via Terme di Tito 96. ℂ 06-481-7952. Reservations recommended. Main courses 15,000L–20,000L (7.80€–10.40€, $7.50–$10). AE, DC, V. Mon–Sat noon–3pm and 7–11pm. Metro: Colosseo. Bus: 85, 87, 75, 175, or 117.

Ristorante al Cardello *Value* ROMAN/ABRUZZI   Conveniently close to the Colosseum, this restaurant dates from the 1920s, when it opened in the semicellar of an 18th-century building. We always love the antipasti buffet, where the flavorful marinated vegetables reveal the bounty of the Italian harvest; at 12,000L (6.25€, $6) per person for a good serving, it's a great deal. You might follow with *bucatini* (thick spaghetti) *all'amatriciana;* tender roast lamb with potatoes, garlic, and mountain herbs; or a thick, hearty stew. A Roman food critic dining with us claimed that he always comes here when he wants to eat like a peasant (and that's a compliment).

Via del Cardello 1 (at the corner of Via Cavour). ℂ 06-474-5259. Reservations recommended. Main courses 14,000L–20,000L (7.30€–10.40€, $7–$10); fixed-price menu 25,000L (13€, $12.50). AE, DC, MC, V. Mon–Sat noon–3pm and 7–11pm. Closed Aug. Metro: Cavour or Colosseo.

6 Near Campo de' Fiori & the Jewish Ghetto
EXPENSIVE

Il Drappo ⊛ SARDINIAN   A favorite of the local artsy crowd, Il Drappo is on a narrow street near the Tiber and is run by a woman known to her regulars only as "Valentina." You have your choice of two tastefully decorated dining rooms festooned with patterned cotton draped from the ceiling. Flowers and candles are everywhere. Fixed-price dinners reflecting diverse choices might begin with wafer-thin *carte di musica* (sheet-music paper) topped with tomatoes, green peppers, parsley, and olive oil, and then followed with fresh spring lamb in season, fish stew made with tuna caviar, or one of the strong-flavored regional specialties. For dessert, try the *seadas* (cheese-stuffed fried cake in special dark honey). Valentina's cuisine is a marvelous change of pace from the typical Roman diet, showing an inventiveness that keeps us coming back.

Vicolo del Malpasso 9. ℂ 06-687-7365. Reservations required. Main courses 20,000L–45,000L (10.40€–23.40€, $10–$22.50); fixed-price menus 65,000L–70,000L (33.80€–36.40€, $32.50–$35). AE, DC, MC, V. Mon–Sat 7pm–midnight. Closed Aug 15–31. Bus: 46, 62, or 64.

Piperno ✦ ROMAN/JEWISH   This longtime favorite, opened in 1856 and now run by the Mazzarella and Boni families, celebrates the Jerusalem artichoke (which is not really an artichoke at all, by the way) and incorporates it into a number of recipes. You'll be served by a uniformed crew of hardworking waiters, whose advice and suggestions are worth considering. You might begin with aromatic *fritto misto vegetariano* (artichokes, cheese-and-rice croquettes, mozzarella, and stuffed squash blossoms) before moving on to a fish filet, veal, succulent beans, or a pasta creation. Many of the foods are fried or deep-fried, but they emerge flaky and dry, not at all greasy.

Via Monte de' Cenci 9. ℂ **06-6880-6629.** Reservations recommended. Main courses 30,000L–40,000L (15.60€–20.80€, $15–$20). AE, DC, MC, V. Tues–Sat noon–2:30pm and 8–10:30pm; Sun noon–2:30pm. Bus: 23.

MODERATE

Da Gigetto ROMAN/JEWISH   Da Gigetto is right next to the Theater of Marcellus, and old Roman columns extend practically to its doorway. Romans flock to this bustling trattoria for its special traditional dishes. None is more typical than *carciofi alla giudia,* baby-tender fried artichokes, a true delicacy. The cheese concoction called *mozzarella in carrozza* is another delight, as are the zucchini flowers stuffed with mozzarella and anchovies, our personal favorite. You could also sample shrimp sautéed in garlic and olive oil or one of Rome's best versions of saltimbocca (veal with ham).

Via del Portico d'Ottavia 21/A. ℂ **06-686-1105.** Reservations recommended. Main courses 18,000L–30,000L (9.35€–15.60€, $9–$15). AE, DC, MC, V. Tues–Sun 12:30–3pm and 7:30–11pm. Closed Aug 1–15. Bus: 62, 64, 75, 90, or 170.

Il Sanpietrino ROMAN   This Jewish Ghetto restaurant, with three formal dining rooms, is stylish but affordable, with a sophisticated selection of both traditional and modern dishes. Chef Marco Cardillo uses market-fresh ingredients to prepare a seasonal cuisine that's varied and inventive at any time of the year. His combinations are often a surprise but generally delightful; for example, cream of *fagioli* (bean) soup comes not only with the traditional ingredients, but also with mussels and even octopus. The medley of fish antipasti, some of it smoked, is so tempting that you might want to make a meal of it, enjoying items like savory fresh anchovies baked between layers of well-seasoned eggplant. Also look for asparagus-flavored tortellini with cheese; spaghetti with fresh anchovies and tomatoes; and a delectable version of cream of monkfish soup. Crème brûlée always makes a tempting dessert.

Piazza Costaguti 15. ℂ **06-68806471.** Reservations recommended. Main courses 28,000L–35,000L (14€–17.50€, $14.55–$18.20). AE, DC, MC, V. Mon–Sat 8–11pm. Metro: Colosseo or Circo Massimo.

Ristorante da Pancrazio ROMAN   This place is popular as much for its archaeological interest as for its food. One of its two dining rooms is gracefully decorated in the style of an 18th-century tavern; the other occupies the premises of Pompey's ancient theater and is lined with carved capitals and bas-reliefs. In this historic setting, you can enjoy time-tested Roman food. Once a simple fishermen's dish, flavorful *risotto alla pescatora* (with seafood) enjoys a certain chic today, and the scampi is grilled to perfection. Two particular classics are prepared with great skill: saltimbocca and tender roast lamb with potatoes. For a superb pasta, opt for the ravioli stuffed with artichoke hearts.

Piazza del Biscione 92. ℂ **06-686-1246.** Reservations recommended. Main courses 18,000L–35,000L (9.35€–18.20€, $9–$17.50); fixed-price menu 50,000L (26€, $25). AE, DC, MC, V. Thurs–Tues noon–3pm and 7:30–11:15pm. Closed 2 weeks in Aug (dates vary). Bus: 46, 62, or 64.

Dining Near Campo de' Fiori, the Jewish Ghetto & Piazza Navona

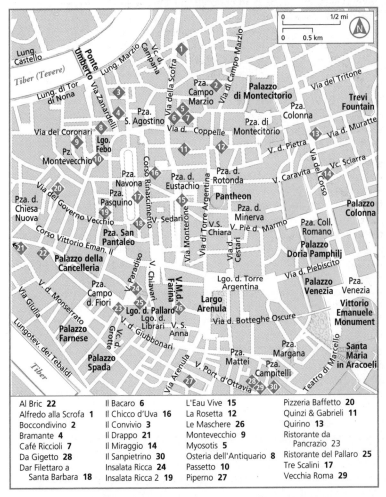

Al Bric **22**	Il Bacaro **6**	L'Eau Vive **15**	Pizzeria Baffetto **20**
Alfredo alla Scrofa **1**	Il Chicco d'Uva **16**	La Rosetta **12**	Quinzi & Gabrieli **11**
Boccondivino **2**	Il Convivio **3**	Le Maschere **26**	Quirino **13**
Bramante **4**	Il Drappo **21**	Montevecchio **9**	Ristorante da
Café Riccioli **7**	Il Miraggio **14**	Myosotis **5**	Pancrazio **23**
Da Gigetto **28**	Il Sanpietrino **30**	Osteria dell'Antiquario **8**	Ristorante del Pallaro **25**
Dar Filettaro a	Insalata Ricca **24**	Passetto **10**	Tre Scalini **17**
Santa Barbara **18**	Insalata Ricca 2 **19**	Piperno **27**	Vecchia Roma **29**

Ristorante del Pallaro ★★ *Value* ROMAN   The cheerful woman in white who emerges with clouds of steam from the bustling kitchen is owner Paola Fazi, who runs two simple dining rooms where value-conscious Romans go for good food at bargain prices. (She also claims—though others dispute it—that Julius Caesar was assassinated on this very site.) The fixed-price menu is the only choice and has made the place famous. Ms. Fazi prepares everything with love, as if she were feeding her extended family. As you sit down, your antipasto, the first of eight courses, appears. Then comes the pasta of the day, followed by roast veal, white meatballs, or (Fri only) dried cod, along with potatoes and eggplant. For your final courses, you're served mozzarella, cake with custard, and fruit in season. The meal also includes bread, mineral water, and half a liter of the house wine.

Largo del Pallaro 15. ✆ **06-6880-1488.** Reservations recommended. Fixed-price menu 34,000L (17.75€, $17). No credit cards. Tues–Sun 1–3pm and 7:30pm–1am. Bus: 40, 46, 60, 62, or 64.

Vecchia Roma ROMAN/ITALIAN   Vecchia Roma is a charming, moderately priced trattoria in the heart of the Ghetto. Movie stars have frequented the
place, sitting at the crowded tables in one of the four small dining rooms (the
back room is the most popular). The owners are known for their *frutti de mare*
(fruits of the sea), a selection of briny fresh seafood. The minestrone is made
with fresh vegetables, and an interesting selection of antipasti, including salmon
or vegetables, is always available. The pastas and risottos are savory, including
linguine alla marinara with calamari—the "green" risotto with porcini mushrooms is reliably good. The chef's specialties are lamb and *spigola* (a type of
white fish).

Via della Tribuna di Campitelli 18. ✆ **06-686-4604**. Reservations recommended. Main courses
24,000L–35,000L (12.50–18.20€, $12–$17.50). AE, DC. Thurs–Tues 1–3pm and 8–11pm. Closed 10 days in
Aug. Bus: 64, 90, 90b, 97, or 774.

INEXPENSIVE

Vegetarians looking for monstrous salads (or anyone who just wants a break
from all those heavy meats and starches) can find great food at the neighborhood
branch of **Insalata Ricca,** Largo dei Chiavari 85 (✆ **06-6880-3656**).

Le Maschere ⭐⭐ *(Finds* CALABRESE   This trattoria specializes in the fragrant, often-fiery cooking of Calabria's Costa Viola, with lots of fresh garlic and
wake-up-your-mouth red peppers. In a cellar from the 1600s, decorated with
artifacts of Calabria, it has enlarged its kitchen and added three dining rooms,
all with fantastic medieval- and Renaissance-inspired murals. Begin with a selection of *antipasti calabresi.* For your first course, try one of the many preparations
of eggplant or a pasta—perhaps with broccoli or with devilish red peppers, garlic, bread crumbs, and more than a touch of anchovy. The chef also grills meats
and fresh swordfish caught off the Calabrian coast—and does so exceedingly
well. If you don't want a full meal, you can visit just for pizza and beer and listen to the music at the piano bar, beginning at 8pm.

Via Monte della Farina 29 (near Largo Argentina). ✆ **06-687-9444**. Reservations recommended. Main
courses 14,000L–22,000L (7.30€–11.45€, $7–$11). AE, DC, MC, V. Tues–Sun 7:30–11pm. Closed Aug. Bus:
46, 62, or 64.

7 Near Piazza Navona & the Pantheon

To locate these restaurants, see the "Dining Near Campo de' Fiori, the Jewish
Ghetto & Piazza Navona" map on p. 105.

VERY EXPENSIVE

La Rosetta ⭐⭐ SEAFOOD   You won't find any meat on the menu at this
sophisticated choice near Piazza Navona, where the Riccioli family has been
directing operations since the late 1960s. This is one of the leading seafood
restaurants of Rome. Only Quinzi & Gabrieli (see below) does it better. An
excellent start is *insalata di frutti di mare,* studded with squid, lobster, octopus,
and shrimp. Menu items include just about every fish native to the Mediterranean, as well as a few from the Atlantic coast of France. There's even a sampling of lobster imported from Maine, which can be boiled with drawn butter
or served Catalan style with tomatoes, red onions, and wine sauce. Hake, monkfish, and sole can be grilled or roasted in rock salt and served with potatoes.
Everyone at our table agreed that the homemade spaghetti garnished with
shrimp, squash blossoms, and pecorino cheese, with a drizzling of olive oil and
herbs adding a savory zing, was tops.

Via della Rosetta 8. ☎ **06-686-1002.** Reservations recommended. Main courses 60,000L–100,000L (31.20–52€, $30–$50). AE, DC, MC, V. Mon–Fri 12:45–2:45pm; Mon–Sat 8–11:30pm. Bus: 70. Metro: Spagna.

Quinzi & Gabrieli ★★★ SEAFOOD We've never found better or fresher seafood than what's served in this 15th-century building. Don't be put off by the rough-and-ready service; come for the great taste instead. (And be prepared to pay for the privilege because fresh seafood is extremely expensive in Rome.) Alberto Quinzi and Enrico Gabrieli have earned their reputation on their simply cooked and presented fresh fish (heavy sauces aren't used to disguise old fish), such as sea urchin, octopus, sole, and red mullet. In fact, the restaurant is known for its raw seafood, including a delicate carpaccio of swordfish, sea bass, and deep-sea shrimp. The house specialty is spaghetti with lobster. Sometimes the headwaiters will prepare wriggling crab or scampi on the grill right before you. In summer, French doors lead to a small dining terrace.

Via delle Coppelle 5–6, 00185 Roma. ☎ **06-687-9389.** Reservation required as far in advance as possible. Main courses 50,000L–80,000L (26€–41.60€, $25–$40). AE, DC, MC, V. Mon–Sat 7:30–11:30pm. Closed Aug. Bus: 44, 46, 55, 60, 61, 62, 64, or 65.

EXPENSIVE

Boccondivino ★ ITALIAN Part of the fun of this restaurant involves wandering through historic Rome to reach it. Inside, you'll find delicious food and an engaging mix of the Italian Renaissance with imperial and ancient Rome, thanks to recycled columns salvaged from ancient monuments by 16th-century builders. Modern art and a hip staff dressed in black and white serve as a tip-off, though, that the menu is completely up-to-date. Dishes vary with the seasons, but you might find fettuccine with shellfish and parsley; carpaccio of beef; various risottos, including a version with black truffles; and grilled steaks and veal. Especially intriguing is whipped codfish resting on spikes of polenta; and tagliolini with cinnamon, prosciutto, and lemon. If you're a seafood lover, look for either the marinated and grilled salmon or a particularly subtle blend of roasted turbot stuffed with foie gras. Desserts feature the fresh fruits of the season, perhaps marinated pineapple or fruit-studded house-made ice creams. The restaurant's name, incidentally, translates as "divine mouthful."

Piazza in Campo Marzio 6. ☎ **06-68308626.** Reservations recommended. Main courses 30,000L–50,000L (15.60€–26€, $14–$25). AE, DC, MC, V. Mon–Sat 1–3:30pm and 8pm–midnight. Bus: 87.

Il Convivio ★ ROMAN/INTERNATIONAL This is one of the most acclaimed restaurants in Rome, and one of the very few to be granted a coveted Michelin star. Its 16th-century building is a classic setting in pristine white with accents of wood. The Troiano brothers turn out an inspired cuisine based on the best and freshest ingredients at the market. Their menu is seasonally adjusted to take advantage of what's good during any month. Start with their giant shrimp tossed with fresh greens. Among the pasta selections, their gnocchi stuffed with zucchini and dribbled with a well-seasoned seafood sauce is fabulous, as is one of the chef's specialties called *petto di faraona* (stuffed chicken spiced up with fresh olives).

Vicolo dei Soldati 31. ☎ **06-686-9432.** Reservations required. Main courses 46,000L (23.90€, $23); 5-course set menu 120,000L (62.40€, $60). AE, DC, MC, V. Mon 8–11pm; Tues–Sat 1–2:30pm and 8–11pm. Bus: 40 and 64. Metro: Piazza di Spagna.

MODERATE

Alfredo alla Scrofa ROMAN/INTERNATIONAL Yes, folks, this is one of two places in Rome claiming to be the birthplace of fettuccine Alfredo, which almost seems as well known in America today as it is in Italy. Douglas Fairbanks and Mary Pickford liked this dish so much they presented a golden spoon and fork to the owners when they parted with the recipe. Thus, a culinary legend was born. If you're not worried about your cholesterol count, you can order the dish that delighted these long-departed silent-screen stars. Although the fettuccine remains the star on the chef's menu, you can try something a little lighter and healthier, perhaps *tagliolini allo scoglio,* delectably concocted from fresh tomatoes and shellfish. We always enjoy the filet mignons; one is offered with a delectable sauce made from Barolo wine, another with a sauce of wine and Gorgonzola. There's another filet mignon dish named after Casanova, prepared with wine sauce, freshly ground pepper, and foie gras. A final offering is the sautéed breast of turkey covered with thin slices of white truffles from Italy's Piedmont district, a truly delightful dish.

Via della Scrofa 104. ✆ **06-6880-6163.** Reservations recommended. Main courses 23,000L–35,000L (11.95€–18.20€, $11.50–$17.50). AE, DC, MC, V. Oct–Apr Wed–Mon 1–3pm and 7:30–11pm; May–Nov daily 1–3pm and 7:30–11pm. Bus: 87, 492, or 680. Metro: Piazza di Spagna.

Bramante ROMAN   In an exquisite 18th-century structure on a cobblestone street behind Piazza Navona, this cafe-restaurant opens onto a delightful small square of vine-draped taverns. Behind the ivy-covered facade, the interior is completely hand painted; white candles illuminate the marble bar, making for a cozy, inviting atmosphere. The owner, Mr. Giuseppe, tries to make visitors appreciate Italian food and traditions, and succeeds admirably. Almost all his dishes are handmade, and the cooks use only the freshest ingredients, such as parmigiano, fresh vegetables, and extra-virgin olive oil. Recipes are simple but rich in Mediterranean flavor. Try wonderful pastas made with fresh tomato sauce, garlic, and pasta, or opt for something heavier, such as braised beef or tender grilled steak flavored with herbs and served with potatoes.

Via della Pace 25. ✆ **06-6880-3916.** Reservations recommended. Main courses 25,000L–32,000L (13€–16.65€, $12.50–$16). AE, DC, MC, V. Daily 5pm–2am. Closed Dec 24. Bus: 44, 46, 55, 60, 61, 62, 64, or 65.

Café Riccioli ✺ JAPANESE/ITALIAN   Stylish and hip, this restaurant builds its reputation on its sashimi-style raw fish, plus a menu of sophisticated and upscale Italian cuisine. The setting is a trio of artfully minimalist dining rooms painted in bright primary colors; after lunch and dinner, this place becomes a buzzing late-night cafe. No one will mind if you order just a light meal (we've often spotted models here doing just that). Food, served by one of the most attractive waitstaffs anywhere, includes platters of sashimi, priced at around 33,000L (17.15€, $16.50) each; salads of raw marinated hake with Italian herbs; more substantial fare such as roast beef with green apples, sea bass with mango sauce; and richly textured chocolate tortes laced with marsala wine.

Piazza delle Coppelle 10A. ✆ **06-6821-0313.** Reservations recommended. Main courses 20,000L–38,000L (10.40€–19.75€, $10–$19). AE, DC, MC, V. Mon–Sat noon–1am. Tram 8. Bus: 64 or 492. Metro: Piazza di Spagna.

Il Bacaro ✺ ITALIAN   Unpretentious and very accommodating to foreigners, this restaurant contains only about a half-dozen tables and operates from an ivy-edged hideaway alley near Piazza di Spagna. The restaurant is well known for its fresh and tasty cheese. This was a palazzo in the 1600s, and some vestiges of the building's former grandeur remain, despite an impossibly cramped kitchen where the efforts of the staff to keep the show moving are nothing short of heroic. The offerings are time-tested and flavorful: homemade ravioli stuffed with mushrooms and parmigiano (in season), grilled beef filet with roasted potatoes, and an unusual version of warm carpaccio of beef. What dish do we prefer year after year? Admittedly, it's an acquired taste, but it's radicchio stuffed with Gorgonzola.

Via degli Spagnoli 27, near Piazza delle Coppelle. (C) **06-686-4110.** Reservations recommended. Main courses 24,000L–30,000L (12.50€–15.60€, $12–$15). MC, V. Mon–Sat 8pm–midnight. Metro: Spagna.

Il Chicco d'Uva ⋆ ITALIAN/INTERNATIONAL   Among Roman foodies, this place just off Piazza Navona is currently a hot ticket. In these two dining rooms, a well-heeled crowd can be seen laughing, drinking, and eating in elegant surroundings softly lit by candles. The site is in an ancient building (who knows how old?), and the decor is classic. The food is secondary here (it's more about the scene), but it has greatly improved lately. We recently had a wonderful fresh fish of the day cooked with chopped tomatoes and perfect seasonings. Among the pastas, we went for the wide noodle, *pappardelle*, which was served with fresh artichokes and calamari, a winning combination. One of the chef's specialties is *embuttiti di vitello*, a lamb sausage.

Corso Rinascimento 70. (C) **06-686-7983.** Reservations required. Main courses 23,000L–35,000L (11.95€–18.20€, $11.50–$17.50). AE, MC, V. Mon–Sat 7:30pm–midnight. Closed 2 weeks in Aug (dates vary). Bus: 87.

L'Eau Vive ⋆ (Finds FRENCH/INTERNATIONAL   Here you'll find an elegant dining experience, with unique food and atmosphere. Fine French cuisine and a daily exotic dish are prepared and served by a lay sisterhood of missionary Christians from five continents who dress in traditional costumes. Nonsmokers can skip the plain stuccoed vaulting downstairs and head to the 16th-century Palazzo Lantante della Rovere, where the high ceilings are gorgeously frescoed. Pope John Paul II dined here when he was archbishop of Krakow, and today some jet-setters have adopted it as their favorite spot. You'll never know until you arrive what the dishes for the evening will be. On previous occasions we've enjoyed beef filet flambé with cognac, toasted goat cheese coated with mustard and almond slivers, and duck filet in Grand Marnier sauce with puff-fried potatoes. The homemade patés are always flavorful. At 10pm, when most customers are finished with dinner, the recorded classical music is interrupted so that the sisters can sing the "Ave Maria of Lourdes," and some evenings they interpret a short Bible story in ballet.

Via Monterone 85. (C) **06-6880-1095.** Reservations recommended. Main courses 15,000L–38,000L (7.80€–19.75€, $7.50–$19); fixed-price menus 15,000L (7.80€, $7.50), 30,000L (15.60€, $15), and 50,000L (26€, $25). AE, MC, V. Mon–Sat 12:30–2:30pm and 8–10:30pm. Closed Aug 1–20. Bus: 64, 70, 81, 87, or 115.

Montevecchio ROMAN/ITALIAN   To find this place, you have to negotiate the winding streets of one of Rome's most confusing neighborhoods, near Piazza Navona. The heavily curtained restaurant on this Renaissance piazza is where both Raphael and Bramante had studios and where Lucrezia Borgia spun many of her intrigues. The entrance opens onto a high-ceilinged room filled with country-style decorations and bottles of wine. Your meal might begin with a strudel of porcini mushrooms followed by the invariably good pasta of the day, perhaps a *bombolotti* succulently stuffed with prosciutto and spinach. Then you might choose roebuck with polenta, roast Sardinian goat, or veal with salmon mousse. Each of these dishes is prepared with flair and technique, and the food takes advantage of the region's bounty.

Piazza Montevecchio 22A. ☎ **06-686-1319.** Reservations required. Main courses 30,000L–40,000L (15.60€–20.80€, $15–$20). AE, MC, V. Tues–Sun 7:30pm–midnight. Closed Aug 10–25 and Dec 26–Jan 9. Bus: 60 or 64. Metro: Spagna.

Myosotis ⭐ ITALIAN Midway between Piazza Navona, the Pantheon, and the Italian Parliament, the building that contains Myosotis is relatively modern and nondescript, but as the name promises (translated from Latin, it means "forget-me-not"), you're likely to remember the food for a long time. Menu items include a cornucopia of fresh-baked bread; tagliatelle with an old-fashioned country recipe that substitutes sautéed bread crumbs instead of beef; grilled buffalo steak; grilled, very fresh prawns served as simply as possible, with virgin olive oil and herbs; and a succulent version of baked swordfish that's stuffed with cheese, bread crumbs, and capers. There's also a mixed fish fry (*frittura mista*) that some diners claim is one of the best dishes served here; and flavorful filet of pork with a sauce of carefully aged pecorino cheese. The array of fresh fish that's available here includes sea bass, gilthead, and the ever-present calamari.

Vicolo della Vaccarella 3–5. ☎ **06-686-5554.** Reservations recommended. Main courses 14,000L–40,000L (7.30€–20.80€, $7–$20). AE, MC, V. Mon–Sat 12:30–3pm and 7:30–11:30pm. Bus: 70, 87, 186, or 492. Metro: Piazza di Spagna.

Osteria dell'Antiquario ⭐ *Finds* INTERNATIONAL/ROMAN This virtually undiscovered osteria enjoys a good location a few blocks down the Via dei Coronari as you leave the Piazza Navona and head toward St. Peter's. In a stone-built stable from the 1500s, this restaurant has three dining rooms used in winter. In nice weather, try to get an outdoor table on the terrace; shaded by umbrellas, they face a view of the Palazzo Lancillotti. We like to begin with a delectable appetizer of sautéed shellfish (usually mussels and clams), but you might opt for the risotto with porcini mushrooms. For a main course, you can go experimental with the filet of ostrich covered by a slice of ham and grated Parmesan, or opt for shellfish flavored with saffron. The fish soup with fried bread is excellent, as is an array of freshly made soups and pastas. This is dining in the classic Roman style.

Piazzetta di S. Simeone 26/27, Via dei Coronari. ☎ **06-687-9694.** Reservations recommended. Main courses 28,000L–40,000L (14.55€–20.80€, $14–$20). AE, DC, MC, V. Tues–Sat 12:30–2:30pm and 8–11pm; Mon 8–11pm. Closed 15 days in mid-Aug, Christmas, and Jan 1–15. Bus: 70, 87, or 90.

Passetto ⭐ ROMAN/ITALIAN Passetto, dramatically positioned at the north end of Piazza Navona, is still drawing patrons after a century and a half with excellent food. The stylish interior consists of a trio of high-ceilinged dining rooms, each outfitted with antique furniture and elaborate chandeliers. In summer, however, you'll want to sit outside looking out on Piazza Sant'Apollinare. The pastas are exceptional, including *farfalle passetto* (pasta with shrimp, mushrooms, and fresh tomatoes). One recommended main dish is *orata al cartoccio* (sea bass baked in a paper bag, to seal in the juices and the aroma, with tomatoes, mushrooms, capers, and white wine). Another house specialty is *rombo passetto* (a fish similar to sole) cooked in cognac and pine nuts. An eternal Roman favorite is lamb in the style of Abruzzi (oven-roasted with potatoes). Fresh fish is often priced by its weight, so be careful—your bill can soar quickly. Fresh vegetables are abundant in summer, and a favorite dessert is seasonal berries with fresh thick cream.

Via Zanardelli 14. ☎ **06-6880-6569.** Reservations recommended. Main courses 24,000L–45,000L (12.50€–23.40€, $12–$22.50). AE, DC, MC, V. Daily noon–3:30pm and 7pm–midnight. Bus: 87.

Quirino ROMAN/ITALIAN/SICILIAN Quirino is a good place to dine after you've tossed your coin into the Trevi. The atmosphere is typical Italian, with hanging Chianti bottles, a beamed ceiling, and muraled walls. We're fond of the mixed fry of tiny shrimp and squid rings, and the vegetarian pastas are prepared only with the freshest ingredients. The regular pasta dishes are fabulous, especially our favorite: homemade pasta with baby clams and porcini mushrooms. A variety of fresh and tasty fish is always available and always grilled to perfection. For dessert, try the yummy chestnut ice cream with hot chocolate sauce or the homemade cannoli.

Via delle Muratte 84. ℂ **06-679-4108.** Reservations recommended. Main courses 20,000L–35,000L (10.40€–18.20€, $10–$17.50); fish dishes 25,000L–30,000L (13€–15.60€, $12.50–$15). AE, MC, V. Mon–Sat 12:30–3:30pm and 7–11pm. Closed 3 weeks in Aug. Metro: Barberini or Spagna.

Tre Scalini ⭐ (Kids) ROMAN/ITALIAN Opened in 1882, this is the most famous restaurant on Piazza Navona—a landmark for ice cream as well as for more substantial meals. Yes, it's crawling with tourists, but its waiters are a lot friendlier and more helpful than those at the nearby Passetto, and the setting can't be beat. The cozy bar on the upper floor offers a view over the piazza, but most visitors opt for the ground-floor cafe or restaurant. During warm weather, try to snag a table on the piazza, where the people-watching is extraordinary.

The Lombard specialty of risotto with porcini mushrooms is excellent, the carpaccio of sea bass is worthy of a fine restaurant in Paris, and the roast duck with prosciutto wins many a devoted fan. One cook confided to us, "I cook dishes to make people love me." If that's the case, try his saltimbocca (veal with ham) and roast lamb Roman style—and you'll fall hard. No one will object if you order just a pasta and salad. The famous tartufo (ice cream coated with bittersweet chocolate, cherries, and whipped cream) makes a fantastic dessert.

Piazza Navona 30. ℂ **06-687-9148.** Reservations recommended. Main courses 30,000L–45,000L (15.60€–23.40€, $15–$22.50). AE, DC, MC, V. Thurs–Tues noon–3pm and 7–11pm. Closed Dec–Feb. Bus: 70, 87, or 90.

INEXPENSIVE

Al Bric (Value) ITALIAN With four separate and artfully minimalist dining rooms in a 16th-century building close to Campo de' Fiori, this well-managed restaurant combines creative cooks with a polite and efficient waitstaff. Many of the dishes include dollops of some kind of Italian cheese, a flavor that seems to make the wines here taste better. Menu items are based on a combination of traditional and creatively modern cuisine. Examples include house-made, ultra-fresh *bucatini alla matriciana; bucatini* flavored with fresh-ground black pepper and aged *caciocavallo* cheese; *tonnarelli* pasta with Sicilian broccoli and aged pecorino cheese; and roasted, aromatic rabbit laden with herbs and Camembert cheese and drenched in apple-flavored Calvados liqueur. There's even a delicious roasted shoulder of lamb drizzled with aged pecorino sauce, or a stuffed filet of veal with French brie and sweet-textured Sicilian broccoli that may have you asking for the recipe.

Via del Pellegrino 51. ℂ **06-687-9533.** Reservations recommended. Main courses 15,000L–30,000L (7.80€–15.60€, $7.50–$15). Tues–Sun 7:30–11:30pm. Closed: Aug. Bus: 64.

Il Miraggio ROMAN/SARDINIAN/SEAFOOD You might want to escape the roar of traffic along Via del Corso by ducking into this informal spot on a crooked side street (about midway between Piazza Venezia and Piazza Colonna). It's a cozy neighborhood setting with rich and savory flavor in every dish. The risotto with scampi or the fettuccine with porcini mushrooms will have you begging for more. Some dishes are classic, such as roast lamb with potatoes, but others are more inventive, such as sliced stew beef with arugula. The grilled scampi always is done to perfection, or you might prefer a steaming kettle of mussels flavored with olive oil, lemon juice, and fresh parsley. We're especially fond of the house specialty, *spaghetti alla bottarga* with roe sauce, especially if it's followed by *spigola alla vernaccia* (sea bass sautéed in butter and vernaccia wine from Tuscany). For dessert, try the typical Sardinian *seadas,* thin-rolled pastry filled with fresh cheese, fried, and served with honey.

Vicolo Sciarra 59. (C) **06-678-0226.** Reservations recommended. Main courses 14,000L–24,000L (7.35€–12.55€, $7–$12). AE, MC, V. Thurs–Tues 12:30–3:30pm and 7:30–11pm. Closed 15 days in Feb. Metro: Barberini. Bus: 56, 60, 62, 81, 85, 95, 160, 175, 492, or 628.

Insalata Ricca 2 *(Value* ITALIAN/VEGETARIAN   This choice fulfills a need for more vegetarian restaurants and lighter low-fat fare in Rome. Most people call ahead for an outdoor table, though on summer days you may prefer the smoke-free air-conditioning inside. The more popular of the oversized salads are the *baires* (lettuce, rughetta, celery, walnuts, apples, Gorgonzola) and *siciliana* (lettuce, rughetta, sun-dried tomatoes, green olives, corn, hard salted ricotta). Also on the menu are dishes like *gnocchi verdi al gorgonzola* (spinach gnocchi with Gorgonzola sauce) and *pasta integrale* (whole-wheat pasta in tomato-and-basil sauce). The branches near Campo de' Fiori and near the Vatican (mentioned under their respective neighborhoods) offer the same basic menu, which can be a refreshing relief after too many days of heavy meals and rich sauces.

Piazza Pasquino 72 (southwest of Piazza Navona). (C) **06-6830-7881.** Reservations recommended. Main courses 12,000L–25,000L (6€–12.50€, $6.25–$13); salads 10,000L–14,000L (5.20€–7.30€, $5–$7). AE, MC, V. Daily 12:15–3:15pm and 7pm–12:30am. Bus: 46, 62, or 64.

Pizzeria Baffetto (★) *(Kids* PIZZA   Our Roman friends always take out-of-towners here when they ask for the best pizza in Rome. Arguably, Pizzeria Baffetto fills the bill and has done so for the past 80 years. Pizzas are sold as *piccolo* (small), *media* (medium), or *grande* (large). Most pizza aficionados order the margherita, which is the simplest version with mozzarella and a delectable tomato sauce, but a wide range of toppings is served. The chef is proud of his pizza Baffetto, the house specialty. It comes with a topping of tomato sauce, mozzarella, mushrooms, onions, sausages, roasted peppers, and eggs. The pizza crusts are delightfully thin, and the pies are served piping hot from the intense heat of the ancient ovens.

Via del Governo Vecchio 114. (C) **06-686-1617.** Reservations not accepted. Pizza 7,000L–15,000L (3.65€–7.80€, $3.50–$7.50). No credit cards. Daily 6:30pm–1am. Closed Aug. Bus: 46, 62, or 64.

8 Near Piazza del Popolo & the Spanish Steps

VERY EXPENSIVE

El Toulà (★★) ROMAN/VENETIAN   El Toulà, offering sophisticated haute cuisine, is the glamorous flagship of an upscale chain that has now gone international. The setting is elegant, with vaulted ceilings, large archways, and a charming bar. The impressive, always-changing menu has one section devoted to Venetian specialties, in honor of the restaurant's origins. Items include tender *fegato* (liver) *alla veneziana,* vegetable-stuffed calamari, a robust *baccala* (codfish mousse with polenta), and *broetto,* a fish soup made with monkfish and clams. Save room for the seasonal selection of sorbets and sherbets (the cantaloupe and fresh strawberry are celestial); you can request a mixed plate if you'd like to sample several. El Toulà usually isn't crowded at lunchtime. The wine list is extensive and varied, but hardly a bargain.

Dining Near the Spanish Steps & Ancient Rome

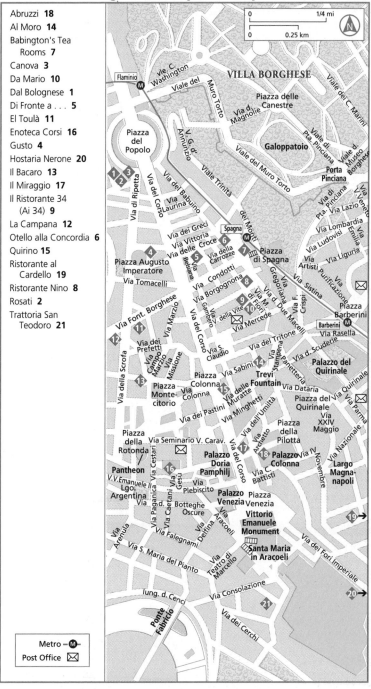

Via della Lupa 29B. © **06-687-3498.** Reservations required for dinner. Main courses 40,000L–46,000L (20.80€–23.90€, $20–$23); five-course menu degustazione 130,000L (67.60€, $65); four-course menu veneto 110,000L (57.20€, $55). AE, DC, MC, V. Tues–Fri noon–3pm and 7:30–11pm; Mon and Sat 7:30–11pm. Closed Aug. Bus: 81, 90, 90b, 628, or 913.

EXPENSIVE

Il Ristorante 34 (Al 34) ⊛ ROMAN/ITALIAN   Il Ristorante 34, very good and increasingly popular, is close to Rome's most famous shopping district. Its long, narrow interior is sheathed in scarlet wallpaper, ringed with modern paintings, and capped with a vaulted ceiling. In the rear, stop to admire a display of *dolce* proudly exhibited near the entrance to the bustling kitchen. The chef might whip caviar and salmon into the noodles to enliven a dish or add generous chunks of lobster into the risotto. He also believes in rib-sticking fare like pasta lentil soup or meatballs in a sauce with "fat" mushrooms. One of his most interesting pastas comes with a pumpkin-flavored cream sauce, and his spaghetti with clams is among the best in Rome.

Via Mario de' Fiori 34. © **06-679-5091.** Reservations required. Main courses 35,000L–60,000L (18.20€– 31.20€, $17.50–$30); fixed-price menu 58,000L (30.15€, $29). AE, DC, MC, V. Tues–Sun 12:30–3pm and 7:30–11pm. Closed 1 week at Easter and 3 weeks in Aug. Metro: Piazza di Spagna.

MODERATE

Al Moro ⊛ ITALIAN   This 1929 trattoria is a difficult-to-locate place behind the Trevi Fountain. Franco, the son of founding father Moro, is in charge. You're not a true Roman until Franco has thrown you out of his joint at least once. In spite of his scowling, locals recommend that you persevere and get a table. Once you've overcome the initial hostility at the door, you're serve some of the most authentic specialties in Rome, including crispy baby goat roasted a dark golden and flavored with fresh rosemary. Roman-style milk-fed lamb is stewed with fresh tomatoes and cooked to perfection, so tender it falls from your fork. Our favorite vegetables are the crispy fried artichokes. For a pasta, go for the typical spaghetti carbonara; we love the light Moro version. The chef likes to cook with salt, so be warned: Don't salt anything before you taste it. The wine list is one of the most unusual in the capital.

Vicolo delle Bollette 13. © **06-678-3495.** Reservations required. Main courses 24,000L–50,000L (12.50€–26€, $12–$25). MC, V. Mon–Sat 1–3pm and 8–10:30pm. Closed: Aug. Metro: Piazza di Spagna. Bus 60 or 62.

Babington's Tea Rooms ENGLISH/MEDITERRANEAN   This is a long-time landmark. When Victoria was on the throne in 1893, an Englishwoman named Anne Mary Babington arrived in Rome and couldn't find a place for "a good cuppa." With stubborn determination, she opened her own tearooms near the foot of the Spanish Steps, and the rooms are still going strong, although the prices are terribly inflated because of its fabulous location. You can order everything from Scottish scones and Ceylon tea to a club sandwich and American coffee. Brunch is served at all hours. Pastries cost 5,000L to 15,000L (2.60€– 7.80€, $2.50–$7.50); a pot of tea (dozens of varieties available) goes for 12,000L (6.25€, $6).

Piazza di Spagna 23. © **06-678-6027.** Main courses 21,000L–39,000L (10.90€–20.30€, $10.50–$19.50); brunch 53,000L (27.55€, $26.50). AE, DC, DISC, MC, V. Sept–June Wed–Mon 9am–8:30pm; July–Aug Mon–Sat 9am–8:30pm. Metro: Spagna.

Da Mario ROMAN/FLORENTINE   Da Mario is noted for its flavor-filled game specialties and excellent Florentine-style dishes (meats marinated in olive oil with fresh herbs and garlic and lightly grilled). The rich bounty of meats available during hunting season makes this a memorable choice, but even if you aren't feeling game (sorry, bad pun), you'll find this a convivial and quintessentially Roman trattoria. A good beginning is the wide-noodle pappardelle, best when served with a game sauce (*caccia*) or with chunks of rabbit (*lepre*), available only in winter. *Capretto* (kid), beefsteaks, and roast quail with polenta are other good choices. The wine cellar is well stocked with sturdy reds, the ideal accompaniment for the meat dishes. For dessert we heartily recommend the *gelato misto,* a selection of mixed velvety ice cream. You can dine in air-conditioned comfort at street level or descend to the cellars.

Via della Vite 55–56. (C) **06-678-3818.** Reservations recommended. Main courses 17,000L–30,000L (8.85€–15.60€, $8.50–$15). AE, DC, MC, V. Mon–Sat 12:30–3pm and 7–11pm. Closed Aug. Metro: Piazza di Spagna.

Dal Bolognese (★) BOLOGNESE   This is one of those rare dining spots that's chic but actually lives up to the hype with truly noteworthy food. Young actors, shapely models, artists from nearby Via Margutta, and even corporate types on expense accounts show up, trying to land one of the few sidewalk tables. To begin, we suggest *misto di pasta:* four pastas, each with a different sauce, arranged on the same plate. Another good choice would be thin slices of savory Parma ham or the delectable prosciutto and vine-ripened melon. For your main course, specialties that win hearts year after year are *lasagne verde* and *tagliatelle alla bolognese.* The chefs also turn out the town's most recommendable veal cutlets bolognese topped with cheese. They're not inventive, but they're simply superb.

You might want to cap your evening by dropping into the **Rosati** cafe next door (or its competitor, the **Canova,** across the street) to enjoy one of the tempting pastries.

Piazza del Popolo 1–2. (C) **06-361-1426.** Reservations required. Main courses 25,000L–30,000L (13€–15.60€, $12.50–$15). AE, DC, MC, V. Tues–Sun 12:30–3pm and 8:15pm–11pm. Closed 20 days in Aug. Metro: Flaminio.

Di Fronte a . . . ITALIAN   After a hard morning shopping in the Piazza di Spagna area, this is an ideal spot for a lunch break. Its name (which translates as "in front of . . .") comes from the fact that the restaurant lies right in front of a stationery shop (owned by the father of the restaurant's proprietor). We prefer the dining room in the rear, with its changing exhibitions of pictures. You'll be seated at a marble table on wrought-iron benches with leather cushions. The chef prepares a tasty cuisine that is simple but good—nothing creative, but a good boost of energy to hit the stores again. Salads are very large, as are the juicy half-pound burgers. You can also order more substantial food such as succulent pastas and tender steaks. The pizza isn't bad, either. For dessert, try the pizza blanca, which is a pizza crust topped with chocolate cream or seasonal fruits.

Via della Croce 38. (C) **06-678-0355.** Reservations recommended for dinner. Main courses 15,000L–30,000L (7.80€–15.60€, $7.50–$15). AE, MC, DC, V. Tues–Sun 12:30–4pm and 7:30–11:30pm. Metro: Spagna.

Gusto (★) (*Finds*) ITALIAN/PACIFIC RIM   This restaurant is made up of two separate parts. The simpler and more informal of the two is a street-level pizzeria, where at least a dozen kinds of homemade pastas and pizzas are offered along with freshly made salads and simple platters of such grilled specialties as veal, chicken, steak, and fish. More upscale, and somewhat calmer, is the upstairs restaurant, where big windows, high ceilings, floors of glowing hardwood, and lots of exposed brick create an appropriately minimalist setting for cutting-edge cuisine. Look for a fusion of Italian and Pacific Rim cuisine in such internationally inspired combinations as spaghetti stir-fried in a Chinese wok with fresh, al dente vegetables; prawns and spring baby vegetables done tempura-style; buffalo mozzarella intriguingly entwined with tuna and arugula; Middle Eastern staples; and stir-fried scallops with Italian herbs.

Piazza Augusto Imperatore 9. © **06-322-6273.** Reservations recommended. Main courses in street-level pizzeria 11,000L–15,000L (5.70€–7.80€, $5.50–$7.50); main courses in upstairs restaurant 25,000L–55,000L (13€–28.60€, $12.50–$27.50). AE, MC, V. Daily 1–2:30pm and 8–11:45pm. Metro: Flaminio.

La Campana ROMAN   If you opt for a meal in this comfortable but not particularly innovative restaurant, you won't be alone. The place has been dishing up traditional Roman specialties since it began welcoming locals and religious pilgrims in 1518 (unlike those folks, you'll enjoy air-conditioning in summer). Look for a well-stocked antipasti buffet, rich pastas, herb-laden roast lamb with potatoes, aromatic roast hen with roasted vegetables, and perfectly grilled fish or squid. We always start with *vignarola,* a soup made with fresh green peas and artichokes. The welcome is always warm, after all those years and all those thousands of diners.

Vicolo della Campana 18. © **06-686-7820.** Reservations recommended. Main courses 20,000L–30,000L (10.40€–15.60€, $10–$15). AE, DC, MC, V. Tues–Sun 12:30–3pm and 7:30–11pm. Metro: Spagna.

Ristorante Nino TUSCAN/ROMAN   Ristorante Nino, off Via Condotti and a short walk from the Spanish Steps, is a mecca for writers, artists, and the occasional model. Hearty, robustly flavored Tuscan home-style dishes that change with the season have made Nino's famous. Beef, shipped in from Florence and charcoal-broiled, is pricier than the rest of the menu items. A plate of cannelloni Nino (the house version of the popular dish, consisting of meat-stuffed pasta) is one of the chef's specialties. Other good dishes include grilled veal liver, *fagiole cotti al fiasco* (beans boiled in white wine, salt, ground black pepper, and herbs), codfish *alla livornese* (codfish cooked with tomatoes and onions), and zucchini pie. The reasonably priced wine list is mainly Tuscan, with some especially good choices among the Chiantis.

Via Borgognona 11. © **06-679-5676.** Reservations recommended. Main courses 27,000L–60,000L (14.05€–31.20€, $$13.50–$30). AE, DC, MC, V. Mon–Sat 12:30–3pm and 7:30–11pm. Closed Aug. Metro: Piazza di Spagna.

INEXPENSIVE

Don't forget to consider the street-level pizzeria in **Gusto,** reviewed above under "Moderate."

Enoteca Corsi ROMAN   Here's a breath of unpretentious fresh air in a pricey neighborhood, an informal wine tavern open for lunch only. Both dining rooms are usually packed and full of festive diners, just as they've always been since 1943. The wine list includes affordable choices from around Italy, to go perfectly with the platters of straightforward cuisine. It's nothing fancy, just hearty fare like bean soup, gnocchi, Roman tripe, and roasted codfish with garlic and potatoes. It's Italian home cooking.

Via del Gesú 87–88. © **06-679-0821.** Reservations not necessary. Main courses 14,000L (7.30€, $7) each; pastas 8,000L (4.15€, $4); vegetable side dishes 4,000L (2.10€, $2). AE, DC, MC, V. Mon–Sat noon–3pm. Closed Aug. Metro: Piazza di Spagna.

Otello alla Concordia *Kids* ROMAN   On a side street amid the glamorous boutiques near the northern edge of the Spanish Steps, this is one of Rome's

Impressions

In Italy, the pleasure of eating is central to the pleasure of living. When you sit down to dinner with Italians, when you share their food, you are sharing their lives.

—Fred Plotkin, *Italy for the Gourmet Traveler* (1996)

most consistently reliable restaurants. A stone corridor from the street leads into the dignified Palazzo Povero. Choose a table in the arbor-covered courtyard or the cramped but convivial dining rooms. Displays of Italian bounty decorate the interior, where you're likely to rub elbows with many of the shopkeepers from the fashion district. The *spaghetti alle vongole veraci* (with clams) is excellent, as are Roman-style saltimbocca (veal with ham), *abbacchio arrosto* (roast lamb), eggplant parmigiana, a selection of grilled or sautéed fish dishes (including swordfish), and several preparations of veal.

Via della Croce 81. ✆ **06-679-1178.** Reservations recommended. Main courses 14,000L–30,000L (7.30€–15.60€, $7–$15); fixed-price menu 40,000L (20.80€, $20). AE, DC, MC, V. Mon–Sat 12:30–3pm and 7:30–11pm. Closed 2 weeks in Jan. Metro: Piazza di Spagna.

9 Near the Vatican

To locate the restaurants in this section, refer to the "Accommodations & Dining Near the Vatican" map on p. 83.

VERY EXPENSIVE

Les Etoiles ⭐⭐ MEDITERRANEAN   Les Etoiles ("The Stars") is a garden in the sky where you'll have an open window over Rome's rooftops—a 360° view of landmarks, especially the floodlit dome of St. Peter's. A flower terrace contains a trio of little towers named Michelangelo, Campidoglio, and Ottavo Colle. In summer everyone wants a table outside, but in winter almost the same view is available near the picture windows. Savor the textures and aromas of sophisticated Mediterranean cuisine with perfectly balanced flavors, perhaps choosing quail in a casserole with mushrooms and herbs, delectable artichokes stuffed with ricotta and pecorino cheeses, Venetian-style risotto with squid ink, and roast suckling lamb perfumed with mint. The creative chef is justifiably proud of his many regional dishes, and the service is refined, with an exciting French and Italian wine list.

In the Hotel Atlante Star, Via Vitelleschi 34. ✆ **06-689-9494.** Reservations required. Main courses 80,000L–120,000L (41.60€–62.40€, $40–$60). AE, DC, MC, V. Daily 12:30–2:30pm and 7:30–11pm. Metro: Ottaviano.

MODERATE

Cesare ROMAN/TUSCAN   The area around the Vatican is not the place to go in a search for great restaurants. But Cesare is a fine old-world dining room known for its deft handling of fresh ingredients. You can select your fresh fish from the refrigerated glass case at the entrance. We come here for the fresh and tender seafood salad, brimming with cuttlefish, shrimp, squid, mussels, and octopus, and dressed with olive oil, fresh parsley, and lemon. Our table was blessed with an order of *spaghetti all'amatriciana* in a spicy tomato sauce flavored with hot peppers and tiny bits of salt pork. The *saltimbocca alla romana*, that classic Roman dish, is a masterpiece as served here—butter-tender veal slices topped with prosciutto and fresh sage and sautéed in white wine. Another specialty is smoked swordfish; you can order fresh sardines and fresh anchovies if you want to go truly Roman.

Via Crescenzio 13, near Piazza Cavour. ℂ **06-6861-227.** Reservations recommended. Main courses 25,000L–50,000L (13€–26€, $12.50–$25). AE, DC, MC, V. June 15–Aug 7 Mon–Sat 12:30–3pm and 7–11:30pm. Off-season Tues–Sun 12:30–3pm and 7–11:30pm. Closed 3 weeks Aug. Bus: 23, 46, 49, or 62.

Ristorante Giardinaccio ITALIAN/MOLISIAN/ROMAN This popular restaurant, operated by Nicolino Mancini, is only a stone's throw from St. Peter's. Unusual for Rome, it offers Molisian specialties from southeastern Italy. It's rustically decorated in the country-tavern style with dark wood and exposed stone. Flaming grills provide succulent versions of perfectly done quail, goat, and other dishes, but perhaps the mutton goulash would be more adventurous. You can order many pastas, including homemade *taconelle* with lamb sauce. Vegetarians will like the large self-service selection of antipasti made from market-fresh ingredients. This is robust peasant fare, a perfect introduction to the cuisine of an area rarely visited by Americans.

Via Aurelia 53. ℂ **06-631-367.** Reservations recommended, especially on weekends. Main courses 22,000L–40,000L (11.45€–20.80€, $11–$20); fixed-price menus 45,000L–50,000L (23.40€–26€, $22.50–$25). AE, DC, MC, V. Daily 12:15–3:15pm and 7:15–11:15pm. Bus: 46, 62, or 98.

Ristorante Il Matriciano ★ *Kids* ROMAN Il Matriciano is a family restaurant with a devoted following and a convenient location near St. Peter's. The food is good but mostly country fare. In summer, try to get one of the sidewalk tables behind a green hedge and under a shady canopy. For openers, you might enjoy a bracing *zuppa di verdura* (vegetable soup) or creamy ravioli di ricotta. From many dishes, we recommend *scaloppa alla valdostana* or *abbacchio* (suckling lamb) *al forno,* each evocative of the region's bounty. The specialty, and our personal favorite, is *bucatini matriciana,* a variation on the favorite sauce in the Roman repertoire, *amatriciana,* richly flavored with bacon, tomatoes, and basil. Dining at the convivial tables, you're likely to see an array of Romans, including prelates and cardinals ducking out of the nearby Vatican for a meal.

Via dei Gracchi 55. ℂ **06-321-2327.** Reservations required. Main courses 18,000L–28,000L (9.35€–14.55€, $9–$14). DC, MC, V. Daily 12:30–3pm and 8pm–midnight. Closed Aug 5–25. Metro: Ottaviano.

INEXPENSIVE

The no. 6 branch of **Insalata Ricca,** the popular chain of salad-and-light-meals restaurants, is across from the Vatican walls at Piazza del Risorgimento 5 (ℂ **06-3973-0387**).

Hostaria dei Bastioni ROMAN This simple but well-managed restaurant is about a minute's walk from the entrance to the Vatican Museums and has been open since the 1960s. Although a warm-weather terrace doubles the size during summer, many diners prefer the inside room as an escape from the roaring traffic. The menu features the staples of Rome's culinary repertoire, including fisherman's *risotto* (a broth-simmered rice dish studded with fresh fish, usually shellfish), a vegetarian fettuccine alla bastione with orange-flavored creamy tomato sauce, an array of grilled fresh fish, and saltimboca (veal with ham). The food is first-rate—and a real bargain at these prices.

Via Leone IV 29. ℂ **06-397-230-34.** Reservations recommended Fri–Sat. Main courses 15,000L–20,000L (7.80€–10.40€, $7.50–$10). AE, DC, MC, V. Mon–Sat noon–3pm and 7–11:30pm. Closed July 15–Aug 1. Metro: Ottaviano.

ugglers, dancers and an assortment of acrobats fill the street.

he shoots you a wide-eyed look as a seven-foot cartoon character approaches.

What brought you here was wanting the kids

o see something magical while they still believed in magic.

America Online Keyword: Travel

Travelocity.com
A Sabre Company
Go Virtually Anywhere.

With 700 airlines, 50,000 hotels and over 5,000 cruise and vaca-

ion getaways, you can now go places you've always dreamed of.

WORLD'S LEADING TRAVEL WEB SITE, 5 YEARS IN A ROW." WORLD TRAVEL AWARDS

10 In Trastevere

EXPENSIVE

Alberto Ciarla ☆☆ SEAFOOD   The Ciarla, in an 1890 building set in an obscure corner of an enormous square, is Trastevere's best restaurant and one of its most expensive. You'll be greeted with a cordial reception and a lavish display of seafood on ice. A dramatically modern decor plays light against shadow for a Renaissance chiaroscuro effect. The specialties include a handful of ancient recipes subtly improved by Signor Ciarla (such as the soup of pasta and beans with seafood). Original dishes include a delectable fish in orange sauce, savory spaghetti with clams, and a full array of delicious shellfish. The sea bass filet is prepared in at least three ways, including an award-winning version with almonds.

Piazza San Cosimato 40. ☎ **06-581-8668.** Reservations required. Main courses 20,000L–48,000L (10.40€–24.95€, $10–$24); fixed-price menus 80,000L–120,000L (41.60€–62.40€, $40–$60). AE, DC, MC, V. Mon–Sat 8:30pm–12:30am. Closed 1 week in Jan and 1 week in Aug. Bus: 44, 75, 170, 280, or 718.

Sabatini ☆ ROMAN/SEAFOOD   This is a real neighborhood spot in a lively location. (You might have to wait for a table even if you have a reservation.) In summer, tables are placed on the charming piazza, and you can look across at the church's flood-lit golden frescoes. The dining room sports beamed ceilings, stenciled walls, lots of paneling, and framed oil paintings. The spaghetti with seafood is excellent, and the fresh fish and shellfish, especially grilled scampi, might tempt you as well. For a savory treat, try *pollo con peperoni,* chicken with red and green peppers. The large antipasti table is excellent, and the delicious pastas, the superb chicken and veal dishes, and the white Frascati wine or the house Chianti continue to delight year after year. (Order carefully, though; your bill can skyrocket if you choose grilled fish or the Florentine steaks.)

Piazza Santa Maria in Trastevere 13. ☎ **06-581-2026.** Reservations recommended. Main courses 40,000L–60,000L (20.80€–31.20€, $20–$30); fixed-price menu 115,000L–140,000L (59.80€–72.80€, $57.50–$70). AE, DC, MC, V. Daily noon–3pm and 8pm–midnight. Closed 2 weeks in Aug (dates vary). Bus: 45, 65, 170, 181, or 280.

MODERATE

Antico Arco ☆ *(Finds)* ITALIAN   Named after one of the gates of early medieval Rome (Arco di San Pancrazio), which rises nearby, this place is set on the Janiculum Hill not far from Trastevere and the American Academy. It's a hip restaurant with a young, stylish clientele. It's run by three investors (Maurizio and Patrizia, who are married, and their friend Domenico) who are likely to be on site themselves, working hard to ensure that food and service flow smoothly. Carefully created menu items include herb-laden versions of onion flan with Parmesan sauce; a palate-awakening truffle and rabbit-meat salad with sliced Parmesan and honey sauce; and a succulent version of spaghetti served with pecorino romano cheese, heavenly fried zucchini blossoms, and fresh-ground pepper. A bitter orange sauce and a sesame-flavored chutney are appropriate foils for roasted duck. Macaroni carbonara and *tagliolini con bottarga* (a Sardinian dish composed of pasta flavored with fish roe) are particularly enticing pastas.

Piazzale Aurelio 7. ☎ **06-581-5274.** Reservations recommended. Main courses 28,000L–39,000L (14.55€–20.30€, $14–$18.50). AE, MC, DC, V. Mon–Sat 8pm–midnight. Bus: 44 or 870.

Asinocotto ITALIAN   Within a pair of cramped dining rooms (one on street level, the other upstairs), you'll be served by a cheerful staff that's well-versed in hauling steaming platters of food up the steep flight of stairs. The simple decor of white-painted walls accented with dark timbers and panels is an appropriate foil for the flavorful dishes that stream from the busy kitchens of Giuliano Brenna. The menu is more sophisticated than you might have thought, thanks to the owner's stint as a chef at the Hotel Eden, one of Rome's more upscale hotels. Menu items include an antipasto that's been compared to a small portion of bouillabaisse. Also look for whole-wheat pasta garnished with lamb stew, swordfish in pesto sauce, and breast of duckling in green tea sauce with tangerine slices. The restaurant's name, incidentally, translates as "cooked donkey meat," but don't look for that on the menu anytime soon.

Via dei Vascellari. ✆ **06-589-8985.** Reservations recommended. Main courses 28,000L–30,000L (14.55€–15.60€, $14–$15). AE, DC, MC, V. Tues–Sun 8–11pm. Tram 8.

La Cisterna ROMAN   If you like traditional home cooking based on the best regional ingredients, head here. La Cisterna, named for an ancient well from imperial times discovered in the cellar, lies deep in the heart of Trastevere. For more than 75 years, it has been run by the wonderful Simmi family. In good weather, you can dine at sidewalk tables. From the ovens emerge Roman-style suckling lamb that's amazingly tender and seasoned with fresh herbs and virgin olive oil. The fiery hot *rigatoni all'amatriciana* is served with red-hot peppers, or you might decide on another delectable pasta dish, *papalini romana,* wide noodles flavored with prosciutto, cheese, and eggs. The shrimp is grilled to perfection, and there's also an array of fresh fish, including flaky sea bass baked with fresh herbs.

Via della Cisterna 13. ✆ **06-581-2543.** Reservations recommended. Main courses 20,000L–35,000L (10.40€–18.20€, $10–$17.50). AE, DC, MC, V. Mon–Sat 7pm–1:30am. Bus: 44, 75, 170, 280, or 710.

Paris ROMAN   For about a century, there's been a restaurant here in this weathered stone building erected about 600 years ago in Trastevere. Over the years, this cramped but convivial place has turned out thousands of platters of authentic Roman cuisine, usually with an emphasis on seafood. This is old-fashioned cooking; don't look for the latest foodie trends. Despite that, you're likely to be very happy here, thanks to heaping portions of such dishes as fried filet of sole; turbot with mushrooms, olive oil, and herbs; several interpretations of scampi; Roman tripe; *coda alla vaccinara* (slow-baked rumpsteak in the Roman style); and succulent grilled baby lamb chops. Vegetarians appreciate one of the house specialties—a beautifully presented platter of fried, very fresh vegetables that can be a main course for one diner or a shared *antipasti* for two or three. We especially love the deep-fried zucchini blossoms stuffed with mozzarella and anchovies, when they're available.

Piazza San Calisto 7A. ✆ **06-581-5378.** Reservations recommended. Main courses 20,000L–34,000L (10.40€–17.70€, $10–$17). AE, DC, MC, V. Tues–Sun noon–3pm and Tues–Sat 7:45am–11pm.

11 In Testaccio

MODERATE

Checchino dal 1887 ⚘ ROMAN   During the 1800s, a wine shop flourished here, selling drinks to the butchers working in the nearby slaughterhouses. In 1887, the ancestors of the restaurant's present owners began serving food, too. Slaughterhouse workers in those days were paid part of their meager salaries with the *quinto quarto* (fifth quarter) of each day's slaughter (the tail, feet, intestines, and other parts not for the squeamish). Following centuries of Roman traditions, Ferminia, the wine shop's cook, somehow transformed these products into

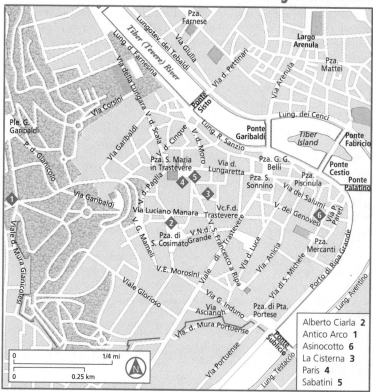

Alberto Ciarla **2**
Antico Arco **1**
Asinocotto **6**
La Cisterna **3**
Paris **4**
Sabatini **5**

the tripe and oxtail dishes that form an integral part of the menu. Many Italian diners come here to relish the *rigatoni con pajata* (pasta with small intestines), *coda alla vaccinara* (oxtail stew), *fagioli e cotiche* (beans with intestinal fat), and other examples of *la cucina povera* (food of the poor). In winter, a succulent wild boar with dried prunes and red wine is served. Safer and possibly more appetizing is the array of salads, soups, pastas, steaks, cutlets, grills, and ice creams. The English-speaking staff is helpful, tactfully proposing alternatives if you're not ready for Roman soul food.

Via di Monte Testaccio 30. (C) **06-574-6318.** Reservations recommended. Main courses 20,000L–35,000L (10.40€–18.20€, $10–$17.50); fixed-price menu 70,000L–80,000L (36.40€–41.60€, $35–$40). AE, DC, MC, V. Tues–Sat 12:30–3pm and 8–11pm; Sun 12:30–3pm. June–Sept closed Sun–Mon. Bus: 75 from Termini Station.

12 The Aventine & the South

MODERATE

La Dolce Vita ROMAN/ITALIAN   This trattoria draws pilgrims on a visit to St. Paul Outside the Walls. The trattoria is separated by a bridge that crosses the Tiber away from the basilica. Its owner, Giorgio Bodoni, has recently been named president of the association of Roman restaurateurs, and, if anything, his chefs are trying harder to impress with his sudden prominence. His fish is fresher and better prepared than ever; try the paper-thin slices of marinated salmon and octopus. No one makes a better skate broth with pasta, tomato, and Roman broccoli than La Dolce Vita.

Via Lungotevere di Pietra Papa 51. ℂ **06-5579-865.** Reservations recommended. Main courses 25,000L–35,000L (13€–18.20€, $12.50–$17.50). DC, MC, V. Tues–Sun 7:30pm–12:30am. Closed 2 weeks in Jan. Metro: Marconi.

13 On the Appian Way

MODERATE

Antica Hostaria l'Archeologia ROMAN/GREEK   A short walk from the catacombs of St. Sebastian, the family-run Hostaria l'Archeologia is like an 18th-century village tavern with lots of atmosphere, strings of garlic and corn, oddments of copper hanging from the ceiling, earth-brown beams, and sienna-washed walls. In summer, you can dine in the garden out back under the wisteria. From the kitchen emerges an array of first-rate dishes, such as gnocchi with wild boar sauce and a special favorite of ours—*veal alla massenzio* (with artichokes, olives, and mushrooms). A longtime favorite is braised beef, tender chunks cooked in a Barolo wine sauce. Of special interest is the wine cellar, excavated in an ancient Roman tomb, with bottles dating from 1800. (You go through an iron gate, down some stairs, and into the underground cavern. Along the way, you can still see the holes once occupied by funeral urns.)

Via Appia Antica 139. ℂ **06-788-0494.** Reservations recommended Sat–Sun. Main courses 20,000L–30,000L (10.40€–15.60€, $10–$15); fixed-price menu from 28,000L (14.55€, $14). AE, DC, MC, V. Mon–Sat 12:30–3:30pm and 7:30–11pm. Bus 218 from San Giovanni or 660 from colli Albani.

14 In Parioli

VERY EXPENSIVE

Relais Le Jardin ✯✯✯ ITALIAN/TRADITIONAL   Relais Le Jardin is one of the best places to go for both traditional and creative cuisine, and a chichi crowd with demanding palates that packs it nightly. There are places in Rome with better views, but not with such an elegant setting, inside one of the capital's most exclusive small hotels. The lighthearted decor combines white lattice work with bold colors and flowers. The service is impeccable.

The pastas and soups are among the finest in town. We were particularly taken with the tonnarelli pasta with asparagus and the smoked ham with concassé tomatoes. The chef can take a dish once served only to the plebes in ancient times, such as bean soup with clams, and make it something elegant. For your main course, you can choose a delectable roast loin of lamb with artichoke romana or the tender grilled beef sirloin with hot chicory and sautéed potatoes. The chef also creates a fabulous risotto with pheasant sauce, asparagus, black truffle flakes, and a hint of fresh thyme—it gets our vote as the best risotto around.

In the Hotel Lord Byron, Via G. de Notaris 5. ℂ **06-361-3041.** Reservations required. Main courses 28,000L–60,000L (14.55€–31.20€, $14–$30). AE, DC, MC, V. Mon–Sat 12:30–2:30pm and 8–10:30pm. Closed Aug. Bus: 52.

MODERATE

Al Ceppo ✯✯ ROMAN   Because the place is somewhat hidden (although only 2 blocks from the Villa Borghese, near Piazza Ungheria), you're likely to rub elbows with more Romans than tourists. It's a longtime favorite, and the cuisine is as good as ever. "The Log" features an open wood-stoked fireplace on which the chef roasts lamb chops, liver, and bacon to perfection. The beefsteak, which hails from Tuscany, is succulent. Other dishes that we continue to delight in are *linguine monteconero* (with clams and fresh tomatoes); savory spaghetti with peppers, fresh basil, and pecorino cheese; swordfish filet filled with grapefruit, parmigiano, pine nuts, and dry grapes; and a fish carpaccio with a green salad, onions, and green pepper. Save room for dessert, especially the apple cobbler, pear-and-almond tart, or chocolate meringue hazelnut cake.

Via Panama 2. © **06-841-9696.** Reservations recommended. Main courses 26,000L–36,000L (13.50€–18.70€, $13–$18). AE, DC, MC, V. Tues–Sun 12:30–3pm and 8–11pm. Closed last 2 weeks of Aug. Bus: 4, 52, or 53.

7

Exploring Rome

Where else but in Rome could you admire a 17th-century colonnade designed by Bernini while resting against an Egyptian obelisk carried off from Heliopolis while Jesus was still alive? Or stand amid the splendor of Renaissance frescoes in a papal palace built on top of the tomb of a Roman emperor? Where else, for that matter, are vestal virgins buried adjacent to the Ministry of Finance?

Rome went all out to spruce up for 2000, and when you visit in 2002, you'll benefit from all those improvements made at the end of the 20th century. For the Jubilee, decades' worth of grime from car exhaust and other pollution was scrubbed from the city's facades, revealing the original glory of the Eternal City (though Rome could still stand even more work on this front), and ancient treasures like the Colosseum were shored up. Many of the most popular areas (such as the Trevi Fountain and Piazza Navona) are sparkling and inviting again.

Whether they're still time-blackened or newly gleaming, the city's ancient monuments are a constant reminder that Rome was one of the greatest centers of Western civilization. In the heyday of the Empire, all roads led to Rome, and with good reason. It was one of the first cosmopolitan cities, importing slaves, gladiators, great art, and even citizens from the far corners of the world. Despite its carnage and corruption, Rome left a legacy of law; a heritage of great art, architecture, and engineering; and an uncanny lesson in how to conquer enemies by absorbing their cultures.

But ancient Rome is only part of the spectacle. The Vatican has had a tremendous influence on making the city a tourism center. Although Vatican architects stripped down much of the city's glory, looting ancient ruins for their precious marble, they created great Renaissance treasures and even occasionally incorporated the old into the new—as Michelangelo did when turning the Baths of Diocletian into a church. And in the years that followed, Bernini adorned the city with the wonders of the baroque, especially his glorious fountains.

SUGGESTED ITINERARIES

If You Have 1 Day

One day is far too brief—after all, Rome wasn't built in a day, and you can't see it in one—but you can make the most of your limited time. You'll basically have to choose between exploring the legacy of imperial Rome or taking in St. Peter's and the Vatican. We'll describe below how to see the best of ancient Rome, and we'll talk about the Vatican in Day 2, but if you have only 1 day, it's equally viable to spend it at St. Peter's and the Vatican Museums.

If you'll be in Rome for a few days, stop by the ticket office of the Galleria Borghese to make a reservation for later.

If you've come to see ancient Rome and the glory of the Caesars, start your stroll at Michelangelo's Campidoglio, or Capitoline Hill. From here you can look out over the Roman Forum area before venturing forth to discover on your own. After this overview, walk east along the Via dei Fori Imperiali, taking in a view of the remains of the Imperial Forums, which can be seen from the street. This route leads you right to the ruins of the Colosseum. After a visit to this amphitheater, cross over to spend the rest of the day exploring the ruins of the Roman Forum and Palatine Hill to the immediate west of the Colosseum. And you can detour north of the Colosseum to look at Domus Aurea, or the "Golden House" of the emperor, Nero.

For a change of pace, stop into the church of San Pietro in Vincoli, which is near ancient Rome. Pop in quickly just to see Michelangelo's *Moses.*

After your day of sightseeing, have dinner near the Pantheon, an area that's packed with restaurants, bars, and cafes. Toss a coin in the Trevi Fountain and promise a return visit to Rome.

If You Have 2 Days

If you elected to see the Roman Forum and the Colosseum on your first day, then spend Day 2 exploring St. Peter's and the Vatican Museums. The tiny walled "city-state of the Vatican," the capital of the Catholic world, contains such a wealth of splendor that you could spend more than a day seeing it all, but most people are content to hit the highlights in 1 busy day. After exploring the treasures of St. Peter's Basilica (including climbing Michelangelo's dome), take a

lunch break and then stroll over to the Vatican Museums, which boast one of the most jaw-dropping collections of art and antiquities in the world, all of it culminating in the gloriously restored Sistine Chapel. By now, you'll probably be exhausted, but if you can keep going, take in the Castel Sant'Angelo.

Have dinner that night in a restaurant in Trastevere.

If You Have 3 Days

On the morning of Day 3, go to the Pantheon in the heart of Old Rome; then, if you were able to make a reservation, take in the Galleria Borghese and spend an hour relaxing in this beautiful park afterward. If you don't have a ticket, head instead to another of Rome's top museums (perhaps the Capitoline Museum and Palazzo dei Conservatori, if you weren't able to squeeze in a visit during your Day 1 in ancient Rome).

Have dinner at a restaurant on Piazza Navona. Then treat yourself to a moonlit stroll. Don't worry about following any set itinerary— just let yourself wander. At night the stunning piazzas and fountains are dramatically lit, as are the ancient ruins, which look even more haunting and evocative when floodlit.

If You Have 4 Days

Spend your first 3 days as previously indicated. On Day 4, you might want to take in one of the museums you didn't get to earlier (consider the National Etruscan Museum or the Galleria Doria Pamphilj). Another great option is to head out the Appian Way to take in the catacombs, an outing that will take up most of the day. Squeeze in a couple of hours of shopping and strolling around the Spanish Steps.

Rome Attractions

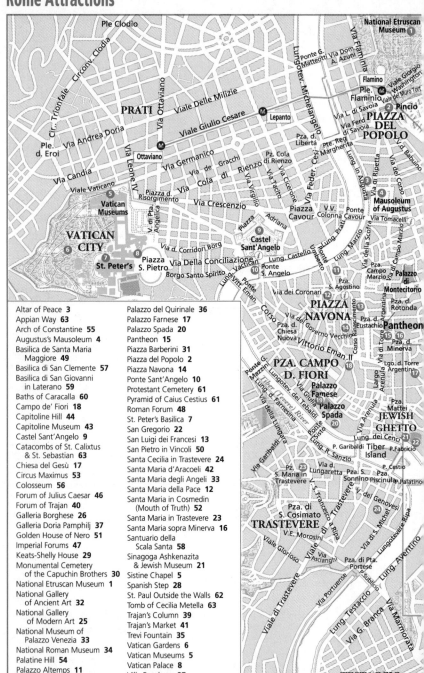

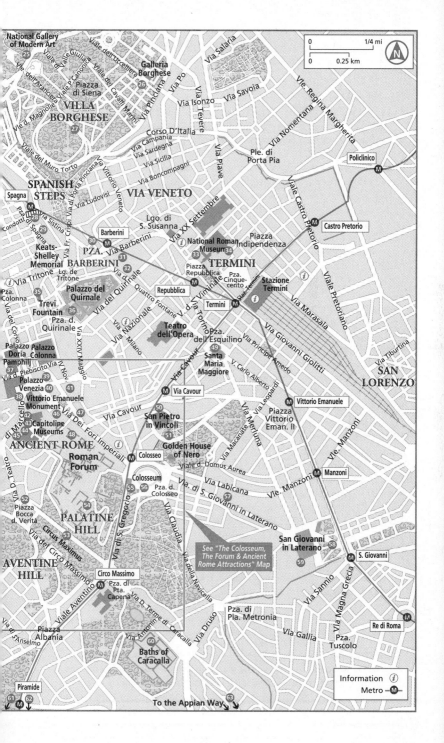

National Gallery
of Modern Art

Galleria
Borghese

Via dell'Uccelliera

Piazza
di Siena

VILLA
BORGHESE

Via Salaria

Via Po

Via Isonzo

Via Savoia

Vle. Regina Margherita

Corso D'Italia

Via Campania

Via Sardegna

Via Sicilia

Via Boncompagni

Ple. di
Porta Pia

Via Nomentana

Policlinico

SPANISH
STEPS

Spagna

VIA VENETO

Via XX Settembre

Viale Castro Pretorio

Castro Pretorio

Barberini

Lgo. di
S. Susanna

National Roman
Museum

Piazza
Indipendenza

Stazione
Termini

PZA.
BARBERINI

Keats-
Shelley
Memorial

Via Tritone

Lgo. de
Tritone

Piazza
Repubblica

TERMINI

Pza.
Cinque-
cento

Stazione Termini

Via Marasala

Pza.
Colonna

Trevi
Fountain

Palazzo del
Quirinale

Repubblica

Termini

Pza. d.
Quirinale

Via Nazionale

Teatro
dell'Opera

Pza.
dell'Esquilino

Via Giovanni Giolitti

SAN
LORENZO

Palazzo
Doria
Pamphilj

Palazzo
Colonna

Santa
Maria
Maggiore

V. Carlo Alberto

Via Tiburtina

Palazzo
Venezia

Vittorio Emanuele
Monument

Via Cavour

Via Cavour

Vittorio Emanuele

Capitoline
Museums

Via Dei Fori Imperiali

San Pietro
in Vincoli

Piazza
Vittorio
Eman. II

ANCIENT ROME

Roman
Forum

Golden House
of Nero

Colosseo

Viale d. Domus Aurea

Via Merulina

Manzoni

Piazza
Bocca
d. Verita

Colosseum

Pza. d.
Colosseo

Via Labicana

Vle. Manzoni

PALATINE
HILL

Circus Maximus

See "The Colosseum,
The Forum & Ancient
Rome Attractions" Map

Via di S. Giovanni in Laterano

San Giovanni
in Laterano

S. Giovanni

AVENTINE
HILL

Circo Massimo

Pza. di
Pta.
Capena

Pza. di
Pla. Metronia

Via Gallia

Re di Roma

Piazza
Albania

Baths of
Caracalla

Via Druso

Pza.
Tuscolo

Piramide

To the Appian Way

Information   *i*
Metro   —Ⓜ

127

1 St. Peter's & the Vatican

If you want to know more about the Vatican, check out its website at **www.vatican.va**.

IN VATICAN CITY

In 1929, the Lateran Treaty between Pope Pius XI and the Italian government created the **Vatican,** the world's second-smallest sovereign independent state. It has only a few hundred citizens and is protected (theoretically) by its own militia, the curiously uniformed (some say by Michelangelo) Swiss guards.

The only entrance to the Vatican for the casual visitor is through one of the glories of the Western world: Bernini's **St. Peter's Square (Piazza San Pietro).** As you stand in the huge piazza, you'll be in the arms of an ellipse partly enclosed by a majestic **Doric-pillared colonnade.** Atop it stands a gesticulating crowd of some 140 saints. Straight ahead is the facade of **St. Peter's Basilica** (Sts. Peter and Paul are represented by statues in front, with Peter carrying the keys to the kingdom), and, to the right, above the colonnade, are the dark brown buildings of the **papal apartments** and the **Vatican Museums.** In the center of the square is an **Egyptian obelisk,** brought from the ancient city of Heliopolis on the Nile delta. Flanking the obelisk are two 17th-century **fountains.** The one on the right (facing the basilica), by Carlo Maderno, who designed the facade of St. Peter's, was placed here by Bernini himself; the other is by Carlo Fontana.

On the left side of Piazza San Pietro is the **Vatican Tourist Office** (*©* 06-6988-4466 or 06-6988-4866), open Monday to Saturday from 8:30am to 7pm. It sells maps and guides that'll help you make more sense of the riches you'll be seeing in the museums. It also accepts reservations for tours of the Vatican Gardens and tries to answer questions.

Basilica di San Pietro (St. Peter's Basilica) *★★★*   In ancient times, the Circus of Nero, where St. Peter is said to have been crucified, was slightly to the left of where the basilica is now located. Peter was allegedly buried here in A.D. 64 near the site of his execution, and in 324 Constantine commissioned a basilica to be built over Peter's tomb. That structure stood for more than 1,000 years, until it verged on collapse. The present basilica, mostly completed in the 1500s and 1600s, is predominantly High Renaissance and baroque. Inside, the massive scale is almost too much to absorb, showcasing some of Italy's greatest artists: Bramante, Raphael, Michelangelo, and Maderno. In a church of such grandeur—overwhelming in its detail of gilt, marble, and mosaic—you can't expect much subtlety. It's meant to be overpowering.

In the nave on the right (the first chapel) stands one of the Vatican's greatest treasures: Michelangelo's exquisite *Pietà* *★★★*, created while the master was still in his early 20s but clearly showing his genius for capturing the human

---

Tips A St. Peter's Warning

St. Peter's has a strict dress code: no shorts, no skirts above the knee, and no bare shoulders. ***You will not be let in if you don't come dressed appropriately.*** In a pinch, men and women alike can buy a big, cheap scarf from a nearby souvenir stand and wrap it around their legs as a long skirt or throw it over their shoulders as a shawl. You also are not supposed to take photographs.

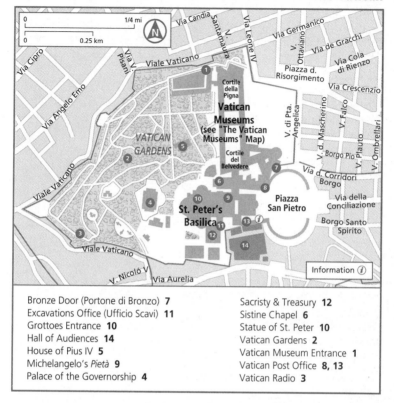

Bronze Door (Portone di Bronzo) **7**
Excavations Office (Ufficio Scavi) **11**
Grottoes Entrance **10**
Hall of Audiences **14**
House of Pius IV **5**
Michelangelo's *Pietà* **9**
Palace of the Governorship **4**

Sacristy & Treasury **12**
Sistine Chapel **6**
Statue of St. Peter **10**
Vatican Gardens **2**
Vatican Museum Entrance **1**
Vatican Post Office **8, 13**
Vatican Radio **3**

form. (The sculpture has been kept behind reinforced glass since a madman's act of vandalism in the 1970s.) Note the incredibly lifelike folds of Mary's robes and her youthful features (although she would've been middle-aged at the time of the Crucifixion, Michelangelo portrayed her as a young woman to convey her purity).

Much farther on, in the right wing of the transept near the Chapel of St. Michael, rests Canova's neoclassic **sculpture of Pope Clement XIII** ✦✦. The truly devout stop to kiss the feet of the 13th-century **bronze of St. Peter** ✦, attributed to Arnolfo di Cambio (at the far reaches of the nave, against a corner pillar on the right). Under Michelangelo's dome is the celebrated twisty-columned **baldacchino** ✦✦ (1524), by Bernini, resting over the papal altar. The 96-foot-high ultrafancy canopy was created in part, so it's said, from bronze stripped from the Pantheon, although that's up for debate.

In addition, you can visit the **treasury** ✦, which is filled with jewel-studded chalices, reliquaries, and copes. One robe worn by Pius XII strikes a simple note in these halls of elegance. The sacristy contains a **Historical Museum (Museo Storico)** ✦ displaying Vatican treasures, including the large 1400s bronze tomb of Pope Sixtus V by Antonio Pollaiuolo and several antique chalices.

You can also head downstairs to the **Vatican grottoes** ✦✦, with their tombs of the popes, both ancient and modern (Pope John XXIII gets the most adulation). Behind a wall of glass is what's assumed to be the tomb of St. Peter himself.

To go even farther down, to the **necropolis vaticana** ✦✦, the area around St. Peter's tomb, you must apply in writing three weeks beforehand to the **excavations office.** Apply in advance at the Ufficio Scavi (✆ **06-6988-5318**), through the arch to the left of the stairs up the basilica. You specify your name, the number in your party, your language, and dates you'd like to visit. They'll notify you by phone of your admission date and time. For 15,000L (7.80€, $7.50), you'll take a guided tour of the tombs that were excavated in the 1940s, 23 feet beneath the church floor. For details, check **www.vatican.va**.

> **Impressions**
>
> *As a whole St. Peter's is fit for nothing but a ballroom, and it is a little too gaudy even for that.*
> —John Ruskin, letter to the Rev. Thomas Dale (1840)

After you leave the grottoes, you'll find yourself in a courtyard and ticket line for the grandest sight: the climb to **Michelangelo's dome** ✦✦✦, about 375 feet high. You can walk up all the steps or take the elevator as far as it goes. The elevator saves you 171 steps, and you'll *still* have 320 to go after getting off. After you've made it to the top, you'll have an astounding view over the rooftops of Rome and even the Vatican Gardens and papal apartments—a photo op, if ever there was one.

Piazza San Pietro. ✆ **06-6988-4466** or 96/688-4466 (for information on celebrations). Basilica (including grottoes) free admission. Guided tour of excavations around St. Peter's tomb 15,000L (7.80€, $7.50); children younger than 15 are not admitted. Stairs to the dome 7,000L (3.65€, $3.50); elevator to the dome 8,000L (4.15€, $4). Sacristy (with Historical Museum) 9,000L (4.70€, $4.50). Basilica (including the sacristy and treasury) Oct–Mar daily 7am–6pm; Apr–Sept daily 7am–7pm. Grottoes daily 8am–5pm. Dome Oct–Mar daily 8am–5pm; Apr–Sept 8am–6pm. Bus: 46. Metro: Ottaviano/San Pietro, then a long stroll.

Vatican Museums (Musei Vaticani) & the Sistine Chapel (Cappella Sistina) ✦✦✦   The Vatican Museums boast one of the world's greatest art collections. They're a gigantic repository of treasures from antiquity and the Renaissance, all housed in a labyrinthine series of lavishly adorned palaces, apartments, and galleries leading you to the real gem: the Sistine Chapel. The Vatican Museums occupy a part of the papal palaces built from the 1200s onward. From the former papal private apartments, the museums were created over a period of time to display the vast treasure trove of art acquired by the Vatican.

You'll climb a magnificent spiral ramp to get to the ticket windows. After you're admitted, you can choose your route through the museum from **four color-coded itineraries** (A, B, C, D) according to the time you have (from 1½–5 hr.) and your interests. You determine your choice by consulting large-size panels on the wall and then following the letter/color of your choice. All four itineraries culminate in the Sistine Chapel. Obviously, 1, 2, or even 20 trips will not be enough to see the wealth of the Vatican, much less to digest it. With that in mind, we've previewed only a representative sampling of the masterpieces on display (in alphabetical order).

Borgia Apartments ✦: Frescoed with biblical scenes by Pinturicchio of Umbria and his assistants, these rooms were designed for Pope Alexander VI (the infamous Borgia pope). They may be badly lit, but they boast great splendor and style. At the end of the Raphael Rooms (see below) is the Chapel of Nicholas V, an intimate room frescoed by the Dominican monk Fra Angelico, the most saintly of all Italian painters.

Chiaramonti Museum: Founded by Pope Pius VII, also known as Chiaramonti, the museum includes the *Corridoio* (Corridor), the Galleria Lapidaria, and the *Braccio Nuovo* (New Side). The Corridor hosts an exposition of more

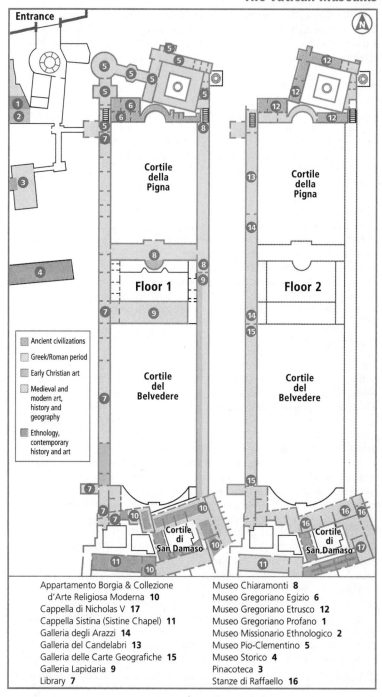

Entrance

N

Cortile della Pigna

Floor 1

Cortile della Pigna

Floor 2

- Ancient civilizations
- Greek/Roman period
- Early Christian art
- Medieval and modern art, history and geography
- Ethnology, contemporary history and art

Cortile del Belvedere

Cortile del Belvedere

Cortile di San Damaso

Cortile di San Damaso

Appartamento Borgia & Collezione
  d'Arte Religiosa Moderna **10**
Cappella di Nicholas V **17**
Cappella Sistina (Sistine Chapel) **11**
Galleria degli Arazzi **14**
Galleria del Candelabri **13**
Galleria delle Carte Geografiche **15**
Galleria Lapidaria **9**
Library **7**

Museo Chiaramonti **8**
Museo Gregoriano Egizio **6**
Museo Gregoriano Etrusco **12**
Museo Gregoriano Profano **1**
Museo Missionario Ethnologico **2**
Museo Pio-Clementino **5**
Museo Storico **4**
Pinacoteca **3**
Stanze di Raffaello **16**

than 800 Greek-Roman works, including statues, reliefs, and sarcophagi. In the Galleria Lapidaria are about 5,000 Christian and pagan inscriptions. You'll find a dazzling array of Roman sculpture and copies of Greek originals in these galleries. In the Braccio Nuovo, built as an extension of the Chiaramonti, you can admire *The Nile* ✯, a magnificent reproduction of a long-lost Hellenistic original and one of the most remarkable pieces of sculpture from antiquity. The imposing statue of Augustus of Prima Porta presents him as a regal commander.

Collection of Modern Religious Art: This museum, opened in 1973, represents American artists' first invasion of the Vatican. Of the 55 rooms, at least 12 are devoted to American artists. All the works chosen were judged on their "spiritual and religious values." Among the American works is Leonard Baskin's 5-foot bronze sculpture of *Isaac.* Modern Italian artists such as De Chirico and Manzù are also displayed, and there's a special room for the paintings of the Frenchman Georges Rouault. You'll also see works by Picasso, Gauguin, Gottuso, Chagall, Henry Moore, Kandinsky, and others.

Egyptian–Gregorian Museum: Experience the grandeur of the pharaohs by studying sarcophagi, mummies, statues of goddesses, vases, jewelry, sculptured pink-granite statues, and hieroglyphics.

Etruscan–Gregorian Museum ✯: This was founded by Gregory XIV in 1837 and then enriched year after year, becoming one of the most important and complete collections of Etruscan art. With sarcophagi, a chariot, bronzes, urns, jewelry, and terra-cotta vases, this gallery affords remarkable insights into an ancient civilization. One of the most acclaimed exhibits is the Regolini–Galassi tomb, unearthed in the 19th century at Cerveteri. It shares top honors with the *Mars of Todi,* a bronze sculpture probably dating from the 5th century B.C.

Ethnological Museum: This is an assemblage of works of art and objects of cultural significance from all over the world. The principal route is a half-mile walk through 25 geographical sections, displaying thousands of objects covering 3,000 years of world history. The section devoted to China is especially interesting.

Historical Museum: This museum tells the history of the Vatican. It exhibits arms, uniforms, and armor, some dating from the early Renaissance. The carriages displayed are those used by the popes and cardinals in religious processions.

Pinacoteca (Picture Gallery) ✯✯✯: The Pinacoteca houses paintings and tapestries from the 11th to the 19th century. As you pass through room 1, note the oldest picture at the Vatican, a keyhole-shaped wood panel of the *Last Judgment* from the 11th century. In room 2 is one of the finest pieces—the *Stefaneschi Triptych* (six panels) by Giotto and his assistants. Bernardo Daddi's masterpiece of early Italian Renaissance art, *Madonna del Magnificat,* is also here. And you'll see works by Fra Angelico, the 15th-century Dominican monk who distinguished himself as a miniaturist (his *Virgin with Child* is justly praised—check out the Madonna's microscopic eyes).

In the **Raphael salon** ✯✯✯ (room 8), you can view three paintings by the Renaissance giant himself: the *Coronation of the Virgin,* the *Virgin of Foligno,* and the massive *Transfiguration* (completed shortly before his death). There are also eight tapestries made by Flemish weavers from cartoons by Raphael. In room 9, seek out Leonardo da Vinci's masterful but uncompleted **St. Jerome with the Lion** ✯✯, as well as Giovanni Bellini's *Pietà* and one of Titian's greatest works, the *Virgin of Frari.* Finally, in room 10, feast your eyes on one of the masterpieces of the baroque, **Caravaggio's *Deposition from the Cross*** ✯✯.

Tips **Buy the Book**

In the Vatican Museums you'll find many overpacked galleries and few labels on the works. At the Vatican Tourist Office (mentioned earlier), you can buy a detailed guide that'll help you make more sense of the incredible riches you'll be seeing here.

Pio Clementino Museum ⚝⚝⚝: Here you'll find Greek and Roman sculptures, many of which are immediately recognizable. The rippling muscles of the *Belvedere Torso* ⚝⚝⚝, a partially preserved Greek statue (1st century B.C.) much admired by the artists of the Renaissance, especially Michelangelo, reveal an intricate knowledge of the human body. In the rotunda is a large gilded bronze of *Hercules* from the late 2nd century B.C. Other major sculptures are under porticoes opening onto the Belvedere courtyard. From the 1st century B.C., one sculpture shows *Laocoön* ⚝⚝⚝ and his two sons locked in an eternal struggle with the serpents. The incomparable *Apollo Belvedere* ⚝⚝⚝ (a late Roman reproduction of an authentic Greek work from the 4th c. B.C.) has become the symbol of classic male beauty, rivaling Michelangelo's *David.*

Raphael Rooms ⚝⚝: While still a young man, Raphael was given one of the greatest assignments of his short life: to decorate a series of rooms in the apartments of Pope Julius II. The decoration was carried out by Raphael and his workshop from 1508 to 1524. In these works, Raphael achieves the Renaissance aim of blending classic beauty with realism. In the first chamber, the Stanza dell'Incendio, you'll see much of the work of Raphael's pupils but little of the master—except in the fresco across from the window. The figure of the partially draped Aeneas rescuing his father (to the left of the fresco) is sometimes attributed to Raphael, as is the surprised woman with a jug balanced on her head to the right.

Raphael reigns supreme in the next and most important salon, the Stanza della Segnatura, the first room decorated by the artist, where you'll find the majestic *School of Athens* ⚝⚝⚝, one of his best-known works, depicting such philosophers from the ages as Aristotle, Plato, and Socrates. Many of the figures are actually portraits of some of the greatest artists of the Renaissance, including Bramante (on the right as Euclid, bent over and balding as he draws on a chalkboard), Leonardo da Vinci (as Plato, the bearded man in the center pointing heavenward), and even Raphael himself (looking out at you from the lower-right corner). While he was painting this masterpiece, Raphael stopped work to walk down the hall for the unveiling of Michelangelo's newly finished Sistine Chapel ceiling. He was so impressed that he returned to his *School of Athens* and added to his design a sulking Michelangelo sitting on the steps. Another well-known masterpiece here is the *Disputa del Sacramento.*

The *Stanza d'Eliodoro,* also by the master, manages to flatter Raphael's papal patrons (Julius II and Leo X) without compromising his art (although one rather fanciful fresco depicts the pope driving Attila from Rome). Finally, there's the *Sala di Constantino,* which was completed by his students after Raphael's death. The loggia, frescoed with more than 50 scenes from the Bible, was designed by Raphael, but the actual work was done by his loyal students.

Sistine Chapel ⚝⚝⚝: Michelangelo considered himself a sculptor, not a painter. While in his 30s, he was commanded by Julius II to stop work on the

Papal Audiences

When the pope is in Rome, he gives a public audience every Wednesday beginning at 10:30am (sometimes at 10am in summer). It takes place in the Paul VI Hall of Audiences, although sometimes St. Peter's Basilica and St. Peter's Square are used to accommodate a large attendance. Anyone is welcome, but you must first obtain a **free ticket** from the office of the Prefecture of the Papal Household, accessible from St. Peter's Square by the Bronze Door, where the colonnade on the right (as you face the basilica) begins. The office is open from Monday to Saturday 9am to 1pm. Tickets are readily available on Monday and Tuesday; sometimes you won't be able to get into the office on Wednesday morning. Occasionally, if there's enough room, you can attend without a ticket.

You can also write ahead to the **Prefecture of the Papal Household,** 00120 Città del Vaticano (℃ **06-698-83114**), indicating your language, the dates of your visit, the number of people in your party, and (if possible) the hotel in Rome to which the cards should be sent the afternoon before the audience. American Catholics, armed with a letter of introduction from their parish priest, should apply to the **North American College,** Via dell'Umiltà 30, 00187 Roma (℃ **06-690-011**).

At noon on Sunday, the pope speaks briefly from his study window and gives his blessing to the visitors and pilgrims gathered in St. Peter's Square. From about mid-July to mid-September, the Angelus and blessing take place at the summer residence at Castelgandolfo, some 16 miles (26km) out of Rome and accessible by metro and bus.

pope's own tomb and to devote his considerable talents to painting ceiling frescoes (an art form of which the Florentine master was contemptuous). Michelangelo labored for 4 years (1508–12) over this epic project, which was so physically taxing that it permanently damaged his eyesight. All during the task, he had to contend with the pope's incessant urgings to hurry up; at one point, Julius threatened to topple Michelangelo from the scaffolding—or so Vasari relates in his *Lives of the Artists.*

It's ironic that a project undertaken against the artist's wishes would form his most enduring legend. Glorifying the human body as only a sculptor could, Michelangelo painted nine panels, taken from the pages of Genesis, and surrounded them with prophets and sibyls. The most notable panels detail the expulsion of Adam and Eve from the Garden of Eden and the creation of man; you'll recognize the image of God's outstretched hand as it imbues Adam with spirit. (You might want to bring along binoculars so you can see the details better.)

The Florentine master was in his 60s when he began the masterly *Last Judgment* ★★★ on the altar wall. Again working against his wishes, Michelangelo presented a more jaundiced view of people and their fate; God sits in judgment and sinners are plunged into the mouth of hell. A master of ceremonies under Paul III, Monsignor Biagio da Cesena, protested to the pope about the "shameless nudes" painted by Michelangelo. Michelangelo showed that he wasn't above petty revenge by painting the prude with the ears of a jackass in hell. When Biagio complained to the pope, Paul III maintained that he had no jurisdiction in hell. However, Daniele de Volterra was summoned to drape clothing over some of the bare figures, thus earning for himself a dubious distinction as a haberdasher.

On the side walls are frescoes by other Renaissance masters, such as Botticelli, Perugino, Signorelli, Pinturicchio, Roselli, and Ghirlandaio, but because they must compete unfairly with the artistry of Michelangelo, they're virtually ignored by most visitors.

The restoration of the Sistine Chapel in the 1990s touched off a worldwide debate among art historians. The chapel was on the verge of collapse, from both its age and the weather, and restoration took years, as restorers used advanced computer analyses in their painstaking and controversial work. They reattached the fresco and repaired the ceiling, ridding the frescoes of their dark and shadowy look. Critics claim that in addition to removing centuries of dirt and grime—and several of the added "modesty" drapes—the restorers removed a vital second layer of paint as well. Purists argue that many of the restored figures seem flat compared with the originals, which had more shadow and detail. Others have hailed the project for saving Michelangelo's masterpiece for future generations to appreciate and for revealing the vibrancy of his color palette.

Vatican Library ⊛: The library is richly decorated, with frescos created by a team of Mannerist painters commissioned by Sixtus V.

Vatican City, Viale Vaticano (a long walk around the Vatican walls from St. Peter's Square). ☏ 06-6988-4341. Admission 18,000L (9.35€, $9); free for everyone the last Sun of each month (be ready for a crowd). Mid-Mar to late Oct, Mon–Fri 8:45am–3:45pm; Sat and last Sun of the month 8:45am–12:45pm. Off-season, Mon–Sat and last Sun of the month 8:45am–12:45pm. Closed all national and religious holidays (except Easter week) and Aug 15–16. Metro: Ottaviano/San Pietro, then a long walk.

Vatican Gardens ⊛   Separating the Vatican from the secular world on the north and west are 58 acres of lush gardens filled with winding paths, brilliantly colored flowers, groves of massive oaks, and ancient fountains and pools. In the midst of this pastoral setting is a small summer house, Villa Pia, built for Pope Pius IV in 1560 by Pirro Ligorio. The gardens contain medieval fortifications from the 9th century to the present. Water spouts profusely from a variety of fountains.

To make a reservation to visit the Vatican Gardens, send a fax to **06-698-851-00.** Once the reservation is accepted, you must go to the Vatican information office (at Piazza San Pietro, on the left side looking at the facade of St. Peter's) and pick up the tickets 2 or 3 days before your visit. Tours of the gardens are Monday, Tuesday, Thursday, Friday, and Saturday at 10am; they last for 2 hours, and the first half hour is by bus. The cost of the tour is 20,000L (10.40€, $10). For further information, contact the **Vatican Tourism Office** (☏ **06-698-844-66,** or 06-698-848-66).

North and west of the Vatican. See previous paragraph for tour information.

NEAR VATICAN CITY

The trio of arches in the Tiber River's center has been basically unchanged since the **Ponte Sant'Angelo** was built around A.D. 135; the arches abutting the river's embankments were added late in the 19th century as part of a flood-control program. On December 19, 1450, so many pilgrims gathered on this bridge (which at the time was lined with wooden buildings) that about 200 of them were crushed to death.

Since the 1960s, the bridge has been reserved for pedestrians who can stroll across and admire the statues designed by Bernini. On the southern end is **Piazza Sant'Angelo,** the site of one of the most famous executions of the Renaissance. In 1599, Beatrice Cenci and several members of her family were beheaded on orders of Pope Clement VIII. Their crime? Plotting the successful death of their rich and brutal father. Their tale later inspired a tragedy by Shelley and a novel by a 19th-century Italian politician named Francesco Guerrazzi.

Castel Sant'Angelo ⭐ This overpowering castle on the Tiber was built in the 2nd century as a tomb for Emperor Hadrian; it continued as an imperial mausoleum until the time of Caracalla. If it looks like a fortress, it should—that was its function in the Middle Ages. It was built over the Roman walls and linked to the Vatican by an underground passage that was much used by the fleeing papacy, who escaped from unwanted visitors such as Charles V during his 1527 sack of the city. In the 14th century, it became a papal residence, enjoying various connections with Boniface IX, Nicholas V, and Julius II, patron of Michelangelo and Raphael.

But its legend rests largely on its link with Pope Alexander VI, whose mistress bore him two children (those darlings of debauchery, Cesare and Lucrezia Borgia). Even those on a rushed visit to Rome might want to budget time for a stopover here because it's a most intriguing sight, an imposing fortress that has seen more blood, treachery, and turmoil than any other left in Rome. It is Rome's chief citadel and dungeon. An audio guide is available to help you understand what you're seeing.

The highlight here is a trip through the Renaissance apartments with their coffered ceilings and lush decoration. Their walls have witnessed some of the most diabolical plots and intrigues of the High Renaissance. Later, you can go through the dank cells that once echoed with the screams of Cesare's victims of torture. The most famous figure imprisoned here was Benvenuto Cellini, the eminent sculptor/goldsmith, remembered chiefly for his candid *Autobiography.* Now an art museum, the castle halls display the history of the Roman mausoleum, along with a wide-ranging selection of ancient arms and armor. You can climb to the top terrace for another one of those dazzling views of the Eternal City.

The bumper-to-bumper cars and buses that once roared around Castel Sant'Angelo are now gone. The area around the castle has been turned into a new pedestrian zone. Visitors can now walk in peace through the landscaped section with a tree-lined avenue above the Tiber and a formal garden. In 2000, the moat under the ramparts was opened to the public for the first time. You can wander the footpaths and enjoy the new beeches providing shade in the sweltering summer.

Lungotevere Castello 50. ✆ **06-681-9111.** Admission 10,000L (5.20€, $5). Tues–Sun 9am–8pm. Bus: 23, 46, 49, 62, 87, 98, 280, or 910. Metro: Ottaviano, then a long stroll.

2 The Colosseum, the Roman Forum & Highlights of Ancient Rome

THE TOP SIGHTS IN ANCIENT ROME

If you'd like more guidance as you explore this area, turn to "Walking Tour 1: Rome of the Caesars" on p. 170.

The Colosseum (Colosseo) ⭐⭐⭐ Now a mere shell, the Colosseum still remains the greatest architectural legacy from ancient Rome. Vespasian ordered

The Colosseum, the Forum & Ancient Rome Attractions

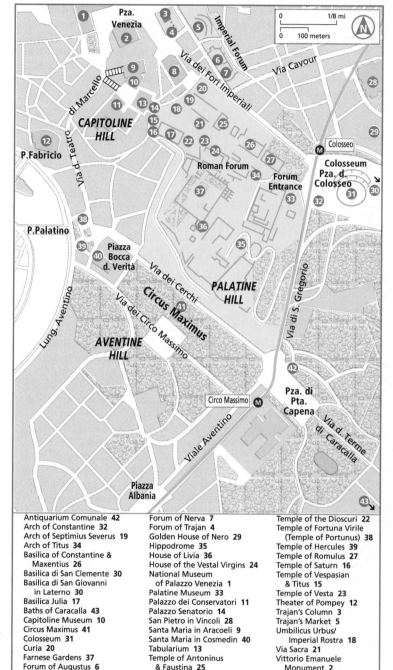

Pza. Venezia

Imperial Forum

Via dei Fori Imperiali

Via Cavour

0 — 1/8 mi
0 — 100 meters

CAPITOLINE HILL

P.Fabricio

Roman Forum

Colosseo

Colosseum
Pza. d.
Colosseo

Forum Entrance

P.Palatino

Piazza Bocca d. Verità

Via dei Cerchi

PALATINE HILL

Circus Maximus

Via dei Circo Massimo

Lung. Aventino

AVENTINE HILL

Via di S. Gregorio

Circo Massimo

Pza. di Pta. Capena

Via d. Terme di Caracalla

Viale Aventino

Piazza Albania

137

the construction of the elliptical bowl, called the Amphitheatrum Flavium, in A.D. 72; it was inaugurated by Titus in A.D. 80 with a bloody combat, lasting many long weeks, between gladiators and wild beasts. At its peak, under the cruel Domitian, the Colosseum could seat 50,000. The vestal virgins from the temple screamed for blood, as more exotic animals were shipped in from the far corners of the Empire to satisfy jaded tastes (lion versus bear, two humans vs. hippopotamus). Not-so-mock naval battles were staged (the canopied Colosseum could be flooded), and the defeated combatants might have their lives spared if they put up a good fight. Many historians now believe that one of the most enduring legends about the Colosseum (that Christians were fed to the lions) is unfounded.

Long after the Colosseum ceased to be an arena to amuse sadistic Romans, it was struck by an earthquake. Centuries later it was used as a quarry, its rich marble facing stripped away to build palaces and churches. On one side, part of the original four tiers remains; the first three levels were constructed in Doric, Ionic, and Corinthian styles, respectively, to lend variety. Inside, the seats are gone, as is the wooden floor.

Efforts are currently underway to restore and shore up the Colosseum, but, like most major projects in Rome, they've been dragging on for years. As of this writing, scaffolding still covers one section, but it could be removed by 2002 unless additional cracks develop. The Colosseum has become the turnstile for Rome's largest traffic circle, around which thousands of cars whip daily, spewing exhaust over this venerable monument. In addition to reinforcing the structure, workers are attempting to clean off a layer of grime. Ambitious plans are also underway to allow visitors to explore the interior more fully by 2002 (see the note "Hail to the Gladiator"). For now, you can explore on your own or rent an audio guide for 7,000L (3.65€, $3.50).

The **Arch of Constantine** 🟉🟉, the highly photogenic memorial next to the Colosseum, was erected by the Senate in A.D. 315 to honor Constantine's defeat of the pagan Maxentius (306). Many of the reliefs have nothing whatsoever to do with Constantine or his works, but they tell of the victories of earlier Antonine rulers (they were apparently lifted from other, long-forgotten memorials).

Historically, the arch marks a period of great change in the history of Rome and thus the history of the world. Converted to Christianity by a vision on the battlefield, Constantine ended the centuries-long persecution of the Christians (during which many devout followers of the new religion had often been put to death in a most gruesome manner). While Constantine didn't ban paganism (which survived officially until the closing of the temples more than half a century later), he espoused Christianity himself and began the inevitable development that culminated in the conquest of Rome by the Christian religion.

Hail to the Gladiator

Good news for fans of the Oscar-winning smash *Gladiator:* You can now get the same center-stage view of the Colosseum that the fighters had before they met a bloody death or glory in the ring. Recent renovations will allow visitors to wander spaces under the Colosseum where elephants, lions, and wild animals from North America once waited to be hoisted up in cages to take on the gladiators.

After visiting the Colosseum, it's convenient to head over to the recently reopened **Domus Aurea (Golden House of Nero)** on the Esquiline Hill; it faces the Colosseum and is adjacent to the Forum (see below).

Piazzale del Colosseo, Via dei Fori Imperiali. ℂ **06-700-4261**. Admission 10,000L (5.20€, $5) all levels. Oct–Jan 15 daily 9am–3pm; Jan 16–Feb 15 daily 9am–4pm; Feb 16–Mar 17 daily 9am–4:30pm; Mar 18–Apr 16 daily 9am–5pm; Apr 17–Sept daily 9am–7pm. Guided tours in English with an archaeologist 3 times per morning on Sun and holidays 6,000L (3.10€, $3). Tickets to Palatine Hill also sold at box office for 12,000L (6.25€, $6).

Golden House of Nero (Domus Aurea) ✪   "Nero's Folly" finally reopened

in 1999 after a 15-year restoration. After the disastrous fire of A.D. 64 swept over Rome (it has never been proven that Nero set the fire, much less fiddled while Rome burned), the emperor seized about three-quarters of the burned-out historic core (more than 200 acres) to create in just 4 years one of the most sumptuous palaces in history. Subsequent emperors destroyed much of the golden palace, but what remains is now on view.

The area that is the Colosseum today was a central ornamental lake reflecting the glitter of the Golden House. At the entrance Nero installed a 150-foot statue of himself in the nude. In the words of Suetonius, "all parts of it were overlaid with gold and adorned with jewels and mother-of-pearl." During the Renaissance, painters such as Raphael chopped holes in the long-buried ceilings to gain admittance and were inspired by the frescoes and small "grotesques" of cornucopia and cherubs. The word *grotto* comes from this palace because the palace is believed to have been built underground. Remnants of these almost-2,000-year-old frescoes and fragments of mosaics remain. Out of the original 250 rooms, 30 are now open to the public. Some of the sculptures that survived are also on view.

Practical matters: To visit the Domus Aurea, you must make a reservation at Centro Servizi per l'Archeologia, Via Amendola 2 (Metro: Colosseo; open Mon–Sat 9am–1pm and 2–5pm). But it's easier to book your visit before you leave home through Select Italy (ℂ **847/853-1661** in the U.S.; www.selectitaly.com). Or, once you're in Rome, call ℂ **06-397-499-07,** where a recorded message in both Italian and English will guide you through the reservation process. Usually you must call at least a week ahead of the date you've scheduled your visit. The guided tours, both with a guide or with audio-guides, last about 1 hour from 9am to 7pm. Visitors enter in groups of no more than 25, with gaps of 15 minutes between groups.

Of particular interest are the Hall of Hector and Andromache (*Sala di Ettore e Andromaca*), once illustrated with scenes from Homer's *Iliad;* the Hall of Achilles (*Sala di Achille*), with a gigantic shell decoration; the Hall of Ninfeo (*Sala di Ninfeo*), which once had a waterfall; and the Hall of the Gilded Vault (*Sala della Volta Dorata*), depicting satyrs raping nymphs, plus Cupid driving a chariot pulled by panthers. You'll be amazed by the beauty of the floral frescoes along the *cryptoportici* (long corridors); the longest is about 200 feet. The most spectacular sight is the Octagonal Hall, Nero's banqueting hall, where the menu included casseroles of flamingo tongues and other rare dishes.

When Nero moved in, he shouted, "At last I can start living like a human being!"

Via della Domus Aurea. ℂ **06-397-499-07.** Admission 12,000L (6.25€, $6). Daily 9am–7:45pm. Last admission 1 hour before closing. Metro: Colosseo.

Tips No More Lines

The endless lines outside Italian museums and attractions are a fact of life. But new reservation services can help you avoid the wait, at least for some of the major museums.

Select Italy offers the possibility to reserve your tickets for the Colosseum, the Palatine Forum & Museum, Palazzo Altemps, the Domus Aurea, the Galleria Borghese, and more, plus many other museums in Florence and Venice. The cost varies from $15 to $24, depending on the museum, and several combination passes are available. Contact Select Italy at (© 847/853-1661), or buy your tickets online at **www.selectitaly.com**.

Roman Forum (Foro Romano), Palatine Hill (Palatino), and Palatine Museum (Museo Palatino) ⭐⭐⭐   When it came to cremating Caesar, purchasing a harlot for the night, or sacrificing a naked victim, the Roman Forum was the place to be. Traversed by the **Via Sacra (Sacred Way)** ⭐, the Broadway of ancient Rome, the Forum was built in the marshy land between the Palatine and Capitoline hills, and flourished as the center of Roman life in the days of the Republic, before it gradually lost prestige to the Imperial Forums.

You'll see only ruins and fragments, an arch or two, and lots of overturned boulders, but with some imagination you can feel the rush of history here. That any semblance of the Forum remains today is miraculous because it was used for years (like the Colosseum) as a quarry. Eventually it reverted to what the Italians call a *campo vaccino* (cow pasture). But excavations in the 19th century began to bring to light one of the world's most historic spots.

By day, the columns of now-vanished temples and the stones from which long-forgotten orators spoke are mere shells. Bits of grass and weeds grow where a triumphant Caesar was once lionized. But at night, when the Forum is silent in the moonlight, it isn't difficult to imagine vestal virgins still guarding the sacred temple fire. (The maidens were assigned to keep the temple's sacred fire burning but to keep their own passions under control. Failure to do the latter sent them to an early grave—alive!) The best view of the Roman Forum at night is from Campidoglio or Capitoline Hill, Michelangelo's piazza from the Renaissance, that overlooks the Forum.

You can spend at least a morning wandering alone through the ruins of the Forum. If you're content with just looking at the ruins, you can do so at your leisure. But if you want the stones to have some meaning, buy a detailed plan at the gate (the temples are hard to locate otherwise).

Turn right at the bottom of the entrance slope to walk west along the old Via Sacra toward the arch. Just before it on your right is the large brick **Curia** ⭐⭐ built by Julius Caesar, the main seat of the Roman Senate (pop inside to see the 3rd-century marble inlay floor).

The triumphal **Arch of Septimius Severus** ⭐⭐ (A.D. 203) displays timebitten reliefs of the emperor's victories in what are today Iran and Iraq. During the Middle Ages, Rome became a provincial backwater, and frequent flooding of the nearby river helped to rapidly bury most of the Forum. This former center of the empire became a cow pasture. Some bits did still stick out above ground, including the top half of this arch, which was used to shelter a barbershop! It wasn't until the 19th century that people really became interested in excavating these ancient ruins to see what Rome in its glory must have been like.

Just to the left of the arch, you can make out the remains of a cylindrical lump of rock with some marble steps curving off it. That round stone was the **Umbilicus Urbus,** considered the center of Rome and of the entire Roman empire; and the curving steps are those of the **Imperial Rostra** 🏛, where great orators and legislators stood to speak and the people gathered to listen. Nearby, the much-photographed trio of fluted columns with Corinthian capitals supporting a bit of architrave form the corner of the **Temple of Vespasian and Titus** 🏛🏛 (emperors were routinely turned into gods upon dying).

Start heading to your left toward the eight Ionic columns marking the front of the **Temple of Saturn** 🏛🏛 (rebuilt 42 B.C.), which housed the first treasury of Republican Rome. It was also the site of one of the Roman year's biggest annual blowout festivals, the December 17 feast of *Saturnalia,* which, after a bit of tweaking, we now celebrate as Christmas. Now turn left to start heading back east, past the worn steps and stumps of brick pillars outlining the enormous **Basilica Julia** 🏛🏛, built by Julius Caesar. Past it are the three Corinthian columns of the **Temple of the Dioscuri** 🏛🏛🏛, dedicated to the Gemini twins, Castor and Pollux. Forming one of the most celebrated sights of the Roman Forum, a trio of columns supports an architrave fragment. The founding of this temple dates from the 5th century B.C.

Beyond the bit of curving wall that marks the site of the little round **Temple of Vesta** (rebuilt several times after fires started by the sacred flame housed within), you'll find the partially reconstructed **House of the Vestal Virgins** 🏛🏛 (A.D. 3rd–4th c.) against the south side of the grounds. This was the home of the consecrated young women who tended the sacred flame in the Temple of Vesta. Vestals were young girls chosen from patrician families to serve a 30-year-long priesthood. During their tenure, they were among Rome's most venerated citizens, with unique powers such as the ability to pardon condemned criminals. The cult was quite serious about the "virgin" part of the job description—if any of Vesta's earthly servants were found to have "misplaced" their virginity, the miscreant Vestal was summarily buried alive. (Her amorous accomplice was merely flogged to death.) The overgrown rectangle of their gardens has lilied goldfish ponds and is lined with broken, heavily worn statues of senior Vestals on pedestals (and, at any given time when the guards aren't looking, two to six tourists are posing as Vestal Virgins on the empty pedestals).

The path dovetails back to join Via Sacra at the entrance. Turn right and then left to enter the massive brick remains and coffered ceilings of the 4th-century **Basilica of Constantine and Maxentius** 🏛🏛. These were Rome's public law courts, and their architectural style was adopted by early Christians for their houses of worship (the reason so many ancient churches are called "basilicas").

Return to the path and continue toward the Colosseum, veering right to the second great surviving triumphal arch, the **Arch of Titus** 🏛🏛 (A.D. 81), on which one relief depicts the carrying off of treasures from Jerusalem's temple—look closely and you'll see a menorah among the booty. The war that this arch glorifies ended with the expulsion of Jews from the colonized Judea, signaling the beginning of the Jewish Diaspora throughout Europe. From here you can enter and climb the only part of the Forum's archaeological zone that still charges admission, the **Palatine Hill** 🏛 (with the same hours as the Forum).

The Palatine, tradition tells us, was the spot on which the first settlers built their huts, under the direction of Romulus. In later years, the hill became a patrician residential district that attracted such citizens as Cicero. In time, however, the area was gobbled up by imperial palaces and drew a famous and infamous roster of tenants, such as Livia (some of the frescoes in the House of Livia are in miraculous condition), Tiberius, Caligula (he was murdered here by members of his Praetorian Guard), Nero, and Domitian.

Only the ruins of its former grandeur remain today, and you really need to be an archaeologist to make sense of them because they're more difficult to understand than those in the Forum. But even if you're not interested in the past, it's worth the climb for the panoramic view of both the Roman and the Imperial Forums, as well as the Capitoline Hill and the Colosseum.

/ **Tips Before & After**

To appreciate the Colosseum, the Roman Forum, and other ruins more fully, buy a copy of the small red book called *Rome Past and Present* (Vision Publications), sold in bookstores or by vendors near the Forum. Its plastic overleafs show you the elaborate way things were 2,000 years ago.

In 1998, the **Palatine Museum (Museo Palatino)** ✪ here finally reopened, displaying a good collection of Roman sculpture from the ongoing digs in the Palatine villas. In summer you can take guided tours in English from Monday to Sunday at noon for 6,000L (3.10€, $3); call in winter to see if they're still available. If you ask the museum's custodian, he might take you to one of the nearby locked villas and let you in for a peek at surviving frescoes and stuccoes. The entire Palatine is slated for renewed excavations, so many areas might be roped off at first, but soon even more will be open to the public.

Via dei Fori Imperiali. ℂ **06-699-0110.** Forum free admission; Palatine Hill 12,000L (6.25€, $6). Apr–Sept daily 9am–8pm; Oct–Mar daily 9am–sunset. Last admission 1 hour before closing. Closed holidays. Metro: Colosseo. Bus: 27, 81, 85, 87, or 186.

Imperial Forums (Fori Imperiali) ✪✪   It was Mussolini who issued the controversial orders to cut through centuries of debris and junky buildings to carve out Via dei Fori Imperiali, thereby linking the Colosseum to the grand 19th-century monuments of Piazza Venezia. Excavations under his fascist regime began at once, and many archaeological treasures were revealed.

Begun by Julius Caesar as an answer to the overcrowding of Rome's older forums, the Imperial Forums were, at the time of their construction, flashier, bolder, and more impressive than the buildings in the Roman Forum. This site conveyed the unquestioned authority of the emperors at the height of their absolute power. On the street's north side, you'll come to a large outdoor restaurant, where Via Cavour joins the boulevard. Just beyond the small park across Via Cavour are the remains of the **Forum of Nerva,** built by the emperor whose 2-year reign (A.D. 96–98) followed that of the paranoid Domitian. You'll be struck by just how much the ground level has risen in 19 centuries. The only really recognizable remnant is a wall of the Temple of Minerva with two fine Corinthian columns. This forum was once flanked by that of Vespasian, which is now gone. It's possible to enter the Forum of Nerva from the other side, but you can see it just as well from the railing.

The next forum you approach is the **Forum of Augustus** ✪✪, built before the birth of Christ to commemorate the emperor's victory over the assassins Cassius and Brutus in the Battle of Philippi (42 B.C.). Like the Forum of Nerva, you can enter this forum from the other side (cut across the wee footbridge).

Continuing along the railing, you'll see the vast semicircle of **Trajan's Market** ★★, Via Quattro Novembre 94 (© **06-679-0048**), whose teeming arcades stocked with merchandise from the far corners of the Roman world collapsed long ago, leaving only a few cats to watch after things. The shops once covered a multitude of levels, and you can still wander around many of them. In front of the perfectly proportioned facade (designed by Apollodorus of Damascus at the beginning of the 2nd century) are the remains of a great library, and fragments of delicately colored marble floors still shine in the sun between stretches of rubble and tall grass. Trajan's Market is worth the descent below street level. To get there, follow the service road you're on until you reach the monumental Trajan's Column on your left; turn right and go up the steep flight of stairs leading to Via Nazionale. At the top, about half a block farther on the right, you'll see the entrance. It's open from Tuesday to Sunday 9am to 4:30pm. Admission is 4,000L (2.10€, $2).

Before you head down through the labyrinthine passages, you might like to climb the **Tower of the Milizie** ★, a 12th-century structure that was part of the medieval headquarters of the Knights of Rhodes. The view from the top (if it's open) is well worth the climb.

You can enter the **Forum of Trajan** ★★ on Via Quattro Novembre near the steps of Via Magnanapoli. Once through the tunnel, you'll emerge into the newest and most beautiful of the Imperial Forums, built between A.D. 107 and 113, and designed by Greek architect Apollodorus of Damascus (who laid out the adjoining market). There are many statue fragments and pedestals bearing still-legible inscriptions, but more interesting is the great Basilica Ulpia, whose gray marble columns rise roofless into the sky. This forum was once regarded as one of the architectural wonders of the world.

Beyond the Basilica Ulpia is **Trajan's Column** ★★★, in magnificent condition, with intricate bas-relief sculpture depicting Trajan's victorious campaign (though, from your vantage point, you'll be able to see only the earliest stages). The next stop is the **Forum of Julius Caesar** ★★, the first of the Imperial Forums. It lies on the opposite side of Via dei Fori Imperiali. This was the site of the Roman stock exchange, as well as the Temple of Venus.

After you've seen the wonders of ancient Rome, you might continue up Via dei Fori Imperiali to **Piazza Venezia** ★★, where the white Brescian marble **Vittorio Emanuele Monument** dominates the scene. (You can't miss it.) Italy's most flamboyant landmark, it was built in the late 1800s to honor the first king of Italy. It has been compared to everything from a frosty wedding cake to a Victorian typewriter and has been ridiculed because of its harsh white color in a city of honey-gold tones. An eternal flame burns at the Tomb of the Unknown Soldier. The interior of the monument has been closed for many years, but you'll come to use it as a landmark as you figure your way around the city.

Via de Fori Imperiali. Free admission. Metro: Colosseo. Keep to the right side of the street.

Circus Maximus (Circo Massimo)   The Circus Maximus, with its elongated oval proportions and ruined tiers of benches, still evokes the setting for *Ben-Hur* on the late show. Today a formless ruin, the once-grand circus was pilfered repeatedly by medieval and Renaissance builders in search of marble and stone. At one time, 250,000 Romans could assemble on the marble seats while the emperor observed the games from his box high on the Palatine Hill. What the

Romans called a "circus" was a large arena enclosed by tiers of seats on three or four sides, used especially for sports or spectacles.

The circus lies in a valley formed by the Palatine on the left and the Aventine on the right. Next to the Colosseum, it was the most impressive structure in ancient Rome, located certainly in one of the most exclusive neighborhoods. For centuries, the pomp and ceremony of imperial chariot races filled this valley with the cheers of thousands.

When the dark days of the 5th and 6th centuries fell, the Circus Maximus seemed a symbol of the complete ruination of Rome. The last games were held in A.D. 549 on the orders of Totila the Goth, who had seized Rome in 547 and established himself as emperor. He lived in the still-glittering ruins on the Palatine and apparently thought the chariot races in the Circus Maximus would lend credibility to his charade of an Empire. It must've been a pretty miserable show because the decimated population numbered something like 500 when Totila recaptured the city. The Romans of these times were caught between Belisarius, the imperial general from Constantinople, and Totila the Goth, both of whom fought bloodily for control of Rome. After the travesty of 549, the Circus Maximus was never used again, and the demand for building materials reduced it, like so much of Rome, to a great dusty field.

Between Via dei Cerchi and Via del Circo Massimo. Metro: Circo Massimo.

Capitoline Museum (Museo Capitolino) and Palazzo dei Conservatori ★★

Of Rome's seven hills, the Capitoline (Campidoglio) is the most sacred—its origins stretch way back into antiquity (an Etruscan temple to Jupiter once stood on this spot). The approach is dramatic as you climb the long, sloping steps by Michelangelo. At the top is a perfectly proportioned square, **Piazza del Campidoglio** ★★, also laid out by the Florentine artist. Michelangelo positioned the bronze equestrian statue of Marcus Aurelius in the center, but it has now been moved inside for protection from pollution (a copy was placed on the pedestal in 1997). The other steps adjoining Michelangelo's approach will take you to Santa Maria d'Aracoeli (see "Other Attractions Near Ancient Rome," below).

One side of the piazza is open; the others are bounded by the **Senatorium (Town Council),** the statuary-filled **Palace of the Conservatori (Curators),** and the **Capitoline Museum.** These museums house some of the greatest pieces of classical sculpture in the world.

The **Capitoline Museum,** built in the 17th century, was based on an architectural sketch by Michelangelo. In the first room is *The Dying Gaul* ★★, a work of majestic skill that's a copy of a Greek original dating from the 3rd century B.C. In a special gallery all her own is the *Capitoline Venus* ★★, who demurely covers herself. This statue was the symbol of feminine beauty and charm down through the centuries (also a Roman copy of a 3rd-c. B.C. Greek original). *Amore* (Cupid) and *Psyche* are up to their old tricks near the window.

The famous **equestrian statue of Marcus Aurelius** ★★, whose years in the piazza made it a victim of pollution, has recently been restored and is now kept in the museum for protection. This is the only bronze equestrian statue to have survived from ancient Rome, mainly because it was thought for centuries that the statue was that of Constantine the Great, and papal Rome respected the memory of the first Christian emperor. It's beautiful, although the perspective is rather odd. The statue is housed in a glassed-in room on the street level, the Cortile di Marforio; it's a kind of Renaissance greenhouse, surrounded by windows.

(**Moments**   A View to Remember a Lifetime

Standing on Piazza del Campidoglio, walk around the right side of the Palazzo Senatorio to a terrace overlooking the city's best panorama of the Roman Forum, with the Palatine Hill and the Colosseum as a backdrop. At night, the Forum is dramatically flood-lit and the ruins look even more impressive and haunting.

Palace of the Conservatori ★★, across the way, was also based on a Michelangelo architectural plan and is rich in classical sculpture and paintings. One of the most notable bronzes, a Greek work of incomparable beauty dating from the 1st century B.C., is *Lo Spinario* ★★★ (a little boy picking a thorn from his foot). In addition, you'll find *Lupa Capitolina (Capitoline Wolf)* ★★★, a rare Etruscan bronze that could date from the 5th century B.C. (Romulus and Remus, the legendary twins who were suckled by the wolf, were added at a later date.) The palace also contains a *Pinacoteca* (Picture Gallery)—mostly works from the 16th and 17th centuries. Notable canvases are Caravaggio's *Fortune-Teller* and his curious *John the Baptist; The Holy Family,* by Dosso Dossi; *Romulus and Remus,* by Rubens; and Titian's *Baptism of Christ.* The entrance courtyard is lined with the remains (head, hands, a foot, and a kneecap) of an ancient colossal statue of Constantine the Great.

Piazza del Campidoglio. ℂ **06-6710-2071.** Admission (to both) 12,000L (6.25€, $6). Free on last Sun of each month. Tues–Sun 9am–7pm. Bus: 44, 89, 92, 94, or 716.

Baths of Caracalla (Terme di Caracalla) ★   Named for the emperor Caracalla, the baths were completed in the early 3rd century. The richness of decoration has faded, and the lushness can be judged only from the shell of brick ruins that remain. In their heyday, they sprawled across 27 acres and could handle 1,600 bathers at one time. A circular room, the ruined caldarium for very hot baths, had been the traditional setting for operatic performances in Rome, until it was discovered that the ancient structure was being severely damaged.

Via delle Terme di Caracalla 52. ℂ **06-575-8626.** Admission 8,000L (4.15€, $4). Oct–Jan daily 9am–4:30pm; Jan 16–Feb 15 daily 9am–5pm; Feb 16–Mar 15 daily 9am–5:30pm; Mar 16–31 daily 9am–5:30pm; Apr–Sept daily 9am–7:30pm. Last admission 1 hour before closing. Closed holidays. Bus: 628.

OTHER ATTRACTIONS NEAR ANCIENT ROME

Basilica di San Clemente ★   From the Colosseum, head up Via San Giovanni in Laterano to this basilica. It isn't just another Roman church—far from it. In this church-upon-a-church, centuries of history peel away. In the 4th century A.D., a church was built over a secular house from the 1st century, beside which stood a pagan temple dedicated to Mithras (god of the sun). Down in the eerie grottoes (which you can explore on your own), you'll discover well-preserved frescoes from the 9th to the 11th century. The Normans destroyed the lower church, and a new one was built in the 12th century. Its chief attraction is the bronze-orange mosaic (from that period) adorning the apse, as well as a chapel honoring St. Catherine of Alexandria with frescoes by Masolino.

Via San Giovanni in Laterano at Piazza San Clemente, Via Labicana 95. ℂ **06-7045-1018.** Basilica free admission; excavations 4,000L (2.10€, $2). Mon–Sat 9am–12:30pm and 3–6pm; Sun 10am–12:30pm and 3–6pm. Metro: Colosseo. Bus: 85, 87, or 810.

Basilica di San Giovanni in Laterano ✿   This church (not St. Peter's) is the cathedral of the diocese of Rome, where the pope comes to celebrate mass on certain holidays. Built in A.D. 314 by Constantine, it has suffered the vicissitudes of Rome, forcing it to be rebuilt many times. Only fragmented parts of the baptistry remain from the original.

The present building is characterized by its 18th-century facade by Alessandro Galilei (statues of Christ and the Apostles ring the top). A 1993 terrorist bomb caused severe damage, especially to the facade. Borromini gets the credit (some say blame) for the interior, built for Innocent X. It's said that, in the misguided attempt to redecorate, frescoes by Giotto were destroyed (remains believed to have been painted by Giotto were discovered in 1952 and are now on display against a column near the entrance on the right inner pier). In addition, look for the unusual ceiling and the sumptuous transept, and explore the 13th-century cloisters with twisted double columns. Next door, **Palazzo Laterano** (not open to the public) was the original home of the popes before they became voluntary "Babylonian captives" in Avignon, France, in 1309.

Across the street is the **Santuario della Scala Santa (Palace of the Holy Steps),** Piazza San Giovanni in Laterano (✆ **06-7049-4619**). It's alleged that the 28 marble steps here (now covered with wood for preservation) were originally at Pontius Pilate's villa in Jerusalem and that Christ climbed them the day he was brought before Pilate. According to a medieval tradition, the steps were brought from Jerusalem to Rome by Constantine's mother, Helen, in 326, and they've been in this location since 1589. Today pilgrims from all over the world come here to climb the steps on their knees. This is one of the holiest sites in Christendom, although some historians say the stairs might date only to the 4th century.

Piazza San Giovanni in Laterano 4. ✆ **06-6988-6433.** Basilica free admission; cloisters 4,000L (2.10€, $2). Summer daily 7am–6:45pm (off-season to 6pm). Metro: San Giovanni. Bus: 4, 16, 30, 85, 87, or 174.

National Museum in Palazzo Venezia (Museo Nazionale di Palazzo Venezia) ✿   The Palazzo Venezia, in the geographic heart of Rome near Piazza Venezia, served as the seat of the Austrian Embassy until the end of World War I. During the Fascist regime (1928–43), it was the seat of the Italian government. The balcony from which Mussolini used to speak to the people was built in the 15th century. You can now visit the rooms and halls containing oil paintings, porcelain, tapestries, ivories, and ceramics. No one particular exhibit stands out—it's the sum total that adds up to a major attraction. The State Rooms occasionally open to host temporary exhibits.

Via del Plebiscito 118. ✆ **06-679-8865.** Admission 8,000L (4.15€, $4). Tues–Sun 8:30am–7:30pm. Bus: 40, 60, 64, or 70.

San Pietro in Vincoli (St. Peter in Chains) ✿   This church, which has undergone recent renovations, was founded in the 5th century to house the chains that bound St. Peter in Palestine (they're preserved under glass). But the drawing card is the tomb of Pope Julius II, with one of the world's most famous sculptures: **Michelangelo's** *Moses* ✿✿✿. Michelangelo was to have carved 44 magnificent figures for the tomb. That didn't happen, of course, but the pope was given a great consolation prize—a figure intended to be "minor" that's now numbered among Michelangelo's masterpieces. In the *Lives of the Artists,* Vasari wrote about the stern father symbol of Michelangelo's *Moses:* "No modern work will ever equal it in beauty, no, nor ancient either."

Fun Fact **Did You Know?**

- Along with miles of headless statues and acres of paintings, Rome has 913 churches.
- Some Mongol khans and Turkish chieftains pushed westward to conquer the Roman empire after it had ceased to exist.
- At the time of Julius Caesar and Augustus, Rome's population reached one million—it was the largest city in the Western world. Some historians claim that by the year A.D. 500 only 10,000 inhabitants were left.
- Pope Leo III sneaked up on Charlemagne and set an imperial crown on his head, a surprise coronation that launched a precedent of Holy Roman Emperors being crowned by popes in Rome.
- More than 90% of Romans live in apartment buildings, some of which rise 10 floors and have no elevators.
- The bronze of Marcus Aurelius in the Capitoline Museums, one of the world's greatest equestrian statues, escaped being melted down because the early Christians thought it was of Constantine.
- The Theater of Marcellus incorporated a gory realism in some of its stage plays: Condemned prisoners were often butchered before audiences as part of the plot.
- Christians may not have been fed to the lions at the Colosseum, but in 1 day 5,000 animals were slaughtered (about one every 10 seconds). North Africa's native lions and elephants were rendered extinct.

Piazza San Pietro in Vincoli 4A (off Via degli Annibaldi). ✆ **06-488-2865.** Free admission. Spring/summer daily 7am–12:30pm and 3:30–7pm (autumn/winter to 6pm). Metro: V. Cavour, then cross the boulevard and walk up the flight of stairs. Turn right, and you'll head into the piazza; the church will be on your left.

Santa Maria d'Aracoeli ⭐   On the Capitoline Hill, this landmark church was built for the Franciscans in the 13th century. According to legend, Augustus once ordered a temple erected on this spot, where a sibyl, with her gift of prophecy, forecast the coming of Christ. In the interior are a coffered Renaissance ceiling and a mosaic of the Virgin over the altar in the Byzantine style. If you're enough of a sleuth, you'll find a tombstone carved by the great Renaissance sculptor Donatello. The church is known for its **Bufalini Chapel,** a masterpiece by Pinturicchio, who frescoed it with scenes illustrating the life and death of St. Bernardino of Siena. He also depicted St. Francis receiving the stigmata. These frescoes are a high point in early Renaissance Roman painting. You have to climb a long flight of steep steps to reach the church, unless you're already on neighboring Piazza del Campidoglio, in which case you can cross the piazza and climb the steps on the far side of the Museo Capitolino (see above).

Piazza d'Aracoeli. ✆ **06-679-8155.** Free admission. Daily 6:30am–5pm. Bus: 44, 46, or 75.

Santa Maria in Cosmedin   This little church was begun in the 6th century but was subsequently rebuilt, and a Romanesque campanile was added at the end of the 11th century, although its origins go back to the 3rd century. The church was destroyed several times by earthquakes or by foreign invasions, but it has always been rebuilt.

People come not for great art treasures, but to see the **"Mouth of Truth,"** a large disk under the portico. As Gregory Peck demonstrated to Audrey Hepburn in the film *Roman Holiday,* the mouth is supposed to chomp down on the hands of liars who insert their paws. (According to local legend, a former priest used to keep a scorpion in back to bite the fingers of anyone he felt was lying.) The purpose of this disk (which is not of particular artistic interest) is unclear. One hypothesis says that it was used to collect the faithful's donations to God, which were introduced through the open mouth.

Piazza della Bocca della Verià 18. ℂ **06-678-1419.** Free admission. Summer daily 9am–7pm; winter daily 9am–5pm. Metro: Circo Massimo.

3 The Pantheon & Attractions Near Piazza Navona & Campo de' Fiori

THE PANTHEON & NEARBY ATTRACTIONS

The Pantheon stands on **Piazza della Rotonda,** a lively square with cafes, vendors, and great people-watching.

The Pantheon ⭐⭐⭐ Of all ancient Rome's great buildings, only the Pantheon ("All the Gods") remains intact. It was built in 27 B.C. by Marcus Agrippa and was reconstructed by Hadrian in the early 2nd century A.D. This remarkable building, 142 feet wide and 142 feet high (a perfect sphere resting in a cylinder) and once ringed with white marble statues of Roman gods in its niches, is among the architectural wonders of the world because of its dome and its concept of space. Hadrian himself is credited with the basic plan, an architectural design that was unique for the time. The once-gilded dome is merely show. A real dome, a perfect hemisphere of cast concrete, rests on a solid ring wall, supporting this massive structure. Before the 20th century, this was the biggest pile of concrete ever constructed. The ribbed dome outside is a series of almost weightless cantilevered brick. Animals were sacrificed and burned in the center, and the smoke escaped through the only means of light, the oculus, an opening at the top 18 feet in diameter. Michelangelo came here to study the dome before designing the cupola of St. Peter's (whose dome is 2 ft. smaller than the Pantheon's). The walls are 25 feet thick, and the bronze doors leading into the building weigh 20 tons each. About 125 years ago, Raphael's tomb was discovered here (fans still bring him flowers). Vittorio Emanuele II, king of Italy, and his successor, Umberto I, are interred here as well.

Piazza della Rotonda. ℂ **06-6830-0230.** Free admission. Mon–Sat 8:30am–7:30pm; Sun 9am–6pm. Bus: 46, 62, 64,170, or 492 to Largo di Torre.

Galleria Doria Pamphilj ⭐ This museum offers a look at what it was like to live in an 18th-century palace. It has been restored to its former splendor and expanded to include four rooms long closed to the public. It's partly leased to tenants (on the upper levels), and there are shops on the street level—but you'll overlook all this after entering the grand apartments of the Doria Pamphilj family, which traces its lineage to before the great 15th-century Genoese admiral Andrea Doria. The apartments surround the central court and gallery. The **ballroom, drawing rooms, dining rooms,** and **family chapel** are full of gilded furniture, crystal chandeliers, Renaissance tapestries, and family portraits. The **Green Room** is especially rich, with a 15th-century Tournay tapestry, paintings by Memling and Filippo Lippi, and a seminude portrait of Andrea Doria by

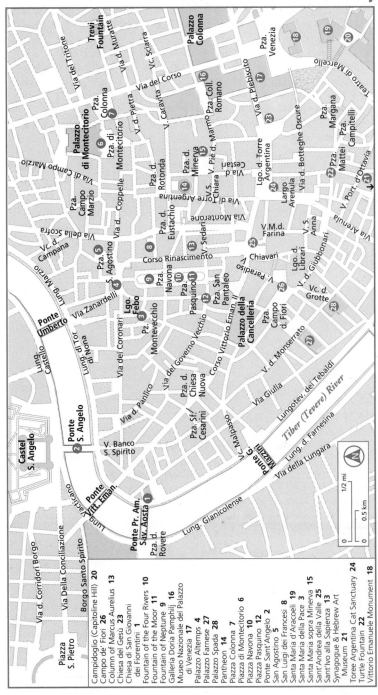

Sebastiano del Piombo. The **Andrea Doria Room,** dedicated to the admiral and to the ship of the same name, contains a glass case with mementos of the great 1950s maritime disaster.

Skirting the central court is a **picture gallery** with a memorable collection of frescoes, paintings, and sculpture. Most important are the portrait of Innocent X, by Velázquez; *Salome,* by Titian; works by Rubens and Caravaggio; the *Bay of Naples,* by Pieter Brueghel the Elder; and a copy of Raphael's portrait of Principessa Giovanna d'Aragona de Colonna (who looks remarkably like Leonardo's *Mona Lisa*). Most of the sculpture came from the Doria country estates: marble busts of Roman emperors, bucolic nymphs, and satyrs.

Piazza del Collegio Romano 2 (off Via del Corso). ℂ 06-679-7323. Admission 14,000L (7.30€, $7) adults, 11,000L (5.70€, $5.50) students/seniors. Fri–Wed 10am–5pm. Private visits can be arranged. Metro: Barberini.

Santa Maria Sopra Minerva   Beginning in 1280, early Christian leaders ordained that the foundation of an ancient temple dedicated to Minerva (goddess of wisdom) be reused as the base for Rome's only Gothic church. Architectural changes and redecorations in the 1500s and 1900s stripped it of some of its magnificence, but it still includes an awe-inspiring collection of medieval and Renaissance tombs. You'll find a beautiful chapel frescoed by Fillipino Lippi and, to the left of the apse, a muscular *Risen Christ* carrying a rather small marble cross carved by Michelangelo (the bronze drapery covering Christ's nudity was added later). Under the altar lie the remains of St. Catherine of Siena. After St. Catherine died, her head was separated from her body, and now the head is in Siena, where she was born. In the passage to the left of the choir, surrounded by a small fence, is the floor tomb of the great monastic painter Fra Angelico. The amusing baby elephant carrying a small obelisk in the piazza outside was designed by Bernini.

Piazza della Minerva 42. ℂ 06-679-3926. Free admission. Daily 7am–noon and 4–7pm. Bus: 64 or 119.

PIAZZA NAVONA & NEARBY ATTRACTIONS

Piazza Navona 👁👁👁, one of the most beautifully baroque sites in all Rome, is an ocher-colored gem, unspoiled by new buildings or traffic. Its shape results from the ruins of the Stadium of Domitian, lying underneath. Great chariot races were once held here (some rather unusual, such as the one in which the head of the winning horse was lopped off as it crossed the finish line and was

---

Moments **Where Emperors Ruled & Cats Now Reign**

At the site where Julius Caesar is believed to have been stabbed to death, right in the heart of historic Rome, you can visit and say "hi" to the city's vast feline population at the **Toree Argentia Cat Sanctuary,** at Largo di Torre Argentina (ℂ **06-687-2133**), at the intersection of via Arenula and via Florida, right off Corso Vittorio Emanuele, a short walk from the Pantheon and Piazza Navona. Where four Republican-era temples dating from 200 to 300 B.C. once stood, some 300 abandoned house cats are cared for by a group of volunteers. Cats in all shapes and sizes are everywhere, craving human attention. Some of them find homes with visitors from around the world. You can visit at any time during the day. The cats will be waiting.

ALPS   ASPEN

AT&T Direct® Service

The easy way to call home from anywhere.

Global | **AT&T**
connection | direct
with the AT&T | service
Network |

For the easy way to call home, take the attached wallet guide.

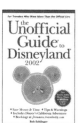
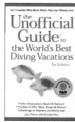
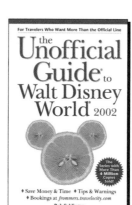

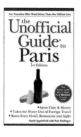
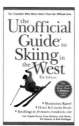

then carried by runners to be offered as a ͟/͟ ͟e by the Vestal Virgins atop the Capitoline). In medieval times, the po͟r ͟ ͟ ͟ ͟ᴜ to flood the piazza to stage mock naval encounters. Today the piazza ͟ ͟ ͟ᴄked with vendors and street performers, and lined with pricey cafes w͟ḥ̲e̲r̲e̲ you can enjoy a cappuccino or gelato and indulge in unparalleled people-watching.

Besides the twin-towered facade of 17th-century Santa Agnes, the piazza boasts several baroque masterpieces. The best known, in the center, is Bernini's **Fountain of the Four Rivers (Fontana dei Quattro Fiumi)** ⍟⍟⍟, whose four stone personifications symbolize the world's greatest rivers: the Ganges, Danube, della Plata, and Nile. It's fun to try to figure out which is which. (*Hint:* The figure with the shroud on its head is the Nile, so represented because the river's source was unknown at the time.) At the south end is the **Fountain of the Moor (Fontana del Moro),** also by Bernini. The **Fountain of Neptune (Fontana di Nettuno),** which balances that of the Moor, is a 19th-century addition; it was restored after a demented 1997 attack by two men who broke off the tail of one of its sea creatures.

Palazzo Altemps ⍟   This branch of the National Roman Museum is housed in a 15th-century palace that was restored and opened to the public in 1997. It is home to the fabled Ludovisi Collection of Greek and Roman sculpture. Among the masterpieces of the Roman Renaissance, you'll find the *Ares Ludovisi,* a Roman copy of the original dated 330 B.C. and restored by Bernini during the 17th century. In the *Sala delle Storie di Mosè* is *Ludovisi's Throne,* representing the birth of Venus. The *Sala delle Feste* (the Celebrations' Hall) is dominated by a sarcophagus depicting the Romans fighting against the Ostrogoth Barbarians; this masterpiece, carved from a single block, dates back to the 2nd century A.D. and nowadays is called *Grande Ludovisi* (Great Ludovisi). Other outstanding art from the collection includes a copy of Phidias's celebrated *Athena,* which once stood in the Parthenon in Athens. (The Roman copy here is from the 1st century B.C. because the original *Athena* is lost to history.) The huge *Dionysus with Satyr* is from the 2nd century A.D.

Piazza San Apollinare 44, near the Piazza Navona. ✆ **06-683-3759.** Admission 10,000L (5.20€, $5). Tues–Sun 9am–7pm. Closed Monday. Last admission one hour before closing. Bus: 70, 81, 87, or 492.

San Luigi dei Francesi   This has been the national church of France in Rome since 1589, and a stone salamander (the symbol of the Renaissance French monarch François I) was subtly carved into its facade. Inside, in the last chapel on the left, is a noteworthy series of oil paintings on canvas by Caravaggio: the celebrated *Calling of St. Matthew* on the left, *St. Matthew and the Angel* in the center, and the *Martyrdom of St. Matthew* on the right.

Via Santa Giovanna d'Arco 5. ✆ **06-688271.** Free admission. Fri–Wed 8am–12:30pm and 3:30–7pm; Thurs 8am–12:30pm. Bus: 70, 81, or 87.

Santa Maria della Pace   According to legend, blood flowed from a statue of the Virgin above the altar here after someone threw a pebble at it. This legend motivated Pope Sixtus to rebuild the church in the 1500s on the foundations of an even older sanctuary. For generations after that, its curved porticos, cupola atop an octagonal base, cloisters by Bramante, and frescoes by Raphael helped make it one of the most fashionable churches for aristocrats residing in the surrounding palazzos.

Vicolo del Arco della Pace 5 (off Piazza Navona). ✆ **06-6861156.** Free admission. Mon–Fri 10am–4pm; Tues–Thurs 9am–noon.

913 Churches, 1 Synagogue: Jews in the Capital of Christendom

Nestled midway between the Isola Tiberina and the monument to Vittorio Emanuele II, Rome's Jewish ghetto was designated during the administration of Pope Paul IV between 1555 and 1559. At the time, it enclosed several thousand people into a cramped, 2½-acre tract of walled-in, overcrowded real estate that did much to contribute to the oppression of the Jews during the Italian Renaissance.

Jews had played an important part in the life of Rome prior to that time. They migrated to the political center of the known world during the 1st century B.C., and within 200 years their community had grown to a very noticeable minority. Most of it was based in Trastevere, a neighborhood that for many years was referred to as the *Contrada Iudaeorum* (Jewish Quarter). By 1309 ordinances were passed that forced Jews to illustrate their religious and cultural backgrounds with special garments, and their ability to worship as they wished depended on the indulgence of the pope.

In 1363 additional ordinances were passed that limited Jewish cemeteries to an area adjacent to the Tiber, near the present-day Church of San Francesco a Ripa. During the 1400s the Jewish population regrouped onto the opposite side of the Tiber, in an area around the square that's known today as Piazza Mattei.

In 1492 Queen Isabella and King Ferdinand of Spain killed, tortured, forcibly converted, or forced the emigration of thousands of Jews from Spain. Many came to Rome, swelling the ranks of the city. Pope Alexander VI (1492–1503), whose political sympathies lay firmly with the Spanish monarchs, grudgingly admitted the refugees into his city, on condition that each pay a hefty fee in gold. His papal bull, *Cum nimis absurdium,* defined the borders of the Jewish ghetto within the boundaries of the Sant'Angelo district and later enlarged them to include the muddy, frequently flooded banks of the Tiber. Water levels often

CAMPO DE' FIORI & THE JEWISH GHETTO

During the 1500s, **Campo de' Fiori** ✿ was the geographic and cultural center of secular Rome, site of dozens of inns. From its center rises a statue of the severe-looking monk Giordano Bruno, whose presence is a reminder that religious heretics were occasionally burned at the stake here. Today, circled by venerable houses, the campo is the site of an **open-air food market** held from Monday to Saturday from early in the morning until around noon (or whenever the food runs out).

Built from 1514 to 1589, the **Palazzo Farnese** ✿, on Piazza Farnese, was designed by Sangallo and Michelangelo, among others, and was an astronomically expensive project for the time. Its famous residents have included a 16th-century member of the Farnese family, plus Pope Paul III, Cardinal Richelieu, and the former Queen Christina of Sweden, who moved to Rome after abdicating. During the 1630s, when the heirs couldn't afford to maintain the palazzo, it became the site of the French Embassy, as it still is (it's closed to reached the third floors of the houses of the poorest families, who were forced, by law and economics, to settle here. Piling humiliation on humiliation, the residents of the nearly uninhabitable riverbanks were forced to pay for the construction of the embankments that prevented the neighborhood from flooding. For centuries, no one could enter or leave the ghetto between sundown and sunrise.

In 1848 the walls that had defined and confined the ghetto were demolished under the auspices of the relatively lenient Pope Leo XII. In 1883, during the surge of nationalism that preceded the unification of Italy, the ghetto was abolished altogether.

Tragically, on October 16, 1943, the segregation of Rome's Jews was reestablished when German Nazi soldiers rounded up most of the Jews from throughout Rome into a re-creation of the medieval ghetto and imposed a flabbergastingly high ransom on them. Amazingly, this fee—more than 100 pounds of gold per resident—was eventually collected. Despite having made the payment, the Jews were rounded up and deported to the death camps anyway, one of the most horrible episodes of Italy's participation in the war years.

Today the neighborhood, centered around Piazza Mattei and its elegant Renaissance fountain, lacks any coherent architectural unity; it's a colorful hodgepodge of narrow, twisting streets and sometimes derelict buildings. One of the most unusual streets is Via del Portico d'Ottavia, where medieval houses and pavements adjoin kosher food stores and simple trattorie that almost invariably feature *carciofi alla Giudeai* (deep-fried Jerusalem artichokes).

Although it bears the scars and honors of centuries of occupation by Jews, today this is a Jewish neighborhood mostly in name only. Its centerpiece is the synagogue on Via Catalana.

the public). For the best view of it, cut west from Via Giulia along any of the narrow streets (we recommend Via Mascherone or Via dei Farnesi).

Palazzo Spada ⊕, Capo di Ferro 3 (© **06-686-1158**), built around 1550 for Cardinal Gerolamo Capo di Ferro and later inhabited by the descendants of several other cardinals, was sold to the Italian government in the 1920s. Its richly ornate facade, covered in high-relief stucco decorations in the Mannerist style, is the finest of any building from 16th-century Rome. The State Rooms are closed, but the richly decorated courtyard and a handful of galleries of paintings are open. Admission is 4,000L (2.10€, $2) from Tuesday to Saturday from 9am to 7pm, and Sunday from 9am to 1pm. To get there, take bus no. 44, 56, 60, 65, 75, 170, or 710.

Also in this neighborhood stands the **Sinagoga Romana** (© **06-6840-061**), open only for services. Trying to avoid all resemblance to a Christian church, the building (1874–1904) evokes Babylonian and Persian details. The synagogue was attacked by terrorists in 1982 and since then has been heavily guarded by *carabinieri* (a division of the Italian army) armed with machine guns. It houses the **Jewish Museum** (© 06-6840-061), open Monday to Thursday 9am to 4:30pm, Friday 9am to 1:30pm, and Sunday 9am to noon. Admission is 10,000L (5.20€, $5). Many rare and even priceless treasures are here, including a Moroccan prayer book from the early 14th century and ceremonial objects from the 17th-century Jewish Ghetto.

4 The Spanish Steps, the Trevi Fountain & Attractions Nearby

ON OR AROUND PIAZZA DI SPAGNA

The **Spanish Steps** ★★ (Scalinata di Spagna; Metro: Spagna) are filled in spring with azaleas and other flowers, flower vendors, jewelry dealers, and photographers snapping pictures of visitors. The steps and the square (Piazza di Spagna) take their names from the Spanish Embassy, which used to be headquartered here. Designed by Italian architect Francesco de Sanctis and built from 1723 to 1725, they were funded almost entirely by the French as a preface to Trinità dei Monti at the top.

The steps and the piazza below are always packed with a crowd: strolling, reading in the sun, browsing the vendors' carts, and people-watching. Near the steps, you'll also find an American Express office, public restrooms (near the Metro stop), and the most sumptuous McDonald's we've ever seen (cause for uproar among the Romans when it first opened).

Keats–Shelley House   At the foot of the Spanish Steps is this 18th-century house where John Keats died of consumption on February 23, 1821, at age 25. Since 1909, when it was bought by well-intentioned English and American literary types, it has been a working library established in honor of Keats and Percy Bysshe Shelley, who drowned off the coast of Viareggio with a copy of Keats in his pocket. Mementos range from the kitsch to the immortal. The apartment where Keats spent his last months, carefully tended by his close friend Joseph Severn, shelters a strange death mask of Keats as well as the "deadly sweat" drawing by Severn.

Piazza di Spagna 26. © 06-678-4235. Admission 5,000L (2.60€, $2.50). Mon–Fri 9am–1pm and 3–6pm; Sat 11am–2pm and 3–6pm. Guided tours by appointment. Metro: Spagna.

Palazzo del Quirinale ★★   Until the end of World War II, this palace was the home of the king of Italy; before that, it was the residence of the pope. Despite its Renaissance origins (nearly every important architect in Italy worked on some aspect of its sprawling premises), it's rich in associations with ancient emperors and deities. The colossal statues of the dioscuri Castor and Pollux, which now form part of the fountain in the piazza, were found in the nearby great Baths of Constantine; in 1793 Pius VI had the ancient Egyptian obelisk moved here from the Mausoleum of Augustus. The sweeping view of Rome from the piazza, which crowns the highest of the seven ancient hills of Rome, is itself worth the trip.

Piazza del Quirinale. Free admission (but a passport or similar ID is required for entrance). Sun 9am–1pm. Metro: Barberini.

Trevi Fountain (Fontana dei Trevi) ★★   As you elbow your way through the summertime crowds around the Trevi Fountain, you'll find it hard to believe that this little piazza was nearly always deserted before the film *Three Coins in the Fountain* brought the stampede of tour buses. Today this newly restored gem is a must on everybody's itinerary.

Attractions Near the Spanish Steps & Piazza del Popolo

American Express
  Office **12**

Ara Pacis
  (Altar of Peace) **9**

Campidoglio
  (Capitoline Hill) **24**

Cimitero Monumentale
  dei Padri Cappucini
  (Capuchin Crypt) **13**

Fountain of the Bees
  (Fontana dei Api) **15**

Fountain of the Triton
  (Fontana del Tritone) **14**

Galleria Nazionale
  d'Arte Antica **2**

Galleria Borghese **3**

Keats-Shelley
  Memorial House **12**

Pantheon **19**

Piazza Barberini **15**

Piazza Colonna
  (Marcus Aurelius
  Column) **18**

Piazza del Popolo **7**

Piazza del Quirinale **17**

Pincio Gardens **5**

Mausoleo Augusteo
  (Augustus's
  Mausoleum) **8**

Museo Nazionale della
  Villa Giuila
  (Etruscan Museum) **1**

Museo Nazionale del
  Palazzo di Venezia **21**

Roman Forum
  (Foro Romano) **25**

Santa Maria d'Aracoeli **23**

Santa Maria del Popolo **6**

Santa Maria sopra
  Minerva **20**

Spanish Steps
  (Scalinata di Trinita
  dei Monti) **11**

Trevi Fountain
  (Fontana di Trevi) **16**

Via dei Condotti **10**

Villa Borghese Park **4**

Vittorio Emanuele
  Monument **22**

Metro **—Ⓜ—**
Post Office ✉

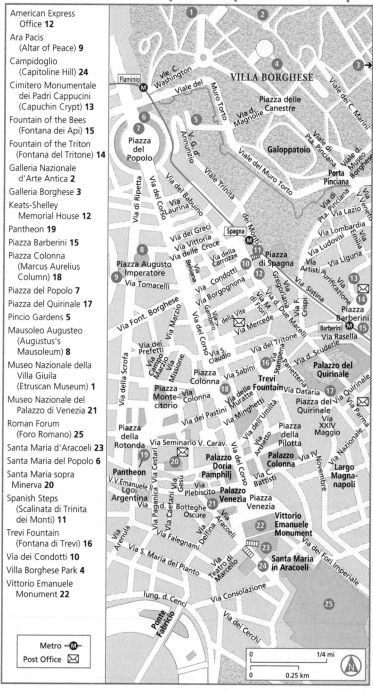

0   1/4 mi
0   0.25 km

(*Finds* **Great Art in the Stables**

Across from the Palazzo del Quirinale, the 18th-century Quirinal stables called the **Scuderie del Quirinale or Scuderie Papali,** via XXIV Maggio 16 (© **06-696-270**), originally built for the pope's horses, have been transformed into an art gallery that hosts changing exhibitions. Check to see what's on. Recent exhibits have ranged from 100 masterpieces on loan from the Hermitage to Botticelli's drawings illustrating Dante's *Divine Comedy.* The stables were built on the site of the 3rd-century Temple of Serapis (some of the ruins can still be seen from the glass-enclosed stairs overlooking a private garden). The galleries are open daily from 10am to 8pm; admission fees vary depending on the exhibit.

Supplied by water from the Acqua Vergine aqueduct and a triumph of the baroque style, it was based on the design of Nicolo Salvi (who's said to have died of illness contracted during his supervision of the project) and was completed in 1762. The design centers on the triumphant figure of Neptunus Rex, standing on a shell chariot drawn by winged steeds and led by a pair of tritons. Two allegorical figures in the side niches represent good health and fertility.

On the southwestern corner of the piazza is a somber, not particularly spectacular-looking church, **SS. Vincenzo e Anastasio,** with a strange claim to fame. Within it survive the hearts and intestines of several centuries of popes. According to legend, the church was built on the site of a spring that burst from the earth after the beheading of St. Paul; the spring is one of the *three* sites where his head is said to have bounced off the ground.

Piazza di Trevi. Metro: Barberini.

AROUND VIA VENETO & PIAZZA BARBERINI

Piazza Barberini lies at the foot of several Roman streets, among them Via Barberini, Via Sistina, and Via Vittorio Veneto. It would be a far more pleasant spot were it not for the heavy traffic swarming around its principal feature, Bernini's **Fountain of the Triton (Fontana del Tritone)** ☆. For more than 3 centuries, the strange figure sitting in a vast open clam has been blowing water from his triton. Off to one side of the piazza is the aristocratic side facade of the **Palazzo Barberini,** named for one of Rome's powerful families; inside is the **Galleria Nazionale d'Arte Antica** (see below). The Renaissance Barberini reached their peak when a son was elected pope as Urban VIII; he encouraged Bernini and gave him great patronage.

As you go up Via Vittorio Veneto, look for the small fountain on the right corner of Piazza Barberini—it's another Bernini, the small **Fountain of the Bees (Fontana delle Api).** At first they look more like flies, but they're the bees of the Barberini, the crest of that powerful family complete with the crossed keys of St. Peter above them (the keys were always added to a family crest when a son was elected pope).

To find these attractions, see the map titled "Attractions Near Stazione Termini, Via Veneto & Piazza Barberini" on p. 165.

National Gallery of Ancient Art (Galleria Nazionale d'Arte Antica) ☆☆
Palazzo Barberini, right off Piazza Barberini, is one of the most magnificent baroque palaces in Rome. It was begun by Carlo Maderno in 1627 and completed in 1633 by Bernini, whose lavishly decorated rococo apartments, the

Gallery of Decorative Art (Galleria d'Arte Decorativa), are on view. This gallery is part of the **National Gallery of Ancient Art.**

The bedroom of Princess Cornelia Costanza Barberini and Prince Giulio Cesare Colonna di Sciarra stands just as it was on their wedding night, and many household objects are displayed in the decorative art gallery. In the chambers, which boast frescoes and hand-painted silk linings, you can see porcelain from Japan and Bavaria, canopied beds, and a wooden baby carriage.

On the first floor is a splendid array of paintings from the 13th to the 16th century, most notably *Mother and Child,* by Simone Martini and works by Fillipino Lippi, Andrea Solario, and Francesco Francia. Il Sodoma has some brilliant pictures here, including *The Rape of the Sabines* and *The Marriage of St. Catherine.* One of the best-known paintings is Raphael's beloved *La Fornarina,* the baker's daughter who was his mistress and who posed for his Madonna portraits. Titian is represented by his *Venus and Adonis.* Also here are Tintorettos and El Grecos. Many visitors come just to see the magnificent Caravaggios, including *Narcissus.*

Via Barberini 18. ✆ **06-481-4430.** Admission 12,000L (6.25€, $6). Tues–Sun 9am–7pm. Metro: Barberini.

Monumental Cemetery of the Capuchin Brothers (Cimitero Monumentale dei Padri Cappuccini) One of the most horrifying sights in all Christendom, this is a series of chapels with hundreds of skulls and crossbones woven into mosaic "works of art." To make this allegorical dance of death, the bones of more than 4,000 Capuchin brothers were used. Some of the skeletons are intact, draped with Franciscan habits. The creator of this chamber of horrors? The tradition of the friars is that it was the work of a French Capuchin. Their literature suggests that you should visit the cemetery while keeping in mind the historical moment of its origins, when Christians had a rich and creative cult for their dead and great spiritual masters meditated and preached with a skull in hand. Those who've lived through the days of crematoriums and other such massacres might view the graveyard differently, but to many who pause to think, this sight has a message. It's not for the squeamish, however. The entrance is halfway up the first staircase on the right of the church.

Beside the Church of the Immaculate Conception, Via Vittorio Veneto 27. ✆ **06-487-1185.** Donation required. Daily 9am–noon and 3–6pm. Metro: Barberini.

NEAR PIAZZA DEL POPOLO

The newly restored **Piazza del Popolo** ★★ is haunted with memories. According to legend, the ashes of Nero were enshrined here, until 11th-century residents began complaining to the pope about his imperial ghost. The **Egyptian obelisk**

Tips **Seeing the Sights at Night**

Some of Rome's most popular monuments, archaeological sites, and museums have begun not only staying open until 8 or 10pm during summer but also engaging in **Art and Monuments Under the Stars.** For these special summer schedules, they reopen one or more nights from around 8:30 to 11:30pm. The offering includes guided tours (often in English), concerts, or simply general admission to sights for night owls, with tours of some ancient areas usually closed to the public, like the Tomb of Augustus and the Stadium of Domitian (under Piazza Navona). Keep your eyes peeled in the events guides from mid-June to September.

dates from the 13th century B.C., removed from Heliopolis to Rome during Augustus's reign (it stood at the Circus Maximus). The piazza was designed in the early 19th century by Valadier, Napoléon's architect. The lovely **Santa Maria del Popolo** 🏛🏛, with two Caravaggios, is at its northern curve, and opposite are almost-twin baroque churches, overseeing the never-ending traffic.

Altar of Peace (Ara Pacis) 🏛 In an airy glass-and-concrete building beside the eastern banks of the Tiber rests a reconstructed treasure from the reign of Augustus. It was built by the Senate as a tribute to that emperor and the peace he had brought to the Roman world. On the marble wall, you can see portraits of the imperial family—Augustus, Livia (his second wife), Tiberius (Livia's son from her first marriage and Augustus's successor), and even Julia (Augustus's unfortunate daughter, who divorced her first husband to marry Tiberius and then was exiled by her father for her sexual excesses). The altar was reconstructed from literally hundreds of fragments scattered in museums for centuries. A major portion came from the foundations of a Renaissance palace on the Corso. The reconstruction (quite an archaeological adventure story in itself) took place during the 1930s.

Lungotevere Augusta 🕓 **06-3600-3471.** Admission 3,750L (1.95€, $1.90). Tues–Sat 9am–7pm; Sun 9am–1pm. Bus: 70,81,186, or 628.

Augustus's Mausoleum (Mausoleo Augusteo) 🏛 This seemingly indestructible pile of bricks has been here for 2,000 years and will probably remain for another 2,000. Like the larger tomb of Hadrian across the river, this was once a circular marble-covered affair with tall cypresses, symmetrical groupings of Egyptian obelisks, and some of Europe's most spectacular ornamentation. Many of the 1st-century emperors had their ashes deposited in golden urns inside, and it was probably because of this crowding that Hadrian decided to construct an entirely new tomb (the Castel Sant'Angelo) for himself in another part of Rome. The imperial remains stayed intact here until the 5th century, when invading barbarians smashed the bronze gates and stole the golden urns, emptying the ashes on the ground outside. After periods when it functioned as a Renaissance fortress, a bullfighting ring, and a private garden, the tomb was restored in the 1930s by Mussolini, who might have envisioned it as a burial place for himself. You can't enter, but you can walk along the four streets encircling it.

Piazza Augusto Imperatore. Admission 5,000L (2.60€, $2.50). Bus: 81, 115, or 590. Metro: Spagna.

5 In the Villa Borghese

Villa Borghese 🏛🏛, in the heart of Rome, is 3½ miles (6km) in circumference. One of Europe's most elegant parks, it was created by Cardinal Scipione Borghese in the 1600s. Umberto I, king of Italy, acquired it in 1902 and presented it to the city of Rome. With lovely landscaped vistas, the greenbelt is crisscrossed by roads, but you can escape from the traffic and seek a shaded area under a pine or oak tree to enjoy a picnic or simply relax. On a sunny weekend afternoon, it's a pleasure to stroll here and see Romans at play, relaxing or in-line skating. There are a few casual cafes and some food vendors throughout; you can also rent bikes here. In the northeast of the park is a small zoo; the park is also home to a few outstanding museums.

Galleria Borghese 🏛🏛🏛 This legendary art gallery shut its doors in 1984 and appeared to have closed forever. However, in early 1997, after a complete restoration, it returned in all its fabulous glory.

This treasure trove includes such masterpieces as Bernini's *Apollo and Daphne*, Titian's *Sacred and Profane Love*, Raphael's *Deposition*, and Caravaggio's *Jerome*. The collection began with the gallery's founder, Scipione Borghese, who, by the time of his death in 1633, had accumulated some of the greatest art of all time, even managing to acquire Bernini's early sculptures. Some paintings were spirited out of Vatican museums and even confiscated when their rightful owners were hauled off to prison until they became "reasonable" about turning over their art. The great collection suffered at the hands of Napoléon's notorious sister, Pauline, who married Prince Camillo Borghese in 1807 and sold most of the ancient collection (many works are now in the Louvre in Paris). One of the most popular pieces of sculpture in today's gallery, ironically, is Canova's life-size sculpture of Pauline in the pose of *Venus Victorious*. (When Pauline was asked whether she felt uncomfortable posing in the nude, she replied, "Why should I? The studio was heated.")

Important information: No more than 300 visitors at a time are allowed on the ground floor, and no more than 90 are allowed on the upper floor. Reservations are essential, so call ℂ **06-328-101** (Mon–Fri 9am–6pm). However, the number always seems to be busy. If you'll be in Rome for a few days, try stopping by in person on your first day to reserve tickets for a later day. Better yet, before you leave home, contact **Select Italy** (ℂ **847/853-1661;** www.selectitaly.com).

Piazza Scipione Borghese 5 (off Via Pinciano). ℂ **06-841-7645** for information. Admission 14,000L (7.30€, $7). Nov–Apr Tues–Sun 9am–7pm; May–Oct Tues–Sun 9am–7pm. Bus: 56 or 910.

National Etruscan Museum (Museo Nazionale di Villa Giulia) ★★★

This 16th-century papal palace shelters a priceless collection of art and artifacts from the mysterious Etruscans, who predated the Romans. Known for their sophisticated art and design, they left a legacy of sarcophagi, bronze sculptures, terra-cotta vases, and jewelry, among other items. If you have time for only the masterpieces, head for room 7, with a remarkable 6th-century B.C. *Apollo from Veio* (clothed, for a change). The other two widely acclaimed statues here are *Dea con Bambino* (*Goddess with a Baby*) and a greatly mutilated but still powerful *Hercules* with a stag. In room 8, you'll see the lions' sarcophagus from the mid–6th century B.C., which was excavated at Cerveteri, north of Rome.

Finally, one of the world's most important Etruscan art treasures is the bride and bridegroom coffin from the 6th century B.C., also dug out of the tombs of Cerveteri (in room 9). Near the end of your tour, another masterpiece of Etruscan art awaits you in room 33: the Cista Ficoroni, a bronze urn with paw feet, mounted by three figures, dating from the 4th century B.C.

Piazzale di Villa Giulia 9. ℂ **06-320-1951.** Admission 8,000L (4.15€, $4). Tues–Sun 8:30am–7:15pm. Metro: Flaminio.

National Gallery of Modern Art (Galleria Nazionale d'Arte Moderna) ★

This gallery of modern art is a short walk from the Etruscan Museum (see above). With its neoclassic and Romantic paintings and sculpture, it makes a dramatic change from the glories of the Renaissance and ancient Rome. Its 75 rooms also house the largest collection in Italy of 19th- and 20th-century works by Balla, Boccioni, De Chirico, Morandi, Manzù, Burri, Capogrossi, and Fontana. Look for Modigliani's *La Signora dal Collaretto* and large *Nudo*. There are also many works of Italian optical and pop art and a good representation of foreign artists, including Degas, Cézanne, Monet, and van Gogh. Surrealism and expressionism are well represented by Klee, Ernst, Braque, Mirò, Kandinsky, Mondrian, and Pollock. You'll also find sculpture by Rodin. Several other important sculptures, including one by Canova, are on display in the museum's gardens. You can see the collection of graphics, the storage rooms, and the Department of Restoration by appointment from Tuesday to Friday.

Viale delle Belle Arti 131. ℂ **06-322-981**. Admission 12,000L (6.25€, $6). Tues–Sun 8:30am–7:20pm. Bus: 56 or 910.

6 The Appian Way & the Catacombs

Of all the roads that led to Rome, **Via Appia Antica** (built in 312 B.C.) was the most famous. It eventually stretched all the way from Rome to the seaport of Brindisi, through which trade with the colonies in Greece and the East was funneled. (According to Christian tradition, it was along the Appian Way that an escaping Peter encountered the vision of Christ, causing him to go back into the city to face subsequent martyrdom.) The road's initial stretch in Rome is lined with the great monuments and ancient tombs of patrician Roman families— burials were forbidden within the city walls as early as the 5th century B.C.— and, beneath the surface, miles of tunnels hewn out of the soft tufa stone.

These tunnels, or catacombs, were where early Christians buried their dead and, during the worst times of persecution, held church services discreetly out of the public eye. A few of them are open to the public, so you can wander through mile after mile of musty-smelling tunnels whose soft walls are gouged out with tens of thousands of burial niches (long shelves made for two to three bodies each). In some dank, dark grottoes (never stray too far from your party or one of the exposed light bulbs), you can still discover the remains of early Christian art. The requisite guided tours, hosted by priests and monks, feature a smidgen of extremely biased history and a large helping of sermonizing.

The Appia Antica has been a popular Sunday lunch picnic site for Roman families (following the half-forgotten pagan tradition of dining in the presence of one's ancestors on holy days). This practice was rapidly dying out in the face of the traffic fumes that for the past few decades have choked the venerable road, but a 1990s initiative has closed the Via Appia Antica to cars on Sundays, bringing back the picnickers and bicyclists—along with in-line skaters and a new Sunday-only bus route to get out here.

You can take bus 218 from the San Giovanni Metro stop, which follows the Appia Antica for a bit and then veers right on Via Ardeatina at Domine Quo Vadis? Church. After another long block, the 218 stops at the square Largo M.F. Via d. Sette Chiese to the San Domitilla catacombs; or, walk left down Via d. Sette Chiese to the San Sebastiano catacombs.

An alternative is to ride the Metro to the Colli Albani stop and catch bus 660, which wraps up the Appia Antica from the south, veering off it at the San Sebastiano catacombs (if you're visiting all three, you can take bus 218 to the first two, walk to San Sebastiano, and then catch bus 660 back to the Metro). On Sundays the road is closed to traffic, but bus 760 trundles from the Circo Massimo Metro stop down the Via Appia Antica, turning around after it passes the Tomb of Cecila Metella.

Of the monuments on the Appian Way, the most impressive is the **Tomb of Cecilia Metella** ✿, within walking distance of the catacombs. The cylindrical tomb honors the wife of one of Julius Caesar's military commanders from the Republican era. Why such an elaborate tomb for such an unimportant person in history? Cecilia Metella happened to be singled out for enduring fame because her tomb has remained and the others have decayed.

Catacombs of St. Callixtus (Catacombe di San Callisto) ⭐⭐   "The most venerable and most renowned of Rome," said Pope John XXIII of these funerary tunnels. The founder of Christian archaeology, Giovanni Battista de Rossi (1822–94), called them "catacombs par excellence." These catacombs are often packed with tour-bus groups, and they have perhaps the most cheesy tour, but the tunnels are simply phenomenal. They're the first cemetery of the Christian community of Rome, burial place of 16 popes in the 3rd century. They bear the name of St. Callixtus, the deacon whom Pope St. Zephyrinus put in charge of them and who was later elected pope (A.D. 217–22) in his own right. The complex is a network of galleries stretching for nearly 12 miles (19km), structured in five levels and reaching a depth of about 65 feet. There are many sepulchral chambers and almost half a million tombs of early Christians. Paintings, sculptures, and epigraphs (with such symbols as the fish, anchor, and dove) provide invaluable material for the study of the life and customs of the ancient Christians and the story of their persecutions.

Entering the catacombs, you see at once the most important crypt, that of nine popes. Some of the original marble tablets of their tombs are still preserved. The next crypt is that of St. Cecilia, the patron of sacred music. This early Christian martyr received three ax strokes on her neck, the maximum allowed by Roman law, which failed to kill her outright. Farther on, you'll find the famous Cubicula of the Sacraments with its 3rd-century frescoes.

Via Appia Antica 170. ✆ **06-513-015-80.** Admission 8,000L (4.15€, $4) adults, 4,000L (2.130€, $2) children 6–15; free for children 5 and under. Apr–Oct Thurs–Tues 8:30am–noon and 2:30–5:30pm (to 5pm Nov–Mar). Bus: 118.

Catacombs of St. Sebastian (Catacombe di San Sebastiano) ⭐   Today the tomb of St. Sebastian is in the basilica, but his original resting place was in the catacombs underneath it. From the reign of Valerian to the reign of Constantine, the bodies of Sts. Peter and Paul were hidden in the catacombs, which were dug from tufa, a soft volcanic rock. The big church was built in the 4th century. The tunnels here, if stretched out, would reach a length of 7 miles (11km). In the tunnels and mausoleums are mosaics and graffiti, along with many other pagan and Christian objects from centuries even before the time of Constantine. The tour here is one of the shortest and least satisfying of all the catacomb visits.

Via Appia Antica 136. ✆ **06-785-0350.** Admission 8,000L (4.15€, $4) adults, 4,000L (2.10€, $2) children 6–15; free for children 5 and under. Mon–Sat 8:30am–noon and 2:30–5pm. Closed mid-Nov to mid-Dec.

Catacombs of St. Domitilla (Catacombe di San Domitilla) ⭐⭐⭐   This oldest of the catacombs is also the hands-down winner for most enjoyable catacomb experience. Groups are small, most guides are genuinely entertaining and personable, and, depending on the mood of the group and your guide, the visit may last anywhere from 20 minutes to over an hour. You enter through a sunken 4th-century church. There are fewer "sights" than in the other catacombs—although the 2nd-century fresco of the Last Supper is impressive—but some of the guides actually hand you a few bones out of a tomb niche. (Incidentally, this is the only catacomb where you'll still see bones; the rest have emptied their tombs to rebury the remains in ossuaries on the inaccessible lower levels.)

Via d. Sette Chiese 283. ✆ **06-511-0342.** Admission 8,000L (4.15€, $4) adults, 4,000L (2.10€, $2) children 6–14. Wed–Mon 8:30am–noon and 2:30–5pm. Closed Jan.

Finds Beneath It All: Touring Roma Sotteranea

Talk about the "underground," and a growing legion of Romans will excitedly take up the story, offering tidbits about where to go, who to talk to, what's been seen, and what's allegedly awaiting discovery around the next bend in the sewer. The sewer? That's right. **Roma Sotteranea (Subterranean Rome)** is neither a subway nor a trendy arts movement, but the vast historic ruins of a city that has been occupied for nearly 3,000 years, the first 2 millennia of which are now largely buried by natural sediment and artificial landfills. Archaeologists estimate that these processes have left the streets of ancient Rome as much as 20 yards beneath the surface.

Consider this: Each year, an inch of dust in the form of pollen, leaves, pollution, sand, and silt from disintegrating ruins settles over Rome. That silt has really taken a toll in its own right. Archaeologists estimate that the ruins of a one-story Roman house will produce debris 6 feet deep over its entire floor plan. When you multiply that by more than 40,000 apartment buildings, 1,800 palaces, and numerous giant public buildings, a real picture of the burial of the ancient city presents itself. You should also take note of the centuries-old Roman tradition of burying old buildings in landfills, which can raise the level of the earth up to several yards all at once. In fact, past builders have often filled up massive stone ruins with dirt or dug down through previous landfills to the columns and vaults of underlying structures, and then laid a foundation for a new layer of Roman architecture.

As a result, many buildings on the streets today actually provide direct access to Rome's inner world. Doorways lead down to hidden crypts and shrines—the existence of which are closely guarded secrets. Nondescript locked doors in churches and other public buildings often open on whole blocks of the ancient city, streets still intact. For example, take **San Clemente,** the 12th-century basilica east of the Colosseum, where a staircase in the sacristy leads down to the original 4th-century church. Not only that, but a staircase near the apse goes down to an earlier Roman apartment building and temple, which in turn leads down to a giant public building dating back to the Great Fire (A.D. **64**). Another interesting doorway to the past is in the south exterior wall of **St. Peter's,** leading down to an intact necropolis. That crumbling brick entry in the gardens on the east side of Esquiline Hill carries you into the vast **Domus Aurea (Golden House),** Nero's residence, built on the ruins left by the Great Fire.

Don't expect a road map of this subterranean world; it's a meandering labyrinth beneath the streets. A guided tour can be useful, especially those focusing on Roman excavations and anything to do with church crypts. Several tour companies now offer selected subterranean views, lasting 90 to 120 minutes and costing 25,000L to 50,000L (13€–26€, $12.50–$25). The best are provided by **Itinera** (© 06-278-00785) and **LUPA** (© 06-574-1974), both run by trained archaeologists. **Città Nascosta** (© 06-321-6059; www.nascosta.cjb.net) offers offbeat tours to less-visited churches and monuments, and advertises the week's schedule via a recorded phone announcement that changes every week.

7 More Attractions
AROUND STAZIONE TERMINI

Basilica di Santa Maria Maggiore 🏛   This great church, one of Rome's four major basilicas, was built by Pope Liberius in A.D. 358 and was rebuilt by Pope Sixtus III from 432 to 440. Its 14th-century **campanile** is the city's loftiest. Much doctored in the 18th century, the church's facade isn't an accurate reflection of the treasures inside. Restoration of the 1,600-year-old church is scheduled for completion in 2000. The basilica is especially noted for the 5th-century Roman mosaics in its nave, as well as for its coffered ceiling, said to have been gilded with gold brought from the New World. In the 16th century, Domenico Fontana built a now-restored "Sistine Chapel." In the following century, Flaminio Ponzo designed the **Pauline (Borghese) Chapel** in the baroque style. The church also contains the **tomb of Bernini,** Italy's most important baroque sculptor/architect. Ironically, the man who changed the face of Rome with his elaborate fountains is buried in a tomb so simple that it takes a sleuth to track it down (to the right near the altar).

Piazza di Santa Maria Maggiore. ✆ **06-488-1094.** Free admission. Daily 7am–7pm. Metro: Termini.

MUSEO NAZIONALE ROMANO
Originally, this museum occupied only the Diocletian Baths. Today it is divided into four different sections: Palazzo Massimo alle Terme; the Terme di Diocleziano (Diocletian Baths), with the annex Octagonal Hall; and Palazzo Altemps (which is near Piazza Navona; see p. 151 for a complete listing).

Palazzo Massimo alle Terme 🏛   If you'd like to go wandering in a virtual garden of classical statues, head for this palazzo, built from 1883 to 1887 and opened as a museum in 1998. Much of the art here, including the frescoes, stuccoes, and mosaics, was discovered in excavations in the 1800s but has never been put on display before.

If you ever wanted to know what all those emperors from your history books looked like, this museum will make them live again, togas and all. In the central hall are works representing the political and social life of Rome at the time of Augustus Caesar. Note the statue of the emperor with a toga covering his head, symbolizing his role as the head priest of state. Other works include an altar from Ostia Antica, the ancient port of Rome, plus a statue of a wounded Niobid from 440 B.C. that is a masterwork of expression and character. Upstairs, stand in awe at all the traditional art from the 1st century B.C. to the Imperial Age. The most celebrated mosaic is of the *Four Charioteers.* In the basement is a rare numismatic collection and an extensive collection of Roman jewelry.

Largo di Villa Peretti 67. ✆ **06-489-035-00.** Admission 12,000L (6.25€, $6); the same ticket will admit you to the Diocletian Baths. Tues–Sun 9am–8pm. Last admission 1 hour before closing. Metro: Termini.

Terme di Diocleziano (Diocletian Bath) and the Aula Ottagona (Octagonal Hall) 🏛   Near Piazza dei Cinquecento, which fronts the rail station, this museum occupies part of the 3rd-century A.D. Baths of Diocletian and part of a convent that may have been designed by Michelangelo. The Diocletian Baths were the biggest thermal baths in the world. Nowadays they host a marvelous collection of funereal art works, such as sarcophagi, and decorations dating back to the Aurelian period. The Baths also have a section reserved for temporary exhibitions.

The **Octagonal Hall** occupies the southwest corner of the central building of the Diocletian Baths. Here you can see the *Lyceum Apollo,* a copy of the 2nd-century A.D. work inspired by the Prassitele. Also worthy of a note is the *Aphrodite of Cyrene,* a copy dating back to the second half of the 2nd century A.D. and discovered in Cyrene, Libya.

Viale E. di Nicola 79. ℂ **06-488-0530.** Admission to the Baths 8,000L (4.15€, $4), Octagonal Hall free admission. The same ticket will admit you to Palazzo Massimo alle Terme. Tues–Sun 9am–6:45pm. Last admission 1 hour before closing. Metro: Termini.

IN THE TESTACCIO AREA, THE AVENTINE & SOUTH

Museo Centrale Di Monte Martini *(Finds*   Hike out to this old power plant if you want to see some of the finest sculptures in ancient Rome, including many items from the Capitoline Museum stockpile that haven't been displayed in Rome since Mussolini was in power. They're displayed against a backdrop of Industrial Age machinery that once supplied electricity to the area. The prize here is the Togato Barberini, a berobed aristocrat from Rome of 90 B.C. He carries two heads, the symbol of an old custom in Republican Rome when patricians maintained hollow wax portrait busts of their former ancestors. They brought these busts out for special celebrations. By carrying the head, they were signifying that they were the stand-in for their illustrious progenitors.

You'll find everything from a Greek Aphrodite from the 5th century B.C. to an endless array of marble busts and statues, many of which might have come from the area of the Imperial Forum. Many of the statues, especially those in the rooms upstairs, are superb Roman copies of Greek originals. The most stunning of these is a towering goddess statue from 100 B.C. that once graced the Temple of Fortuna in Largo di Teatro Argentina.

Via Ostiense 106. ℂ **06-574-8030.** Admission 8,000L (4.15€, $4) adults, free for ages 18 and under. Tues–Sun 10am–7pm. Bus: 23 or 702. Metro: Piramide o Garbatella.

Museo della Civiltà Romana (Museum of Roman Civilization)   Some 3½ miles south of the historic center of Rome is a more modern city conceived by the Fascist-era dictator, Mussolini. At the height of his power, he launched a complex of impersonal modern buildings, many of them in cold marble, to dazzle Europe with a scheduled world's fair in 1942 that never happened. Il Duce got strung up, and EUR—the neighborhood in question—got hamstrung. The new Italian government that followed inherited the unfinished project and turned it into a center of government and administration.

The most intriguing sight here is this Museum of Roman Civilization, in which are housed two fascinating scale models that reproduce Rome in two different epochs: the early Republican Rome, and the city in its imperial heyday in the 4th century A.D. You'll see the then impressive Circus Maximus, the intact Colosseum, the Baths of Diocletian—and lots more. You can also see examples of late Imperial and Paleochristian art, including more than a hundred casts of the reliefs that climb Trajan's Column in the Imperial Forum.

Piazza Giovanni Agnelli 10 (in EUR, south of the city center). ℂ **06-592-6041.** Admission 8,000L (4.15€, $4). Tues–Sat 9am–6:45pm, Sun 9am–1pm. Metro: EUR-Fermi.

Protestant Cemetery (Cimitero Prote Sante)   Near Porta San Paola, in the midst of cypress trees, lies the old cemetery where John Keats is buried. In a grave nearby, Joseph Severn, his "deathbed" companion, was interred beside him 6 decades later. Dejected and feeling his reputation as a poet diminished by the rising vehemence of his critics, Keats asked the following epitaph be written on

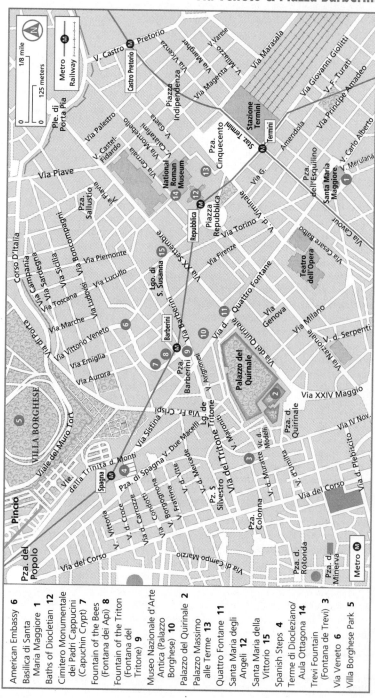

American Embassy **6**

Basilica di Santa
Maria Maggiore **1**

Baths of Diocletian **12**

Cimitero Monumentale
dei Padri Cappucini
(Capuchin Crypt) **7**

Fountain of the Bees
(Fontana dei Api) **8**

Fountain of the Triton
(Fontana del Tritone) **9**

Museo Nazionale d'Arte
Antica (Palazzo
Borghese) **10**

Palazzo del Quirinale **2**

Palazzo Massimo
alle Terme **13**

Quattro Fontane **11**

Santa Maria degli
Angeli **12**

Santa Maria della
Vittorio **15**

Spanish Steps **4**

Terme di Diocleziano/
Aula Ottagona **14**

Trevi Fountain
(Fontana de Trevi) **3**

Via Veneto **6**

Villa Borghese Park **5**

his tombstone: "Here lies one whose name was writ in water." A great romantic poet Keats certainly was, but a prophet, thankfully not. Percy Bysshe Shelley, author of *Prometheus Unbound,* drowned off the Italian Riviera in 1822, before his 30th birthday, and his ashes rest beside those of Edward John Trelawny, a fellow romantic.

Via Caio Cestio 6. (℃) **06-574-1900.** Free admission (but a 1,500L–2,000L [.75€–1€, $.80–$1.05] offering is customary). Apr–Sept Tues–Sun 9am–6pm (Oct–Mar to 4:30pm). Metro: Piramide. Bus: 23 or 27.

Pyramid of Caius Cestius ⋆   From the 1st century B.C., the Pyramid of Caius Cestius, about 120 feet high, looks as if it belongs to the Egyptian landscape. It was constructed during the "Cleopatra craze" in architecture that swept across Rome. You can't enter the pyramid, but it's a great photo op. And who was Caius Cestius? He was a rich magistrate in imperial Rome whose tomb is more impressive than his achievements. You can visit at any time.

Piazzale Ostiense. Metro: Piramide.

St. Paul Outside the Walls (Basilica di San Paolo Fuori le Mura) ⋆   The Basilica of St. Paul, whose origins go back to the time of Constantine, is Rome's fourth great patriarchal church; it's believed to have been erected over the tomb of St. Paul. The basilica fell victim to fire in 1823 and was subsequently rebuilt. It is the second-largest church in Rome after St. Peter's. From the inside, its windows may appear to be stained glass, but they're actually translucent alabaster. With its forest of single-file columns and mosaic medallions (portraits of the various popes), this is one of the most streamlined and elegantly decorated churches in Rome. Its most important treasure is a 12th-century candelabra by Vassalletto, who's also responsible for the remarkable cloisters, containing twisted pairs of columns enclosing a rose garden. Of particular interest is the *baldachino* (richly embroidered fabric of silk and gold, usually fixed or carried over an important person or sacred object) of Arnolf di Cambio, dated 1285, that miraculously wasn't damaged in the fire. The Benedictine monks and students sell a fine collection of souvenirs, rosaries, and bottles of Benedictine every day except Sunday and religious holidays.

Via Ostiense 184. (℃) **06-541-0341.** Free admission. Basilica daily 7am–6:30pm; cloisters daily 9am–1pm and 3–6pm. Metro: San Paolo Basilica.

Santa Sabina ⋆ *Finds*   A rarity, Santa Sabina is the best remaining example of a Paleochristian church, dating from 422 A.D., with its original wooden doors from that time still intact. The doors alone are worth the trek here. They are handsomely carved with Bible scenes, including one that depicts the Crucifixion, one of the earliest examples of this in the art of the Western world. You'll find it carved on a door at the end of a "porch" from the 1400s. The porch itself contains ancient sarcophagi.

   Santa Sabina was the site of the temple of Juno Regina, the patroness of Rome's Etruscan arch-rival, Veii, who was seduced into switching sides in 392 B.C. She was martyred to the Christian cause. In 1936 much of the church was restored to its original appearance, and today it is one of Rome's most beautiful churches. The surviving two dozen Corinthian columns may have come from the Temple of Juno. The windows of great delicacy were pieced together from 9th-century fragments. In the floor of the nave is Rome's only surviving mosaic, tomb, circa 1300.

Piazza Pietro d'Iliria. (℃) **06-574-3573.** Free admission. Daily 7:30am–12:30pm and 3:30–5:30pm. Bus: 81 or 160.

IN TRASTEVERE

Rome boasts many wonderful views, but one of the best spots for a memorable vista is the **Janiculum Hill (Gianicolo)** ✦✦, across the Tiber. It's not considered one of the "Seven Hills" of Rome, but it's certainly one of the most visited (and a stop on many bus tours). Not even included within the original city walls, the area was built by Urban VII for defensive purposes but today most of Gianicolo has been turned into parkland. We like to come here at dawn and watch the sun rise over Rome. Here you can also look at the Tempietto of Bramante, the most evocative work of the High Renaissance in Rome.

Legend has it that Gianicolo was the site of the city founded by the god Janus. One of his kids, Tiber, lent his name to the river of Rome. For the best view, position yourself at the open space in front of the church, San Pietro in Montorio, which was constructed at the end of the 1400s during the reign of Sixtus IV. There is no grander panorama of Rome than the one you'll see here, extending from Monte Mario. Later you can follow the Passeggiata del Gianicolo or Janiculum Walk, which winds along the crest of the hill.

If you don't want to walk up the hill, you can catch bus 41 from the Ponte Sant' Angelo. But we prefer to walk along the medieval Via Garibaldi reached from Via della Scale in Trastevere. You'll reach the summit of the hill in about 15 minutes of steady climbing.

Galleria Nazionale di Palazzo Corsini   After you've seen Italy's National Gallery of Art at the Palazzo Barberini, head to Trastevere to view the other half of the collection. This collection is installed in what was the 18th-century mansion of Pope Clemente XII (whose real name was Lorenzo Corsini, of the famous banking family). Before it was damaged by French attacks in 1849, the palace was once the grandest in Rome. Queen Christina died here in her bedroom (room 5) in 1689, and Napoléon's mother, Letizia, once lived here as well. The palace is still rich in neoclassical works of the Napoleonic era.

The gallery hosts a wide array of paintings from the 16th and 17th centuries, although they are bunched together and badly displayed. Nonetheless, this is an outstanding treasure trove of such European masters as Van Dyck, although Italian artists dominate. Seek out, in particular, Caravaggio's *St. John the Baptist,* and also a rendition of the same subject by Guido Reni who painted *Salome with the Head of St. John the Baptist.* Murillo's *Madonna and Bambino* is one of his less saccharine efforts, and some Rubens paintings are a bit overripe, notably a *St. Sebastian* and a *Madonna.* For sheer gore, Salvator Rosa tops them all with his version of *Prometheus.*

Via della Lungara 10. ✆ **06-6880-2323.** Admission 8,000L (€4, $4.15) adults, 4,000L (€2, $2.10) 17 and under. Tues–Sun 9am–7pm. Bus: 23 or 280.

Santa Cecilia in Trastevere ✦   A cloistered and still-functioning convent with a fine garden, Santa Cecilia contains *The Last Judgment,* by Pietro Cavallini (c. 1293), a masterpiece of Roman medieval painting. Another treasure is a late-13th-century baldachino by Arnolfo di Cambio over the altar. The church is built on the reputed site of Cecilia's long-ago palace, and for a small fee you can descend under the church to inspect the ruins of some Roman houses as well as peer through a gate at the stuccoed grotto beneath the altar.

Piazza Santa Cecilia 2. ✆ **06-589-9289.** Church free admission; Cavallini frescoes 3,000L (1.55€, $1.50); excavations 3,000L (1.55€, $1.50). Main church and excavations daily 8am–noon and 3–7pm; frescoes Tues and Thurs 10–11:30am, Sun 11:30am–noon. Bus: 44, 75, 170, or 181.

Attractions in Trastevere

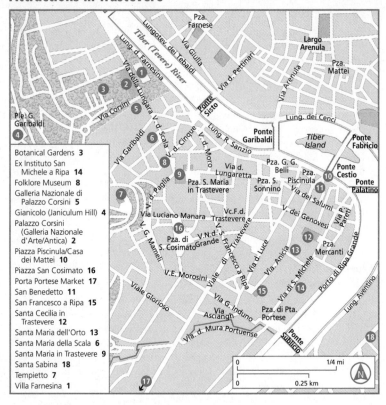

Botanical Gardens **3**
Ex Instituto San
  Michele a Ripa **14**
Folklore Museum **8**
Galleria Nazionale di
  Palazzo Corsini **5**
Gianicolo (Janiculum Hill) **4**
Palazzo Corsini
  (Galleria Nazionale
  d'Arte/Antica) **2**
Piazza Piscinula/Casa
  dei Mattei **10**
Piazza San Cosimato **16**
Porta Portese Market **17**
San Benedetto **11**
San Francesco a Ripa **15**
Santa Cecilia in
  Trastevere **12**
Santa Maria dell'Orto **13**
Santa Maria della Scala **6**
Santa Maria in Trastevere **9**
Santa Sabina **18**
Tempietto **7**
Villa Farnesina **1**

Santa Maria in Trastevere ✸ This Romanesque church at the colorful center of Trastevere was built around A.D. 350 and is one of the oldest in Rome. The body was added around 1100, and the portico was added in the early 1700s. The restored mosaics on the apse date from around 1140, and below them are the 1293 mosaic scenes depicting the life of Mary done by Pietro Cavallini. The faded mosaics on the facade are from the 12th or 13th century, and the octagonal fountain in the piazza is an ancient Roman original that was restored and added to in the 17th century by Carlo Fontana.

Piazza Santa Maria in Trastevere. ✆ **06-581-4802.** Free admission. Daily 7:30am–8pm. Bus: 44, 75, 170, or 181.

8 Organized Tours

Because of the sheer number of sights to see, some first-time visitors like to start out with an organized tour. While few things can really be covered in any depth on these overview tours, they're sometimes useful for getting your bearings.

One of the leading tour operators is **American Express,** Piazza di Spagna 38 (✆ **06-67641;** Metro: Spagna). One popular tour is a 4-hour orientation of Rome and the Vatican, which departs most mornings at 9:30am and costs 70,000L (36.40€, $35) per person. Another 4-hour tour, which focuses on the Rome of antiquity (including visits to the Colosseum, the Roman Forum, the ruins of the Imperial Palace, and San Pietro in Vincoli), costs 60,000L (31.20€, $30). From April to October, a popular excursion outside Rome is a 5-hour bus tour to Tivoli, where tours are conducted of the Villa d'Este and its spectacular gardens and the ruins of the Villa Adriana, all for 70,000L (36.40€ $35) per person.

Enjoy Rome, Via Varese 39 (© **06-445-18-43;** www.enjoyrome.com), makes the 1-day sprint from Rome to Pompeii as inexpensive and painless as possible with a daily tour from 8:30am to 5:30pm round-trip by air-conditioned minivan (seating eight passengers); it costs 75,000L (39€, $37.50). The trip is 3 hours one way, with an English-speaking driver. You're on your own once you reach the archaeological site, and there's no imposed restaurant lunch: That's what keeps their prices the lowest around.

Another option is **Scala Reale,** Via Varese 52 (© **888/467-1986** in the U.S., or 06-4470-0898), a cultural association founded by American architect Tom Rankin. He offers small-group tours and excursions focusing on the architectural and artistic significance of Rome. Tours include visits to monuments, museums, and piazzas, as well as to neighborhood trattorie. Custom-designed tours are available. Prices begin at 50,000L (26€, $25). Children 12 and under are admitted free to walking tours. Tour discounts are available for a group of four.

Walks of Rome, Via Urbana 38 (© **06-484-853**), features tours ranging from 1 to 5 hours. Some itineraries concentrate on major attractions, while other specialized tours take visitors to offbeat sights. Guides are young, native English speakers, usually art or history students, who know how to make the monuments come alive.

One of the most unusual tours of Rome, a first for visitors, was recently announced by **Passetto del Borgo** (© **06-390-80730**). Reserve in advance for these tours, conducted Saturday and Sunday at 3pm. You'll start inside the Castel Sant'Angelo and move toward the Passetto del Borgo, a covered walkway that joins the medieval castle to the Vatican. Built in the 13th century, and reconstructed at the end of the 15th century under Alexander VI, it was an escape route for the popes when threatened at their castle. When the murderous troops of Charles V arrived in 1527, Pope Clement VII ran for his life, his skirts flying in the wind. After a walk through the first 250 feet of the passageway, you reenter the open air and head for the Vatican, taking in a private glimpse of the life of Borgo dwellers along the way, complete with their hanging laundry and balconied herb gardens.

8

Strolling Through Rome

Rome is a great city for walking—be sure to allow yourself enough time to just wander and let yourself get lost. Those of you who want more guidance in your exploration may enjoy the walking tours we've designed in this chapter. Visitors with very limited time might want to concentrate on Walking Tour 1, "Rome of the Caesars," and Walking Tour 2, "The Heart of Rome." Those with more time can try out Walking Tour 3, "Renaissance Rome" and Walking Tour 4, "Trastevere." Many of the major sights along these routes, especially on Walking Tours 2 to 4, are covered fully in chapter 7. These tours serve both to string the sights together—for those who have limited time or want more structure—and they'll also reveal some lesser-known hidden gems along the way.

WALKING TOUR 1: ROME OF THE CAESARS

Start:	Via Sacra, in the Roman Forum.
Finish:	Circus Maximus.
Time:	5½ hours.
Best Times:	Any sunny day.
Worst Times:	After dark, or when the place is overrun with tour groups.

This tour takes in the most central of the monuments and ruins that attest to the military and architectural grandeur of ancient Rome. As a whole, they make up the most famous and evocative ruins in the world, despite such drawbacks as the roaring traffic that's the bane of the city's civic planners and a general dustiness and heat that might test even the hardiest amateur archaeologists.

After the collapse of Rome and during the Dark Ages, the forums and many of the other sites on this tour were lost to history, buried beneath layers of debris, their marble mined by medieval builders, until Benito Mussolini set out to restore the grandeur of Rome by reminding his compatriots of their glorious past.

THE ROMAN FORUM

The western entrance to the Roman Forum (there are two entrances) is at the corner of Via dei Fori Imperiali and Via Cavour, adjacent to Piazza Santa Maria Nova. The nearest Metro is the Colosseo stop. As you walk down into the Forum along a masonry ramp, you'll be heading for Via Sacra, the ancient Roman road that ran through the Forum connecting the Capitoline Hill, to your right, with the Arch of Titus (1st century A.D.), off to your left. The Roman Forum is the more dignified and more austere of the two forums you'll visit on this walking tour. Although it consists mostly of artfully evocative ruins scattered confusingly around a sun-baked terrain, it represents almost 1,000

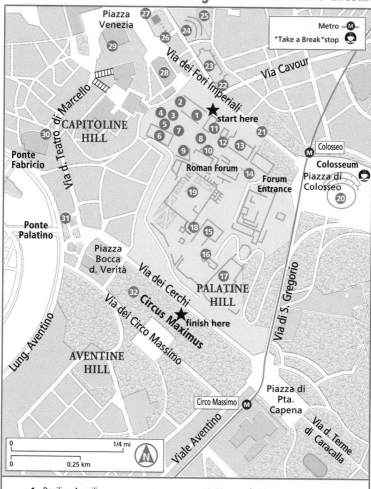

Metro — M
"Take a Break"stop Ⓢ

Piazza Venezia

Piazza Venezia

Via dei Fori Imperiali

Via Cavour

CAPITOLINE HILL

Via d. Teatro di Marcello

Ponte Fabricio

start here

Roman Forum

Forum Entrance

Colosseo

Colosseum

Piazza di Colosseo

Ponte Palatino

Piazza Bocca d. Verità

Via dei Cerchi

PALATINE HILL

Via di S. Gregorio

Circus Maximus

finish here

Via dei Circo Massimo

Lung. Aventino

AVENTINE HILL

Circo Massimo

Piazza di Pta. Capena

Viale Aventino

Via d. Terme di Caracalla

0   1/4 mi
0   0.25 km

N

1 Basilica Aemilia	**18** House of Livia
2 Curia	**19** Orti Farnesiani (Farnese Gardens)
3 Lapis Niger	**20** The Colosseum
4 Arch of Septimius Severus	Ⓢ Bar Martini
5 Rostra	**21** Via dei Fori Imperiali
6 Basilica Julia	**22** Forum of Nerva
7 Column of Phocas	**23** Forum of Augustus
8 Temple of Julius Caesar	**24** Trajan's Market
9 Temple of the Castors	**25** Tower of the Milizie
10 Temple of Vesta	**26** Forum of Trajan (Foro Traiano)
11 Temple of Antoninus and Faustina	**27** Trajan's Column
12 Temple of Romulus	**28** Forum of Julius Caesar
13 Basilica of Constantine	**29** Vittorio Emanuele Monument
14 Arch of Titus	**30** Teatro di Marcello
15 Flavian Palace	**31** Temple of Fortuna Virile
16 Domus Augustana	**32** Circus Maximus
17 Hippodrome	

years of Roman power during the severely disciplined period that preceded the legendary decadence of the later Roman emperors.

During the Middle Ages, when this was a cow pasture and all these stones were underground, there was a dual column of elm trees connecting the Arch of Titus with the Arch of Septimius Severus (A.D. 200), to your right.

Arriving at Via Sacra, turn right. The random columns on the right as you head toward the Arch of Septimius Severus belong to the:

❶ Basilica Aemilia

This was once the site of great meeting halls and shops, all maintained for centuries by the noble Roman family who gave it its name. At the corner nearest the Forum entrance are some traces of melted bronze decoration that was fused to the marble floor during a great fire set by invading Goths in A.D. 410.

The next important building is the:

❷ Curia, or Senate house

It's the large brick building on the right that still has its roof. Romans had been meeting on this site for centuries before the first structure was erected, and that was still centuries before Jesus. The present building is the fifth (if you count all the reconstructions and substantial rehabilitations) to stand on the site. Legend has it that the original building was constructed by an ancient king with the curious name of Tullus Hostilius. The tradition he began was noble indeed, and our present legislative system owes much to the Romans who met in this hall. Unfortunately, the high ideals and inviolate morals that characterized the early Republican senators gave way to the bootlicking of imperial times, when the Senate became little more than a rubber stamp. Caligula, who was only the third emperor, had his horse appointed to the Senate, which pretty much sums up the state of the Senate by the middle of the 1st century A.D.

The building was a church until 1937, when the fascist government tore out the baroque interior and revealed what we see today. The original floor of Egyptian marble and the tiers that held the seats of the senators have miraculously survived. In addition, at the far end of the great chamber we can see the stone on which rested the fabled golden statue of Victory. Originally installed by Augustus, it was disposed of in the 4th century by a fiercely divided Senate whose Christian members convinced the emperor that it was improper to have a pagan statue in such a revered place.

Outside, head down the Curia stairs to the:

❸ Lapis Niger

These are the remains of black marble blocks that reputedly mark the tomb of Romulus. Today, they bask under a corrugated metal roof. Go downstairs for a look at the excavated tomb. There's a stone here with the oldest Latin inscription in existence, which unfortunately is nearly illegible. All that can be safely assumed is that it genuinely dates from the Rome of the kings, an era that ended in a revolution in 510 B.C.

Across from the Curia, the:

❹ Arch of Septimius Severus

The arch was dedicated at the dawn of the troubled 3rd century to the last decent emperor to govern Rome for some time. The friezes on the arch depict victories over Arabs and Parthians by the cold but upright Severus and his two dissolute sons, Geta and Caracalla. Severus died on a campaign to subdue the unruly natives of Scotland. At the end of the first decade of the 3rd century, Rome unhappily fell into the hands of the young Caracalla, chiefly remembered today for the baths he ordered built.

Walk around to the back of the Severus arch, face it, and look to your right. There amid the rubble can be discerned a semi-circular stair that led to the famous:

❺ Rostra

This was the podium from which dictators and caesars addressed the throngs of the Forum below. You can just imagine the emperor, shining in his white toga, surrounded by imperial guards and distinguished senators, gesticulating grandly like one of the statues on a Roman roofline. The motley crowd falls silent, the senators pause and listen, the merchants put down their measures, even the harlots and unruly soldiers lower their voices in such an august presence. Later emperors didn't have much cause to use the Rostra; they made their policies known through edicts and assassinations instead.

Now, facing the colonnade of the Temple of Saturn, once the public treasury, and going to the left, you'll come to the ruins of the:

❻ Basilica Julia

Again, little more remains other than a foundation. The basilica gets its name from Julius Caesar, who dedicated the first structure in 46 B.C. Like many buildings in the Forum, the basilica was burned and rebuilt several times, and the last structure dated from those shaky days after the Gothic invasion of A.D. 410. Throughout its history, it was used for the hearing of civil court cases, which were conducted in the pandemonium of the crowded Forum, open to anyone who happened to pass by. The building was also reputed to be particularly hot in the summer, and it was under these sweaty and unpromising circumstances that Roman justice, the standard of the world for a millennium, was meted out.

Walking back down the ruined stairs of the Basilica Julia and into the broad area whose far side is bounded by the Curia, you'll see the:

❼ Column of Phocas

Probably lifted from an early structure in the vicinity, this was the last monument to be erected in the Roman Forum, and it commemorates the Byzantine emperor Phocas's generous donation of the Pantheon to the pope of Rome, who almost immediately transformed it into a church.

Now make your way down the middle of the Forum, nearly back to the ramp from which you entered. The pile of brick with the semi-circular indentation that stands in the middle of things was the:

❽ Temple of Julius Caesar

It was erected some time after the dictator was deified, and judging from the reconstruction, it was quite an elegant building.

As you stand facing the ruins, with the entrance to the Forum on your left, you'll see on your right three columns originally belonging to the:

❾ Temple of the Castors

This temple perpetuated the legend of Castor and Pollux, who appeared out of thin air in the Roman Forum and were observed watering their horses at the fountain of Juturna (still visible today), just as a major battle against the Etruscans turned in favor of Rome. Castor and Pollux, the heavenly twins (and the symbol of the astrological sign Gemini) are a favorite of Rome.

The next major monument is the circular:

❿ Temple of Vesta

Here dwelt the sacred flame of Rome and the Atrium of the Vestal Virgins. A vestal virgin was usually a girl of good family who signed a contract for 30 years. During that time she lived in the ruin you're standing in right now. Of course, back then it was an unimaginably rich marble building with two floors. There were only six vestal virgins at a time during the imperial period, and even though they had the option of going back out into the world at the end of their 30 years, few did. The cult of Vesta came to an end in A.D. 394, when a Christian Rome secularized all its pagan temples. A man standing on this site before then would have been put to death immediately.

Stand in the atrium with your back to the Palatine and look beyond those fragmented statues of the former vestals to the:

⑪ Temple of Antoninus and Faustina

It's the building with the freestanding colonnade just to the right of the ramp where you first entered the Forum. Only the colonnade dates from imperial times; the building behind it is a much later church dedicated to San Lorenzo.

After you inspect the beautifully proportioned Antoninus and Faustina temple, head up Via Sacra away from the entrance ramp toward the Arch of Titus. Pretty soon, on your left, you'll see the twin bronze doors of the:

⑫ Temple of Romulus

It's the doors themselves that are really of note here—they're the original Roman doors, swinging on the same massive hinges they were mounted on in A.D. 306. In this case, the temple is not dedicated to the legendary cofounder of Rome, but to the son of its builder, Emperor Maxentius, who named his son Romulus in a fit of antiquarian patriotism. Unfortunately for both father and son, they competed with a general who deprived them of their empire and lives. That man was Constantine, who, while camped outside Rome during preparations for one of his battles against Maxentius, saw the sign of the cross in the heavens with the insignia *In hoc signo vinces* (in this sign shall you conquer). Raising the standard of Christianity above his legions, he defeated Maxentius and became the first Christian emperor.

Those three gaping arches up ahead on your left were part of the:

⑬ Basilica of Constantine

At the time of Constantine's victory (A.D. 306), the great basilica was only half finished, having been started by the unfortunate Maxentius. However, Constantine finished the job and affixed his name to this, the largest and most impressive building in the Forum. To our taste, the more delicate, Greek-influenced temples are more attractive, but you have to admire the scale and the engineering skill that erected this monument. The fact that portions of the original coffered ceiling are still intact is amazing. The basilica once held a statue of Constantine so large that his little toe was as wide as an average man's waist. You can see a few fragments from this colossus—the remnants were found in 1490—in the courtyard of the Conservatory Museum on the Capitoline Hill. As far as Roman emperors went, Christian or otherwise, ego knew no bounds.

From Constantine's basilica, follow the Roman paving stones of Via Sacra to a low hill just ahead, where you'll find the:

⑭ Arch of Titus

Titus was the emperor who sacked the great Jewish temple in Jerusalem, and the bas-relief sculpture inside the arch shows the booty of the Jews being carried in triumph through the streets of Rome, while Titus is crowned by Victory, who comes down from heaven for the occasion. You'll notice in particular the candelabrum, for centuries one of the most famous pieces of the treasure of Rome. In all probability it lies at the bottom of the Busento River in the secret tomb of Alaric the Goth.

THE PALATINE HILL

When you've gathered your strength in the shimmering sun, head up the Clivus Palatinus, the road to the palaces of the Palatine Hill, or

Palatino. With your back to the Arch of Titus, it's the road going up the hill to the left.

It was on the Palatine Hill that Rome first became a city. Legend tells us that the date was 753 B.C. The new city originally consisted of nothing more than the Palatine, which was soon enclosed by a surprisingly sophisticated wall, remains of which can still be seen on the Circus Maximus side of the hill. As time went on and Rome grew in power and wealth, the boundaries were extended and later enclosed by the Servian Wall. When the last of the ancient kings was overthrown (510 B.C.), Rome had already extended over several of the adjoining hills and valleys. As Republican times progressed, the Palatine became a fashionable residential district. So it remained until Tiberius—who, like his predecessor, Augustus, was a bit too modest to call himself "emperor" out loud—began the first of the monumental palaces that eventually covered the entire hill.

It's difficult today to make sense out of the Palatine. First-time viewers might be forgiven for suspecting it to be an entirely artificial structure built on brick arches. Those arches, which are visible on practically every flank of the hill, are actually supports that once held imperial structures. Having run out of building sites, the emperors, in their fervor, simply enlarged the hill by building new sides on it.

The road goes on only a short way, through a small sort of valley filled with lush, untrimmed greenery. After about 5 minutes (for slow walkers), you'll see the ruins of a monumental stairway just to the right of the road. The Clivus Palatinus turns sharply to the left here, skirting the monastery of San Bonaventura, but we'll detour to the right and take a look at the remains of the:

🕚 **Flavian Palace**

As you walk off the road and into the ruins, you'll be able to discern that there were once three rooms here. But it's impossible for anyone but the most imaginative to comprehend quite how splendid these rooms were.

The entire Flavian Palace was decorated in the most lavish of colored marbles and gold. Much of the decoration survived as late as the 18th century, when the greedy duke of Parma removed most of what was left. The room closest to the Clivus Palatinus was called the Lararium and held statues of the divinities that protected the imperial family. The middle room was the grandest of the three. It was the imperial throne room, where sat the ruler of the world, the emperor of Rome. The far room was a basilica and, as such, was used for miscellaneous court functions, among them audiences with the emperor. This part of the palace was used entirely for ceremonial functions.

Adjoining these three rooms are the remains of a spectacularly luxurious peristyle. You'll recognize it by the hexagonal remains of a fountain in the middle. Try, if you can, to imagine this fountain surrounded by marble arcades planted with mazes and equipped with mica-covered walls. On the opposite side of the peristyle from the throne room are several other great reception and entertainment rooms. The banquet hall was here; beyond it, looking over the Circus Maximus, are a few ruins of former libraries. Although practically nothing remains except the foundations, every now and then you'll catch sight of a fragment of colored marble floor in a subtle, sophisticated pattern.

Toward the Circus Maximus, slightly to the left of the Flavian Palace, is the:

🕧 **Domus Augustana**

This is where the imperial family lived. The remains lie toward the Circus Maximus, slightly to the left of the Flavian Palace. The new building that stands here—it looks old to us, but in Rome it qualifies as a new building—is a museum (usually closed). It stands in the absolute center of the Domus Augustana. In the field adjacent to the stadium well into the present century stood the Villa Mills, a gingerbread Gothic villa of the 19th century. It was quite a famous place, owned by a rich Englishman who came to Rome from the West Indies. The Villa Mills was the scene of fashionable entertainment in Victorian times, and it's interesting to note, as H. V. Morton pointed out, that the last dinner parties that took place on the Palatine Hill were given by an Englishman. At any of several points along this south-facing gazebo of the Palatine Hill, you'll be able to see the faraway oval walls of the Circus Maximus.

Continue with your exploration of the Palatine Hill by heading across the field parallel to the Clivus Palatinus until you come to the north end of the:

⑰ Hippodrome, or Stadium of Domitian

The field was apparently occupied by parts of the Domus Augustana, which in turn adjoined the enormous stadium. The stadium itself is worth examination, although sometimes it's difficult to get down inside it. The perfectly proportioned area was usually used for private games staged for the amusement of the imperial family. As you look down the stadium from the north end, you can see, on the left side, the semicircular remains of a structure identified as Domitian's private box. Some archaeologists claim that this stadium was actually an elaborate sunken garden.

The aqueduct that comes up the wooded hill used to supply water to the Baths of Septimius Severus, whose difficult-to-understand ruins lie in monumental poles of arched brick at the far end of the stadium.

Returning to the Flavian Palace, leave the peristyle on the opposite side from the Domus Augustana and follow the signs for the:

⑱ House of Livia

They take you down a dusty path to your left. Although legend says that this was the house of Augustus's consorts, it actually was Augustus's all along. The place is notable for some rather well preserved murals showing mythological scenes. But more interesting is the aspect of the house itself—it's smallish, and there never were any great baths or impressive marble arcades. Augustus, even though he was the first emperor, lived simply compared to his successors. His wife, Livia, was a fiercely ambitious aristocrat who divorced her first husband to marry the emperor (the ex-husband was made to attend the wedding, incidentally) and, according to some historians, the true power behind Roman policy between the death of Julius Caesar and the ascension of Tiberius. She even controlled Tiberius, her son, since she had engineered his rise to power through a long string of intrigues and poisonings.

After you've examined the frescoes in Livia's parlor, head up the steps that lead to the top of the embankment to the north. Once on top, you'll be in the:

⑲ Farnese Gardens (Orti Farnesiani)

This was the 16th-century horticultural fantasy of a Farnese cardinal. They're constructed on top of the Palace of Tiberius, which, you'll remember, was the first of the great imperial palaces to be built on this hill. It's impossible to see any of it, but the gardens are cool and nicely laid out. You might stroll up to the promontory above the Forum and admire the view of the ancient temples and the Capitoline heights off to the left.

You've now seen the best of the Forum and the Palatine. To leave the archaeological area, continue walking eastward along the winding road that meanders steeply down from the Palatine Hill to Via di San Gregorio. When you reach the roaring traffic of that busy thoroughfare, walk north toward the ruins so famous that they symbolize the city itself:

⑳ The Colosseum

Its crumbling, oval bulk is the greatest monument of ancient Rome, and visitors are impressed with its size, its majesty, and its ability to conjure up the often cruel games that were played out for the pleasure of the Roman masses. Visit it now or return later.

TAKE A BREAK
On a hill in back of the landmark Colosseum is the **Bar Martini**, Piazza del Colosseo 3A (✆ **06-700-4431**), surrounded by flowery shrubs. Have your coffee, cool drink, plate of pasta, or simple sandwich outside at one of the tables and absorb one of the world's greatest architectural views: that of the Colosseum itself.

THE IMPERIAL FORUMS

Begun by Julius Caesar as an answer to the overcrowding of Rome's older forums during the days of the empire, the imperial forums were at the time of their construction flashier, bolder, and more impressive than the old Roman Forum, and as such represented the unquestioned authority of the Roman emperors at the height of their absolute power. After the collapse of Rome and during the Dark Ages, they, like many other ancient monuments, were lost to history, buried beneath layers of debris. Mussolini, in an egomaniacal attempt to draw comparisons between his fascist regime and the glory of ancient Rome, later helped restore the grandeur of Rome.

With your back to the Colosseum, walk westward along the:

㉑ Via dei Fori Imperiali

Keep to the right side of the street. It was Mussolini who issued the controversial orders to cut through centuries of debris and junky buildings to reveal many archaeological treasures and carve out this boulevard linking the Colosseum to the grand 19th-century monuments of Piazza Venezia. The vistas over the ruins of Rome's imperial forums from the northern side of the boulevard make for one of the most fascinating walks in Rome.

Some of the rather confusing ruins you'll see from the boulevard include the shattered remnants of the colonnade that once surrounded the Temple of Venus and Roma. Next to it, you'll see the back wall of the Basilica of Constantine.

Shortly, on the street's north side, you'll come to a large outdoor restaurant, where Via Cavour joins the boulevard. Just beyond the small park across Via Cavour are the remains of the:

㉒ Forum of Nerva

Your best view is from the railing that skirts it on Via dei Fori Imperiali. It was built by the emperor whose 2-year reign (A.D. 96–98) followed that of the paranoid Domitian. You'll be struck by just how much the ground level has risen in 19 centuries. The only really recognizable remnant is a wall of the Temple of Minerva with two fine Corinthian columns. This forum was once flanked by that of Vespasian, which is now completely gone. It's possible to enter the Forum of Nerva from the other side, but you can see it just as well from the railing.

The next forum you approach is the:

㉓ Forum of Augustus

This was built to commemorate the emperor's victory over the assassins Cassius and Brutus in the Battle of Philippi (42 B.C.). Fittingly, the temple that once dominated this forum—its remains can still be seen—was that of Mars Ultor, or Mars the Avenger, in which stood a mammoth statue of Augustus that unfortunately has vanished completely. You can enter the Forum of Augustus from the other side (cut across the wee footbridge).

Continuing along the railing, you'll see next the vast semicircle of:

㉔ Trajan's Market

Its teeming arcades, stocked with merchandise from the far corners of the Roman empire, long ago collapsed, leaving only the ubiquitous cats to watch over things. The shops once covered a multitude of levels, and you can still wander around many of them. In front of the perfectly proportioned semicircular facade, designed by Apollodorus of Damascus at the beginning of the 2nd century, are the remains of a great library. Fragments of delicately colored marble floors still shine in the sunlight between stretches of rubble and tall grass.

Although the view from the railing is interesting, it's worth your time to descend below street level. To get here, follow the service road you're on until you reach the monumental Trajan's Column on your left, where you turn right and go up the steep flight of stairs that leads to Via Nazionale. At the top of the stairs, about half a block farther on the right, you'll see the entrance to the market. It's open Tuesday to Sunday from 9am to 6pm. Admission is 12,000L (6.25€, $6) for adults, 6,000L (3.10€, $3) for students, and free for children age 17 and under.

Before you head down through the labyrinthine passageways, you might like to climb the:

㉕ Tower of the Milizie

This 12th-century structure was part of the medieval headquarters of the Knights of Rhodes. The view from the top (if it's open) is well worth the climb. From the tower, you can wander where you will through the ruins of the market, admiring the sophistication of the layout and the sad beauty of the bits of decoration that still remain.

When you've examined the brick and travertine corridors, head out in front of the semicircle to the site of the former library; from here, scan the retaining wall that supports the modern road and look for the entrance to the tunnel that leads to the:

㉖ Forum of Trajan

It's entered on Via IV Novembre near the steps of Via Magnanapoli. Once through the tunnel, you'll emerge in the newest and most beautiful of the imperial forums, designed by the same man who laid out the adjoining market. There are many statue fragments and pedestals that bear still-legible inscriptions, but more interesting is the great Basilica Ulpia, with gray marble columns rising roofless into the sky. You wouldn't know it to judge from what's left, but the Forum of Trajan was once regarded as one of the architectural wonders of the world. Constructed between A.D. 107 and 113, it was designed by the Greek architect Apollodorus of Damascus.

Beyond the Basilica Ulpia is:

㉗ Trajan's Column

This column is in magnificent condition, with intricate bas-relief sculpture depicting Trajan's victorious campaign (although from your vantage point you'll only be able to see the earliest stages). The emperor's ashes were kept in a golden urn at the base of the column. If you're fortunate, someone on duty at the stairs next to the column will let you out there. Otherwise, you'll have to walk back the way you came.

The next stop is the:

㉘ Forum of Julius Caesar

This is the first of the imperial forums. It lies on the opposite side of Via dei Fori Imperiali, the last set of sunken ruins before the Victor Emmanuel monument. Though it's possible to go right down into the ruins, you can see everything just as well from the railing. This was the site of the Roman stock exchange, as well as of the Temple of Venus, a few of whose restored columns stand cinematically in the middle of the excavations.

ON TO THE CIRCUS MAXIMUS

From here, retrace your last steps until you're in front of the white Brescian marble monument around the corner on Piazza Venezia, the:

㉙ Vittorio Emanuele Monument

The most flamboyant landmark in Italy (it's been compared to a frosted wedding cake or a Victorian typewriter), it was constructed in the late 1800s to honor the first king of Italy. An eternal flame burns at the Tomb of the Unknown Soldier. The interior of the monument has been closed to the public for many years.

Keep close to the monument and walk to your left, in the opposite direction from Via dei Fori Imperiali. You might like to pause at the fountain that flanks one of the monument's great white walls and splash some icy water on your face. Stay on the same side of the street and just keep walking around the monument. You'll be on Via del Teatro Marcello, which takes you past the twin lions that guard the sloping stairs and on along the base of the Capitoline Hill.

Keep walking along this street until you come to the:

㉚ Teatro di Marcello

It'll be on your right, and you'll recognize the two rows of gaping arches, which are said to be the models for the Colosseum. Julius Caesar is credited with starting the construction of this theater, but it was finished many years after his death (in 11 B.C.) by Augustus, who dedicated it to his favorite nephew, Marcellus. A small corner of the 2,000-year-old arcade has been restored to what presumably was the original condition. Here, as everywhere, there are numerous cats stalking around the broken marble.

The bowl of the theater and the stage were adapted many centuries ago as the foundation for the Renaissance palace of the Orsini family. The other ruins belong to old temples. To the right is the Porticus of Octavia, dating from the 2nd century B.C. Note how later cultures used part of the Roman structure without destroying its original character. There's another good example of this on the other side of the theater. Here you'll see a church with a wall that completely incorporates part of an ancient colonnade.

Keep walking along Via del Teatro Marcello away from Piazza Venezia for 2 more long blocks, until you come to Piazza della Bocca della Verità. The first item to notice in the attractive piazza is the rectangular:

㉛ Temple of Fortuna Virile

You'll see it on the right, a little off the road. Built a century before the birth of Jesus, it's still in magnificent condition. Behind it is another temple, dedicated to Vesta. Like the one in the Roman Forum, it is round, symbolic of the prehistoric huts where continuity of the hearth fire was a matter of survival.

About a block to the south you'll pass the facade of the Church of Santa Maria in Cosmedin, set on Piazza della Bocca della Verità. Even more noteworthy, a short walk to the east, is the:

㉜ Circus Maximus

Its elongated oval proportions and ruined tiers of benches will make you think of *Ben-Hur*. Today a formless ruin, the victim of countless raids on its stonework by medieval and Renaissance builders, the remains of the once-great arena lie directly behind the church. At one time 250,000 Romans could assemble on the marble seats, while the emperor observed the games from his box high on the Palatine Hill.

The circus lies in a valley formed by the Palatine Hill on the left and the Aventine Hill on the right. Next to the

Colosseum, it was the most impressive structure in ancient Rome, located certainly in one of the most exclusive neighborhoods. Emperors lived on the Palatine, and the great palaces of patricians sprawled across the Aventine, which is still a nice neighborhood. For centuries the pomp and ceremony of imperial chariot races filled this valley with the cheers of thousands.

When the dark days of the 5th and 6th centuries fell on the city, the Circus Maximus seemed a symbol of the complete ruination of Rome. The last games were held in 549 on the orders of Totilla the Goth, who had seized Rome in 547 and established himself as emperor. He lived in the still-glittering ruins on the Palatine and apparently thought that the chariot races in the Circus Maximus would lend credence to his charade of empire. It must have been a pretty miserable show, as the decimated population numbered something like 500 when Totilla recaptured the city. The Romans of those times were caught between Belisarius, the imperial general from Constantinople, and Totilla the Goth, both of whom fought bloodily for control of Rome. After the travesty of 549, the Circus Maximus was never used again, and the demand for building materials reduced it, like so much of Rome, to a great dusty field.

To return to other parts of town, head for the bus stop adjacent to the Church of Santa Maria in Cosmedin, or walk the length of the Circus Maximus to its far end and pick up the Metro to Termini or anywhere else in the city that appeals to you.

WALKING TOUR 2:   THE HEART OF ROME

Start:	Palazzo del Quirinale.
Finish:	Piazza Santi Apostoli.
Time:	3½ hours.
Best Times:	Sunday mornings.
Worst Times:	Morning and afternoon rush hours on weekdays.

This walking tour will lead you down narrow, sometimes traffic-clogged streets that have witnessed more commerce and religious fervor than any other neighborhood in Rome. Be prepared for glittering and very unusual shops that lie cheek by jowl with churches dating back to A.D. 500.

Begin in the monumental, pink-toned:

❶ Piazza del Quirinale

Crowning the highest of the seven ancient hills of Rome, this is where Augustus's Temple of the Sun once stood (the steep marble steps that now lead to Santa Maria d'Aracoeli on the Capitoline Hill once serviced this spot), and part of the fountains in the piazza were built from the great Baths of Constantine, which also stood nearby. The palace, today home to the president of Italy, is open to the public only on Sunday mornings.

You can admire a view overlooking Rome from the piazza's terrace, then meander along the curiously lifeless streets that surround it before beginning your westward descent along Via della Dataria and your northerly descent along Via San Vincenzo to one of the most famous waterworks in the world, the:

❷ Trevi Fountain

Supplied by water from the Acqua Vergine aqueduct, and a triumph of the baroque style, it was based on the design of Nicolo Salvi (who is said to have died of illness contracted during his supervision of the project) and

Walking Tour: The Heart of Rome

1 Piazza del Quirinale
2 Trevi Fountain
3 Piazza della Trinità dei Monti
4 Spanish Steps (Scalinata della Trinita dei Monti)
5 Keats-Shelley Memorial (Casina Rossa)
☕ Babington's Tea Rooms
6 Collegio di Propoganda Fide
7 Via Condotti
8 Augustus's Mausoleum (Mausoleo Augusteo)
9 Altar of Peace (Ara Pacis)
10 Borghese Palace (Palazzo Borghese)
11 Via del Corso
12 Palazzo Ruspoli
13 Chiesa di San Lorenzo in Lucina
14 Piazza Colonna
15 Piazza di Montecitorio
16 Chiesa San Marcello al Corso
17 Chiesa S.S. Apostoli

"Take A Break" Stop ☕
Metro —Ⓜ—
Post Office ✉

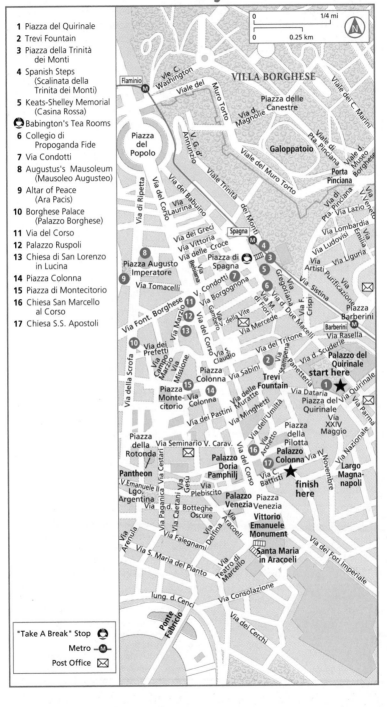

181

completed in 1762. On the south-western corner of the fountain's piazza you'll see a somber, not particularly spectacular church (Chiesa S.S. Vincenzo e Anastasio) with a strange claim to fame: In it are contained the hearts and intestines of several centuries' worth of popes. This was the parish church of the popes when they resided at the Quirinal Palace on the hill above, and for many years each pontiff willed those parts of his body to the church. According to legend, the church was built on the site of a spring that burst from the earth after the beheading of St. Paul, at one of three sites where his head is said to have bounced off the ground.

Throw a coin or two into the fountain to ensure your return to Rome, then walk around to the right of the fountain along streets whose names will include Via di Stamperia, Via del Tritone, and Via F. Crispi. These lead to a charming street, Via Gregoriana, whose relatively calm borders and quiet apartments flank a narrow street that inclines upward to one of the most spectacular public squares in Italy:

❸ Piazza della Trinità dei Monti

Partly because of its position at the top of the Spanish Steps (which you'll descend in a moment), partly because of its soaring Egyptian obelisk, and partly because of its lavish and perfect baroque symmetry, this is one of the most theatrical piazzas in Italy. Flanking the piazza are buildings that have played a pivotal role in French (yes, French) politics for centuries, including the Church of Trinità dei Monti, begun by the French monarch Louis XII in 1502, and restored during Napoléon's occupation of Rome in the early 1800s. The eastern edge of the square, adjacent to Via Gregoriana, is the site of the 16th-century Palazzetto Zuccaro, built for the mannerist painter Federico Zuccaro with doorways and window openings fashioned into deliberately grotesque shapes inspired by the mouths of sea monsters. (It lies between Via Gregoriana,

Via Sistina, and Piazza Trinità dei Monti.) In this building, at the dawn of the French Revolution, David painted the most politicized canvas in the history of France, *The Oath of the Horatii* (1784), which became a symbol of the Enlightenment then sweeping through the salons of Paris. Today the palazzetto is owned by the German Institute for Art History.

Begin descending the most famous staircase in the world, the:

❹ Spanish Steps

This azalea-flanked triumph of landscape design takes its name from the Spanish Embassy, which was in a nearby palace during the 19th century. The Spanish, however, had nothing to do with the construction of the steps. Designed by Italian architect Francesco de Sanctis between 1723 and 1725, they were funded almost entirely by the French as a preface to the above-mentioned French church, Trinità dei Monti.

The Spanish Steps are at their best in spring, when they're filled with flowers that seem to cascade down into Piazza di Spagna, a piazza designed like two interconnected triangles. It's interesting to note that in the early 19th century the steps were famous for the sleek young men and women who lined the travertine steps, flexing muscles and exposing ankles in hopes of attracting an artist and being hired as a model.

The boat-shaped Barcaccia fountain, in the piazza at the foot of the steps, was designed by Bernini's father at the end of the 16th century.

There are two nearly identical houses at the foot of the steps on either side. One is the home of Babington's Tea Rooms (see "Take a Break," below); the other is the house where the English romantic poet John Keats lived—and died. That building, at 26 Piazza di Spagna, contains the:

❺ Keats-Shelley Memorial

Keats died here on February 23, 1821, at the age of 25, during a trip he made to Rome to improve his failing health. Since 1909, when well-intentioned English and American aficionados of English literature bought the building, it has been a working library established in honor of Keats as well as Shelley, who drowned off the coast of Viareggio with a copy of Keats's work in his pocket. Mementos inside range from the kitschy to the immortal and are almost relentlessly laden with literary nostalgia.

TAKE A BREAK
Opened in 1893 by Miss Anna Maria Babington, **Babington's Tea Rooms,** Piazza di Spagna 23 (© 06-678-6027), has been serving homemade scones and muffins, along with a good cuppa, ever since, based on her original recipes. Celebrities and thousands of tourists have stopped off here to rest in premises inspired by England's Victorian age. Prices are high, however.

In the past, the Piazza di Spagna area was a favorite of English lords, who rented palaces hereabouts and parked their coaches on the street. Americans now dominate the scene, especially since the main office of American Express is right on Piazza di Spagna and dispenses all those letters (and money) from home. Much to the dismay of many Romans, the piazza is also home to a **McDonald's,** though it's not your average Golden Arches— we've never seen one so lavish, and it's a good place to duck in if you need a restroom.

To the extreme southern edge of the square—flanked by Via Due Macelli, Via Propaganda, and Piazza di Spagna—is an odd vestige of the Catholic church's sense of missionary zeal, the:

6 Collegio di Propoganda Fide
Established in 1627 as the headquarters of a religious organization devoted to the training of young missionaries, it later grew into one of the most important centers for missionary work in the world. Owned and administered by the Vatican, and therefore exempt from most of the laws and legalities of Italy, it contains design elements by two of the 17th century's most bitter artistic rivals, Bernini and Borromini.

The street that runs east-west as the logical continuation of the descent of the Spanish Steps is one of the most celebrated for style and fashion in Italy:

7 Via Condotti
It's lined with windows displaying the latest offerings from the Italian fashion industry. Even the least materialistic will enjoy window shopping along this impressive line-up of the most famous names in international design. (Via Condotti is only the most visible of several upscale shopping streets in the neighborhood. For more of the same kind of temptation, detour onto a smaller but equally glamorous parallel street, Via della Croce, 2 blocks to the north, and wander at will with your platinum card in hand. You'll need to walk to Via Condotti eventually for the continuation of this walking tour.)

Via Condotti ends at a shop-lined plaza, Largo Goldoni, where your path will fork slightly to the right onto Via Tomacelli. Staying on the right-hand (northern) edge of the street, turn right at the second intersection into Piazza Augusto, site of the:

8 Augustus Mausoleum
Once covered with marble and cypress trees, this tomb housed the ashes of many of the emperors of the 1st century all the way up to Hadrian (who built what is now Castel Sant'Angelo across the river for his own tomb). The imperial remains stayed intact within this building until the 5th century, when invading barbarians smashed the bronze gates and stole the golden urns, probably emptying the ashes onto the ground outside. The tomb was restored by Mussolini,

and although you cannot enter the mausoleum itself, you can walk around it.

At the mausoleum's southwestern corner (Largo San Rocco), veer northwest until you reach the edge of the Tiber, stopping for a view of a bizarre, almost surreal compendium of ancient archaeological remnants restored, and in some cases enhanced, by Mussolini. It sits in an airy glass-and-concrete building beside the eastern banks of the Tiber at Ponte Cavour. Inside is one of the treasures of antiquity, the:

⑨ Altar of Peace (Ara Pacis)

The altar was built by the Senate as a tribute to Augustus and the peace he had brought to the Roman world. Look closely at the marble walls for portraits of Augustus's imperial family. Mussolini collected the few fragments of this monument that were scattered in museums throughout the world and gave his archaeological engineers a deadline for digging out the bulk of the altar, which remained underground—below the water table and forming part of the foundation of a Renaissance palace on the Corso. Fearful of failing Il Duce, the engineers hit on the idea of chemically freezing the water surrounding the altar and simply chipping the relic out in huge chunks of ice, building new supports for the palace overhead as they went.

Proceed southward along Via Ripetta, cross over Piazza di Porto di Ripetta, then fork left, walking southeast along Via Borghese for a block until you reach the austere entrance to the:

⑩ Borghese Palace (Palazzo Borghese)

Although many of the art treasures that once graced its interior now form part of the Galleria Borghese collections (for details, see the listing on p. 158—you can't just duck in quickly on a whim), this huge and somewhat disjointed palazzo retains its status as the modern-day Borghese family's seat of power and prestige. Bought from another family in 1605 by the cardinal who later became Pope Paul V, it was later occupied by Pauline Borghese, Napoléon's scandalous sister, a noted enemy of opera composer Rossini. Regrettably, the palace, carefully preserving its status as one of the most prestigious private homes in the world, is not open to the public.

From your vantage point, walk in a westerly direction along Via Fontanella Borghese back to a square you've already visited, Largo Goldoni, the western terminus of Via Condotti. The busy avenue on your right is one of the most richly stocked treasure troves of Italian merchandise in Rome:

⑪ Via del Corso

When compared to the many meandering streets with which it merges, the rigidly straight lines of Via del Corso are unusual. In the 18th century, residents of Rome commandeered the street to race everything from horses to street urchins, festooning the windows of buildings on either side of the narrow street with banners and flags. Although today its merchandise is not as chic (nor as expensive) as what you'll find along Via Condotti, it's well worth a browse to see what's up in the world of Italian fashion.

Walk south along Via del Corso's western edge, turning right (west) after 1 block into Piazza San Lorenzo in Lucina. The severely massive building on the piazza's northern edge is the:

⑫ Palazzo Ruspoli

This is a 16th-century testament to the wealth of the Florentine Rucellai family. Family members commissioned the same architect (Bartolommeo Ammannati) who designed parts of the Pitti Palace in Florence to build their Roman headquarters. Today the building belongs to a private foundation, although it's occasionally open for temporary, infrequently scheduled exhibitions. The entrance is at Via del Corso 418A, although your best vantage point will be from Piazza San Lorenzo in Lucina.

On the piazza's southern edge rises the:

⑬ Chiesa di San Lorenzo in Lucina

Most of what you'll see today was rebuilt around 1650, although if you look carefully, the portico and most of the bell tower have survived almost unchanged since the 1100s. According to tradition, this church was built on the site of the mansion of Lucina, a prosperous Roman matron who salvaged the corpses of Christian martyrs from prisons and amphitheaters for proper burials. The church was founded by Sixtus III, who reigned for 8 years beginning in A.D. 432. Inside, look for the tomb of the French painter Poussin (1594–1665), which was carved and consecrated on orders of the French statesman Chateaubriand in 1830.

After your visit, retrace your steps back to Via del Corso and walk southward until you reach the venerable perimeter of:

⑭ Piazza Colonna

Its centerpiece is one of the most dramatic obelisks in town, the Column of Marcus Aurelius, a hollow bronze column rising 83 feet above the piazza. Built between A.D. 180 and 196, and restored (some say "defaced") in 1589 by a pope who replaced the statue of the Roman warrior on top with a statue of St. Paul, it's one of the ancient world's best examples of heroic bas-relief and one of the most memorable sights of Rome. Beside the piazza's northern edge rises the Palazzo Chigi, official residence of the Italian prime minister.

Continue walking west from Piazza Colonna into another square a few steps to the east and you'll find yourself in a dramatic piazza designed by Bernini:

⑮ Piazza di Montecitorio

This was the site during ancient times of the cremations of the Roman emperors. In 1792 the massive obelisk of Psammetichus II, originally erected in Egypt in the 6th century B.C., was

placed here as the piazza's centerpiece. Brought to Rome by barge from Heliopolis in 10 B.C., it was unearthed from a pile of rubble in 1748 at a site close to the Church of San Lorenzo in Lucina. The Palazzo di Montecitorio, which rises from the piazza's northern edge, is the modern-day site of the Italian legislature (the Chamber of Deputies) and is closed to the public.

Retrace your steps back to Via del Corso, then walk south, this time along its eastern edge. Within 6 blocks, just after crossing over Via dell'Umiltà, you'll see the solid stone walls of the namesake church of this famous shopping boulevard:

⑯ Chiesa San Marcello al Corso

Originally founded in the 4th century and rebuilt in 1519 after a disastrous fire, it was ornamented in the late 1600s with a baroque facade by Carlo Fontana. A handful of ecclesiastical potentates from the 16th and 17th centuries, many resting in intricately carved sarcophagi, are contained inside.

After your visit, return to the piazza in front of the church, then continue walking for half a block south along Via del Corso. Turn left (eastward) onto Via S.S. Apostoli, then turn right onto Piazza S.S. Apostoli, and conclude this tour with a visit to a site that has witnessed the tears of the penitent since the collapse of the Roman empire, the:

⑰ Chiesa S.S. Apostoli

Because of alterations to the site, especially a not-very-harmonious rebuilding that began in the early 1700s, there's very little to suggest the ancient origins of this church of the Holy Apostles. Pope Pelagius founded it in the dim, early days of the Roman papacy, sometime between A.D. 556 and 561, as a thanksgiving offering for the short-term defeat of the Goths at a battle near Rome. The most interesting parts of this ancient site are the fluted stone columns at the end of the south aisle, in the Cappella del Crocifisso; the building's front portico, added in the 1300s, which managed to incorporate a frieze from ancient Rome; and one of the first works executed by Canova, a painting near the high altar completed in 1787 shortly after his arrival in Rome. The church is open daily from 6:30am to noon and 4 to 7pm.

WALKING TOUR 3: RENAISSANCE ROME

Start:	Via della Conciliazione (Piazza Pia).
Finish:	Galleria Doria Pamphili.
Time:	4 hours, not counting a tour of the Castel Sant'Angelo and visits to the Palazzo Spada and the Galleria Doria Pamphili.
Best Times:	Early and mid-mornings.
Worst Times:	After dark.

The threads that unify this tour are the grandiose tastes of Rome's Renaissance popes and the meandering Tiber River that has transported building supplies, armies, pilfered treasures from other parts of Europe, and such famous personages as Cleopatra and Mussolini into Rome. Slower and less powerful than many of Italy's other rivers (such as the mighty Po, which irrigates the fertile plains of Lombardy and the north), the Tiber varies, depending on the season, from a sluggish ribbon of sediment-filled water only 4 feet deep to a 20-foot-deep torrent capable of flooding the banks that contain it.

The last severe flood to destroy Roman buildings occurred in 1870. Since then, civic planners have built mounded barricades high above its winding banks, a development that has diminished the river's visual appeal. The high embankments, as well as the roaring traffic arteries that parallel them, obscure views of the water along most of the river's trajectory through Rome. In any event, the waters of the Tiber are so polluted that many modern Romans consider their concealment something of a plus.

Begin your tour at Piazza Pia. (Don't confuse Piazza Pia with nearby Piazza Pio XII.) Piazza Pia is the easternmost end of Rome's most sterile and impersonal boulevard. Start at:

❶ Via della Conciliazione
Conceived by Mussolini as a monumental preface to the faraway dome of St. Peter's Basilica, construction required the demolition of a series of medieval neighborhoods between 1936 and 1950, rendering it without challenge the most disliked avenue in Rome.

Walk east toward the massive and ancient walls of the:

❷ Castel Sant'Angelo
Originally built by Emperor Hadrian in A.D. 135 as one of the most impressive mausoleums in the ancient world, it was adapted for use as a fortress, a treasure vault, and a pleasure palace for the Renaissance popes. Visit its interior, noting the presence near the entrance of architectural models showing the castle at various periods of its history. Note the building's plan (a circular tower set atop a square foundation), and the dry moats (used today for impromptu soccer games by neighborhood kids), which long ago were the despair of many an invading army.

After your visit, walk south across one of the most ancient bridges in Rome:

❸ Ponte Sant'Angelo
The trio of arches in the river's center is basically unchanged since the bridge was built around A.D. 135; the arches that abut the river's embankments

Walking Tour: Renaissance Rome

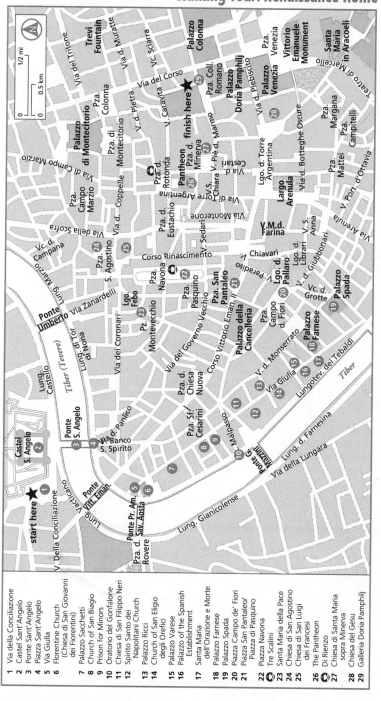

1   Via della Conciliazione
2   Castel Sant'Angelo
3   Ponte Sant'Angelo
4   Piazza Sant'Angelo
5   Via Giulia
6   Florentine Church
    (Chiesa di San Giovanni
    dei Fiorentini)
7   Palazzo Sacchetti
8   Church of San Biagio
9   Prison for Minors
10 Oratorio del Gonfalone
11 Chiesa di San Filippo Neri
12 Spirito Santo dei
    Napolitani Church
13 Palazzo Ricci
14 Church of San Eligio
    degli Orefici
15 Palazzo Varese
16 Palazzo of the Spanish
    Establishment
17 Santa Maria
    dell'Orazione e Morte
18 Palazzo Farnese
19 Palazzo Spada
20 Piazza Campo de' Fiori
21 Piazza San Pantaleo/
    Piazza di Pasquino
22 Piazza Navona
23 Tre Scalini
24 Santa Maria della Pace
25 Chiesa di San Agostino
26 Chiesa di San Luigi
    dei Francesi
27 The Pantheon
    Di Rienzo
28 Chiesa di Santa Maria
    sopra Minerva
29 Chiesa del Gesu
30 Galleria Doria Pamphilj

were added late in the 19th century as part of a flood-control program. On December 19, 1450, so many pilgrims gathered on this bridge (which at the time was lined with wooden buildings) that about 200 of them were crushed to death. Today the bridge is reserved exclusively for pedestrians; vehicular traffic was banned in the 1960s.

On the southern end of the bridge is the site of one of the most famous executions of the Renaissance:

④ Piazza Sant'Angelo

Here, in 1599, Beatrice Cenci and several members of her family were beheaded on the orders of Pope Clement VIII. Their crime? Successfully plotting the death of their very rich and very brutal father. Their tale later inspired a tragedy by Shelley and a novel by 19th-century Italian politician Francesco Guerrazzi.

From the square, cut southwest for 2 blocks along Via Paola (crossing the busy traffic of Corso Vittorio Emanuele in the process) onto:

⑤ Via Giulia

Laid out during the reign of Pope Julius II (1503-13), Via Giulia's straight edges were one of Renaissance Rome's earliest examples of urban planning. Designed to facilitate access to the Vatican, it was the widest, straightest, and longest city street in Rome at the time of its construction and was bordered by the 16th-century homes of such artists as Raphael, Cellini, and Borromini and the architect Sangallo. Today the street is lined with some of the most spectacular antiques stores in Rome.

At the terminus of Via Paola, the first building on Via Giulia you're likely to see is the soaring dome of the:

⑥ Florentine Church (Chiesa di San Giovanni dei Fiorentini)

This is the premier symbol of the city of Florence in papal Rome. Its design is the result of endless squabbling between such artistic rivals as Sansovino, Sangallo, and Maderno, each of

whom added embellishments of his own. Michelangelo also submitted a design for the church, although his drawing did not prevail during the initial competition. Although most of the building was completed during the 1620s, Lorenzo Corsini added the facade during the 1700s.

Now walk in a southeasterly direction along Via Giulia, making special note of houses at **no. 82** (built in the 1400s, it was offered by Pope Julius II to the Florentine community), **no. 85** (the land it sits on was once owned by Raphael), and **no. 79** (built in 1536 by the architect Sangallo as his private home, it was later snapped up by a relative of Cosimo de' Medici).

In less than 3 short blocks, on the northwest corner of Vicolo del Cefalo, rises the symmetrical bulk of the:

⑦ Palazzo Sacchetti

Completed by Vasari in the mid-1500s, it was built for the Sacchetti family, a Florence-based clan of bankers and merchants who moved to Rome after they lost an epic power struggle with the Medicis.

Continue walking south along Via Giulia. On your right rises the baroque facade of the unpretentious:

⑧ Church of San Biagio

Although its front was added in the early 1700s, it's actually one of the oldest churches in Rome, rebuilt from an even earlier model dating to around 1070. The property of an Armenian Christian sect based in Venice, the church is named after an early Christian martyr (St. Biagio), a portion of whose throat is included among the sacred objects inside.

Walk another short block south along Via Giulia. Between Via del Gonfalone and Vicolo della Scimia are the barred windows of what was originally built early in the 19th century as a:

⑨ Prison for Minors

This, along with another nearby building (at Via Giulia 52, a few blocks to the south, which was built during the mid-1600s) incarcerated juvenile delinquents, political prisoners, debtors, common rogues, and innocent victims of circumstance for almost a hundred years. During its Industrial Revolution heyday, armed guards supervised all comings and goings along this section of Via Giulia.

Turn right onto Vicolo della Scimia and descend toward the Tiber. On your left, at no. 18, is a building used since the early 1500s as a guildhall for the flag-bearers of Rome, the:

⑩ Oratorio del Gonfalone

The guild of flag-bearers had, by the time this building was constructed, evolved into a charitable organization of concerned citizens and a rather posh social and religious fraternity. The frescoes inside were painted in 1573 by Zuccari. Restored during the early 1980s, they now form a backdrop for concerts held inside. The building is usually open Monday to Saturday from 9:30am to noon.

Walk to the very end of Vicolo della Scimia and make a hard left onto Vicolo Prigioni, which will eventually lead back to Via Giulia. At this point, as you continue to walk south along Via Giulia, you'll notice a swath of trees and a curious absence of buildings flanking the corner of Via Moretta. In 1940 Mussolini ordered the demolition of most of the buildings along Via Moretta for the construction of a triumphal boulevard running from east to west. His intention—which was never fulfilled—was to link together the nearby Ponte Mazzini with Corso Vittorio Emanuele. One building that suffered was the building near the corner with a baroque facade, the:

⑪ Chiesa di San Filippo Neri

Originally funded during the early 1600s by a wealthy but ailing benefactor in hopes of curing his gout, the church retains only its facade—the rest of the building was demolished. Where choirs once sang and candles burned during masses, there is now a market for fruits and vegetables.

About another block to the south, on your right, rises the bulk of the:

⑫ Spirito Santo del Napolitani Church

Once one of the headquarters of the Neapolitan community in Rome, the version you see today is a product of a rebuilding during the 1700s, although parts of the foundation were originally constructed during the 1300s.

Slightly farther south, at Via Giulia 146, rises the:

⑬ Palazzo Ricci

This is one of the many aristocratic villas that once flanked this historic street. For a better view of its exterior frescoes, turn left from Via Giulia into Piazza Ricci to admire this building from the rear.

Returning to Via Giulia, walk south for a block, then turn right onto Via Barchetta. At the corner of Via di San Eligio, notice the:

⑭ Church of San Eligio degli Orefici

According to popular belief, this church was designed by Raphael in 1516. Completed about 60 years later, it was dedicated to (and funded by) the city's gold- and silversmiths.

Return to Via Giulia and notice, near its terminus, at Via Giukua 16, the:

⑮ Palazzo Varese

This structure was built as an aristocratic residence in the Tuscan style.

Nearby, at Via Giulia 151, is the:

⑯ Palazzo of the Spanish Establishment

Constructed in anticipation of the 1862 visit of Queen Elizabeth II of Spain, for the occasion of her charitable visit to Rome, it was designed by Antonio Sarti.

Continue walking south along Via Giulia, past the faded grandeur of at least another half-dozen palazzi. These will include the **Palazzo Cisterno** (from about 1560) at no. 163; **Palazzo Baldoca/Muccioli/Rodd** (about 1700) at no. 167; and **Palazzo Falconieri** (about 1510) at no. 1.

Opposite the corner of Via dei Farnesi rise the walls of one of the most macabre buildings in Rome, the church of:

⑰ Santa Maria dell'Orazione e Morte

Built around 1575, and reconstructed about 160 years later, it was the property of an order of monks whose job it was to collect and bury the unclaimed bodies of the indigent. Notice the depictions of skulls decorating the church's facade. During the Renaissance, underground chambers lined with bodies led from the church to the Tiber, where barges carried the corpses away. Although these vaults are not open to the public, the church's interior decoration carries multiple reminders of the omnipresence of death.

After exiting the church, notice the covered passageway arching over Via Giulia. Built in 1603 and designed by Michelangelo, it connected the:

⑱ Palazzo Farnese

The rear side of the palazzo rises to your left, with the Tiber and a series of then-opulent gardens and villas that no longer exist. The Palazzo Farnese was designed by Sangallo and Michelangelo, among others, and has housed dignitaries ranging from Pope Paul III to Queen Christina of Sweden. Today the French Embassy, it's closed to the public. For the best view of the building, cut west from Via Giulia along any of the narrow streets (Via Mascherone or Via dei Farnesi will do nicely) to reach Piazza Farnese.

To the southwest is a satellite square, Piazza Quercia, at the southern corner of which rises the even more spectacular exterior of the:

⑲ Palazzo Spada

Built around 1550 for Cardinal Gerolamo Capo di Ferro, its ornate facade is stuccoed in high-relief in the mannerist style. Although the staterooms are closed to the public, the courtyard and several galleries are open.

From here, walk 2 blocks north along either Vicolo del Grotte or Via Balestrari until you reach one of the most famous squares of Renaissance Rome:

⑳ Piazza Campo de' Fiori

During the 1500s this square was the geographic and cultural center of secular Rome, with inns and the occasional burning at the stake of religious heretics. Today the campo hosts a morning open-air food market every day except Sunday.

After your visit, continue to walk north for 3 meandering blocks along the narrow confines of Via Baullari to:

㉑ Piazza San Pantaleo/Piazza di Pasquino

Its edges are the site of both the Palazzo Massimo (to the east) and the Palazzo Braschi (Museo di Roma) to the north. The Palazzo Massimo (currently home to, among other things, the Rome campus of Cornell University) was begun as a private home in 1532 and designed with an unusual curved facade that corresponded to the narrow confines of the street. Regrettably, because it's open to the public only 1 day a year (March 17), it's viewed as a rather odd curiosity from the Renaissance by most passersby. More accessible is the **Palazzo Braschi,** built during the late 1700s by Pope Pius IV Braschi for his nephews. Severe and somewhat drab, it was the last palace ever constructed in Rome by a pope. Since 1952 it has contained the exhibits of the Museo di Roma, a poorly funded entity whose visiting hours and future are uncertain.

Continue walking north for 2 blocks until you reach the southernmost entrance of the most thrilling square in Italy:

㉒ Piazza Navona

Originally laid out in A.D. 86 as a stadium by Emperor Domitian, stripped of its marble in the 4th century by Constantine, and then embellished during the Renaissance into the lavish baroque form you'll see today, it has witnessed as much pageantry and heraldic splendor as any other site in Rome. The fact that it's reserved exclusively for pedestrians adds enormously to its charm, but makes parking in the neighborhood around it almost impossible.

TAKE A BREAK
Established in 1882, **Tre Scalini**, Piazza Navona 28 (*©* **06-687-9148**), is the most famous cafe on the square. Literally hundreds of people go here every day to sample its tartufo (ice cream disguised with a coating of bittersweet chocolate, cherries, and whipped cream). There are simpler versions of gelato as well.

After you've perked yourself up with sugar or caffeine or both, head for the piazza's northwestern corner, adjacent to the startling group of heroic fountains at the square's northern edge, and exit onto Via di Lorenesi. Walk westward for 2 crooked blocks, forking to the left onto Via Parione until you reach the edge of one of the district's most charming churches:

㉓ Santa Maria della Pace

According to legend, blood flowed from a statue of the Virgin above the altar after someone threw a pebble at it. This legend motivated Pope Sixtus IV to rebuild the church in the 1500s on the foundations of an even older sanctuary. For generations after that, its curved porticos, cupola atop an octagonal base, and frescoes by Raphael helped make it one of the most fashionable churches for aristocrats residing in the surrounding palazzos.

After admiring the subtle, counterbalancing curves of the church, retrace your steps to the welcoming confines of Piazza Navona, then exit from it at its northernmost (narrow) end. Walk across the broad expanse of Via Zanardelli to its northern edge, then head east for 2 blocks to Piazza San Agostino, on whose northern flank rises the:

㉔ Chiesa di San Agostino

Built between 1479 and 1483 and originally commissioned by the archbishop of Rouen, France, it was one of the first churches erected in Rome during the Renaissance. Its interior was altered and redecorated in the 1700s and 1800s. A painting by Caravaggio, *Madonna of the Pilgrims* (1605), hangs over the first altar on the left, as you enter.

After your visit, continue walking east along Via Zanardelli, turning south in about a block onto Via della Scrofe. Be alert to the fact that this street changes its name, in rapid order, to Largo Toniolo and Via Dogana, but regardless of how it's marked, walk for about 2 blocks south until, on the right, you'll see a particularly charming church, the:

㉕ Chiesa di San Luigi dei Francesi

This has functioned as the national church of France in Rome since 1589. Subtly carved into its facade is a stone salamander, the symbol of the Renaissance French monarch François I. Inside are a noteworthy series of frescoes by Caravaggio, *The Martyrdom of St. Matthew.*

Continue walking south for less than a block along Via Dogana, then turn left for a 2-block stroll along the Salita dei Crescenzi. Suddenly, at Piazza della Rotonda, there will emerge a sweeping view of one of our favorite buildings in all of Europe:

㉖ The Pantheon

Rebuilt by Hadrian around A.D. 125, it's the best-preserved ancient monument in Rome, a remarkable testimony to the skill of ancient masons, whose (partial) use of granite helped ensure the building's longevity. Originally dedicated to all the gods, it was transformed into a church (Santa Maria ad Martyres) by Pope Boniface IV in A.D. 609. Many archaeologists find the building's massive, slightly battered dignity thrilling. Its flattened dome is the widest in the world, exceeding the width of the dome atop St. Peter's by about 2 feet.

TAKE A BREAK
Di Rienzo, Piazza della Rotunda 8–9 (✆ **06-686-9097**), is a great cafe. Here you can sit at a table enjoying a pick-me-up while you view not only one of the world's premier ancient monuments but also the lively crowd of people who come and go on this square, one of the most interesting in Rome. Open daily 7am to 3am.

After your coffee, walk southward along the eastern flank (Via Minerva) of the ancient building. That will eventually lead you to Piazza di Minerva. On the square's eastern edge rises the massive and severe bulk of a site that's been holy for more than 3,000 years:

② Chiesa di Santa Maria Sopra Minerva

Beginning in 1280, early Christian leaders ordained that the foundation of an already ancient temple dedicated to Minerva (goddess of wisdom) be reused as the base for Rome's only Gothic church. Unfortunately, architectural changes and redecorations during the 1500s and the 1900s weren't exactly improvements. Despite that, the awe-inspiring collection of medieval and Renaissance tombs

inside creates an atmosphere that's something akin to a religious museum.

After your visit, exit Piazza di Minerva from the square's easternmost edge, following Via del Gesù in a path that proceeds eastward, then meanders to the south. Continue walking southward until you eventually cross over the roaring traffic of Corso Vittorio Emanuele II/Via del Plebiscito. On the southern side of that busy avenue, you'll see a church that for about a century after the Protestant Reformation was one of the most influential in Europe, the:

② Chiesa del Gesù

Built between 1568 and 1584 with donations from a Farnese cardinal, this was the most powerful church in the Jesuit order for several centuries. Conceived as a bulwark against the perceived menace of the Protestant Reformation, it's sober, monumental, and historically very important to the history of the Catholic Counter-Reformation. The sheathing of yellow marble that covers part of the interior was added during the 1800s.

After your visit, cross back over the roaring traffic of Via del Plebiscito, walk eastward for 2 blocks, and turn left (north) onto Via de Gatta. Pass through the first piazza (Piazza Grazioli), then continue northward to Piazza del Collegi Romano, site of the entrance to one of Rome's best-stocked museums, the:

② Galleria Doria Pamphili

This wonderful museum has a full listing on p. 148.

WALKING TOUR 4: **TRASTEVERE**

Start: Isola Tiberina.
Finish: Palazzo Corsini.
Time: 3 hours, not counting museum visits.
Best Times: Daylight hours during weekday mornings, when the outdoor food markets are open, or early on a Sunday, when there's very little traffic.
Worst Times: After dark.

Not until the advent of the Fellini films did Trastevere make a name for itself. Set on the western bank of the Tiber, away from the main tourist path, Trastevere (whose name translates as "across the Tiber") seems a world apart from the rest of Rome. Its residents have traditionally been considered more insular than the Romans across the river.

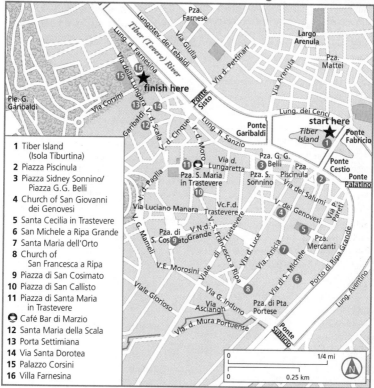

finish here

start here

1 Tiber Island
   (Isola Tiburtina)
2 Piazza Piscinula
3 Piazza Sidney Sonnino/
   Piazza G.G. Belli
4 Church of San Giovanni
   dei Genovesi
5 Santa Cecilia in Trastevere
6 San Michele a Ripa Grande
7 Santa Maria dell'Orto
8 Church of
   San Francesca a Ripa
9 Piazza di San Cosimato
10 Piazza di San Callisto
11 Piazza di Santa Maria
   in Trastevere
☕ Café Bar di Marzio
12 Santa Maria della Scala
13 Porta Settimiana
14 Via Santa Dorotea
15 Palazzo Corsini
16 Villa Farnesina

Because only a fraction of Trastevere has been excavated, it remains one of Rome's most consistently unchanged medieval neighborhoods, despite a trend toward gentrification. Dotted with ancient and dimly lit churches, crumbling buildings angled above streets barely wide enough for a Fiat, and very articulate inhabitants who have stressed their independence from Rome for many centuries, the district is the most consistently colorful of the Italian capital.

Be warned that street crime, pickpockets, and purse snatchers are more plentiful here than in Rome's more frequently visited neighborhoods, so leave your valuables behind and be alert to what's going on around you.

Your tour begins on the tiny but historic:

❶ **Tiber Island (Isola Tiburtina)**
Despite its location in the heart of Rome, this calm and sun-flooded island has always been a refuge for the sick. The oldest bridge in Rome, the Ponte Fabricio, constructed in 62 B.C., connects the island to the Tiber's eastern bank. The church at the island's eastern end, **San Bartolomeo,** was built during the 900s by Holy Roman

Emperor Otto III, although dozens of subsequent renovations have removed virtually everything of the original structure. The complex of structures at the island's western end contain the hospital of Fatebenefratelli, whose foundations and traditions date back to the ancient world (the island was associated with the healing powers of the god Aesculapius, son of Apollo).

Walk south along the bridge (Ponte Cestio) that connects the island to the western bank of the Tiber. After crossing the raging traffic, which runs parallel to the riverbanks, continue south for a few steps. Soon you'll reach:

❷ Piazza Piscinula

Named after the Roman baths (piscina) that once stood here, the square contains the tiny but ancient Church of San Benedetto, whose facade was rebuilt in a simplified baroque style during the 1600s. It's classified as the smallest Romanesque church in Rome and supposedly is constructed on the site where St. Benedict, founder of the Benedictine order, lived as a boy. Directly opposite the church rises the intricate stonework of the Casa dei Mattei. Occupied during the Renaissance by one of the city's most powerful and arrogant families (the Mattei), it was abandoned as unlucky after several family members were murdered during a brawl at a wedding held inside. In reaction, the family moved to more elegant quarters across the Tiber.

Exit the piazza at the northwest corner, walking west along either the narrow Via Gensola or the somewhat wider Via della Lungaretta. In about 2 jagged blocks you'll reach the first of a pair of connected squares:

❸ Piazza Sidney Sonnino

This first square was named after the Italian minister of foreign affairs during World War I. A few hundred feet to the north, facing the Tiber, is **Piazza G. G. Belli,** with a statue commemorating Giuseppe Gioacchino Belli (1791-1863), whose more than 2,000 satirical sonnets (written in Roman dialect) on Roman life have made him a particular favorite of the Trasteverans. From one edge of the piazza rise the 13th-century walls of the Torre degli Anguillara and the not-very-famous church of St. Agatha, and on the southern edge, across the street, stand the walls of the Church of San

Crisogono. Founded in the 500s and rebuilt in the 1100s (when the bell tower was added), it contains stonework and mosaics that merit a visit.

Now, from a point near the southernmost expanses of these connected squares, cross the traffic-clogged Viale di Trastevere and head southeast into a maze of narrow alleyways. We suggest that you ask a passerby for Via dei Genovesi, as street signs in this maze of piazzas might be hard to find. Walking along Via dei Genovesi, traverse Via della Luce, then turn right onto Via Anicia (which was named after the family that produced the medieval leader Pope Gregory the Great). Then, at Via Anicia 12, on the west side of the street, you'll see the simple but dignified walls of the:

❹ Church of San Giovanni dei Genovesi

Built during the 1400s for the community of Genoan sailors who labored at the nearby port, it has a tranquil garden on the opposite side of the street, which you may or may not be able to visit according to the whim of the gatekeeper.

After your visit, look across Via Anicia to the forbidding rear walls and ancient masonry of:

❺ Santa Cecilia in Trastevere

To reach its entrance, continue walking another block southeast along Via dei Genovesi, then turn right onto Via Santa Cecilia, which soon funnels into Piazza dei Mercanti. A cloistered and still-functioning convent with a fine garden, Santa Cecilia contains in its inner sanctum hard-to-visit frescoes by Cavallini. (If you want to see the frescoes, call ✆ **06-589-9289** to make an appointment. Viewing hours are Tues or Thurs 10–11:30am.) The church is more easily visited and contains a white marble statue of the saint herself. The church is built on the reputed site of Saint Cecilia's long-ago palace and contains sections dating from the 12th to the 19th century. Admission to see the frescoes is

3,000L (1.55€, $1.50), and admission to the subterranean areas is 4,000L (2.10€, $2). Open daily 9:30am to noon and 3:45 to 6:30pm.

St. Cecilia, who proved of enormous importance in the history of European art as a symbol of the struggle of the early church, was a wealthy Roman aristocrat condemned for her faith by a Roman prefect around A.D. 300. According to legend, her earthly body proved extraordinarily difficult for Roman soldiers to slay, affording the saint ample opportunity to convert bystanders to the Christian cause as she slowly bled to death over a period of 3 days.

TAKE A BREAK
About half a dozen cafes are near this famous church. Any of them will serve frothy cups of cappuccino, tasty sandwiches, ice cream, and drinks.

After your snack, take the opportunity to wander randomly down three or four of the narrow streets outward from Piazza dei Mercanti. Of particular interest might be Via del Porto, which stretches south to the Tiber. The largest port in Rome once flourished at this street's terminus (Porto di Ripa Grande). During the 1870s redesign of the riverfront, when the embankments were added, the port was demolished.

Retrace your steps northward along Via del Porto, turning left onto Via di San Michele. At no. 22, inside a stucco-covered, peach-colored building that never manages to lose its bureaucratic anonymity despite its age, you'll see:

⑥ San Michele a Ripa Grande
For many years this was the temporary home of the paintings of the Borghese Gallery until that gallery was restored and reopened.

After your visit, turn north onto Via Madonna dell'Orto, a narrow street that intersects Via di San Michele. One block later, at the corner of Via Anicia, you'll see the baroque:

⑦ Santa Maria dell'Orto
This church was originally founded by the vegetable gardeners of Trastevere during the early 1400s, when the district provided most of the green vegetables for the tables of Rome. Famous for the obelisks that decorate its cornices (added in the 1760s) and for the baroque gilding inside, it's one of the district's most traditional churches.

Now walk southwest along Via Anicia. In 2 blocks the street funnels into Piazza di San Francesco d'Assisi. On your left, notice the ornate walls of the:

⑧ Church of San Francesco a Ripa
Built in the baroque style, and attached to a medieval Franciscan monastery, the church contains a mannerist statue by Bernini depicting Ludovica Albertoni. It's Bernini's last known sculpture and supposedly one of his most mystically transcendental.

Exit from Piazza di San Francesco d'Assisi and walk north along Via San Francesco a Ripa. After traversing the feverish traffic of Viale di Trastevere, take the first left onto a tiny street with a long name, Via Natale del Grande Cardinale Merry di Val. (Its name is sometimes shortened to simply "Via Natale," if it's marked at all on your map.) This funnels into:

⑨ Piazza di San Cosimato
A busy food market operates here every weekday from early morning until around noon. On the north side of the square lies the awkwardly charming church of San Cosimato, sections of which were built around A.D. 900; it's closed to the public.

Exit from the piazza's north side, heading up Via San Cosimato (its name might not be marked). This will lead into:

⑩ Piazza di San Callisto
Much of the real estate surrounding this square, including the 17th-century

Palazzo San Callisto, belongs to the Vatican.

The edges of this piazza will almost imperceptibly flow into one of the most famous squares of Rome:

⓫ Piazza di Santa Maria in Trastevere

The Romanesque church that lends the piazza its name (**Santa Maria in Trastevere**) is the most famous building in the entire district. Originally built around A.D. 350 and thought to be one of the oldest churches in Rome, it sports a central core that was rebuilt around 1100 and an entrance and portico that were added in the 1840s. The much-restored mosaics on both the facade and in the interior, however, date from around 1200. Its sense of timelessness is enhanced by the much-photographed octagonal fountain in front (and the hundreds of pigeons).

TAKE A BREAK
Try one of the many cafes that line this famous square. We especially like the **Café Bar di Marzio**, Piazza di Santa Maria in Trastevere 14B (✆ **06-581-6095**), where rows of tables, both inside and out, offer an engaging view of the ongoing carnival of Trastevere. Open Tuesday to Sunday 6am to 3am.

After your stop, walk to the church's north side, toward its rear. Stretching from a point beginning at its northwestern edge is an ancient square, Piazza di San Egidio, with its own drab and rather nondescript 16th-century church (Chiesa di San Egidio) set on its western edge. Use it as a point of reference for the left-hand street that funnels from its base in a northeasterly direction, Via della Scalla.

The next church you'll see on your left, just after Via della Scalla, is:

⓬ Santa Maria della Scala

This 17th-century baroque monument belongs to the Discalced Carmelite order of nuns. The interior contains works by Caravaggio and his pupils. There's also a pharmacological oddity in the annexes associated with the building: They include a modern pharmacy as well as a room devoted to arcane jars and herbal remedies that haven't changed very much since the 18th century.

In about 5 blocks, you'll reach a triumphal archway that marks the site of one of the ancient Roman portals to the city, the:

⓭ Porta Settimiana

During the 3rd century it was a vital link in the Roman defenses of the city, but its partially ruined masonry provides little more than poetic inspiration today. Much of its appearance dates from the age of the Renaissance popes, who retained it as a site marking the edge of the ancient Aurelian wall.

The narrow medieval-looking street leading off to the right is:

⓮ Via Santa Dorotea

Site of a rather drab church (**Chiesa San Dorotea,** a few steps from the intersection with Via della Scala), the street also marks a neighborhood that was, according to legend, the home of La Fornarina, the baker's daughter. She was the mistress of Raphael, and he painted her as the Madonna, causing a scandal in his day.

Return to Via della Scala (which at this point has changed its name to Via della Lungara) and continue walking north. After Via Corsini, the massive palace on your left is the:

⓯ Palazzo Corsini

Built in the 1400s for a nephew of the pope, it was acquired by Queen Christina of Sweden, the fanatically religious monarch who abdicated the Protestant throne of Sweden for a life of devotion to Catholic causes. Today it houses some of the collection of the **National Gallery of Ancient Art,** plus European paintings of the 17th and 18th centuries. It's open Tuesday to Sunday from 9am to 2pm.

After your visit, cross Via della Lungara, heading east toward the Tiber, for a look at what was once the most fashionable villa in Italy, the:

⑯ Villa Farnesina

It was built between 1508 and 1511 by a Sienese banker, Agostino Chigi (Il Magnifico), who was believed to be the richest man in Europe at the time. After his death in 1520, the villa's frescoes and carvings were partially sacked by German armies in 1527. After years of neglect, the building was bought by the Farnese family, after whom it is named today, and in the 18th century by the Bourbons of Naples. Graced with sculpture and frescoes (some by Raphael and his studio), it now belongs to the Italian government and is the home of the National Print Cabinet (Gabinetto Nazionale delle Stampe), whose collections are open for view only by appointment. The public rooms, however, are open Monday to Saturday from 9am to 1pm, and also on Tuesday afternoon from 3 to 5:30pm.

9

Shopping

Rome offers temptations of every kind. You might find hidden oases of charm and value in lesser-known neighborhoods, but in our limited space below, we've summarized certain streets known throughout Italy for their shops. The monthly rent on these places is very high and those costs are passed on to you. Nonetheless, a stroll down some of these streets presents a cross section of the most desirable wares in Italy.

Though Rome has many wonderful boutiques, you'll find better shopping in Florence and Venice. If you're continuing on to either of these cities, hold off a bit.

Shopping hours are generally Monday from 3:30 to 7:30pm, and Tuesday to Saturday from 9:30 or 10am to 1pm and from 3:30 to 7 or 7:30pm. Some shops are open on Monday mornings, however, and some shops don't close for the afternoon break.

1 The Shopping Scene

SHIPPING   Shipping can be a problem, but—for a price—any object can be packed, shipped, and insured. For major purchases, you should buy an all-risks insurance policy to cover damage or loss in transit. Because these policies can be expensive, check into whether using a credit or charge card to make your purchase will provide automatic free insurance.

TAX REBATES ON PURCHASES IN ITALY   Visitors are sometimes appalled at the high taxes and add-ons that seem to make so many things expensive in Italy. Those taxes, totaling as much as 19% to 35% for certain goods, apply to big-ticket purchases of more than 300,000L (150€, $156), but can be refunded if you plan ahead and perform a bit of sometimes tiresome paperwork. When you make your purchase, be sure to get a receipt from the vendor. When you leave Italy, find an Italian Customs agent at the point of your exit from the country. The agent will want to see the item you've bought, confirm that it's physically leaving Italy, and stamp the vendor's receipt.

You should then mail the stamped receipt (keeping a photocopy for your records) back to the original vendor. The vendor will, sooner or later, send you a check representing a refund of the tax you paid at the time of your original purchase. Reputable stores view this as a matter of ordinary paperwork and are very businesslike about it. Less honorable stores might lose your receipts. It pays to deal with established vendors on purchases of this size.

MAJOR SHOPPING STREETS

VIA BORGOGNONA   This street begins near Piazza di Spagna, and both the rents and the merchandise are chic and ultra-expensive. Like its neighbor, Via Condotti, Via Borgognona is a mecca for wealthy well-dressed women and men from around the world. Its storefronts have retained their baroque or neoclassical facades.

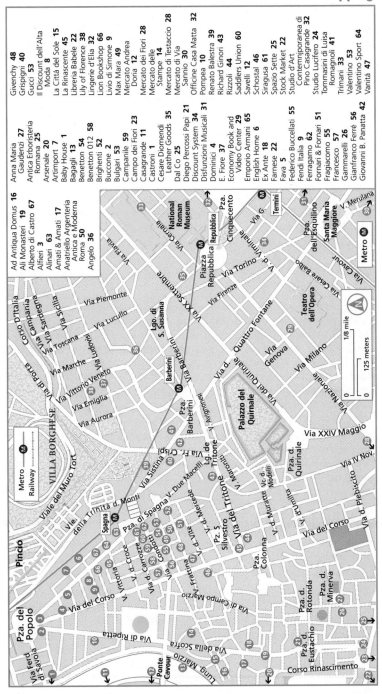

Ad Antiqua Domus **16**
Ali Monasteri **19**
Alberto di Castro **67**
Alfieri **3**
Alinari **63**
Amati & Amati **17**
Anatriello Argenteria
 Antica e Moderna
 Roma **50**
Angelo **36**

Anna Maria
 Gaudenzi **27**
Antica Erboristeria
 Romana **25**
Arsenale **20**
Artimport **7**
Baby House **1**
Bagagli **13**
Benetton **54**
Benetton 012 **58**
Brighenti **52**
Buccone **2**
Bulgari **53**
Campanile **59**
Campo dei Fiori **23**
Casagrande **11**
Castroni **1**
Cesare Diomendi
 Leather Goods **35**
Dal Co **25**
Diego Percossi Papi **21**
Discount System **34**
Disfunzioni Musicali **31**
Dominici **4**
E. Fiore **37**
Economy Book and
 Video Center **29**
Emporio Armani **65**
English Home **6**
Ex Ante **18**
Farnese **22**
Fava **5**
Federico Buccellati **55**
Fendi Italia **9**
Ferragamo **62**
Fornari & Fornari **51**
Fragiacomo **55**
Francesco **57**
Gammarelli **26**
Gianfranco Ferré **56**
Giovanni B. Panatta **42**

Givenchy **48**
Grispigni **40**
Gucci **53**
Il Discount dell'Alta
 Moda **8**
La Città del Sole **15**
La Rinascente **45**
Libreria Babele **22**
Lily of Florence **38**
Lingerie d'Elia **32**
Lion Bookshop **66**
Livio di Simone **9**
Max Mara **49**
Mercato Andrea
 Doria **12**
Mercato dei Fiori **28**
Mercato delle
 Stampe **14**
Mercato di Testaccio **28**
Mercato di Via
 Sannio **30**
Officine Casa Matta **32**
Pompea **10**
Renato Balestra **39**
Richard Ginori **43**
Rizzoli **44**
Saddlers Union **60**
Savelli **12**
Schostal **46**
Siragusa **61**
Spazio Sette **25**
Stock Market **22**
Studio d'Art
 Contemniporanea di
 Pino Casagrande **32**
Studio Lucifero **24**
Tommasini di Luisa
 Romagnoli **41**
Trimani **33**
Valentino **53**
Valentino Sport **64**
Vanità **47**

VIA COLA DI RIENZO Bordering the Vatican, this long, straight street runs from the Tiber to Piazza Risorgimento. Since the street is wide and clogged with traffic, it's best to walk down one side and then up the other. Via Cola di Rienzi is known for stores selling a wide variety of merchandise at reasonable prices—from jewelry to fashionable clothes and shoes.

VIA CONDOTTI Easy to find because it begins at the base of the Spanish Steps, this is Rome's poshest and most prominent shopping street—the Madison Avenue of Rome. Even the recent incursion of some less elegant stores hasn't diminished the allure of Via Condotti as a consumer's playground for the rich and super rich. For us mere mortals, it's a great place for window-shopping and people-watching.

VIA DEL CORSO Not attempting the stratospheric image or prices of Via Condotti or Via Borgognona, Via del Corso boasts styles aimed at younger consumers. There are, however, some gems scattered amid the shops selling jeans and sporting equipment. The most interesting stores are nearest the fashionable cafes of Piazza del Popolo.

VIA FRANCESCO CRISPI Most shoppers reach this street by following Via Sistina (below) 1 long block from the top of the Spanish Steps. Near the intersection of these streets are several shops well suited for unusual and less expensive gifts.

VIA FRATTINA Running parallel to Via Condotti, it begins, like its more famous sibling, at Piazza di Spagna. Part of its length is closed to traffic. Here the concentration of shops is denser, though some aficionados claim that its image is slightly less chic and prices are slightly lower than at its counterparts on Via Condotti. It's usually thronged with shoppers who appreciate the lack of motor traffic.

VIA NAZIONALE The layout recalls 19th-century grandeur, but the traffic is horrendous; crossing Via Nazionale requires a good sense of timing and a strong understanding of Italian driving patterns. It begins at Piazza della Repubblica and runs down almost to the 19th-century monuments of Piazza Venezia. You'll find an abundance of leather stores (more reasonable in price than those in many other parts of Rome) and a welcome handful of stylish boutiques.

VIA SISTINA Beginning at the top of the Spanish Steps, Via Sistina runs to Piazza Barberini. The shops are small, stylish, and based on the tastes of their owners. The pedestrian traffic is less dense than on other major streets.

VIA VITTORIO VENETO Via Veneto is filled these days with expensive hotels and cafes and an array of relatively expensive stores selling shoes, gloves, and leather goods.

BEST BUYS

Because of the Italians' consummate skill as manufacturers and designers, it's no surprise that consumers from all over the world flock to Italy's shops, trade fairs, and design studios to see what's new, hot, and salable back home.

The most obvious draw is **fashion.** Milan may be the center of the fashion industry, but Rome is a principal distribution center. There are literally hundreds of famous designers for both men and women, most of whom make eminently stylish garments. Materials include silks, leathers, cottons, synthetics, and wool, often of the finest quality.

Italian design influences everything from typewriter keyboards to kitchen appliances to furniture. The Italian studios of Memphis-Milan and Studio

Alchimia are two of the leaders in this field, and many of their products (and many rip-offs) are now highly visible in machines and furnishings throughout the world. Alessi has become a world-renowned name in witty, innovative houseware design. You can preview many of Italy's new products and designs by reading a copy of *Domus,* a monthly photographic magazine that reports on many different aspects of the country's design scene.

Food and wine never go out of style, and many gourmets bring some of Italy's bounty home with them. Many Roman shops sell chocolates, pastries, liqueurs, wines, and limited-edition olive oils. Be alert to restrictions against importing certain food products into North America, including anything fresh, such as fruit, as well as prosciutto. Italian wines include many excellent vintages, and bottles of liqueurs (which are sometimes distilled from herbs and flowers) make unusual gifts. You can bring home only 1 liter of wine or spirits duty free.

The **glassware** of Italy (and especially of Venice) is famous throughout the world and sold all over Rome. It's fragile enough that you should look into shipping it directly home with insurance.

Italy's **porcelain** may be elegant and sought after, but personally we prefer the hand-painted rustic plates and bowls of thick-edged **stoneware** known as Laveggio. Done in strong and clear glazes and influenced by their rural origins, the bowls and plates are often used at the most formal dinners for their originality and style. The **tiles** and **mosaics** of Italy are virtually without equal in the world, whether used individually as drink coasters or decorative ornaments, or in groups set into masonry walls.

Lace was, for many years, made in convents by nuns. Venice became the country's headquarters. Handmade Italian lace is exquisite and justifiably expensive, crafted into a wide array of tablecloths, napkins, clothing, and bridal veils. Beware of machine-made imitations; although with a bit of practice, you'll soon be able to recognize the shoddy copies.

Paper goods, stationery, elegantly bound books, prints, and engravings are specialties of Italy. The engravings you find amid stacks of dozens of others will invariably look stately when framed and hanging on a wall back home.

Fabrics, especially silk, are made near Lake Como, in the foothills of the Italian Alps. Known for their supple beauty and their ability to hold color for years (the thicker the silk, the more desirable), these silks are rivaled only by the finest of India, Thailand, and China. Their history in Italy goes back to the era of Marco Polo, possibly much earlier.

Finally, Rome is the home to a **religious objects** industry. Centered on the streets near the Church of Santa Maria Sopra Minerva are dozens of shops selling pictures, statues, and reliefs of most of the important saints, the Madonna, Jesus, and John the Baptist. And some shops cross the line of good taste and into the realm of high camp—we've even seen snow globes of the pope blessing Rome.

2 Shopping A to Z

ANTIQUES
Some visitors to Italy consider the treasure trove of antiques for sale the country's greatest treasure. But prices have risen to alarming levels as increasingly wealthy Europeans outbid one another in a frenzy. Any antiques dealer who risks the high rents of central Rome is acutely aware of valuations. So you might find gorgeous pieces, but you're not likely to find any bargains.

Beware of fakes; remember to insure anything you have shipped home; and for larger purchases—anything more than 300,000L (150€, $156) at any one store—keep your paperwork in order to obtain your tax refund (see section 1 of this chapter).

Via dei Coronari, buried in a colorful section of the Campo Marzio, is lined with stores offering magnificent vases, urns, chandeliers, chaises, refectory tables, and candelabra. To find the street's entrance, turn left out of the north end of Piazza Navona and pass the excavated ruins of Domitian's Stadium—it will be just ahead. There are more than 40 antiques stores in the next 4 blocks, offering inlaid secretaries, gilded consoles, vases, urns, chandeliers, marble pedestals, chaises, refectory tables—you name it. Bring your pocket calculator and keep in mind that stores are frequently closed between 1 and 4pm.

Via del Babuino is another major street for antiques in Rome, with some of the most prestigious stores found here, including Alberto di Castro (our favorite store for prints—see "Art," below), but many others as well.

A few minutes south of Piazza del Popolo, via Laurina lies midway between via del Corso and via del Babuino. It is filled with beautiful stores where you can find anything from an antique print to a 17th-century chandelier.

Ad Antiqua Domus   This shop practically feels like a museum of Italian furniture design through the ages. You'll find Italian furniture from the days of Caesar through the 19th century for sale here. Via Paola 25–27. ✆ 06-686-1530. Bus: 41, 46B, or 98. There's a second location at Via dei Coronari 41 (✆ 06-686-1186).

ArtImport   An antiques shopper's dream, this bazaar always has something for sale that's intriguing and tasteful—that is, if you can agree on a price. The store's motto is "In the service of the table," so there's an emphasis on silver, although the objects run the gamut. The goblets, elegant bowls, candlesticks, and candelabra sold here are almost without equal in Rome. Via del Babuino 150. ✆ 06-322-1330. Metro: Spagna.

ART

Alberto di Castro   Alberto di Castro is one of the largest dealers in antique prints and engravings in Rome. You'll find rack after rack of depictions of everything from the Colosseum to the Pantheon, each evocative of the best architecture in the Mediterranean world, priced between $25 and $10,000, depending on the age and rarity of the engraving. Via del Babuino 71. ✆ 06-361-3752. Metro: Spagna.

Giovanni B. Panatta Fine Art Shop   In business since 1890, this store is up the hill toward the Villa Borghese. Here you'll find excellent prints in color and black-and-white, covering a variety of subjects from 18th-century Roman street scenes to astrological charts. There's a good selection of attractive and reasonably priced reproductions of medieval and Renaissance art as well. Via Francesco Crispi 117. ✆ 06-679-5948. Metro: Spagna or Barberini.

Studio d'Arte Contemporanea Pino Casagrande *(Finds)*   You can skip the dull galleries aimed at the tourist market and head here to see what's hot and happening in Rome's contemporary art scene. An industrial elevator carries you to the fifth floor of this battered old former pasta factory. Pino Casagrande, the owner, displays some of the city's most avant-garde art work on his all-white walls. Local artists hang out here, and it's fun to meet and talk with them, and perhaps purchase one of their works. Via degli Ausoni 7A. ✆ 06-466-3480. Metro: Piazza Vittorio or Termini.

BOOKSTORES

Economy Book and Video Center *Value*   Catering to the expatriate English-speaking communities of Rome and staffed by native English speakers, this bookstore sells only English-language books (both new and used, paperback and hardcover), greeting cards, and videos. Via Torino 136. ✆ **06-474-6877**. Metro: Repubblica.

Libreria Babele   This is Rome's only gay and lesbian bookstore. Besides the usual stock, it sells a gay map of the city. Via dei Banchi Vecchi 116. ✆ **06-6876628**. Bus: 40, 62, 64.

The Lion Bookshop   The Lion Bookshop is the oldest English-language bookshop in town, specializing in both American and English literature. It also sells children's books and photographic volumes on both Rome and Italy. A vast choice of English-language videos is for sale or rent. Closed in August. Via del Greci 33. ✆ **06-3265-4007**. Metro: Spagna.

Rizzoli   Rizzoli has one of the largest collections of Italian-language books in Rome. If your native language happens to be French, English, German, or Spanish, the endless shelves will have a section to amuse, enlighten, and entertain you. Largo Chigi 15. ✆ **06-6796641**. Metro: Barberini or Spagna.

CHINA, PORCELAIN & GLASSWARE

Richard Ginori   One of the city's most prestigious retail outlets for porcelain, both artworks and plates, contains a glittering assortment of the impeccably crafted porcelain of Richard Ginori. Founded in 1735, it offers china and glassware as well. Anything you buy here can be shipped, but if you prefer to buy at Ginori's outlets in North America (which include Tiffany's in New York), you can at least check out the dozens of patterns. Piazza Trinità dei Monti 18B. ✆ **06-679-3836**. Metro: Spagna.

COSMETICS & PERFUMES

Antica Erboristeria Romana *Finds*   Charles Dickens might call it the curiosity shop. Since the 18th century it has been dispensing "wonders" from its tiny wooden drawers, some of which are labeled with skulls and crossbones. Scented aper, licorice, hellbane, and herbal remedies . . . it's all here and more. Via di Torre Argentina 15. ✆ **06-687-9493**. Metro: Spagna or Barberini.

CRAFTS

Officine Casa Matta *Finds*   This funky, offbeat choice is the domain of Francesca Moscarelli, an expert craftsperson who can take almost anything, even a piece of flea market junk and reshape it into something you'd love to have around the house . . . even furniture that has been tossed out on the street. Via dei Latini 78–80. ✆ **06-445-3658**. Metro: Piazza Vittorio or Termini.

DEPARTMENT STORES

La Rinascente   This upscale department store offers clothing, hosiery, perfume, cosmetics, and other goods. It also has its own line of clothing (Ellerre) for men, women, and children. This is the largest of the Italian department-store chains. Piazza Colonna, Via del Corso 189. ✆ **06-679-7691**. Bus: 117.

DISCOUNT SHOPPING

Certain stores that can't move their merchandise at any price often consign their unwanted goods to discounters. In Italy, the original labels are usually still inside the garment (and you'll find some very chic labels strewn in with mounds of more generic garments). Know in advance, however, that these pieces couldn't be sold at higher prices in more glamorous shops, and some garments are either the wrong size, are the wrong look, or have a stylistic mistake. If you're willing to sift through a lot, you might find a gem, though.

Discount System   Discount System sells men's and women's wear by many of the big names (Armani, Valentino, Nino Cerruti, Fendi, and Krizia). Even if an item isn't from a famous designer, it often comes from a factory that produces some of the best quality Italian fashion. If you find something you like, it will be priced at around 50% of its original price tag in its original boutique. Via del Viminale 35. ✆ 06-482-3917. Metro: Repubblica.

Il Discount dell'Alta Moda   The honest and genuinely helpful staff here will help you pick through the constantly changing racks of women's and men's clothing, with discounts of up to 50% on such labels as Versace, Donna Karan, Armani, Krizia, and Ferré. The shop also sells irregulars and overstock at cut-rate tabs. Near the Spanish Steps at Via di Gesù e Maria 16A. ✆ 06-361-3796. Metro: Spagna. Another branch is near Termini at Via Viminale 35 (✆ 06-482-3917). Metro: Termini.

FASHION
See also "Department Stores," "Discount Shopping," "Leather," "Lingerie," and "Shoes."

FOR MEN
Angelo   Angelo is a custom tailor for discerning men and has been featured in *Esquire* and *GQ*. He employs the best cutters and craftspeople, and his taste in style and design is impeccable. Custom shirts, suits, dinner jackets, even casual wear, can be made on short notice. A suit, for instance, takes about 8 days. If you haven't time to wait, Angelo will ship anywhere in the world. Via Bissolati 34. ✆ 06-474-1796. Metro: Barberini.

Emporio Armani   This store stocks relatively inexpensive menswear crafted by the couturier who has dressed perhaps more stage and screen stars than any other designer in Italy. The designer's more expensive line—sold at sometimes staggering prices that are nonetheless up to 30% less than what you'd pay in the United States—is a short walk away at **Giorgio Armani,** Via Condotti 77. (✆ **06-699-1460**). Via del Babuino 140. ✆ 06-3600-2197. Metro: Spagna.

Schostal   Dating to 1870, this is the clothing store for men who like their fashion conservative and well crafted. It features everything from underwear to cashmere overcoats. The prices are more reasonable than you might think, and a devoted staff is both courteous and attentive. Via del Corso 158. ✆ 06-679-1240. Bus: 117.

Valentino   This is a swank emporium for the men's clothing of the acclaimed designer. Here, if you can afford the high prices, you can become the most fashionable man in town. Valentino's women's haute couture is sold around the corner in an even bigger showroom at Via Bocca di Leone 15 (✆ **06-679-5862**). Via dei Condotti 13. ✆ 06-673-9420. Metro: Spagna.

FOR WOMEN
Arsenale   Most of the inventory that's displayed in this shop for women is the creative statement of owner Patrizia Pieroni. Her design preferences include lots of ultra-rich fabrics, nothing too frilly or girlish, and a dignified kind of severity that many foreign visitors find captivating. Favorite colors at this place include a spectrum of pinks, pale grays, and lilacs, with accents of bright orange, celadon green, Bordeaux, and off-whites. Via del Governo Vecchio 64. ✆ 06-686-1380. Bus: 30, 81, or 87.

Benetton   Despite the gracefully arched ceiling and its prized location, this branch of the worldwide sportswear distributor has down-to-earth prices and some of the same stock you'd find at its other branches around the world. Famous for woolen sweaters, tennis wear, blazers, and resort wear, this company has suffered (like every other clothier) from inexpensive copies of its designs. The original, however, is still best for guaranteed quality. Their men's line is also worth a look. Via Condotti 18. ℂ **06-679-7982.** Metro: Spagna.

Gianfranco Ferré   Here you'll find the women's line by this famous designer whose clothes have been called "adventurous." Via Borgognona 42B. ℂ **06-679-7445.** Metro: Spagna.

Givenchy   This is the Roman headquarters of one of the great design houses of France, a company known since World War I for its couture. In its Roman branch, the company emphasizes stylish ready-to-wear garments for women, appropriate for the warm Italian weather. Tasteful shirts and pullovers for men are also featured. Via Borgognona 21. ℂ **06-678-4058.** Metro: Spagna.

Max Mara   Max Mara is one of the best outlets in Rome for chic women's clothing. The fabrics are appealing, and the alterations are free. Via Frattina 28 (at Largo Goldoni). ℂ **06-679-3638.** Metro: Spagna.

Renato Balestra   Rapidly approaching the stratospheric upper levels of Italian fashion is Renato Balestra, whose women's clothing exudes a lighthearted elegance. This branch carries a complete line of the latest Balestra ready-to-wear. Via Sistina 67. ℂ **06-679-5424.** Metro: Spagna.

FOR CHILDREN

Baby House   Baby House offers stylish clothing for the under-15 set. This shop is for the budding young fashion plate, with threads by Valentino, Bussardi, and Biagiotti. Via Cola di Rienzo 117. ℂ **06-321-4291.** Metro: Spagna.

Benetton 012   Benetton isn't as expensive as you might expect. This store is the famous sportswear manufacturer's outlet for children's clothes (from infants to age 12), as well as adult garments for men and women. You can find rugby shirts, corduroys and jeans, and accessories in a wide selection of colors and styles. Via Condotti 59. ℂ **06-679-7982.** Metro: Spagna.

SPORTSWEAR FOR MEN & WOMEN

Valentino Sport   Specializing exclusively in sportswear for men and women, this is the least expensive line of clothing offered by normally wallet-denting designer Valentino. His easy-to-wear, stylish clothing has warm climates in mind. In summer, there's more emphasis on women's clothes than men's, but the rest of the year, the inventories are about equally divided. Via del Babuino 61. ℂ **06-3600-1906.** Metro: Spagna.

FOOD
See also "Markets," below.

Castroni   At this old-fashioned store, you'll find an amazing array of unusual foodstuffs from around the Mediterranean. If you want herbs from Apulia, pepperoncino oil, cheese from the Valle d'Aosta, or that strange brand of balsamic vinegar whose name you can never remember, Castroni will have it. Filled to the rafters with the abundance of agrarian Italy, it also carries foods that are exotic in Italy but commonplace in North America, like taco shells, corn curls, and peanut butter. (Remember, there are restrictions against importing certain food

---

Tips **Shopping Tips**

Remember to bring your pocket calculator with you and keep in mind that stores are often closed between 1 and 4pm. Most important? Save your receipts! See section 1 of this chapter for important money-saving information on obtaining a tax refund.

---

products into North America, including prosciutto and fresh produce.) Via Cola di Rienzo 196. ℃ **06-687-4383**. Bus: 32 or 81.

GIFTS

Amati & Amati   This intimate shop sells antique jewelry, high-fashion clothing, and exotic handcrafts. Good examples include mirrors framed in assorted seashells and lavishly carved chests from North Africa that might inspire you to store your wedding mementos. And if you're on the hunt for exotic fashion accessories, this is the place for you. Via dei Pianellari 21. ℃ **06-686-4319**. Metro: Spagna.

Ex Ante *Finds*   You can find some of the most exquisite and exotic gifts in Rome here, though you should expect to find a hefty price tag attached. If you're looking for a gift item from Italy, France, China, the Middle East, or some other faraway land, this is the place for you. Examples include handcrafted silver frames embedded with amber or trunks from Asia. You'll find it near the Pantheon. There's another location at Via Vittoria 13 (℃ **06-3265-0534**), with smaller and more affordable items. Largo Toniolo 4. ℃ **06-6880-1107**. Bus: 70, 81, 119, or 170.

Grispigni   Here you'll find a constantly changing array of gifts, including a large assortment of leather-covered boxes, women's purses, compacts, desk sets, and cigarette cases. Via Francesco Crispi 59 (at Via Sistina). ℃ **06-679-0290**. Metro: Spagna or Barberini.

HOUSEWARES

Bagagli   Here you'll find a good selection of Alessi, Rose and Tulipani, and Villeroy & Boch china in a pleasantly kitschy old Rome setting that comes complete with cobblestone floors. Via Campo. Marzio 42. ℃ **06-687-1406**. Bus: 70, 81, 115, 186, or 628.

c.u.c.i.n.a.   This is a stainless steel shrine to everything you need for a proper Italian kitchen, sporting designs that are as beautiful in their simplicity as they are utilitarian. Via Mario de' Fiori 65. ℃ **06-679-1275**. Metro: Spagna.

English Home *Finds*   It's amazing how so many intriguing items can be packed into such a small space. Here you'll find everything from painted pillows to handmade wooden frames, even mosaic incense holders or beaded jewelry. Via del Babuino 41A. ℃ **06-3600-1721**. Metro: Spagna.

Spazio Sette   This is far and away Rome's best housewares emporium, a design boutique of department store proportions. It goes way beyond the Alessi tea kettles to fill three huge floors with the greatest names, and latest word, in Italian and international design. Via D. Barberi, off Largo di Torre Argentina. ℃ **06-686-9747**. Metro: Spagna or Barberini.

Stock Market *Value*   Bargain hunters will find mouthwatering prices on last year's models, overstock, slight irregulars, and artistic misadventures in design that the pricier boutiques haven't been able to move. Most is moderately funky household stuff, but you never know when you'll find a gem of design hidden on the shelves. Via D. Banchi Vecchi 51–52. ✆ **06-686-4238.** Bus: 40, 46, 62, or 64. Another location is near the Vatican at Via Tacito 60. ✆ **06-3600-2343.** Metro: Ottaviano.

JEWELRY

Since the days when the ancient Romans imported amethysts and pearls from the distant borders of their empire, and when the great trading ships of Venice and Genoa carried rubies and sapphires from Asia, Italians have collected jewelry. Styles range from the most classically conservative to neo-punk-rock frivolous, and part of the fun is shopping for something you might never before have considered wearing.

Bulgari   Bulgari is the capital's most prestigious jeweler and has been since the 1890s. The shop window, on a conspicuously affluent stretch of Via Condotti, is a visual attraction in its own right. Bulgari designs combine classical Greek aesthetics with Italian taste. Over the years, Bulgari has managed to follow changes in style while still maintaining its tradition. Prices range from affordable to insane. Via Condotti 10. ✆ **06-696-261.** Metro: Spagna.

Diego Percossi Papi   Look here for the ornate jewelry Lucrezia Borgia might wear if she were alive and kicking. Most of the designs are inspired by Renaissance themes, many of them crafted from colored gemstones, and in some cases, accented with iridescent patches of enameling. Jade, opal, and semi-precious gemstones are heavily featured. Via Sant'Eustachio 16. ✆ **06-6880-1466.** Metro: Barberini or Colosseo. Bus: 64.

E. Fiore   This store near Via Veneto is as multifaceted as its jewels. You can select a stone and have it set according to your specifications; choose from a rich assortment of charms, bracelets, necklaces, rings, brooches, corals, pearls, cameos, watches, silverware, and goldware; or have Fiore expertly repair your own jewelry and watches. Closed in August. Via Ludovisi 31. ✆ **06-481-9296.** Bus: 95 or 115.

Federico Buccellati *(Finds)*   At this, one of the best gold- and silversmiths in Italy, neo-Renaissance creations will change your thinking about gold and silver designs. You'll discover the Italian tradition and beauty of handmade jewelry and hollowware whose principles sometimes hark back to the designs of Renaissance gold master Benvenuto Cellini. Via Condotti 31. ✆ **06-679-0329.** Metro: Spagna.

LEATHER

Italian leather is among the very best in the world, and at its best, can attain butter-soft textures more pliable than cloth. You'll find hundreds of leather stores in Rome, many of them excellent.

Alfieri   You'll find virtually any leather garment imaginable in this richly stocked store. Established in the 1960s, with a somewhat more funky and counterculture slant than Casagrande or Campanile, Alfieri prides itself on leather jackets, boots, bags, belts, shirts, hats, and pants for men and women; shorts reminiscent of German lederhosen; and skirts that come in at least 10 different, sometimes neon colors. Although everything sold is made in Italy, this place prides itself on reasonable prices rather than ultra-high quality. So, although you'll definitely find whimsy, an amazingly wide selection, and affordable prices, check the stitching and zippers carefully before you invest. Via del Corso 1–2. ✆ **06-361-1976.** Bus: 117.

Campanile   Belying the postmodern sleekness of its premises, this outfit has a pedigree going back to the 1870s and an impressive inventory of well-crafted leather jackets, belts, shoes, bags, and suitcases for both men and women. Quality is relentlessly high (as are prices), and as such, the store might function as the focal point of your window-shopping energies along either side of Rome's most glamorous shopping street. Via Condotti 58. ✆ 06-678-3041. Metro: Spagna.

Casagrande   If famous names in leather wear appeal to you, you'll find most of the biggies here. Names signifying quality include Fendi and its youth-conscious offspring, Fendissime, plus Cerruti, Mosquino, and Valentino. This well-managed store has developed an impressive reputation for quality and authenticity since the 1930s. The prices are more reasonable than those for equivalent merchandise in some other parts of town. Via Cola di Rienzo 206. ✆ 06-687-4610. Bus: 32 or 81.

Cesare Diomedi Leather Goods   Located in front of the Grand Hotel, this store offers one of the most outstanding collections of leather goods in Rome. And leather isn't all you'll find in this small, two-story shop; many other distinctive items, such as small gold cigarette cases and jeweled umbrellas, make this a good stopping-off point for that last gift. Up the spiral staircase is a wide assortment of elegant leather luggage and accessories. Via Vittorio Emanuele Orlando 96–97. ✆ 06-488-4822. Metro: Piazza della Repubblica.

Fendi Italia   The House of Fendi is mainly known for its leather goods, but it also has furs, stylish purses, ready-to-wear clothing, and a new men's line of clothing and accessories. Gift items, home furnishings, and sports accessories are also sold here, all emblazoned with an "F." Closed Saturday afternoons from July to September. Via Borgognona 36–40. ✆ 06-696-661. Metro: Spagna.

Francesco Rogani   Francesco Rogani has become one of Rome's most famous leather stores, offering a wide selection of bags for every occasion. At Rogani, you'll find a good price-quality relation also for wallets, belts, and handmade ties. Via Condotti 47. ✆ 06-678-4036. Metro: Spagna.

Gucci   Of course, Gucci has been a legend since 1900. It sells high-class leather goods, such as suitcases, handbags, wallets, shoes, and desk accessories. It also has departments complete with elegant men's and women's wear, including tailored shirts, blouses, and dresses, as well as ties and scarves of numerous designs. *La bella figura* is alive and well at Gucci, and prices have never been higher. Among the many temptations is Gucci's own perfume. Via Condotti 8. ✆ 06-679-0405. Metro: Spagna.

Pompea   Fine leather, some of it made to order, is the main focus at this store, where leather bags of all shapes and sizes are sold in a quality that rivals that of the best stores in Italy. You can buy anything on display, but if you have something of a flair for design, you can specify the size, number of compartments, and color of the leather from which your bag will be crafted. Most of the leather goods involve women's purses and bags, although a selection of men's suitcases, briefcases, and garment bags is also sold. Via di Ripetta 150. ✆ 06-687-9165. Metro: Spagna.

Saddlers Union   This is a great place to look for well-crafted leather accessories, such as bags, belts, wallets, shoes, briefcases, and more. Via Condotti 26. ✆ 06-679-8050. Metro: Spagna.

LINGERIE

Brighenti   Brighenti sells strictly lingerie *di lusso*, or perhaps better phrased, haute corseterie. The shop is amid several famous neighbors on Via Frattina; you may run across a lacy, seductive fantasy you just have to have. Closed 2 weeks in August. Via Frattina 7–8. ✆ 06-6791484. Metro: Spagna.

One-of-a-Kind Shops

Alinari, Via Alibert 16A (℅ **06-679-2923**; Metro: Spagna), takes its name from the famed Florentine photographer of the 19th century. Original Alinari prints are almost as prized as paintings in national galleries, and they record the Rome of a century ago.

Fava, Via del Babuino 180 (℅ **06-361-0807**; Metro: Spagna), recaptures the era when Neapolitans sold 17th- and 18th-century pictures of the eruptions of Mount Vesuvius, once highly sought by collectors.

Siragusa, Via delle Carrozze 64 (℅ **06-679-7085**; Metro: Spagna), is more like a museum than a shop, specializing in unusual jewelry, based on ancient carved stones or archaeological pieces mounted in 24K gold. Handmade chains, for example, often hold coins and beads discovered in Asia Minor that date from the 3rd to the 4th century B.C.

Tomassini di Luisa Romagnoli   This shop offers delicately beautiful lingerie and negligees, all original designs of Luisa Romagnoli. Most of the merchandise sold here is of shimmery Italian silk; other items, to a lesser degree, are of fluffy cotton or frothy nylon. Very revealing garments are sold either ready-to-wear or are custom-made. Via Sistina 119. ℅ **06-488-1909**. Metro: Spagna or Barberini.

Vanità   The lingerie selection here spans the spectrum. Yes, you can get black or white, but take the time to browse and you'll find underthings from over, under, and all around the rainbow, including hues you've never dreamed of. Via Frattina 70. ℅ **06-679-1743**. Metro: Spagna.

LUGGAGE

Livio di Simone   Unusual suitcases in many shapes and sizes, into which hand-painted canvas has been sewn, are sold here. This outlet has one of the most tasteful yet durable collections in Rome. Via San Giacomo 23. ℅ **06-3600-1732**. Metro: Spagna.

MARKETS

Piles of fresh vegetables arranged above ancient pavements in the streaming Italian sunshine—well, what visitor can resist? Here's a rundown on the Roman markets known for the freshest produce, the most uninhibited merchants, and the longest-running traditions.

Campo de' Fiori   During the Renaissance, this neighborhood contained most of the inns that pilgrims and merchants from other parts of Europe used for lodgings. Today its battered and slightly shabby perimeter surrounds about a hundred merchants who arrange their produce artfully every day. Campo de' Fiori. Bus: 46, 62, or 64.

Mercato Andrea Doria   After a visit to this open-air festival, you'll never look at the frozen vegetable section in your local supermarket the same way. Set near the Vatican, on a large, sun-baked stretch of pavement between Via Tunisi and Via Santamaura, the merchandise includes meats, poultry, eggs, dairy products, wines, an endless assortment of *frutta e verdura* (fruits and vegetables), and even some scruffy-looking racks of secondhand clothing. Via Andrea Doria. Metro: Ottaviano.

Mercato dei Fiori   Most of the week this vast covered market sells flowers only to retail florists, who resell them to consumers. Every Tuesday, however, the industrial-looking premises open to the public, who crowd in for access to exotic, Mediterranean flowers at bargain-basement prices. Open to the public Tuesday from 10:30am to 1pm. Via Trionfale. Metro: Ottaviano.

Mercato delle Stampe   Virtually everything that's displayed in the dozens of battered kiosks here is dog-eared and evocatively ragtag. You'll find copies of engravings, books, magazines from the 1960s (or before), and prints and engravings that are either worthless or priceless, depending on your taste. If your passion is the printed word, this is your place, and bargaining for value is part of the experience. Largo della Fontanella di Borghese. Bus: 81, 115, or 117.

Mercato di Testaccio   Because their stalls are covered from the wind, rain, and dust of the rest of Rome, the vendors here are able to retain an air of permanence about their set-ups that most outdoor markets simply can't provide. Inside you'll find fishmongers, butchers, cheese sellers, a wide array of dairy products, and the inevitable fruits and vegetables of the Italian harvest. Piazza Testaccio. Bus: 27 or 92.

Mercato di Via Sannio   If you like street fairs loaded with items that verge on the junky, but that contain occasional nuggets of value or eccentric charm, this is the market for you. Regrettably, rare or unusual items are getting harder to find here, as every antiques dealer in Italy seems to have combed through the inventories long before your arrival. Despite that, you'll find some ragtag values in the endless racks of clothing that await cost-conscious buyers. Via Sannio. Metro: S. Giovanni.

Piazza Vittorio Emanuele   Near Santa Maria Maggiore, the largest open-air food market in Rome takes place Monday through Saturday at Piazza Vittorio Emanuele. For browsing Roman style, head here any time between 7am and noon. Most of the vendors at this gigantic square sell fresh fruit, vegetables, and other foodstuffs, although many stalls are devoted to such items as cutlery, clothing, and other merchandise. The place has little to tempt the serious shopper, but it's great for discovering a slice of Roman life. Metro: Vittorio Emanuele.

Porta Portese Flea Market   On Sundays from 7am to 1pm, every peddler from Trastevere and the surrounding Castelli Romani sets up a temporary shop at the sprawling Porta Portese open-air flea market. The vendors are likely to sell merchandise ranging from secondhand paintings of Madonnas and termite-eaten Il Duce wooden medallions, to pseudo-Etruscan hairpins, bushels of rosaries, 1947 TVs, and books printed in 1835. Serious shoppers can often ferret out a good buy. If you've ever been impressed with the bargaining power of the Spaniard, you haven't seen anything till you've bartered with an Italian. By 10:30am the market is full of people. As at any street market, beware of pickpockets. Near the end of Viale Trastevere. Bus: 75 to Porta Portese, then take a short walk to Via Portuense.

Underground   This vast underground car park near the via Veneto blossoms into a bustling flea market two days a month and sells almost anything. From pure junk to genuine antiques there are some real finds here. It's open the first weekend of each month from October to June, from 10am to 8pm. Via Francesco Crispi 96. ℂ 06-3600-5345. Metro: Barberini.

MARQUETRY

Farnese   The entrepreneurs who are the backbone of this outfit are expert restorers of marquetry and inlay work and have been commissioned to help renovate floors as far away as the Kremlin in Moscow. If you want to commission a floor or an entire room sheathed with marquetry crafted from wood, marble, or terra-cotta, this place will send out teams of artisans to install one. But if you're merely in the market for a table, an elaborate cigar or jewel box, or a modest wall plaque that's crafted in a dozen hues of hardwood, look no further. Via Garibaldi 52. ✆ **06-689-6109.** Bus: 16.

MOSAICS

Savelli   This company specializes in the manufacture and sale of mosaics, an art form as old as the Roman empire itself. Many of the objects in the company's gallery were inspired by ancient originals discovered in thousands of excavations throughout the Italian peninsula, including those at Pompeii and Ostia. Others, especially the floral designs, rely on the whim and creativity of the artists. Objects include tabletops, boxes, and vases. The cheapest mosaic objects begin at around $125 and are unsigned products crafted by students at a school for artists that is partially funded by the Vatican. Objects made in the Savelli workshops that are signed by the individual artists tend to be larger and more elaborate. The outlet also contains a collection of small souvenir items, such as keychains and carved statues. Via Paolo VI 27–29. ✆ **06-6830-7017.** Metro: San Paola.

MURALS

Studio Lucifero   Chances are that you won't walk away from this store with a minor purchase, as its specialty involves the creation of full-scale, wall-size murals, each specifically commissioned for the size of the room being decorated and usually based on bucolic or ancient themes. Although the artisans from this shop have actually traveled to execute their works on plaster, the more common motif involves painting a series of large-scale canvas panels, which are then stretched as displays for the room being decorated. The headquarters are within a deconsecrated church near Campo de' Fiori. Here teams of artisans also duplicate such long-ago techniques as trompe l'oeil, gold leafing, and marbelizing techniques known as *faux-marbre.* Via Grottapinta 21. ✆ **06-689-6277.** Bus: 46, 62, or 64.

MUSIC

Disfunzioni Musicali   Sought out by vinyl lovers and used vinyl collectors from Europe and America, this shop has some serious goods. Come here for the rarities. Was that Mick Jagger we spotted searching old labels? Via Degli Etrushi 4–14. ✆ **06-446-1984.** Metro: Piazza Vittorio.

PORCELAIN

Richard Ginori   One of the most prestigious retail outlets for porcelain in the city, this shop contains a roster of the most impeccably crafted pieces by Richard himself. Anything you buy can be shipped. Piazza Trinità dei Monti 18B. ✆ **06-679-3836.** Metro: Spagna.

RELIGIOUS ART & FASHION

Anna Maria Gaudenzi   Set in a neighborhood loaded with purveyors of religious art and icons, this shop claims to be the oldest of its type in Rome. If you collect depictions of Mary, paintings of the saints, exotic rosaries, chalices, small statues, or medals, you can feel secure knowing that thousands of pilgrims have spent their money here before you. Whether you view this type of merchandise as devotional aid or bizarre kitsch, this shop has it all. Piazza della Minerva 69A. ✆ **06-790-431.** Bus: 116.

Gammarelli   Few laypersons ever really think about how or where a clergy-man might clothe himself for mass, but in the Eternal City, the problem is almost universal. If you're looking for a gift for your parish priest or a nephew who has decided to take the vows, head to this store that's known as the "Armani" of the priestly garment biz. Established 200 years ago, it employs a battalion of embroiderers, usually devout Catholics in their own right, who wield needles and either purple, scarlet, or gold threads like the legendary swords of the Counter-Reformation. The inventories are so complete that priests, bishops, and cardinals from around the world consider this a worthwhile stopover during their pilgrimages to Rome. The store does not stock any garments for nuns. Via Santa Chiara 34. ✆ 06-6801314. Bus: 116.

SHOES

Dal Co *(Finds)*   If you've ever suspected that a shoe fetish might be lurking deep inside you, a visit to this store will probably unleash it. Everything inside is handmade and usually can be matched to a handbag that, if it doesn't match exactly, at least provides a reasonably close approximation. Most of the shoes are low-key and conservative, but a few are wild, whimsical, and outrageous enough to appeal even to RuPaul for a night on the town. Only women's shoes are stocked. Via Vittoria 65. ✆ 06-678-6536. Metro: Spagna.

Dominici   An understated facade a few steps from Piazza del Popolo shelters an amusing and lighthearted collection of men's and women's shoes in a rainbow variety of vivid colors. The style is aggressively young-at-heart, and the children's shoes are adorable. Via del Corso 14. ✆ 06-361-0591. Bus: 117.

Ferragamo   Ferragamo sells elegant and fabled footwear, plus ties, women's clothing, and accessories in an atmosphere full of Italian style. The name became famous in America when such silent-screen vamps as Pola Negri and Greta Garbo began appearing in Ferragamo shoes. There are always many customers waiting to enter the shop; management allows them to enter in small groups. (Wear comfortable shoes for what may well be a 30-min. wait.) Via Condotti 73–74. ✆ 06-679-8402. Metro: Spagna.

Fragiacomo   Here you can buy shoes for both men and women in a champagne-colored showroom with gilt-touched chairs and big display cases. Via della Carrozze, 28. ✆ 06-79-8780. Metro: Spagna.

Lily of Florence   This famous Florentine shoemaker now has a shop in Rome, with the same merchandise that made the outlet so well known in the Tuscan capital. Colors come in a wide range, the designs are stylish, and leather texture is of good quality. Shoes for both men and women are sold, and American sizes are a feature. Via Lombardia 38 (off Via Vittorio Veneto). ✆ 06-474-0262. Bus: 116.

SILVER

Anatriello Argenteria Antica e Moderna Roma   This store is known for stocking an inventory of new and antique silver, some of it among the most unusual in Italy. All the new items are made by Italian silversmiths, in designs ranging from the whimsical to the severely formal and dignified. Also on display are antique pieces from England, Germany, and Switzerland. Via Frattina 123. ✆ 06-678-9601. Metro: Spagna.

Fornari & Fornari   This two-story showroom is filled with silver, lamps, porcelain, crystal, furniture, and upscale gift items from many different manufacturers throughout Italy and Europe. Virtually anything can be shipped around the world. Closed in August. Via Frattina 133. ✆ 06-678-0105. Metro: Spagna.

TOYS

La Città del Sole   Other than the branch in Milan, this is the largest and best stocked of any of the stores in its 40-member chain. It specializes in amusements for children and adults, with a wide range of toys and games that don't make beeping noises. Many of the games are configured in English, others in Italian. You'll find role-playing games, battlefield strategy games, family games, and children's games that will challenge a young person's gray matter and probably drive their parents crazy. Also for sale are such rainy-day distractions as miniature billiards tables and tabletop golf sets. Via della Scrofe 65. ℂ **06-687-5404.** Metro: Spagna. Bus: 87 or 492.

WINES & LIQUORS

Ai Monasteri   Italy produces a staggering volume of wines, liqueurs, and after-dinner drinks, and here you'll find a treasure trove of selections: liquors (including liqueurs and wines), honey, and herbal teas made in monasteries and convents all over Italy. You can buy excellent chocolates and other candies here as well. The shop will ship some items home for you. In a quiet atmosphere, reminiscent of a monastery, you can choose your spirits as they move you. Corso Rinascimento 72 (2 blocks from Piazza Navona). ℂ **06-6880-2783.** Bus: 70, 81, or 87.

Buccone   This is a historic wine shop, right near Piazza del Popolo. Its selection of wines and gastronomic specialties is among the finest in Rome. Via Ripetta 19. ℂ **06-361-2154.** Bus: 698 or 926.

Trimani   Established in 1821, Trimani sells wines and spirits from Italy, with a selection of thousands of bottles. Purchases can be shipped to your home. It collaborates with the Italian wine magazine *Gambero Rosso*, organizing some lectures about wine in which enthusiasts can improve their knowledge and educate their taste buds. Via Goito 20. ℂ **06-446-9661.** Metro: Castel Pretorio. Bus: 3, 4, or 36.

10

Rome After Dark

When the sun goes down, lights across the city bathe palaces, ruins, fountains, and monuments in a theatrical white light. There are few evening pursuits as pleasurable as a stroll past the solemn pillars of old temples or the cascading torrents of Renaissance fountains glowing under the blue-black sky.

Of these fountains, the **Naiads** (Piazza della Repubblica), the **Tortoises** (Piazza Mattei), and, of course, the **Trevi** are particularly beautiful at night. The **Capitoline Hill** or Campidoglio is magnificently lit after dark, with its measured Renaissance facades glowing like jewel boxes. The view of the Roman Forum seen from the rear of the trapezoidal piazza del Campidoglio is the grandest in Rome, more so than even the Colosseum. Bus 48, 89, 92, 94, or 716 takes you here at night, or else you can ask for a taxi. If you're across the Tiber, **Piazza San Pietro** (in front of St. Peter's Basilica) is particularly impressive at night, when the tour buses and crowds have departed. A combination of illuminated architecture, Renaissance fountains, sidewalk stage shows, and art expos enliven **Piazza Navona.**

Even if you don't speak Italian, you can generally follow the listings of special events and evening entertainment featured in *La Repubblica,* one of the leading Italian newspapers. *Trova-Roma,* a special weekly entertainment supplement (good for the coming week) is published in this paper on Thursday. The mini-mags *Metropolitan* and *Wanted in Rome* (www.wantedinrome.com) have listings of jazz, rock, and such and give an interesting look at expat Rome. The daily *Il Messaggero* lists current cultural news, especially in its Thursday magazine supplement, *Metro. Un Ospite a Roma,* available free from the concierge desks of top hotels, is full of details on what's happening. There's now a Rome edition of *Time Out,* too, with entertainment and cultural listings available on its website at **www.timeout.co.uk**.

1 The Performing Arts

Rome's premier cultural venue is the **Teatro dell'Opera** (see below), which may not be Milan's legendary La Scala, but offers stellar performances nevertheless. The outstanding local troupe is the **Rome Opera Ballet** (see below).

Rome doesn't have a major center for classical music concerts, although performances of the most important orchestra, the **RAI Symphony Orchestra,** most often take place at the RAI Auditorium, as well as at the Academy of St. Cecilia (see below).

Rome is also a major stopover for international stars. Rock headliners often perform at **Stadio Flaminio, Foro Italico,** and at two different places in the EUR, the **Palazzo della Civiltà del Lavoro** and the **Palazzo dello Sport.** Most of the concerts are at the Palazzo dello Sport.

CLASSICAL MUSIC

Academy of St. Cecilia   Concerts given by the orchestra of the Academy of St. Cecilia usually take place at Piazza di Villa Giulia, site of the Etruscan Museum, from the end of June to the end of July; in winter, they're held in the academy's concert hall on Via della Conciliazione. Sometimes other addresses are selected for concerts, including a handful of historic churches. Performance nights are usually Friday to Tuesday. Via della Conciliazione 4. ✆ **06-6880-1044.** Tickets 33,000L–85,000L (17.15€–44.20€, $16.50–$42.50). Bus: 62 or 982.

Teatro Olimpico   Large and well publicized, this echoing stage hosts a widely divergent collection of singers, both classical and pop, who perform according to a schedule that sometimes changes at the last minute. Occasionally the space is devoted to chamber orchestras or visits by foreign orchestras. Piazza Gentile da Fabriano. ✆ **06-323-4890.** Tickets 20,000L–80,000L (10.40€–41.60€, $10–$40), depending on the event. Metro: Flaminio.

OPERA

Teatro dell'Opera   If you're in the capital for the opera season—usually from the end of December until June—you may want to attend a performance at the historic Rome Opera House, located off Via Nazionale. Nothing is presented here in August; in summer, the venue usually changes. Call ahead or ask your hotel concierge before you go. You can buy tickets at the box office (closed Mon), at any Banca di Roma bank, or by phone at ✆ **147/882-211.** Piazza Beniamino Gigli 1 off Via Nazionale. ✆ **06-481-601.** Tickets 30,000L–300,000L (15.60€–156€, $15–$150). Metro: Termini.

BALLET & DANCE

Performances of the Rome Opera Ballet are given at the **Teatro dell'Opera** (see above). The regular repertoire of classical ballet is supplemented by performances of internationally acclaimed guest artists, and Rome is on the agenda for major troupes from around the world. Watch for announcements in the weekly entertainment guides to see what's happening at the time of your visit and to check on other venues, including the Teatro Olimpico and open-air performances.

A MEAL & A SONG

Frankly, the places below are touristy and cheesy. But thousands upon thousands of visitors love this type of after-dark diversion. Touristy or not, the places are packed every night, so they seem to know what appeals to the mass.

Da Ciceruacchio   This restaurant was once a sunken jail; the ancient vine-covered walls date from the 18th century. Folkloric groups appear throughout the evening, especially singers of Neapolitan songs, accompanied by guitars and harmonicas. It's a rich repertoire of old-time favorites, some with bawdy lyrics. There are charcoal-broiled steaks and chops along with lots of local wine, and bean soup is a specialty. On Piazza dei Mercanti, at Via del Porto 1, in Trastevere. ✆ **06-580-6046.** 40,000L–60,000L (20.80€–31.20€, $20–$30). Tues–Sun 7:30pm–midnight. Bus: 23.

Da Meo Patacca   Da Meo Patacca would have pleased Barnum and Bailey. On a gaslit piazza from the Middle Ages, it serves bountiful self-styled "Roman country" meals to flocks of tourists. The atmosphere is one of extravaganza—primitive, colorful, and theatrical in a carnival sense. It's touristy, all right, but good fun if you're in the mood. Downstairs is a vast cellar with strolling musicians and singers. Many offerings are as adventurous as the decor (wild boar, wild hare, and quail), but you'll also find corn on the cob, pork and beans, thick-cut sirloins, and chicken on a spit. You'll get fun and entertainment—not refined cuisine. In summer, you can dine at outdoor tables. Piazza dei Mercanti 30, in Trastevere. ✆ **06-5833-1086.** From 70,000L (36.40€, $35). Daily 8–11:30pm. Bus: 23.

Fantasie di Trastevere Roman rusticity is combined with theatrical flair at Fantasie di Trastevere, the people's theater where the famous actor Petrolini made his debut. In the 16th century, this restaurant was an old theater built for Queen Cristina of Sweden and her court. The cuisine is bountiful, though hardly subtle. Such dishes as the classic saltimbocca (ham with veal) are preceded by tasty pasta, and everything is helped along by Castelli Romani wines. Accompanying the main dishes is a big basket of warm, country-coarse herb bread. Some two dozen folk singers and musicians in regional attire make it a festive affair. Via di Santa Dorotea 6. ✆ **06-588-1671.** Cover (including the first drink) 35,000L (18.20€, $17.50), or 80,000L–120,000L (41.60€–62.40€, $40–$60) including dinner. Meals daily from 8pm; piano bar music 8:30–9:30pm; show 9:30–10:30pm. Bus: 23, 65, or 280.

2 The Club & Music Scene
NIGHTCLUBS/DANCE CLUBS

Alien In a futuristic setting of exposed pipes and ventilation ducts, Alien provides a bizarre space-age dance floor, bathed in strobe lights and rocking to the sounds of house/techno music. Occasionally, a master of ceremonies will interject brief interludes of cabaret or comedy. The crowd does tend to be young. Via Vellertri 13–19. ✆ **06-841-2212.** Cover (including the first drink) 30,000L–35,000L (15.60€–18.20€, $15–$17.50). Tues–Sat 11pm–5am. Bus 3, 4, or 57.

Alpheus One of Rome's largest and most energetic nightclubs, Alpheus contains three sprawling rooms, each with a different musical sound and an ample number of bars. You'll find areas devoted to Latin music, to rock, and to jazz. Live bands come and go, and there's enough cultural variety in the crowd to keep virtually anyone amused throughout the course of the evening. Both locals and visitors frequent this club, and the clients represent a wide age range. Via del Commercio 36. ✆ **06-574-7826.** Cover 10,000L–20,000L (5.20€–10.40€, $5–$10). Tues–Sun 10pm–4am. Bus: 713.

Berimbau This hot spot is South American *latino,* the decor evokes the southern Mediterranean, and the rhythms are pure Caribbean, including Brazilian, Cuban, and Dominican sounds. Via di Fienaroli 30B. ✆ **06-581-3249** weekends. Cover 15,000L–25,000L (7.80€–13€, $7.50–$12.50), including first drink. Fri–Sat 10:30pm–dawn. Bus: 56 or 60.

Black Out If you're looking for a little counterculture edge, where you might hear the latest indie music from the U.K., head for Black Out, which occupies an industrial-looking site. Whenever it can manage, a live band is presented on Thursday—very late. The recorded music includes punk, retro, R&B, grunge, and whatever else happens to be in fashion. There's always one room (with an independent sound system) set aside as a lounge. This club lures a crowd, mainly Romans, in their 20s and 30s. Via Saturnia 18. ✆ **06-704-96791.** Cover (including the first drink) 10,000L–15,000L (5.20€–7.80€, $5–$7.50). Thurs–Sat 10:30pm–4am. Metro: Re di Roma.

Club Picasso This high-energy dance spot attracts everyone, usually young Romans, from teeny-boppers to 50-year-olds (who remember some of the music as original to their college years) and lots of high-energy people-watchers in between. A strict bouncer at the door bars any potential trouble-makers. There's

> **Tips Nightlife Tips**
>
> In addition to high charges (all nightclubs in Rome are expensive), many otherwise legitimate clubs have add-on expenses in the form of hookers plying their trade.
>
> Another important warning: During the peak of summer tourism, usually in August, all nightclub proprietors seem to lock their doors and head for the seashore, where they operate alternate clubs. Some of them close at different times each year, so it's hard to keep up-to-date. Always have your hotel check to see whether a club is operating before you trek out to it.
>
> Testaccio may be radical chic personified, but it's also a neighborhood with an edge (you don't want to wander around here alone at night). However, Testaccio is the place to find out what's hot in Rome—ask around.

a pizzeria, where you can grab a cheap bite. Via Monte di Testaccio 63. ✆ **06-574-2975.** No cover Tues–Thurs; 15,000L (7.80€, $7.50) Fri; 20,000L (10.40€, $10) Sat. Tues–Sun 8pm–4am. Bus: 95.

Gilda   Gilda is a combination of nightclub, disco, and restaurant known for its glamorous acts (past performances include Diana Ross and splashy, Paris-type revues). The artistic direction assures first-class shows, a well-run restaurant (featuring international cuisine), and disco music played between the live acts. The disco offers music from the 1960s to the present. The attractive piano bar, Swing, features Italian and Latin music. Via Mario de' Fiori 97. ✆ **06-678-4838.** Cover (including the first drink) 40,000L (20.80€, $20); meals from 45,000L (23.40€, $22.50). Disco Tues–Sun midnight–4am; restaurant from 9:30pm. Metro: Piazza di Spagna.

Jackie O   Close to the American Embassy and Via Veneto, Jackie O is a glittery club that draws an affluent, well-dressed, over-30 crowd, mostly foreign. If you opt to go dancing here (it's not as frenzied as some might like), you might begin your evening with a drink at the piano bar, then perhaps end it in the restaurant. Via Boncompagni 11. ✆ **06-4288-5457.** Cover (including the first drink) 50,000L (26€, $25). Meals 100,000L (52€, $50) without wine. Tues–Sun 8:30pm–4am. Metro: Barberini.

Magic Fly   Small-scale and somewhat cramped when it really begins to rock, this club is more elegant than the norm and lies about 3 miles to the northeast, outside the ring road that encircles the center of Rome. Music changes nightly; depending on the schedule, you might hear anything from Latin salsa and merengue to American-style rock or British new wave. There's a posh feel throughout (enhanced by the many men in neckties). You'll need to take a taxi to get here. Via Bassanello 15, Cassia-Grottarossa. ✆ **06-3326-8956.** Cover (including the first drink) 10,000L–30,000L (5.20€–15.60€, $5–$15). Wed–Sat 10:30pm–dawn.

Radio Londra   Radio Londra has a counterculture edge, complete with revelers of the chartreuse-haired, nose-pierced variety from London. Since Radio Londra is near the popular gay L'Alibi (see below), the downstairs club attracts many brethren, though the crowd is mixed with both Roman and foreign. Upstairs is a pub/pizzeria where bands often appear; you can even order a veggie burger with a Bud. Via Monte Testaccio 67. No phone. No cover. Club: Wed–Fri 11:30am–4am; pub/pizzeria: Sun–Mon and Wed–Fri 9pm–3am, Sat 9pm–4am. Bus: 95.

Giardini di Adone If you're young (and we mean barely of legal drinking age), and enjoy a loud and wild atmosphere, head here. Local bands slice the air waves with music heard across town as you rock against the backdrop of a mirror ball and frescoes of Adonis. It's all a bit kitschy but fun. Via dei Reti, 38A. ℂ **06-445-1250**. 10,000L (5.20€, $5) cover charge. Tues–Sat 9pm–1:30am. Closed Aug. Metro: Termini.

Locanda Atlantide Don't be put off by the facade thinking you might have just arrived at a bunker for a Gestapo interrogation. Inside, this San Lorenzo club in a former warehouse is today the setting of a nightclub, bar, concert hall, and theater. Every day a different event is staged—perhaps jazz on Tuesday, a play on Wednesday, or a concert on Thursday, giving way to dance club action on Friday and Saturday with music provided by a DJ. Via dei Lucani. ℂ **06-4470-4540**. Cover 5,000L–10,000L (2.60€–5.20€, $2.50–$5), depending on the evening. Tues–Sun 10pm–3:30am. Closed June 15–Sept 15. Metro: Piazza Vittorio.

JAZZ & OTHER LIVE SOUNDS

The places we've recommended appeal to a wide age group, especially the jazz joints. As one local put it, "You don't get over your love of jazz just because you turned 35."

Alexanderplatz At this leading jazz club, you can listen to the music or enjoy the good kitchen, which serves everything from pesto alla genovese to gnocchi alla romana to Japanese cuisine. Via Ostia 9. ℂ **06-3974-2171**. Club membership (valid for 3 months) 12,000L (6.25€, $6). Mon–Sat 9pm–2am, live music from 10:15pm. Bus: 23.

Arciliuto This place reputedly once housed Raphael's studio, but now it's home to one of the most romantic candlelit spots in Rome. Guests listen to both a guitarist and a lute player in an intimate setting. The evening's presentation also includes Neapolitan love songs, old Italian madrigals, even current hits from New York's Broadway or London's West End. Highly recommended, it's hard to find, but is within walking distance of Piazza Navona. From the west side of Piazza Navona, take Via di S. Agnese in Agone, which leads to Via di Tor Milliana, then follow this street into Piazza Monte Vecchio. Piazza Monte Vecchio 5. ℂ **06-6879419**. Cover (including the first drink) 35,000L (18.20€, $17.50). Mon–Sat 10pm–2am. Closed July 20–Sept 3. Bus: 42, 62, or 64.

Big Mama Big Mama is a hangout for jazz and blues musicians, where you're likely to meet the up-and-coming jazz stars of tomorrow and sometimes even the big names. Vicolo San Francesco a Ripa 18. ℂ **06-581-2551**. Cover 20,000L–30,000L (10.40€–15.60€, $10–$15) for big acts (free for minor shows), plus 20,000L (10.40€, $10) seasonal membership fee. Mon–Sat 9pm–1:30am. Closed July–Sept. Bus: 44, 75, or 170.

Fonclea Fonclea offers live music every night—jazz, Dixieland, rock, rhythm and blues, and funk. This is basically a cellar jazz bar that attracts folks from all walks of Roman life. There's also a restaurant that features moderately priced grilled meats, salads, and crepes; if you want dinner it's best to reserve a table. Music usually starts at 9:15pm and lasts until about 12:30am. Via Crescenzio 82A. ℂ **06-689-6302**. No cover Sun–Fri; 10,000L (5.20€, $5) Sat. Sun–Thurs 7pm–2am, Fri–Sat 7pm–3:30am. Closed July–Aug. Bus: 32 or 39.

GAY & LESBIAN CLUBS

Two English-speaking gay and lesbian organizations can be found in Rome: **ARCI-Gay**, Via Primo Acciaresi 7 (ℂ **06-862-02-728**; Bus: 71) and **Circolo Mario Mieli**, Via Efeso 2 (ℂ **06-54-13-985**; Metro: San Paolo). Both are helpful with political and social information.

Angelo Azzuro   This is a gay hot spot deep in the heart of Trastevere. Men dance with men to recorded music, though women are also invited (Friday is for women only). Via Cardinal Merry del Val 13. ☎ 06-580-0472. Cover (including 1 drink) 20,000L (10.40€, $10). Fri–Sun 11pm–4am. Bus: 44, 75, or 170.

The Hangar   Having survived since 1984, the Hangar is a landmark on the gay nightlife scene. It's on one of Rome's oldest streets, adjacent to the Forum, on the site of the palace once inhabited by Claudius's deranged wife Messalina. Each of the Hangar's two bars has an independent sound system. Women are welcome any night except Monday, when the club features videos and entertainment for men. The busiest nights are Saturday, Sunday, and Monday, when as many as 500 people cram inside. Via in Selci 69. ☎ 06-4881397. No cover. Club membership 12,000L (6.25€, $6). Wed–Mon 10:30pm–2:30am. Closed 3 weeks in Aug. Metro: Cavour.

Joli Coeur   This bar caters to lesbians; Saturdays are reserved for women only. A fixture in the city's lesbian night scene, it also attracts women from around Europe. Information about Joli Coeur ("pretty heart") can be had by contacting The Hangar (see above), as Joli Coeur can be difficult to reach directly. Via Sirte 5. ☎ 06-8621-6240. Cover (including the first drink) 20,000L (10.40€, $10). Sat–Sun 11pm–5am. Bus: 52 or 56.

L'Alibi   L'Alibi, in the Testaccio sector away from the heart of Rome, is a year-round stop on many a gay man's agenda. The crowd, however, tends to be mixed: Roman and international, straight and gay, male and female. One room has a dance floor. Via Monte Testaccio 44. ☎ 06-574-3448. Cover 15,000L–20,000L (7.80€–10.40€, $7.50–$10). Wed–Sun 11pm–4am. Bus: 30N.

3 The Cafe & Bar Scene

It seems there's nothing Romans like better than sitting and talking over their favorite beverage—usually wine or coffee. Unless you're dead set on making the Roman nightclub circuit, try what might be a far livelier and less expensive scene—sitting late at night on **Via Veneto, Piazza della Rotonda, Piazza del Popolo,** or one of Rome's other piazzas, all for the cost of an espresso, a cappuccino, or a Campari.

If you're looking for some scrumptious **ice cream,** refer to the listings below for Café Rosati and Giolitti, as well as the box titled "Take a Gelato Break" on p. 98.

CAFES
ON VIA VENETO

Back in the 1950s (a decade *Time* magazine gave to Rome, in the way it conceded the 1960s and later the 1990s to London), **Via Vittorio Veneto** rose in fame as the hippest street in Rome, crowded with aspiring and actual movie stars, their directors, and a fast-rising group of card-carrying members of the jet set. Today, the beautiful people wouldn't be caught dead on Via Veneto—it's become touristy. But, regardless of that, visitors flock here by the thousands every night. Times Square in New York is very touristy, but millions still head there. As one Roman cafe owner told us, "You can see Romans all over the city. But on the via Veneto sit at one of our tables and catch people from all over the world go by. It's worth the price we charge for an espresso."

Caffè de Paris   This spot has been around for decades. It's popular in summer, when the tables spill right out onto the sidewalk and the passing crowd

Moments **The Ruin to Beat All Ruins**

There is no more dramatic sight in all of Rome at night than that of the Colosseum lit up. In the harsh light of day it looks like a ruin, but at night your imagination goes into overdrive. Over the centuries earthquakes, pollution, traffic, and pillage have taken a toll on the arena. But at night, Rome's greatest marvel emerges in its beauty.

walks through the maze. This is the most famous cafe in all of Rome for people watching along the via Veneto, although locals shun it. Via Vittorio Veneto 90. ℂ 06-488-5284. Wed–Mon 8am–1:30am (Tues till midnight). Metro: Barberini.

Harry's Bar   Sophisticated Harry's Bar is a perennial favorite of the post-40 foreign visitors. Locals rarely show up here. Every major Italian city (like Florence and Venice) seems to have one, and Rome is no exception, though this one has no connection with the others. In summer, tables are placed outside. For those who wish to dine outdoors but want to avoid the scorching sun, there's an air-conditioned sidewalk cafe open from May to November. Meals inside cost about double what you'd pay outside. In back is a small dining room serving some of the finest (and priciest) food in central Rome. The restaurant inside is open Monday to Saturday 12:30 to 3pm and 7:30pm to 1am. Outside you can eat from noon to midnight. The bar is open Monday to Saturday 11am to 2am (closed Aug 1–10), and the piano bar is open nightly from 9:30pm, with live music starting at 11pm. Via Vittorio Veneto 150. ℂ 06-484-643. Metro: Barberini.

NEAR THE TERMINI

Bar Marini   This century-old coffee bar by the marketplace attracts all kinds— students, visitors, Japanese tourists, shopkeepers, artists, pickpockets, and rock stars. Its espresso is one of the lures, as is the delicious ice cream. Try to grab a table on the vine-covered terrace. Via dei Volsci, 57. ℂ 06-490-016. Metro: Termini.

NEAR PIAZZA NAVONA

Bar della Pace   Bar della Pace has elegant neighbors, such as Santa Maria della Pace, a church with sibyls by Raphael and a cloister designed by Bramante. The bar dates from the beginning of the 20th century and is decorated with wood, marble, and mirrors. Via della Pace 3–5. ℂ 06-686-1216. Mon 3pm–3am; Tues–Sun 9am–3am. Bus: 64.

NEAR THE PANTHEON

The **Piazza della Rotonda,** across from the Pantheon, is the hopping place to be after dark, especially in summer. Although it's touristy, locals come here, too, because it's a dramatic place to be at night when the Pantheon is lit up.

Caffè Sant'Eustachio   Strong coffee is liquid fuel to Italians, and many Romans will walk blocks and blocks for what they consider a superior brew. Caffè Sant'Eustachio is one of Rome's most celebrated espresso shops, where the water supply is funneled into the city by an aqueduct built in 19 B.C. Rome's most experienced espresso judges claim the water plays an important part in the coffee's flavor, though steam forced through ground Brazilian coffee roasted on the premises has a significant effect as well. Buy a ticket from the cashier for as many cups as you want, then leave a small tip (about 1,000L/U.S.50¢) for the counter-person when you present your receipt. Piazza Sant'Eustachio 82. ℂ 06-686-1309. Tues–Fri and Sun 8:30am–1am; Sat 8:30am–1:30am. Bus: 116.

Ciampini   This stylish, breezy spot has a staff that's usually hysterically over-burdened, with little time for small talk. But despite the fact that service might be slow, a crowd of midday office workers loyally returns for morning shots of espresso; affordable, filling salads at lunch; and tea in the afternoon. Piazza San Lorenzo in Lucina 29. © **06-687-6606.** Mon–Sat 7:30am–9pm. Bus: 116.

Di Rienzo   This is the top cafe on this piazza. In fair weather, you can sit at one of the sidewalk tables (if you can find a free one). In cooler weather, you can retreat inside, where the walls are inlaid with the type of marble found on the Pantheon's floor. Many types of pastas appear on the menu, as does *risotto alla pescatora* (fisherman's rice) and several meat courses. You can also order pizzas. Piazza della Rotonda 8–9. © **06-686-9097.** Daily 7am–1 or 2am. Bus: 116.

La Caffettiera   In a comfortable, albeit bustling setting, you can enjoy a refreshingly light and easy meal, like a sandwich or a slice of quiche, or just a quick fix of caffeine. Lots of folks drop in for the Neapolitan-style ice-cream confections in the afternoon. Piazza di Pietra 65. © **06-679-8147.** Mon–Sat 7am–9pm. Bus: 116.

Riccioli Café   Formally known as Hemingway's Pub, this recently trans-formed sleek night spot is a fast-rising oyster and champagne bar. In elegant yet informal surroundings, you can order drinks, of course, as well as oysters on the half shell. It's a scene, but the food in the upscale loft-like wine cellar is actually quite good. Piazza delle Coppelle 10A. © **06-6821-0313.** Bus: 64.

Riva Gauche   Adapting a chic Parisian name, this spot evokes the best of some of the new bars popping up in Rome to attract yuppies who are deserting their traditional glass of wine to sample one of the more than three dozen types of whisky on sale here. As part of "Castro chic," people also drink a variety of rum-laced drinks as well. Via dei Sabelli, 43. © **06-445-6722.** Daily 8pm–2:30am. Metro: Termini.

Tazza d'Oro   This cafe is known for serving its own brand of espresso. Another specialty, ideal on a hot summer night, is *granità di caffè* (coffee that has been frozen, crushed into a velvety slushlike ice, and placed in a glass between layers of whipped cream). Piazza della Rotonda, Via degli Orfani 84. © **06-678-2792.** Daily 7:30am–1am. Bus: 116.

ON THE CORSO & PIAZZA COLONNA

Autogrill   Autogrill is a monumental cafe that's often filled with busy shop-pers. There's a stand-up sandwich bar with dozens of selections and a cafeteria, both self-serve and with a sit-down area. The decor includes high coffered ceil-ings, baroque wall stencils, globe lights, crystal chandeliers, and black stone floors. Via del Corso 181. © **06-678-9135.** Daily 7am–10pm. Metro: Piazza di Spagna.

Giolitti   Near Piazza Colonna, this is one of the city's most popular nighttime gathering spots and the oldest ice-cream shop. Some of the sundaes look like Vesuvius about to erupt. Many people take gelato out to eat on the streets; oth-ers enjoy it in the post-empire splendor of the salon inside. You can have your "coppa" daily 7am to 2am (closed at 1am in winter). There are many excellent, smaller gelaterie throughout Rome, wherever you see the cool concoction adver-tised as *produzione propria* (homemade). Via Uffici del Vicario 40. © **06-699-1243.** Bus: 116.

ON OR NEAR PIAZZA DEL POPOLO

According to legend, the ashes of Nero were enshrined here until 11th-century residents began complaining to the pope about his imperial ghost. The Egyptian obelisk seen here today dates from the 13th century B.C.; it was removed from Heliopolis to Rome during the reign of Augustus (it originally stood at the Circus Maximus). The present piazza was designed in the early 19th century by Valadier, Napoléon's architect. Two almost-twin baroque churches stand on the square, overseeing the never-ending traffic.

Café Rosati   Café Rosati, which has been around since 1923, attracts guys and dolls of all persuasions, both foreign and domestic, who drive up in Maseratis and Porsches. It's really a combination of sidewalk cafe, ice-cream parlor, candy store, confectionery, and *ristorante* that has been swept up in the fickle world of fashion. The later you go, the more interesting the action. Piazza del Popolo 5A. © 06-322-5859. Daily noon–11pm. Bus: 117.

Canova Café   Though the management has filled it with boutiques selling expensive gift items, like luggage and cigarette lighters, many Romans still consider Canova Café *the* place to be on the piazza. The Canova has a sidewalk terrace for people-watching, plus a snack bar, a restaurant, and a wine shop. In summer, you'll have access to a courtyard whose walls are covered with ivy and where flowers grow in terra-cotta planters.   Piazza del Popolo 16. © 06-361-2231. Restaurant daily noon–3:30pm and 7–11pm; bar daily 8am to midnight or 1am. Bus: 117.

NEAR THE SPANISH STEPS

Antico Caffè Greco   Since 1760, this has been Rome's poshest coffee bar. Stendhal, Goethe, Keats, and D'Annunzio have sipped coffee here before you. In fact, a list of former guests reads like a syllabus for Romanticism 101. Today, you're more likely to see ladies who lunch and Japanese tourists, but there's plenty of atmosphere. In front is a wooden bar and beyond is a series of small salons. You sit at marble-topped tables of Napoleonic design, against a backdrop of gold or red damask, romantic paintings, and antique mirrors. It was Giorgio De Chirico who suggested that this is the cafe where you sit and await the end. The house specialty is *paradisi,* made with lemon and orange. Via Condotti 84. © 06-679-1700. Mon–Sat 8am–9pm. Closed 10 days in Aug. Metro: Piazza di Spagna.

La Buvette   This place is both a cafe and an unpretentious restaurant. No one will mind if you come here just for an espresso, but if you're hungry, consider ordering one of the meal-sized salads, which serious shoppers from the nearby Via Condotti order as a pick-me-up in the heat and humidity of a hot Roman midday. More elaborate platters are also available. Via Vittoria 44–47. © 06-679-0383. Mon–Sat 7am–8:30pm. Metro: Piazza di Spagna.

IN TRASTEVERE

Several cafes in Trastevere, across the Tiber, are attracting crowds. Fans who saw Fellini's *Roma* know what **Piazza Santa Maria in Trastevere** looks like at night. The square, filled with milling throngs in summer, is graced with an octagonal fountain and a 12th-century church. Children run and play on the piazza, and occasional spontaneous guitar fests break out when the weather's good.

Café-Bar di Marzio   This warmly inviting place, which is strictly a cafe (not a restaurant), has narrow wood paneled furnishings and outdoor tables at the edge of the square with the best view of its famous fountain. Everybody from blue-collar workers to artists and writers, goes here to see and be seen. Piazza di Santa Maria in Trastevere 15. © 06-581-6095. Daily 7am–2am. Closed Mon in Feb. Bus: 44, 75, or 170.

Pasquino-Net   If you want to send an e-mail, surf the Web, or flirt with an anonymous stranger online, head here. You can go online for 7,500L to 9,900L (3.90€–5.15€, $3.75–$4.95) per hour, depending on when you show up. A brief look-see at your e-mail, if you remain online for less than about 10 minutes, goes for 2,000L (1.05€, $1). You can also enjoy drinks and affordable burgers, pastas, salads, and steaks. It's associated with the also-recommended Pasquino Cinema. Piazza San Egidio, just off Piazza di Santa Maria in Trastevere. € 06-580-3622. Daily 4pm–midnight. Bus: 44, 75, or 170.

WINE BARS

Enoteca Fratelli Roffi Isabelli   A stand-up drink in this dark, atmospheric spot is the perfect ending to a visit to the nearby Spanish Steps. Set behind a discreet facade in a chic shopping district, this is the city's best repository for Italian wines, brandies, and grappa. You can opt for a postage-stamp–sized table in the back or stay at the bar with its impressive display of wines stacked on shelves in every available corner. Via della Croce 76B. € 06-679-0896. Restaurant daily 12:30–3:30pm and 7:30–11pm; bar daily 11:30am–1am. Metro: Piazza di Spagna.

Il Goccetto   Set near Campo de' Fiori, Il Goccetto specializes in French and Italian wines by the glass at prices that range from 5,000L (2.60€, $2.50) for a simple Chianti to as much as 18,000L (9.35€, $9) for a glass of French champagne. Platters of food are on hand to assuage your hunger pangs, but don't expect anything hot, as there are no real kitchen facilities. Instead, you'll be presented with an extensive list of Italian cheeses and processed meats, especially salami and pâtés, as well as an occasional salad. Overall, this place provides an excellent site for the *degustazione* of a wide assortment of unusual Italian wines, many of them from less-well-known small producers. Via dei Banchi Vecchi 14. € 06-686-4268. Mon–Sat 11am–2pm and 5–11pm. Bus: 46, 62, or 64.

La Bottega del Vino   This old-fashioned setting comes complete with terracotta floors and long, battered wooden tables. Everything acts as a foil for the Italian and French wines served here. Priced at 5,000L to 15,000L (2.60€–7.80€, $2.50–$7.50) per glass, depending on the vintage, they derive from well-known or obscure vineyards throughout Italy. Affordable snacks and cold platters are available as accompaniment. Lunch features more elaborate offerings, like crushed crabmeat served in a roulade of smoked salmon, or a spinach, pear, and walnut salad. In other hours, the snacks are simpler, consisting mostly of salami, bread, and cheese, but always a good foil for the wines. Via Santa Maria del Pianto 9A-12. € 06-686-5970. Lunch Mon–Sat 12:30–3pm; wine bar and snacks Mon–Sat 12:30–3:30pm and 5–8:30pm. Bus: 44 or 46.

IRISH PUBS

The two most popular Irish pubs, both near Piazza di Santa Maria Maggiore and listed first below, draw mostly English-speaking expatriates. You can always see a cluster of disoriented local teenagers here and there, but their Italian is drowned in the sea of English, Scottish, Irish, Canadian, Australian, and sometimes American accents.

Druid's Den   At the popular Druid's Den you can enjoy a pint of beer while listening to Irish music. One night we saw a group of young Irishmen dancing an Irish jig, much to the delight of the Roman onlookers. Via San Martino ai Monti 28. € 06-488-0258. Daily 5pm–12:30am. Metro: Termini.

Fiddler's Elbow   Fiddler's Elbow, near Piazza di Santa Maria Maggiore and the railway station, is reputedly the oldest pub in the capital. Sometimes, however, the place is so packed you can't find room to drink. Via dell'Olmata 43. € 06-4872110. Daily 4:30pm–12:30am. Metro: Termini.

Night & Day   It sounds like an old Cole Porter song, but it's actually one of the most popular Irish pubs near Piazza del Popolo. It really heats up around 2am, when many dance clubs close for the evening. American music is played as you down your Harps and Guinness. Amazingly, foreigners are issued drink cards, making all their drinks 6,000L (3.10€, $3) instead of the 8,000L (4.15€, $4) usually charged. A young man in his 20s, who introduces himself only as "Simone," is your host and often works behind the bar himself. Via dell'Oca 50. ② 06-320-2300. Daily 5pm–5am. Bus: 117.

4 At the Movies

Pasquino Cinema   Just off the corner of Piazza Santa Maria in Trastevere, the little Pasquino draws faithful English-speaking fans, both Italians and expatriates. You might catch the occasional classic amid the more recent releases. Most are in their original language (usually English) with Italian subtitles. There are three theaters with screenings daily, as well as a bookshop selling videotapes and movie posters, an Internet cafe (Pasquino-Net, which is recommended separately), and a bar. Films usually start at 4pm, with the day's last film usually beginning at 10:30pm. Piazza San Egidio, just off Piazza di Santa Maria in Trastevere. ② 06-580-3622. Tickets 15,000L (7.80€, $7.50). Bus: 45, 65, 170, 181, or 280.

11

Side Trips from Rome

Most European capitals are surrounded with a number of worthwhile
attractions, but Rome tops them all
for sheer variety. Just a few miles from
Rome, you can go back to the dawn of
Italian history and explore the dank
tombs the Etruscans left as their legacy
or drink the golden wine of the towns
in the Alban Hills (Castelli Romani).
You can wander the ruins of Hadrian's
Villa, the "queen of villas of the

ancient world," or be lulled by the
music of the baroque fountains in the
Villa d'Este. You can turn yourself
bronze on the beaches of Ostia di Lido
or explore the remarkable ruins of
Ostia Antica, Rome's ancient seaport.

If you have time, the attractions in
the environs can fill at least 3 days.
We've highlighted the best of the lot
below.

1 Tivoli & the Villas ⋆/⋆

Tivoli, known as Tibur to the ancient Romans, is 20 miles (32km) east of Rome
on Via Tiburtina, about an hour's drive with traffic. If you don't have a car, take
Metro Line B to the end of the line, the Rebibbia station. After exiting the station, board an Acotral bus for the trip the rest of the way to Tivoli. Generally,
buses depart about every 20 minutes during the day. For information about the
town, check with **Azienda Autonoma di Turismo,** Largo Garibaldi (✆ 0774/
334-522), Tivoli. Opening hours are Tuesday to Saturday 9am to 2:30pm, and
Tuesday and Thursday 9am to 2pm and 3 to 6pm.

EXPLORING THE VILLAS

Villa d'Este ⋆⋆ Like Hadrian centuries before, Cardinal Ippolito d'Este of
Ferrara believed in heaven on earth, and in the mid–16th century he ordered
this villa built on a hillside. The dank Renaissance structure, with its second-rate
paintings, is not that noteworthy; the big draw for visitors are the **spectacular
gardens** below (designed by Pirro Ligorio).

You descend the cypress-studded slope to the bottom and, on the way, are
rewarded with everything from lilies to gargoyles spouting water, torrential
streams, and waterfalls. The loveliest fountain is the Ovato Fountain (Fontana dell
Ovato) by Ligorio. But nearby is the most spectacular achievement: the **Fountain
of the Hydraulic Organ (Fontana dell'Organo Idraulico),** dazzling with its
water jets in front of a baroque chapel, with four maidens who look tipsy. The
work represents the genius of Frenchman Claude Veanard. The moss-
covered Fountain of the Dragons (Fontana dei Draghi), also by Ligorio, and the
so-called Fountain of Glass (Fontana di Vetro), by Bernini, are the most intriguing. The best walk is along the promenade, with 100 spraying fountains. The garden is worth hours of exploration, but it's a lot of walking, with some steep climbs.

Piazza Trento, Viale delle Centro Fontane. ✆ 0774/312-070. Admission 8,000L (4.15€, $4). The bus from
Rome stops near the entrance.

Villa Gregoriana ✦ The Villa d'Este dazzles with artificial glamour, but the Villa Gregoriana relies more on nature. The gardens were built by Pope Gregory XVI in the 19th century. At one point on the circuitous walk carved along a slope, you can stand and look out onto the most panoramic waterfall (Aniene) at Tivoli. The trek to the bottom on the banks of the Anio is studded with grottoes and balconies that open onto the chasm. The only problem is that if you do make the full descent, you might need a helicopter to pull you up again (the climb back up is fierce). From one of the belvederes, there's a panoramic view of the Temple of Vesta on the hill.

Largo Sant'Angelo. ✆ **0774/334-522**. Admission 3,500L (1.80€, $1.75). May–Aug daily 10am–7:30pm; Sept daily 9:30am–6:30pm; Oct–Mar daily 9:30am–4:30pm; Apr daily 9:30am–6pm. The bus from Rome stops near the entrance.

Hadrian's Villa (Villa Adriana) ✦✦✦ In the 2nd century A.D., the globe-trotting Hadrian spent the last 3 years of his life in the grandest style. Less than 4 miles (6km) from Tivoli, he built one of the greatest estates ever erected, and he filled acre after acre with some of the architectural wonders he'd seen on his many travels. Perhaps as a preview of what he envisioned in store for himself, the emperor even created a representation of hell. Hadrian was a patron of the arts, a lover of beauty, and even something of an architect. He directed the staggering feat of building much more than a villa: It was a self-contained world for a vast royal entourage and the hundreds of servants and guards they required to protect them, feed them, bathe them, and satisfy their libidos.

Hadrian erected theaters, baths, temples, fountains, gardens, and canals bordered with statuary throughout his estate. He filled the palaces and temples with sculpture, some of which now rest in the museums of Rome. In later centuries, barbarians, popes, and cardinals, as well as anyone who needed a slab of marble, carted off much that made the villa so spectacular. But enough of the fragmented ruins remain for us to piece together the story. For a glimpse of what the villa used to be, see the plastic reconstruction at the entrance.

After all the centuries of plundering, there's still a bit left. The most outstanding remnant is the **Canopo,** or Canopus, a re-creation of the town of Canope with its famous Temple of the Serapis. The ruins of a rectangular area, **Piazza d'Oro,** are still surrounded by a double portico. Likewise, the **Sala dei pilastri dorici,** or Doric Pillared Hall, remains to delight with its pilasters with Doric bases and capitals holding up a Doric architrave. The ruins of the **Baths** remain, revealing rectangular rooms with concave walls. The apse and the ruins of some magnificent vaulting are still found at the Great Baths. Only the north wall remains of the **Pecile,** or Poikile, which Hadrian discovered in Athens and had reproduced here. The best is saved for last—the **Teatro Marittimo,** a circular maritime theater in ruins with its central building enveloped by a canal spanned by small swing bridges. For a closer look at some of the items excavated, you can visit the museum on the premises and a museum and visitor center near the villa parking area.

Via di Villa Adriana. ✆ **0774/530-203**. Admission 12,000L (6.25€, $6). Daily 9am–sunset (about 6:30pm in summer, 4pm Nov–Mar). Closed New Year's Day, May Day, and Christmas. Bus: 2 or 4 from Tivoli.

DINING

Albergo Ristorante Adriano ITALIAN In a stucco-sided villa a few steps from the ticket office sits an idyllic stop for either before or after you visit Hadrian's Villa. It offers terrace dining under plane trees or indoor dining in a high-ceilinged room with terra-cotta walls, neoclassical moldings, and white

Side Trips from Rome

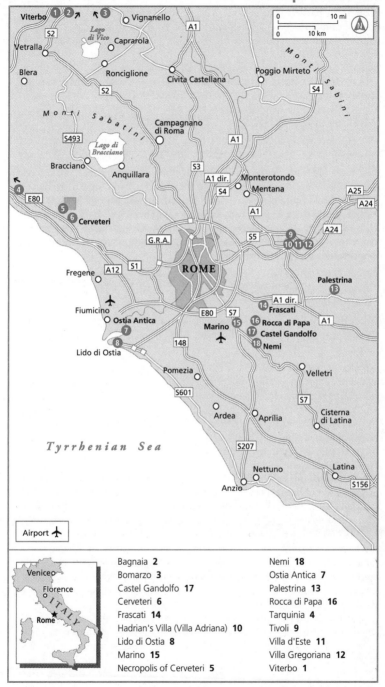

Viterbo ① ② ↗ ↖ ③ Vignanello
S2
Vetralla
Blera
Caprarola
Ronciglione
Civita Castellana
Poggio Mirteto
Lago di Vico
A1
S2
Monti Sabatini
Campagnano di Roma
S493
Lago di Bracciano
Bracciano
Anquillara
S3
A1 dir.
S4
Monterotondo
Mentana
A1
Monti Sabini
S4
A25
A24
④ E80
⑤ ⑥ Cerveteri
G.R.A.
S5
⑨ ⑩ ⑪ ⑫
A24
Fregene
A12
S1
ROME
Palestrina ⑬
Fiumicino
Ostia Antica ⑥
⑦
E80
S7
⑭ A1 dir. Frascati
Marino
⑮ ⑯ Rocca di Papa
⑰ Castel Gandolfo
A1
⑧
Lido di Ostia
148
⑱ Nemi
Pomezia
Velletri
S601
S7
Ardea
Aprília
Cisterna di Latina
Tyrrhenian Sea
S207
Nettuno
Latina
Anzio
S156

Airport ✈

Venice
Florence
ITALY
Rome

Bagnaia **2**	Nemi **18**
Bomarzo **3**	Ostia Antica **7**
Castel Gandolfo **17**	Palestrina **13**
Cerveteri **6**	Rocca di Papa **16**
Frascati **14**	Tarquinia **4**
Hadrian's Villa (Villa Adriana) **10**	Tivoli **9**
Lido di Ostia **8**	Villa d'Este **11**
Marino **15**	Villa Gregoriana **12**
Necropolis of Cerveteri **5**	Viterbo **1**

0   10 mi
0   10 km

227

Corinthian pilasters. The cooking is home-style, and the menu includes roast lamb, saltimbocca (veal cooked with ham), a variety of veal dishes, deviled chicken, salads and cheeses, and simple desserts. They're especially proud of their homemade pastas.

Via di Villa Adriana 194. ✆ **0774/535-028.** Reservations recommended. Main courses 24,000L–32,000L (12.50€–16.65€, $12–$16). AE, DC, MC, V. Mon–Sat 12:30–2:30pm and 8–10pm; Sun 12:30–2:30pm. Bus: 2 or 4 from Tivoli.

Le Cinque Statue ROMAN   This restaurant takes its name from the five old statues (Apollo Belvedere, gladiators, and so on) decorating the place. Today this comfortable place is maintained by a hardworking Italian family that prepares an honest, unpretentious cuisine. Everything is accompanied by the wines of the hill towns of Rome. Begin with a pastiche of mushrooms, or make a selection from the excellent antipasti. Try the rigatoni with fresh herbs, tripe fried Roman style, or mixed fry of brains and vegetables. All the pasta is freshly made. The restaurant also has a wide array of ice creams and fruits.

Via Quintillio Varo 8. ✆ **0774/335-366.** Reservations recommended. Main courses 14,000L–26,000L (7.30€–13.50€, $7–$13). AE, DC, MC, V. Thurs–Sat 12:30–3pm and 7–11pm; Sun 12:30–3pm. Closed Aug 16–25. The Acotral bus from Rome stops nearby.

2 Palestrina

24 miles (39km) E of Rome

Like Tibur, ancient Preneste (as Palestrina was called) was a superb holiday spot. It was the favorite of Horace, Pliny, and even Hadrian, who maintained a villa here.

GETTING THERE
Buses leave every 30 to 45 minutes during the day from Rome; departures are from Via Castro Pretorio (take the Metro to the stop at Castro Pretorio to catch the bus). It takes about an hour to reach Palestrina and costs about 2,500L (1.25€, $1.30).

Take either Via Prenestina (much less trafficked than Via Tiburtina), or the Autostrada (A2) and get off at Valmontana; the latter route is much quicker.

EXPLORING THE TOWN
If you go out of Rome through the Porta Maggiore and travel on Via Prenestina for about 24 miles, you'll eventually come to Palestrina, a medieval hillside town that overlooks a wide valley.

When U.S. airmen flew over in World War II and bombed part of the town, they never imagined their actions would launch Palestrina as an important tourist attraction. After the debris was cleared, a pagan temple (once one of the greatest in the world) emerged: the **Fortuna Primigenia,** rebuilt in the days of the empire but dating from centuries before. In Palestrina you'll also find a **Duomo** dating from 1100, with a mostly intact bell tower.

Palestrina predates the founding of Rome by several hundred years. It resisted conquest by the early Romans and later took the wrong side in the civil war between Marius and Sulla. When Sulla won, he razed every stone in the city except the Temple of Fortune and then built a military barracks on the site. Later, as a favorite vacation spot for the emperors and their entourages, it sheltered some of the most luxurious villas of the Roman empire. Its most famous child was Pier Luigi da Palestrina, recognized as the father of polyphonic harmony.

Galleria Nazional d'Arte Antica in Barberini Palace ★★   High on a hill overlooking the valley, the palace today houses Roman statuary found in the ruins, plus Etruscan artifacts, such as urns the equal of those in Rome's Villa Giulia. But worth the trip itself is the **Nile Mosaic** ★★★, a well-preserved ancient Roman work and the most remarkable ever uncovered. The mosaic details the flooding of the Nile, a shepherd's hunt, mummies, ibises, and Roman warriors, among other things.

Palazzo Barberini. ℂ **06-481-4591**. Admission 12,000L (6.25€, $6) adults, free for children ages 17 and under. Tues–Sun 9am–7pm. Follow the signs from the center to the top of the town.

ACCOMMODATIONS & DINING

Albergo Ristorante Stella (Restaurant Coccia)   A contemporary hotel and restaurant, the Stella is in the commercial district of town on a cobblestone square filled with parked cars, trees, and a small fountain. The bedrooms remain rather basic, but comfortable. All units contain bathrooms containing shower-tub combinations. The simple lobby is filled with warm colors and contains curved leather couches and autographed photos of local sports heroes.

The sunny restaurant, open daily for lunch and dinner, serves affordable, zesty Roman cuisine.

Piazza della Liberazione 3, Palestrina, 00036 Roma. ℂ **06-953-8172**. Fax 06-957-3360. www.hotelstella.it. 28 units. 100,000L (52€, $50) double; 160,000L (83.20€, $80) suite. AE, DC, V. Free parking. **Amenities:** Restaurant, bar; room service. *In room:* TV, hair dryer.

3 The Castelli Romani ★★

For the Roman emperor and the wealthy cardinal in the heyday of the Renaissance, the **Castelli Romani (Roman Castles)** exerted a powerful lure, and they still do. The Castelli aren't castles but hill towns—many of them with an ancient history and several producing well-regarded wines.

The ideal way to explore the hill towns is by car. But you can get a limited overview by taking one of the buses (costing 2,500L, 1.30€, $1.25) that leaves every 20 minutes from Rome's Subaugusta stop on Metro Line A.

MARINO

Marino, the closest to Rome (only 15 miles/24km away), is about 4½ miles (7.2km) off Via Appia Nuova, quite near Ciampino Airport. Much of Marino's original charm has fallen victim to modern builders, but the town is still the place to go each October during the **grape harvest.** Check with the Rome tourist office for the actual dates, as they vary from year to year. At that time, the town's fountains are switched from water to wine, and everyone drinks for free.

ROCCA DI PAPA ★

The most attractive of the hill towns lies only some 6 miles (9.6km)from Marino. It's a lovely spot, on the slopes of Monte Cavo facing the Alban lakes and its enveloping hills. By car, the best route is 217 to the junction with 218, where you make a left turn. Before the intersection, you'll be high on a ridge above Lake Albano, where the views of the lake, the far woods, and the papal palace of Castel Gandolfo on the opposite mountain are superb.

Just before Rocca di Papa is the entrance to the toll road to **Monte Cavo.** A temple of Jove once stood on top of this mountain, and before that, the tribes of the area met with King Tarquin (the Proud) before Rome was a republic. At the top of the mountain is one of the most dramatic panoramic views in the hill towns, giving you a wide survey of the Alban Hills and the Castelli Romani.

Down below, Rocca di Papa is a tangle of old streets and churches. A legend of dubious origin claims that Hannibal once camped just below the town in a wooded hollow.

NEMI

The Romans flock to **Nemi** in droves, particularly from April to June, for the succulent **strawberries** grown here, acclaimed by some gourmets as Europe's finest. In May, there's a strawberry festival. A COTRAL bus departs from Nemi and other hill towns from the Anagnina Metro stop in Rome. Service is about every 30 minutes during the day.

Nemi was also known to the ancients. A temple to the huntress Diana was erected on **Lake Nemi** 🛪, which was said to be her "looking glass." In A.D. 37, Caligula built luxurious barges to float on the lake. The boats, lavishly fitted with bronze and marble, were sunk during Claudius's reign (he succeeded the insane Caligula) and were entirely forgotten until Mussolini drained the lake in the 1930s. Then the barges were found, set up in a lakeside museum, and remained as a wonder of ancient Rome until the Nazis burned them during their retreat.

At the **Roman Ship Museum (Museo delle Navi)** 🛪, Via di Diana 15 (② **06-939-8040**), you can see two scale models of the ships destroyed by the Nazis. The major artifacts on display are mainly copies, as the originals now rest in world-class museums. The museum is open daily from 9am to 7pm. Admission is 4,000L (2.10€, $2). To reach the museum, head from the center of Nemi toward the lake.

The 15th-century **Palazzo Ruspoli,** a private baronial estate, is the focal point of Nemi, but the town itself invites exploration—particularly the alleyways the locals call streets and the houses with balconies jutting out over the slopes.

DINING

Ristorante Il Castagnone 🛪 ROMAN/SEAFOOD   This well-managed dining room of the town's best hotel takes a definite pride in a Roman-based cuisine emphasizing seafood above meat. The attentive formal service is usually delivered with a kind of gentle humor. Amid neoclassical accessories and marble, you can order delectable veal, chicken, beef, and fish dishes like fried calamari, spaghetti with shellfish in garlicky tomato-based sauce, and roasted lamb with potatoes and Mediterranean herbs. As you dine, expect a sweeping lake view from the restaurant's windows.

In the Diana Park Hotel, Via Nemorense 44. ② **06-936-4041.** Reservations recommended. Main courses 18,000–30,000L (9.35€–15.60€, $9–$15). AE, DC, MC, V. Tues–Sun noon–3pm and 8–10pm. Closed Nov.

EN ROUTE TO CASTEL GANDOLFO

The road to Gandolfo leads us through a few worth-a-visit towns on the way. **Genzano,** on the other side of Lake Nemi, has views of the countryside and a 17th-century palace that belonged to the Sforza-Cesarini.

Ariccia is an ancient town that sent representatives to meet with Tarquin the Proud on top of Monte Cavo 2,500 years ago. After many centuries of changing hands, especially between medieval and Renaissance families, it has taken on a suburban look. The palace in the middle of town is still private and belongs to the Chigi family.

Albano practically adjoins Castel Gandolfo. It has a long history; this is the reputed site of Alba Longa, the so-called mother city of Rome, but it's quite built up and modern today. Trains going to Albano leave from Stazione Termini in Rome.

Tips **Reserving Winery Tours**

While exploring the Castelli Romani, the hill towns around Rome, you might want to visit some of the better-known wineries. The region's most famous producers of Frascati are **Fontana Candida,** Via di Fontana Candida, 00040 Monte Porzio Catone, Roma (✆ **06-942-0066**), whose winery, 14 miles southwest of Rome, was built around 1900; and **Gotto D'Oro-Cantina Sociale di Marino,** Via del Divino Amore 115, 00040 Frattocchie, Roma (✆ **06-935-6931** and 06-935-6932). To arrange visits, contact the **Gruppo Italiano Vini,** Villa Belvedere, 37010 Calmasino, Verona (✆ **045/626-9600**).

CASTEL GANDOLFO ✦

Now we come to the summer residence of the pope. The papal palace, a 17th-century edifice designed by Carlo Maderno, stands practically on the foundations of another equally regal summer residence, the villa of Emperor Domitian. Unfortunately, the palace, the gardens, and the adjoining Villa Barberini can't be visited. You'll have to content yourself with a visit to **Piazza della Libertà,** the piazza out front with its church, Chiesa di San Tomaso di Villanova, and fountain by Bernini.

If you're here for lunch, as many are, your best bet is **Antico Ristorante Pagnanelli,** Via Gramsci 4 (✆ **06-9360004**), which serves both regional and pan-Italian dishes, with meals starting at 60,000L (31.20€, $30), with a high of 90,000L (46.80€, $45) for the fresh seafood dishes. The restaurant is open Monday to Wednesday noon to 3pm and 7pm to midnight.

FRASCATI ✦

About 13 miles (21km) from Rome on Via Tuscolana and some 1,073 feet (322m) above sea level, Frascati is one of the most beautiful hill towns. It's known for the wine to which it lends its name, as well as for its villas, which were restored after the severe destruction caused by World War II bombers. To get there, take one of the COTRAL buses leaving from the Anagina stop of Metro Line A. From there take the blue COTRAL bus to Frascati. Again, the transportation situation in Italy is constantly in a state of flux, so check your route at the station.

Although Frascati wine is exported, and served in many of Rome's restaurants and trattorie, tradition holds that it's best near the vineyards from which it came. Romans drive up on Sunday just to drink it. To sample some of the golden white wine, head for **Cantina Comandini,** Via E. Filiberto 1 (✆ **06-942-0915**), right off Piazza Roma. The Comandini family welcomes you to the wine cellar, a regional tavern in which they sell Frascati from their own vineyards. You can drink the wine on the spot for 6,000L (3.10€, $3) per liter, or 2,000L (1.05€, $1) per glass, and you can buy sandwiches to go with your vino. The tavern is open Monday to Saturday from 4 to 8pm. Reservations are required.

Stand in the heart of Frascati, at Piazza Marconi, to see the most important of the estates: **Villa Aldobrandini** ✦, Via Massala. The finishing touches to this 16th-century villa were added by Maderno, who designed the facade of St. Peter's in Rome. You can visit only the gardens, not the interior, but, still, with its grottoes, yew hedges, statuary, and splashing fountains, it's a nice outing. The gardens are open from Monday to Friday from 9am to 1pm and 3 to 5pm (to

6pm in summer), although you must go to the **Azienda di Soggiorno e Turismo,** Piazza Marconi 1 (☎ **06-942-0331**), to ask for a free pass. The office is open Monday to Saturday from 8am to 2pm, and also Tuesday to Friday from 3:30 to 6:30pm in winter and 4 to 7pm in summer.

You also might want to visit the bombed-out **Villa Torlonia,** adjacent to Piazza Marconi. Its grounds have been converted into a public park whose chief treasure is the Theater of the Fountains, designed by Maderno.

If you have a car, you can continue about 3 miles (5km) past the Villa Aldobrandini to **Tuscolo,** an ancient spot with the ruins of an amphitheater dating from about the 1st century B.C. It offers what may be one of Italy's most panoramic views.

DINING

Cacciani Restaurant ROMAN   Cacciani is the top restaurant in Frascati, where the competition has always been tough. It boasts a terrace commanding a view of the valley, and the kitchen is exposed to the public. To start, we recommend the pasta specialties, such as pasta *cacio e pepe* (pasta with caciocavallo cheese and black pepper), or the original spaghetti with seafood and lentils. For a main course, the lamb with a sauce of white wine and vinegar is always fine. Of course, there is a large choice of wine. If you call ahead, the Cacciani family will arrange a visit to several of Frascati's wine-producing villas, along with a memorable meal at their restaurant.

Via Armando Diaz 13. ☎ 06-942-0378. Reservations required on weekends. Main courses 20,000L–35,000L (10.40€–18.20€, $10–$17.50). AE, DC, MC, V. Tues–Sun 12:30–3pm and 7:30–10:30pm. Closed Jan 7–19 and Aug 18–27.

4 Ostia ✸

16 miles (25.7km) SW of Rome

Ostia Antica is one of the area's major attractions, particularly interesting to those who can't make it to Pompeii. If you want to see both ancient and modern Rome, grab your swimsuit, towel, and sunblock, and take the Metro Line B from Stazione Termini to the Magliana stop. Change here for the Lido train to Ostia Antica, about 16 miles (26km) from Rome. Departures are about every half hour, and the trip takes only 20 minutes. The Metro lets you off across the highway that connects Rome with the coast. It's just a short walk to the excavations.

Later, board the Metro again to visit the **Lido di Ostia,** the beach. Italy might be a Catholic country, but you won't detect any religious conservatism in the skimpy bikinis on the beach here. There's a carnival atmosphere, with dance halls, cinemas, and pizzerias. The Lido is set off best at Castelfusano, against a backdrop of pinewoods. This stretch of shoreline is referred to as the Roman Riviera.

Ostia Antica's Ruins ✸✸   Ostia was the port of ancient Rome and a city in its own right. The currents and uneven bottom of the Tiber River prevented Mediterranean shipping from going farther upstream, so merchandise was transferred to barges for the remainder of the trip. Ostia's fate was tied closely to that of the empire. At the peak of Rome's power, the city had 100,000 inhabitants—hard to imagine looking at today's ruins. Ostia was important enough to have had a theater (still standing in reconstructed form), numerous temples and baths, great patrician houses, and a large business complex. Successive emperors, notably Claudius and Trajan, enlarged and improved the facilities, but by Constantine's time (4th century A.D.), the worm had turned. The barbarian sieges of Rome in the 5th century spelled the end of Ostia.

A prosperous city developed, full of temples, baths, theaters, and patrician homes. Ostia flourished for about 8 centuries before it began to wither away. Gradually it became little more than a malaria bed, a buried ghost city that faded into history. A papal-sponsored commission launched a series of digs in the 19th century; however, the major work of unearthing was carried out under Mussolini's orders from 1938 to 1942 (the work had to stop because of the war). The city is only partially dug out today, but it's believed that all the chief monuments have been uncovered. There are quite a few visible ruins unearthed, so this is no dusty field like the Circus Maximus.

These principal monuments are clearly labeled. The most important spot is **Piazzale delle Corporazioni,** an early version of Wall Street. Near the theater, this square contained nearly 75 corporations, the nature of their businesses identified by the patterns of preserved mosaics. Greek dramas were performed at the **ancient theater,** built in the early days of the empire. The classics are still aired here in summer (check with the tourist office for specific listings), but the theater as it looks today is the result of much rebuilding. Every town the size of Ostia had a forum, and during the excavations a number of pillars of the ancient **Ostia Forum** were uncovered. At one end is a 2nd-century B.C. temple honoring a trio of gods, Minerva, Jupiter, and Juno (little more than the basic foundation remains). In addition, in the enclave is a well-lit **museum** displaying Roman statuary along with some Pompeii-like frescoes. Also of special interest are the ruins of **Thermopolium,** which was a bar; its name means "sale of hot drinks." The ruins of **Capitolium and Forum** remain; this was once the largest temple in Ostia, dating from the 2nd century A.D. A lot of the original brick remains, including a partial reconstruction of the altar. Of an insula, a block of apartments, **Casa Diana** remains, with its rooms arranged around an inner courtyard. There are perfect picnic spots beside fallen columns or near old temple walls.

Viale dei Romagnoli 717. © **06-5635-8099.** Admission 8,000L (4.15€, $4). Tues–Sun 9am–6pm. Metro: Ostia Antica Line Roma–Ostia–Lido.

5 Fregene ⊛

24 miles (38.6km) N of Rome

The fame of this coastal city north of the Tiber dates back to the 1600s, when the land belonged to the Rospigliosi, a powerful Roman family. Pope Clement IX, a member of that wealthy family, planted a forest of pine that extends along the shoreline for 2½ miles (4km) and stands half a mile deep to protect the land from the strong winds of the Mediterranean. Today, the wall of pines makes a dramatic backdrop for the golden sands and luxurious villas of the resort. If you'd like to sample an Italian beach, head here instead of to the more polluted beaches along Ostia's Lido.

GETTING THERE

You can catch the Fregene bus, which leaves from the Lepanto Metro stop in Rome and carries passengers to the center of Fregene. A ticket costs 4,800L (2.50€, $2.40) and travel time is 1 hour.

If you're driving, follow Autostrada 1 (also known as Via Aurelia Malagrotta) heading west, crossing over the bypass that encircles Rome. After Castello di Guido, 14 miles (22.5km) west of Central Rome, exit onto the secondary road marked MACCARESE-FREGENE. Then continue southwest for another 10 miles, following the signs to Fregene. There is no tourist information office.

ACCOMMODATIONS & DINING

La Conchiglia ⚜ La Conchiglia means "The Shell," and it's an appropriate name for this hotel and restaurant right on the beach with views of the water and the pines. It features a circular lounge with built-in curving wall banquettes facing a cylindrical fireplace. The guest rooms are comfortable and well furnished, ranging from medium to spacious, each with a fine mattress and a bathroom equipped with a shower-tub combination.

It's also possible to stop by just for a good moderately priced meal. Try, for example, spaghetti with lobster and grilled fish or one of many excellent meat dishes. Meals start at 50,000L (€25, $26). The restaurant is open daily for lunch and dinner.

Lungomare di Ponente 4, Fregene, 00050 Roma. ℂ **06-668-5385.** Fax 06-665-63185. www.laconchiglia.it. 36 units. 160,000L–220,000L (83.20€–114.40€, $80–$110) double. Rates include breakfast. AE, DC, MC, V. Free parking. **Amenities:** Restaurant, lounge; pool ; room service. *In room:* A/C, TV, minibar, hair dryer, safe.

6 Etruscan Historical Sights

CERVETERI (CAERE)

As you walk through Rome's Etruscan Museum (Villa Giulia), you'll often see *Caere* written under a figure vase or sarcophagus. This is a reference to the nearby town known today as Cerveteri, one of Italy's great Etruscan cities, whose origins could date from as far back as the 9th century B.C.

Of course, the Etruscan town has long since faded, but not the **Necropolis of Cerveteri** ⚜⚜ (ℂ **06-994-0001**). The effect is eerie; Cerveteri is often called a "city of the dead." When you go beneath some of the mounds, you'll discover the most striking feature: The tombs are like rooms in Etruscan homes. The main burial ground is the Necropolis of Banditacca. Of the graves thus far uncovered, none is finer than the **Tomba Bella** (or the Reliefs' Tomb), the burial ground of the Matuna family. Articles such as utensils and even house pets were painted in stucco relief. Presumably these paintings were representations of items that the dead family would need in the world beyond. The necropolis is open Tuesday to Sunday from 9am to 4pm. Admission is 8,000L (4.15€, $4).

Relics from the necropolis are displayed at the **Museo Nazionale Cerite,** Piazza Santa Maria Maggiore (ℂ **06-994-1354**). The museum, housed within the ancient walls and crenellations of Ruspoldi Castle, is open Tuesday to Sunday from 9am to 7pm. Admission is free.

You can reach Cerveteri by bus or car. If you're driving, head out Via Aurelia, northwest of Rome, for 28 miles (45km). By public transport, take Metro Line A in Rome to the Lepanto stop; from Via Lepanto, you can catch a COTRAL bus (ℂ **06-324-4724**) to Cerveteri; the trip takes about an hour and costs 5,000L (2.60€, $2.50). Once you're at Cerveteri, it's a 1¼-mile (2km) walk to the necropolis; follow the signs pointing the way.

TARQUINIA ⚜

If you want to see tombs even more striking and more recently excavated than those at Cerveteri, go to Tarquinia. The medieval turrets and fortifications atop the rocky cliffs overlooking the sea seem to contradict the Etruscan name of Tarquinia. Actually, Tarquinia is the adopted name of the old medieval community of Corneto, in honor of the major Etruscan city that once stood nearby.

The main attraction in the town is the **Tarquinia National Museum** ⚜, Piazza Cavour (ℂ **0776/856-036**), devoted to Etruscan exhibits and sarcophagi excavated from the necropolis a few miles away. The museum is housed in the Palazzo Vitelleschi, a Gothic palace from the mid–15th century. Among the exhibits are gold jewelry, black vases with carved and painted bucolic scenes, and sarcophagi decorated with carvings of animals and relief figures of priests and military leaders. But the biggest attraction is in itself worth the ride from Rome: the almost life-size pair of **winged horses** ✯✯ from the pediment of a Tarquinian temple. The finish is worn here and there, and the terra-cotta color shows through, but the relief stands as one of the greatest Etruscan masterpieces ever discovered. The museum is open Tuesday to Sunday from 9am to 7pm, and charges 8,000L (4.15€, $4) admission.

An 8,000L (4.15€, $4) admission admits you to the **Etruscan Necropolis** ✯✯ (✆ **0766/856-308**), covering more than 2½ miles (4.5km) of rough terrain near where the ancient Etruscan city once stood. Thousands of tombs have been discovered, some of which haven't been explored even today. Others, of course, were discovered by looters, but many treasures remain even though countless pieces were removed to museums and private collections. The **paintings** on the walls of the tombs have helped historians reconstruct the life of the Etruscans— a heretofore impossible feat without a written history. The paintings depict feasting couples in vivid colors mixed from iron oxide, lapis lazuli dust, and charcoal. One of the oldest tombs (from the 6th century B.C.) depicts young men fishing while dolphins play and colorful birds fly high above. Many of the paintings convey an earthy, vigorous, sexuality among the wealthy Etruscans. The tombs are generally open Tuesday to Sunday from 8:30am to 4:30pm. You can reach the grave sites by taking a bus from the Barriera San Giusto to the Cimitero stop. Or, try the 20-minute walk from the museum. Inquire at the museum for directions.

To reach Tarquinia by car, take Via Aurelia outside Rome and continue on the autostrada toward Civitavecchia. Bypass Civitavecchia and continue another 13 miles (21km) north until you see the exit signs for Tarquinia. As for public transport, a diretto train from Roma Ostiense station takes 50 minutes. Eight buses a day leave from the Via Lepanto stop in Rome for the 2-hour trip to the town of Barriera San Giusto, 1½ miles (2km) from Tarquinia. Bus schedules are available at the **tourist office** in Barriera San Giusto (✆ **0766/856-384**), open from Monday to Saturday 8am to 1pm.

7 Viterbo ✯

61 miles (98km) N of Rome

The 2,000 years that have gone into the creation of the city of Viterbo make it one of the most interesting day trips from Rome. Although it traces its history back to the Etruscans, the bulk of its historical architecture dates from the Middle Ages and the Renaissance, when the city was a residence (and hideout) for the popes. The old section of the city is still surrounded by the thick stone walls that once protected the inhabitants from papal (or antipapal, depending on the situation at the time) attacks.

ESSENTIALS

GETTING THERE From Rome take Metro Linea A to Flaminio. At the Flaminio station, follow the signs pointing to Roma Nord station. Once there, purchase a combined rail and bus ticket to Viterbo, costing 13,000L (6.75€, $6.50) round-trip. The train takes you to Saxa Rubra in just 15 minutes. At Saxa Rubra, take an Acotral bus for the 1½-hour trip to Viterbo. Especially if you're trying to see Viterbo on a day trip, it might be worth the extra money to take a taxi from Saxa Rubra the remainder of the way.

If you're driving, take Autostrada 2 north to the Orte exit.

VISITOR INFORMATION **Tourist information** is available at Piazza San Careluccio (☎ **0761-304-795**); the office is open Monday to Saturday from 7:30am to 1:30pm.

SEEING THE SIGHTS

The only way to see Viterbo properly is to wander through the narrow cobblestone streets of the medieval town. **Piazza del Plebiscito,** dominated by the 15th-century town hall, impresses visitors with the fine state of preservation of Viterbo's old buildings. The courtyard and fountain in front of the town hall and the 13th-century governor's palace are favorite meeting places for townsfolk and visitors alike.

Just down Via San Lorenzo is **Piazza San Lorenzo** 👁👁, the site of Viterbo's cathedral, which sits atop the former Etruscan acropolis. The **Duomo,** dating from 1192, is a composite of architectural styles, from its pagan foundations to its Renaissance facade to its gothic bell tower. Next door is the 13th-century **Palazzo Papale** 👁👁, built as a residence for the pope, but also serving as a hideout when the pope was in exile. It was the site of three papal elections. The exterior staircase and the colonnaded loggia combine to make up one of the finest examples of civil Roman architecture from the gothic period.

The finest example of medieval architecture in Viterbo is the **San Pellegrino Quarter** 👁👁, reached from Piazza San Lorenzo by a short walk past Piazza della Morte. This quarter, inhabited by working-class Viterboans, is a maze of narrow streets, arched walkways, towers, steep stairways, and ornamental fountains.

Worth a special visit is the **Convent of Santa Maria della Verita,** dating from 1100. The church contains 15th-century frescoes by Lorenzo da Viterbo, student of Piero della Francesca.

Park of the Monsters (Parco dei Mostri) 👁 About 8 miles (12.8km) east of Bagnaia at Bomarzo lies the Park of the Monsters. Prince Vicino Orsini had it built in a deep valley that's overlooked by the Orsini Palace and the houses of the village. On the other side of the valley are stone cliffs. Prince Orsini's park, Bosco Sacro (sacred wood), is filled with grotesque figures carved from natural rock. Nature and art have created a surrealistic fantasy; the Mouth of Hell (an ogre's face so big that people can walk into its gaping mouth), a crude Hercules slaying an Amazon, nymphs with butterfly wings, a huge tortoise with a statue on its shell, a harpy, a mermaid, snarling dogs, lions, and much, much more.

Villa delle Meraviglie, Bomarzo. ☎ 0761-924-029. Admission 15,000L (7.80€, $7.50). Daily 8am–dusk. Bus: 6 from Piazza Martiri d'Ungheria in Viterbo.

Villa Lante 👁👁 The English author Sacheverell Sitwell called Villa Lante, located in Bagnaia, a suburb of Viterbo, "the most beautiful garden in Italy." Water from Monte Cimino flows down to the fountains of the villa, running from terrace to terrace until it reaches the central pool of the regal garden, with statues, stone banisters, and shrubbery. Two symmetrical Renaissance palaces make up the villa. The estate is now partly a public park open during the day. The gardens that adjoin the villa, however, can only be visited on a guided tour. (The gatekeeper at the guard house will show you through, usually with a group that has assembled.) The interiors of the twin mansions can't be visited.

Via Giacopo Barrozzi 1, Bagnaia. ☎ 0761-288-008. Admission 4,000L (2.10€, $2). Nov–Feb Tues–Sun 9am–4:30pm; Mar Tues–Sun 9am–5:30pm; mid-Apr and Sept–Oct 9am–6:30pm; mid-Apr to Aug 9am–7:30pm. Bus: 6 from Viterbo.

Appendix A:
Rome in Depth

Rome, according to legend, was built on seven hills. These hills rise from the marshy lowlands of the Campagna and are mostly on the left bank of the Tiber River. They include the Quirinale (seat of the modern Italian government), Esquiline, Viminal, Caelian, and Aventine—and all combine to form a crescent-shaped plateau of great historical fame. In its center rises the Palatine Hill, the all-powerful seat of the imperial residences of ancient Rome, which looks down on the ancient Forum and the Colosseum. To the northwest rises the Capitoline Hill. Some historians have suggested that Rome's geography—set above a periphery of marshy and swelteringly hot lowlands—contributed to the fall of the Roman empire because of its propensity to breed malaria-inducing mosquitoes.

The modern city of Rome is composed of 22 districts, covering an area of nearly 10 square miles. The Tiber makes two distinct bends within Rome, below Ponte Cavour, one of the city's major bridges, and again at the history-rich island of Tiberina.

With bloodlines including virtually every race ever encompassed by the borders of the ancient Roman empire, the people of Rome long ago grew accustomed to seeing foreign influences come and go. Picking their way through the architectural and cultural jumble of Rome, they are not averse to complaining (loudly) of the city's endless inconveniences, yet they are the first to appreciate the historical and architectural marvels that surround them. Cynical, but hearty and filled with humanity, modern Romans propel themselves through the business of life with an enviable sense of style.

The crowds of pilgrims and the vast numbers of churches and convents exist side by side with fleshier and more earthbound distractions, the combination of which imbues many Romans with an overriding interest in pursuing the pleasures and distractions of the moment. This sense of theatricality can be seen in Roman driving habits; in animated conversations and gesticulations in restaurants and cafes; in the lavish displays of flowers, fountains, food, and architecture, the nation's trademark; and in the 27 centuries of building projects dedicated to the power and egos of long-dead potentates.

Despite the crowds, the pollution, the heat, and the virtual impossibility of efficiency, Romans for the most part take life with good cheer and *pazienza*. Translated as "patience," it seems to be the frequently uttered motto of modern Rome, and an appropriate philosophy for a city that has known everything from unparalleled glory to humiliation and despair. Romans know that since Rome wasn't built in a day, its charms should be savored slowly and with an appreciation for the cultures that contributed to this panoply.

1 Rome Past & Present

Many of the key events that shaped the rich and often gory tapestry of Italian history originated in Rome. Although parts of Italy (especially Sardinia and Sicily) were inhabited as early as the Bronze Age, the region around Rome was occupied relatively late. Some historians claim that the presence of active volcanoes in the region during the Bronze Age prevented prehistoric tribes from living here, but whatever the reason, Rome has unearthed far fewer prehistoric graves and implements than have neighboring Tuscany and Umbria.

THE ETRUSCANS Among the early inhabitants of Italy, the most significant were the Etruscans—but who were they? No one knows, and the many inscriptions they left behind (mostly on graves) are of no help, since the Etruscan language has never been deciphered by modern scholars. It's thought they arrived on the eastern coast of Umbria several centuries before Rome was built, around 800 B.C. Their religious rites and architecture show an obvious contact with Mesopotamia; the Etruscans may have been refugees from Asia Minor who traveled westward about 1200 to 1000 B.C. Within 2 centuries, they had subjugated Tuscany and Campania and the Villanova tribes who lived there.

While the Etruscans built temples at Tarquinia and Caere (present-day Cerveteri), the few nervous Latin tribes who remained outside their sway gravitated to Rome, then little more than a sheepherding village. As its power grew, however, Rome increasingly profited from the strategically important Tiber crossing where the ancient Salt Way (Via Salaria) turned northeastward toward the central Apennines.

From their base at Rome, the Latins remained free of the Etruscans until about 600 B.C. But the Etruscan advance was inexorable, and though the tribes concentrated their forces at Rome for a last stand, they were swept away by the sophisticated Mesopotamian conquerors. The new overlords introduced gold tableware and jewelry, bronze urns and terra-cotta statuary, and the best of Greek and Asia Minor art and culture; they also made

Dateline

- **Bronze Age** Tribes of Celts, Teutonics, and groups from the eastern Mediterranean inhabit the Italian peninsula.
- **1200 B.C.** The Etruscans migrate from the eastern Mediterranean (probably Mesopotamia) and occupy territory north and south of Rome.
- **800 B.C.** Sicily and southern Italy (especially Naples) flourish under Greek and Phoenician protection; independent of most outside domination, Rome evolves as an insignificant community of shepherds with loyalties divided among several Latin tribes.
- **753 B.C.** Rome's traditional founding date.
- **660 B.C.** Etruscans occupy Rome as the capital of their empire; the city grows rapidly and a major seaport (Ostia) opens at the mouth of the Tiber.
- **510–250 B.C.** The Latin tribes, still centered in Rome, maintain a prolonged revolt against the Etruscans; alpine Gauls attack the Etruscans from the north and Greeks living in Sicily destroy the Etruscan navy.
- **250 B.C.** The Romans and their allies finally purge the Etruscans from Italy; Rome flourishes as a republic and begins the accumulation of a vast empire.
- **250–50 B.C.** Rome obliterates its chief rival, Carthage, during two Punic Wars; Carthage's defeat allows unchecked Roman expansion into Spain, North Africa, Sardinia, and Corsica.
- **44 B.C.** Julius Caesar is assassinated; his successor, Augustus, transforms Rome from a city of brick to a city of marble and solidifies Rome's status as a dictatorship.
- **40 B.C.** Rome and its armies control the entire Mediterranean world.
- **3rd century A.D.** Rome declines under a series of incompetent and corrupt emperors.
- **4th century A.D.** Rome is fragmented politically as administrative capitals are established in such cities as Milan and Trier, Germany.

continues

Rome the governmental seat of all Latium. Roma is an Etruscan name, and the kings of Rome had Etruscan names: Numa, Ancus, Tarquinius, and even Romulus.

Under the combined influences of the Greeks and the Mesopotamian east, Rome grew enormously. A new port was opened at Ostia, near the mouth of the Tiber. Artists from Greece carved statues of Roman gods to resemble Greek divinities. From this enforced (and not always peaceable) mixture of Latin tribes and Etruscans grew the roots of what eventually became the Republic of Rome.

The Estruscans ruled until the Roman revolt around 510 B.C., and by 250 B.C., the Romans and their Campania allies had vanquished the Etruscans, wiping out their language and religion. However, many of the former rulers' manners and beliefs remained, assimilated into the culture. Even today, certain Etruscan customs and bloodlines are believed to exist in Italy, especially in Tuscany.

The best places to see the legacy left by these mysterious people are in Cerveteri and Tarquinia outside Rome. Especially interesting is the Etruscan necropolis, just 4 miles southeast of Tarquinia, where thousands of tombs have been discovered. See chapter 11 for details on all these sites. To learn more about the Etruscans, visit the National Etruscan Museum (Museo Nazionale di Villa Giulia) in Rome itself (see chapter 7).

THE ROMAN REPUBLIC Gauls from the alpine regions invaded the northern Etruscan territory around 600 B.C., and the Latin tribes revolted in about 510 B.C., toppling the Etruscan-linked rulers from their power bases and establishing the southern boundary of Etruscan influence at the Tiber. Greeks from Sicily ended Etruscan sea power in 474 B.C. during the battle of Cumae off the

- 395 The empire splits: Constantine establishes a "New Rome" at Constantinople (Istanbul); Goths invade Rome's provinces in northern Italy.
- 410–55 Rome is sacked by barbarians—Alaric the Goth, Attila the Hun, and Galseric the Vandal.
- 475 Rome falls, leaving only the primate of the Catholic church in control; the pope slowly adopts many of the responsibilities and the prestige once reserved for the Roman emperors.
- 731 Pope Gregory II renounces Rome's spiritual and political link to the authorities in Constantinople.
- 800 Charlemagne is crowned Holy Roman Emperor by Pope Leo III; Italy dissolves into a series of small warring kingdoms.
- 1065 The Holy Land falls to the Muslim Turks; the Crusades are launched.
- 1303–77 A papal schism occurs when a rival pope is established at Avignon.
- 1377 The "antipope" is removed from Avignon, and the Roman popes emerge as sole contenders to the legacy of St. Peter.
- Mid-1400s Originating in Florence, the Renaissance blossoms throughout Italy; Italian artists receive multiple commissions from the ecclesiastical communities of Rome.
- 1508 Ordered by the pope, Michelangelo begins work on the ceiling of the Vatican's Sistine Chapel.
- 1527 Rome is attacked and sacked by Charles V, who—to the pope's rage—is elected Holy Roman Emperor the following year.
- 1796–97 Napoléon's military conquests of Italy arouse Italian nationalism.
- 1861 Rome is declared the capital of the newly established Kingdom of Italy; the Papal States (but not the Vatican) are absorbed into the new nation.
- 1929 A concordat between the Vatican and the Italian government delineates the rights and responsibilities of both parties.
- 1935 Italian invasion of Abyssinia (Ethiopia).
- 1941 Italian invasion of Yugoslavia.

continues

Italian coastline just north of Naples. By 250 B.C., the Romans and their allies in Campagna had vanquished the Etruscans, wiping out their language and religion.

Tempered in the fires of military adversity, the stern Roman republic was characterized by belief in the gods, the necessity of learning from the past, strength of the family, education through books and public service, and, most important, obedience. The all-powerful Senate presided as Rome defeated rival powers one after the other in a steady stream of staggering military successes.

As the population grew, the Romans gave to their Latin allies and then to conquered peoples partial or complete Roman citizenship, always with the obligation of military service. Colonies of citizens were established on the borders of the growing empire and were populated with soldiers/farmers and their families. Later, as seen in the history of Britain and the European continent, colonies began to thrive as semi-autonomous units on their own, heavily fortified and linked to Rome by well-maintained military roads and a well-defined hierarchy of military command.

The final obstacle to the unrivaled supremacy of Rome was the defeat,

- **1943** General Patton lands in Sicily and soon controls the island.
- **1945** Mussolini killed by a mob in Milan.
- **1946** Establishment of Rome as the capital of the newly created Republic of Italy.
- **1960s** Rise of left-wing terrorist groups; flight of capital from Italy; continuing problems of the impoverished south cause an exodus from the countryside into such cities as Rome.
- **1980s** *Il Sorpasso* imbues Rome (and the rest of Italy) with dreams of an economic rebirth.
- **1994** Right-wing forces win in Italian national elections.
- **1996** Dini steps down as prime minister, as the president dissolves both houses of Parliament; in general elections, the center-left coalition known as the Olive Tree sweeps both the Senate and the Chamber of Deputies; Romano Prodi becomes prime minister.
- **1997–98** Prodi survives Neo-Communist challenge and continues to press for budget cuts in an effort to join Europe in 1999.
- **1999** Rome officially goes under the euro umbrella as it prepares for the millennium.
- **2000** Italy welcomes Jubilee visitors in wake of political discontent.
- **2001** Silvio Berlusconi, one of the richest men in the world, becomes premier of Italy.

during the 3rd century B.C., of the city-state of Carthage during the two Punic Wars. An ancient Phoenician trading post on the coast of Tunisia, Carthage had grown into one of the premier naval and agricultural powers of the Mediterranean with strongly fortified positions in Corsica, Sardinia, and Spain. Despite the impressive victories of the Carthaginian general Hannibal, Rome eventually eradicated Carthage in one of the most famous defeats in ancient history. Rome was able to immediately expand its power into North Africa, Sardinia, Corsica, and Iberia.

THE ROMAN EMPIRE   By 49 B.C., Italy ruled all of the Mediterranean world either directly or indirectly, with all political, commercial, and cultural pathways leading directly to Rome. The wealth and glory to be found in Rome lured many there, but drained other Italian communities of human resources. As Rome transformed itself into an administrative headquarters, imports to the city from other parts of the empire hurt local farmers and landowners. The seeds for civil discord were sown early in the empire's existence, although, as Rome was embellished with temples, monuments, and the easy availability of slave labor from conquered territories, many of its social problems were overlooked in favor of expansion and glory.

No figure was more towering during the republic than Julius Caesar, the charismatic conqueror of Gaul—"the wife of every husband and the husband of every wife." After defeating the last resistance of the Pompeians in 45 B.C., he came to Rome and was made dictator and consul for 10 years. He was at that point almost a king. Conspirators led by Marcus Junius Brutus stabbed him to death in the Senate on March 15, 44 B.C. Beware the ides of March.

Marc Antony then assumed control by seizing Caesar's papers and wealth. Intent on expanding the Republic, Antony met with Cleopatra at Tarsus in 41 B.C. She seduced him, and he stayed in Egypt for a year. When Antony eventually returned to Rome, still smitten with Cleopatra, he made peace with Caesar's willed successor, Octavius, and, through the pacts of Brundisium, soon found himself married to Octavius's sister, Octavia. This marriage, however, didn't prevent him from openly marrying Cleopatra in 36 B.C. The furious Octavius gathered western legions and defeated Antony at the Battle of Actium on September 2, 31 B.C. Cleopatra fled to Egypt, followed by Antony, who committed suicide in disgrace a year later. Cleopatra, unable to seduce his successor and, thus, retain her rule of Egypt, followed suit with the help of an asp.

Born Gaius Octavius in 63 B.C., Augustus, the first Roman emperor, reigned from 27 B.C. to A.D. 14. His reign, called "the golden age of Rome," led to the Pax Romana, or 2 centuries of peace. He had been adopted by, and eventually became the heir of, his great-uncle Julius Caesar. In Rome you can still visit the remains of the Forum of Augustus, built before the birth of Christ, and the Domus Augustana, where the imperial family lived on the Palatine Hill.

On the eve of the birth of Jesus, Rome was a mighty empire whose generals had brought all of the Western world under the influence of Roman law, values, and civilization. Only in the eastern third of the Mediterranean did the existing cultures—notably the Greek—withstand the Roman incursions. Despite its occupation by Rome, Greece, more than any other culture, permeated Rome with new ideas, values, and concepts of art, architecture, religion, and philosophy.

The emperors, whose succession started with Augustus's principate after the death of Julius Caesar, brought Rome to new, almost giddy, heights. Augustus transformed the city from brick to marble, much the way Napoléon III transformed Paris many centuries later. But success led to corruption. The emperors wielded autocratic power, and the centuries witnessed a steady decay in the ideals and traditions on which the empire had been founded. The army became a fifth column of barbarian mercenaries, the tax collector became the scourge of the countryside, and for every good emperor (Augustus, Claudius, Trajan, Vespasian, and Hadrian, to name a few) there were three or four debased heads of state (Caligula, Nero, Domitian, Caracalla, and more).

The ideals of democratic responsibility in the heart of the empire had begun to break down. The populace began to object violently to a government that took little interest in commerce and seemed interested only in foreign politics. As taxes and levies increased, the poor emigrated in huge and idle numbers to Rome and the rich cities of the Po Valley. Entire generations of war captives, forced into the slave-driven economies of large Italian estates, were steeped in hatred and ignorance.

Christianity, a new and revolutionary religion, probably gained a foothold in Rome about 10 years after Jesus's crucifixion. Feared far more for its political implications than for its spiritual resuppositions, it was at first brutally suppressed before moving through increasingly tolerant stages of acceptability.

After Augustus died (by poison, perhaps), his widow, Livia—a crafty social climber who had divorced her first husband to marry Augustus—set up her son, Tiberius, as ruler through a series of intrigues and poisonings. A long series of murders ensued, and Tiberius, who ruled during Pontius Pilot's trial and crucifixion of Christ, was eventually murdered in an uprising of land-owners. In fact, murder was so common that a short time later, Domitian (A.D. 81–96) became so obsessed with the possibility of assassination he had the walls of his palace covered in mica so he could see behind him at all times. (He was killed anyway.)

Excesses and scandal ruled the day: Caligula (a bit overfond of his sister Drusilla) appointed his horse a lifetime member of the Senate, lavished money on foolish projects, and proclaimed himself a god. Caligula's successor, his uncle Claudius, was deceived and publicly humiliated by one of his wives, the lascivious Messalina (he had her killed for her trouble); he was then poisoned by his final wife, his niece Agrippina, to secure the succession of Nero, her son by a previous marriage. Nero's thanks was later to murder not only his mother but also his wife, Claudius's daughter, and his rival, Claudius's son. The disgraceful Nero was removed as emperor while visiting Greece; he committed suicide with the cry, "What an artist I destroy."

By the 3rd century A.D., corruption was so prevalent there were 23 emperors in 73 years. How bad had things gotten? So bad that Caracalla, to secure control of the empire, had his brother Geta slashed to pieces while lying in his mother's arms.

As the decay progressed, the Roman citizen either lived on the increasingly swollen public dole and spent his days at gladiatorial games and imperial baths or was a disillusioned patrician at the mercy of emperors who might murder him for his property. The 3rd century saw so many emperors that it was common, as H. V. Morton tells us, to hear in the provinces of the election of an emperor together with a report of his assassination.

The 4th-century reforms of Diocletian held the empire together, but at the expense of its inhabitants, who were reduced to tax units. He reinforced imperial power while paradoxically weakening Roman dominance and prestige by dividing the empire into east and west halves and establishing administrative capitals at outposts like Milan and Trier, Germany. Diocletian instituted not only heavy taxes but also a socioeconomic system that made professions hereditary. This edict was so strictly enforced, the son of a silversmith could be tried as a criminal if he attempted to become a sculptor instead.

Constantine became emperor in A.D. 306, and in 330 he made Constantinople (or Byzantium) the new capital of the Empire, moving the administrative functions away from Rome altogether, an act that sounded a death knell for a city already threatened by the menace of barbarian attacks. The sole survivor of six rival emperors, Constantine recognized Christianity as the official religion of the Roman empire and built an entirely new, more easily defended capital on the banks of the Bosporus. Named in his honor (Constantinople, or Byzantium), it was later renamed Istanbul by the Ottoman Turks. When he moved to the new capital, Constantine and his heirs took with them the best of the artisans, politicians, and public figures of Rome. Rome, reduced to little more than a provincial capital controlling the threatened western half of the once-mighty empire, continued to founder and decay. As for the Christian church, although the popes of Rome were under the nominal auspices of an exarch from Constantinople, their power increased slowly and steadily as the power of the emperors declined.

THE EMPIRE FALLS   The eastern and western sections of the Roman Empire split in 395, leaving Italy without the support it once received from east of the Adriatic. When the Goths moved toward Rome in the early 5th century, citizens in the provinces, who had grown to hate and fear the cruel bureaucracy set up by Diocletian and followed by succeeding emperors, welcomed the invaders. And then the pillage began.

Rome was first sacked by Alaric in August 410. The populace made no attempt to defend the city (other than trying vainly to buy off the Goth, a tactic that had worked 3 years before); most people simply fled into the hills or headed to their country estates if they were rich. The feeble Western emperor Honorius hid out in Ravenna the entire time.

More than 40 troubled years passed until the siege of Rome by Attila the Hun. Attila was dissuaded from attacking, thanks largely to a peace mission headed by Pope Leo I in 452. Yet, relief was short-lived: In 455, Gaiseric the Vandal carried out a 2-week sack that was unparalleled in its pure savagery. The empire of the West lasted for only another 20 years; finally the sacks and chaos ended it in 476, and Rome was left to the popes, under the nominal auspices of an exarch from Byzantium (Constantinople).

The last would-be Caesars to walk the streets of Rome were both barbarians: The first was Theodoric, who established an Ostrogoth kingdom at Ravenna from 493 to 526; and the second was Totila, who held the last chariot races in the Circus Maximus in 549. Totila was engaged in a running battle with Belisarius, the general of the Eastern emperor Justinian, who sought to regain Rome for the Eastern Empire. The city changed hands several times, recovering some of its ancient pride by bravely resisting Totilla's forces but eventually being entirely depopulated by the continuing battles.

THE HOLY ROMAN EMPIRE   A ravaged Rome entered the Middle Ages; its once-proud population scattered and unrecognizable in rustic exile. A modest population started life again in the swamps of the Campus Martius, while the seven hills, now without water since the aqueducts were cut, stood abandoned and crumbling.

After the fall of the Western Empire, the pope took on more and more imperial powers; yet, there was no political unity. Decades of rule by barbarians and then Goths were followed by takeovers in different parts of the country by various strong warriors, such as the Lombards. Italy was thus divided into several spheres of control. In 731, Pope Gregory II renounced Rome's dependence on Constantinople and, thus, ended the twilight era of the Greek exarch who had nominally ruled Rome.

Papal Rome turned toward Europe, where the papacy found a powerful ally in Charlemagne, a king of the barbarian Franks. In 800, he was crowned emperor by Pope Leo III. The capital he established at Aachen (Aix-la-Chapelle in French) lay deep within territory known to the Romans a half millennium ago as the heart of the barbarian world. Though Charlemagne pledged allegiance to the church and looked to Rome and its pope as the final arbiter in most religious and cultural affairs, he launched northwestern Europe on a course toward bitter political opposition to the meddling of the papacy in temporal affairs.

The successor to Charlemagne's empire was a political entity known as the Holy Roman Empire (962–1806). The new empire defined the end of the Dark

Ages but ushered in a period of long bloody warfare. The Lombard leaders battled Franks. Magyars from Hungary invaded northeastern Lombardy and were in turn defeated by the increasingly powerful Venetians. Normans gained military control of Sicily in the 11th century, divided it from the rest of Italy, and altered forever the island's racial and ethnic makeup and its architecture. As Italy dissolved into a fragmented collection of city-states, the papacy fell under the power of Rome's feudal landowners. Eventually, even the process for choosing popes came into the hands of the increasingly Germanic Holy Roman emperors, though this power balance would very soon shift.

Rome during the Middle Ages was a quaint rural town. Narrow lanes with overhanging buildings filled many areas that had been planned as showcases of ancient imperial power, like the Campus Martius. Great basilicas were built and embellished with golden-hued mosaics. The forums, mercantile exchanges, temples, and theaters of the Imperial Era slowly disintegrated and collapsed. The decay of ancient Rome was assisted by periodic earthquakes, centuries of neglect, and, in particular, the growing need for building materials. Rome receded into a dusty provincialism. As the seat of the Roman Catholic church, the state was almost completely controlled by priests, who had an insatiable need for new churches and convents.

By the end of the 11th century, the popes shook off control of the Roman aristocracy, rid themselves of what they considered the excessive influence of the emperors at Aachen, and began an aggressive expansion of church influence and acquisitions. The deliberate organization of the church into a format modeled on the hierarchies of the ancient Roman Empire put it on a collision course with the empire and the other temporal leaders of Europe, resulting in an endless series of power struggles.

THE MIDDLE AGES   The papacy soon became essentially a feudal state, and the pope became a medieval (later Renaissance) prince engaged in many of the worldly activities that brought criticism on the church in later centuries. The fall of the Holy Land to the Turks in 1065 catapulted the papacy into the forefront of world politics, primarily because of the Crusades, most of which were judged to be military and economic disasters and many of which the popes directly caused or encouraged. During the 12th and 13th centuries, the bitter rivalries that rocked the secular and spiritual bastions of Europe took their toll on the stability of the Holy Roman Empire, which grew weaker as city-states buttressed by mercantile and trade-related prosperity grew stronger. Also, France emerged as a strong nation in its own right during this period. Each investiture of a new bishop to any influential post became a cause for endless jockeying for power among many political and ecclesiastical factions.

These conflicts achieved their most visible impasse in 1303 with the full-fledged removal of the papacy from Rome to the French city of Avignon. For more than 70 years, until 1377, viciously competing popes (one in Rome, another under the protection of the French kings in Avignon) made simultaneous claims to the legacy of St. Peter, underscoring as never before the degree to which the church was both a victim and a victimizer of European politics.

The seat of the papacy was eventually returned to Rome, where a series of popes proved every bit as fascinating as the Roman emperors they replaced. The great families—Barberini, Medici, Borgia—enhanced their status and fortunes impressively whenever one of their sons was elected pope.

In the mid–14th century, the Black Death ravaged Europe, killing a third of Italy's population. Despite such setbacks, northern Italian city-states grew wealthy from Crusade booty, trade with one another and with the Middle East, and banking. These wealthy principalities and pseudorepublics ruled by the merchant elite flexed their muscles in the absence of a strong central authority.

THE RENAISSANCE   The story of Italy from the dawn of the Renaissance in the 15th century to the Age of Enlightenment in the 17th and 18th centuries is as varied and fascinating as that of the rise and fall of the empire.

Despite the centuries that had passed since the collapse of the Roman Empire, the age of siege wasn't yet over. In 1527, Charles V, king of Spain, carried out the worst sack of Rome ever. To the horror of Pope Clement VII (a Medici), the entire city was brutally pillaged by the man who was to be crowned Holy Roman Emperor the next year.

During the years of the Renaissance, the Reformation, and the Counter-Reformation, Rome underwent major physical changes. The old centers of culture reverted to pastures and fields, and great churches and palaces were built with the stones of ancient Rome. This construction boom, in fact, did far more damage to the temples of the Caesars than any barbarian sack had done. Rare marbles were stripped from the imperial baths and used as altarpieces or sent to lime kilns. So enthusiastic was the papal destruction of Imperial Rome that it's a miracle anything is left.

This era is best remembered because of its art. The great ruling families, especially the Medicis in Florence, the Gonzagas in Mantua, and the Estes in Ferrara, not only reformed law and commerce but also sparked a renaissance in art. Out of this period arose such towering figures as Leonardo da Vinci and Michelangelo. Many visitors come to Italy to view what's left of the art and glory of that era, including Michelangelo's Sistine Chapel ceiling at the Vatican.

THE MOVE TOWARD A UNITED ITALY   During the 17th, 18th, and 19th centuries the fortunes of Rome rose and fell with the general political and economic situation of the rest of Italy. Since the end of the 13th century, Italy had been divided into a series of regional states, each with mercenary soldiers, its own judicial system, and an interlocking series of alliances and enmities that had created a network of intensely competitive city-states. (Some of these families had attained formidable power under such *signori* as the Este family in Ferrara, the Medici in Florence, and the Sforza in Milan.) Rome, headquarters of the Papal States, maintained its independence and (usually) the integrity of its borders, although at least some of the city's religious power had been diluted as increasing numbers of Europeans converted to Protestantism.

Napoléon made a bid for power in Italy beginning in 1796, fueling his propaganda machines with what was considered a relatively easy victory. During the 1815 Congress of Vienna, which followed Napoléon's defeat, Italy was once again divided among many different factions: Austria was given Lombardy and Venetia, and the Papal States were returned to the popes. Some duchies were put back into the hands of their hereditary rulers; whereas, southern Italy and Sicily went to a newly imported dynasty related to the Bourbons. One historic move, which eventually assisted in the unification of Italy, was the assignment of the former republic of Genoa to Sardinia (which at the time was governed by the House of Savoy).

By now, political unrest had become a fact of Italian (and Roman) life, at least some of it encouraged by the rapid industrialization of the north and the almost total lack of industrialization in the south. Despite these barriers, in 1861 the Kingdom of Italy was proclaimed, and Victor Emmanuel II of the House of Savoy, king of Sardinia, became head of the new monarchy. In 1861 the designated capital of the newly united country, following a 2,000-year-old precedent, became Rome.

Garibaldi, the most respected of all Italian heroes, must be singled out for his efforts, which included taking Sicily, then returning to the mainland and marching north to meet Victor Emmanuel II at Teano, and finally declaring a unified Italy (with the important exception of Rome itself). It must have seemed especially sweet to a man whose efforts at unity had caused him to flee the country fearing for his life on four occasions. It's a tribute to the tenacity of this red-bearded hero that he never gave up, even in the early 1850s, when he was forced to wait out one of his exiles as a candlemaker on Staten Island in New York.

In a controversial move that engendered resentment many decades later, the borders of the Papal States were eradicated from the map as Rome was incorporated into the new nation of Italy. The Vatican, however, did not yield its territory to the new order despite guarantees of nonintervention proffered by the Italian government, and relations between the pope and the political leaders of Italy remained rocky until 1929.

WORLD WAR II & THE AXIS   On October 28, 1922, Benito Mussolini, who had started his Fascist Party in 1919, knew the time was ripe for change. He gathered 50,000 supporters for a march on Rome. Inflation was soaring and workers had just called a general strike, so King Victor Emmanuel II, rather than recognizing a state under siege, recognized Mussolini as the new government leader. In 1929, Il Duce defined the divisions between the Italian government and the Vatican by signing a concordat granting political and fiscal autonomy to Vatican City. It also made Roman Catholicism the official state religion—but that designation was removed in 1978 through a revision of the concordat.

During the Spanish Civil War (1936–39), Mussolini's support of Franco's Fascist party, which staged a coup against the democratically elected government of Spain, helped encourage the formation of the "Axis" alliance between Italy and Nazi Germany. Despite its outdated military equipment, Italy added to the general horror of the era by invading Abyssinia (Ethiopia) in 1935. In 1940, Italy invaded Greece through Albania and, in 1942, it sent thousands of Italian troops to assist Hitler in his disastrous campaign along the Russian front. In 1943, Allied forces, under the command of U.S. Gen. George Patton and British Gen. Bernard Montgomery, landed in Sicily and quickly secured the island as they prepared to move north toward Rome.

In the face of likely defeat and humiliation, Mussolini was overthrown by his own cabinet (Grand Council). The Allies made a separate deal with Victor Emmanuel III, who had collaborated with the Fascists during the previous 2 decades and now easily shifted allegiances. A politically divided Italy watched as battalions of fanatical German Nazis released Mussolini from his Italian jail cell to establish the short-lived Republic of Salò, headquartered on the edge of Lake Garda. Mussolini had hoped for a groundswell of popular opinion in favor of Italian Fascism, but events quickly proved this nothing more than a futile dream.

In April 1945, with almost half a million Italians rising in a mass demonstration against him and the German war machine, Mussolini was captured by

---

Impressions

It is not impossible to govern Italians. It is merely useless.

—Benito Mussolini

Italian partisans as he fled to Switzerland. Along with his mistress, Claretta Petacci, and several others of his intimates, he was shot and strung upside-down from the roof of a Milan gas station.

MODERN ROME   Disaffected with the monarchy and its identification with the fallen Fascist dictatorship, Italian voters in 1946 voted for the establishment of a republic. The major political party that emerged following World War II was the Christian Democratic Party, a right-of-center group whose leader, Alcide De Gasperi (1881–1954), served as premier until 1953. The second-largest party was the Communist Party; however, by the mid-1970s it had abandoned its revolutionary program in favor of a democratic form of "Eurocommunism" (in 1991, the Communists even changed their name, to the Democratic Party of the Left).

Though after the war Italy was stripped of all its overseas colonies, it quickly succeeded, in part because of U.S. aid under the Marshall Plan (1948–52), in rebuilding its economy. By the 1960s, as a member of the European Community (founded in Rome in 1957), Italy had become one of the world's leading industrialized nations, prominent in the manufacture of automobiles and office equipment.

But the country continued to be plagued by economic inequities between the prosperous industrialized north and the economically depressed south. It suffered an unprecedented flight of capital (frequently aided by Swiss banks only too willing to accept discreet deposits from wealthy Italians) and an increase in bankruptcies, inflation (almost 20% during much of the 1970s), and unemployment.

During the late 1970s and early 1980s, Italy was rocked by the rise of terrorism, instigated both by neo-Fascists and by left-wing intellectuals from the Socialist-controlled universities of the north.

THE 1990s & INTO THE NEW MILLENNIUM   In the 1990s, some 6,000 businesspeople and politicians were implicated in a billion-dollar government graft scandal. Such familiar figures as Bettino Craxi, former head of the Socialist party, and Giulio Andreotti, a seven-time prime minister, were accused of corruption.

Hoping for a renewal after all this exposure of greed, Italian voters in March 1994 turned to the right wing to head their government. In overwhelming numbers, voters elected a former cruise-ship singer turned media billionaire, Silvio Berlusconi, as their new leader. His Forza Italia (Go, Italy) party formed an alliance with the neo-fascist National Alliance and the secessionist Northern League to sweep to victory. These elections were termed "the most critical" for Italy in 4 decades. The new government was beset with an almost hopeless array of new problems, including destabilization caused by the Mafia and its underground economies and, when the Northern League defected from the coalition in December 1994, Berlusconi resigned.

Treasury Minister Lamberto Dini, a nonpolitical international banker, replaced him. Dini signed on merely as a transitional player in Italy's topsy-turvy political game. His austerity measures enacted to balance Italy's budget, including cuts in pensions and health care, were not popular among the mostly blue-collar Italian workers or the very influential labor unions. Pending a predicted defeat in a no-confidence vote, Dini also stepped down. His resignation in January 1996 left beleaguered Italians shouting *Basta!* (enough). This latest shuffling in Italy's political deck prompted President Oscar Scalfaro to dissolve both houses of the Italian Parliament.

Know Your Gods & Goddesses

Although modern visitors know Rome as the headquarters of Catholicism, the city also developed one of the world's most influential bodies of ancient mythology.

During the days when Rome was little more than a cluster of sheepherder's villages, a body of gods whose characters remained basically unchanged throughout the course of Roman history were worshipped. To this panoply, however, were added and assimilated the deities of other conquered territories (especially Greece) until the roster of Roman gods bristled with imports from around the Mediterranean. In its corrupted (later) version, the list grew impossibly unwieldy as more or less demented emperors forced their own deification and worship on the Roman masses. After the Christianizing of Europe, the original and ancient gods retained their astrological significance and have provided poetic fodder for endless literary and lyrical comparisons.

A brief understanding of each of the major gods' functions will add insights during your explorations of the city's museums and excavations.

Apollo was the representative of music, the sun, prophecy, healing, the arts, and philosophy. He was the brother of **Diana** (symbol of chastity and goddess of the hunt, the moon, wild animals, and later, of commerce) and the son of **Jupiter** (king of the gods and god of lightning), by a lesser female deity named Leto. **Cupid** was the god of falling in love.

Juno, the wife of Jupiter, was attributed with vague but awesome powers and a very human sense of outrage and jealousy. Her main job seemed to be wreaking vengeance against the hundreds of nymphs that Jupiter seduced and punishment of the thousands of children he supposedly fathered.

Mars, the dignified but bloodthirsty god of war, was reputed to be the father of **Romulus,** cofounder of Rome.

Once again Italians were faced with forming a new government. Elections in April 1996 proved quite a shocker, not only for the defeated politicians but also for the victors. The center-left coalition known as the Olive Tree, led by Romano Prodi, swept both the Senate and the Chamber of Deputies. The Olive Tree, whose roots stem from the old Communist party, achieved victory by shifting toward the center and focusing its campaign on a strong platform protecting social benefits and supporting Italy's bid to become a solid member of the European Union. Prodi carried through on his commitment when he announced a stringent budget for 1997 in a bid to be among the first countries to enter the monetary union.

The year 1997 saw further upheavals as the Prodi government continued to push ahead with cuts to the country's generous social security system. In the autumn of 1997 Prodi was forced to submit his resignation when he lost critical support in Parliament from the Communist Refounding party, which balked at further pension and welfare cuts in the 1998 budget. The party eventually backed off with its demands, and Prodi was returned to office.

Mercury, symbol of such Geminis (twins) as Romulus and Remus, was one of the most diverse and morally ambiguous of the gods. He served as the guide to the dead as they approached the underworld, and as the patron of eloquence, travel, negotiation, diplomacy, good sense, prudence, and (to a very limited extent) thieving.

Neptune, god of the sea, was assigned almost no moral attributes but represents solely the watery domains of the earth.

Minerva was the goddess of wisdom, arts and crafts, and (occasionally) of war. A goddess whose allure was cerebral and whose discipline was severe, she wears a helmet and breastplate emblazoned with the head of **Medusa** (the snake-haired monster whose gaze could turn men into stone). During the Renaissance she became a symbol much associated, oddly enough, with the wisdom and righteousness of the Christian popes.

Venus, whose mythological power grew as the empire expanded, was the goddess of gardens and every conceivable variety of love. She was reportedly the mother of **Aeneas,** mythical ancestor of the Romans. Both creative and destructive, Venus's appeal and duality are as primeval as the earth itself.

Ceres, goddess of the earth and of the harvest, mourned for half of every year (during winter) when her daughter, **Proserpine,** abandoned her to live in the house of **Pluto,** god of death and the underworld.

Vulcan was the half-lame god of metallurgy, volcanoes, and furnaces, whose activities at his celestial forge crafted superweapons for an array of military heroes beloved by the ancient Romans.

Finally, **Bacchus,** the god of wine, undisciplined revelry, drunkenness, and absence of morality, gained importance in Rome as the city grew decadent and declined.

Italy and the United States faced tense relations in the spring of 1999 when a military jury cleared marine captain Richard J. Ashby of charges brought against him for flying his plane over a ski resort and severing gondola cables, plunging 20 people to their deaths in 1998. After a year of painful recriminations on both sides of the Atlantic and a bitter, 3-week-long trial, the not-guilty verdict came in with stunning finality.

The big financial news in 1999 was Italy's decision to switch its currency to the euro (a transition that will enter its final phase in 2002, as the lire is gradually withdrawn from circulation in favor of this new continent-wide currency).

In December 1999, under Prime Minister Massimo D'Alema, Italy received its 57th new government since 1945. But it didn't last long. In April 2000, former prime minister Giuliano Amato, a onetime Socialist, returned to power.

As 1999 neared its end, Rome rushed to put the finishing touches on its many monuments, including churches and museums, and everybody was ready for the scaffolding to come down before the arrival of 2000. Italy spent all of 2000 welcoming Jubilee Year visitors from around the world, as its political cauldron bubbled. One particularly notable clash in 2000 pitted the church and social conservatives against more progressive young Italians, as the pope lashed out at the World Gay Pride rally held in the summer of 2000. His condemnation sparked much debate in the media, but the actual event went off without a hitch and, in fact, was labeled as rather tame when compared to more raucous Gay Pride rallies elsewhere around the globe.

The richest man in Italy, billionaire media tycoon Silvio Berlusconi (owner of three private TV networks), swept to victory in May 2001 as prime minister, winning with right-wing support. Calling for a "revolution" in Italy, Berlusconi has promised a million and a half new jobs, pension hikes, epic tax cuts, anti-crime bills, and beefed-up public works projects, and has signaled his readiness to be a conservative ally of U.S. President George W. Bush on environmental issues, unlike other European leaders.

2 Recommended Books

GENERAL & HISTORY

Presenting a "warts and all" view of the Italian character, Luigi Barzini's **The Italians** should almost be required reading for anyone contemplating a trip to Rome. It's lively, fun, and not at all academic.

Edward Gibbon's 1776 **The History of the Decline and Fall of the Roman Empire** is published in six volumes, but Penguin issues a manageable abridgement. This work has been hailed as one of the greatest histories ever written. No one has ever captured the saga of the glory that was Rome the way Gibbon did.

One of the best books on the long history of the papacy—detailing its excesses, triumphs, defeats, and most vivid characters—is Michael Walsh's **An Illustrated History of the Popes: Saint Peter to John Paul II.**

In the 20th century, the most fascinating period in Italian history was the rise and fall of fascism, as detailed in countless works. One of the best biographies of Il Duce is Denis M. Smith's **Mussolini: A Biography.** Another subject that's always engrossing is the Mafia, which is detailed, godfathers and all, in Pino Arlacchi's **Mafia Business: The Mafia Ethic and the Spirit of Capitalism.**

William Murray's **The Last Italian: Portrait of a People** is his second volume of essays on his favorite subject—Italy, its warm people, and astonishing civilization. The *New York Times* called it "a lover's keen, observant diary of his affair."

Once Upon a Time in Italy: The Vita Italiana of an American Journalist, by Jack Casserly, is the entertaining and affectionate memoir of a former bureau chief in Rome from 1957 to 1964. He captures the spirit of Italia *sparita* (bygone Italy) with such celebrity cameos as Maria Callas and the American expatriate singer Bricktop.

ART & ARCHITECTURE

From the Colosseum to Michelangelo, T. W. Potter provides one of the best accounts of the art and architecture of Rome in **Roman Italy,** which is also illustrated. Another good book on the same subject is **Roman Art and Architecture,** by Mortimer Wheeler.

The Sistine Chapel: A Glorious Restoration, by Michael Hirst and others, uses nearly 300 color photographs to illustrate the lengthy and painstaking restoration of Michelangelo's 16th-century frescoes in the Vatican.

Giorgio Vasari's *Lives of the Artists* **Vols. I and II** is a collection of biographies of the great artists from Cimabue up to Vasari's 16th-century contemporaries. It's an interesting read, full of anecdotes and Vasari's theories on art practice. For a more modern art history take, the indispensable tome is Frederick Hartt's *History of Italian Renaissance Art.* For an easier and more colorful introduction, get Michael Levey's *Early Renaissance* and *High Renaissance.*

FICTION & BIOGRAPHY

No one does it better than John Hersey in his Pulitzer Prize–winning *A Bell for Adano,* a frequently reprinted classic. It's a well-written and disturbing story of the American invasion of Italy.

One of the best known Italian writers published in England is Alberto Moravia, born in 1907. His neorealistic novels are immensely entertaining and are read around the world. Notable works include *Roman Tales, The Woman of Rome,* and *The Conformist.*

For the most wildly entertaining books on ancient Rome, detailing its most flamboyant personalities and excesses, read *I, Claudius* and *Claudius the God,* both by Robert Graves. Borrowing from the histories of Tacitus and Suetonius, the series begins at the end of the Emperor Augustus's reign and ends with the death of Claudius in the first century A.D. In 1998, the Modern Library placed *I, Claudius* at number 14 on its list of the 100 finest English-language novels published this century.

Colleen McCullough's "Masters of Rome" series is rich, fascinating, and historically detailed, bringing to vivid life such greats as Gaius Marius (*The First Man in Rome*), Lucius Cornelius Sulla (*The Grass Crown*), and Julius Caesar (*Fortune's Favorites* and *Caesar's Women*).

Michelangelo, a Biography, by George Bull, is a well-written scholarly take on the life of the artist penned by a Renaissance expert and one of the most respected translators of Italian classic literature.

Irving Stone's *The Agony and the Ecstasy,* filmed with Charlton Heston playing Michelangelo, is the easiest to read and the most pop version of the life of this great artist. Heston still views it as his greatest role and still tries to keep Michelangelo from coming out of the closet.

Many other writers have tried to capture the peculiar nature of Italy. Notable works include Italo Calvino's *The Baron in the Trees,* Umberto Eco's *The Name of the Rose,* E. M. Forster's *Where Angels Fear to Tread* and *A Room with a View,* Henry James's *The Aspern Papers,* Giuseppe di Lampedusa's *The Leopard,* Carlo Levi's *Christ Stopped at Eboli,* Susan Sontag's *The Volcano Lover,* and Mark Helprin's underappreciated masterwork, *A Soldier of the Great War.*

Appendix B:
Molto Italiano

1 Basic Vocabulary

English	Italian	Pronunciation
Thank you	**Grazie**	*graht*-tzee-yey
You're welcome	**Prego**	*prey*-go
Please	**Per favore**	*pehr* fah-*vohr*-eh
Yes	**Sì**	see
No	**No**	noh
Good morning or Good day	**Buongiorno**	bwohn-*djor*-noh
Good evening	**Buona sera**	*bwohn*-ah *say*-rah
Good night	**Buona notte**	*bwohn*-ah *noht*-tay
How are you?	**Come sta?**	*koh*-may *stah*
Very well	**Molto bene**	*mohl*-toh *behn*-ney
Goodbye	**Arrivederci**	ahr-ree-vah-*dehr*-chee
Excuse me (to get attention)	**Scusi**	*skoo*-zee
Excuse me (to get past someone)	**Permesso**	pehr-*mehs*-soh
Where is . . . ?	**Dovè . . . ?**	doh-*vey*
the station	**la stazione**	lah stat-tzee-*oh*-neh
a hotel	**un albergo**	oon ahl-*behr*-goh
a restaurant	**un ristorante**	oon reest-ohr-*ahnt*-eh
the bathroom	**il bagno**	eel *bahn*-nyoh
To the right	**A destra**	ah *dehy*-stra
To the left	**A sinistra**	ah see-*nees*-tra
Straight ahead	**Avanti (or sempre diritto)**	ahv-*vahn*-tee (*sehm*-pray dee-*reet*-toh)
How much is it?	**Quanto costa?**	*kwan*-toh *coh*-sta?
The check, please	**Il conto, per favore**	eel *kon*-toh pehr fah-*vohr*-eh
When?	**Quando?**	*kwan*-doh
Yesterday	**Ieri**	ee-*yehr*-ree
Today	**Oggi**	*oh*-jee
Tomorrow	**Domani**	doh-*mah*-nee
Breakfast	**Prima colazione**	*pree*-mah coh-laht-tzee-*ohn*-ay
Lunch	**Pranzo**	*prahn*-zoh
Dinner	**Cena**	*chay*-nah
What time is it?	**Che ore sono?**	kay *or*-ay *soh*-noh
Monday	**Lunedì**	loo-nay-*dee*
Tuesday	**Martedì**	mart-ay-*dee*
Wednesday	**Mercoledì**	mehr-cohl-ay-*dee*
Thursday	**Giovedì**	joh-vay-*dee*

Friday	**Venerdì**	ven-nehr-*dee*
Saturday	**Sabato**	*sah*-bah-toh
Sunday	**Domenica**	doh-*mehn*-nee-kah

NUMBERS

1	**uno** (*oo*-noh)	
2	**due** (*doo*-ay)	
3	**tre** (tray)	
4	**quattro** (*kwah*-troh)	
5	**cinque** (*cheen*-kway)	
6	**sei** (say)	
7	**sette** (*set*-tay)	
8	**otto** (*oh*-toh)	
9	**nove** (*noh*-vay)	
10	**dieci** (dee-*ay*-chee)	
11	**undici** (*oon*-dee-chee)	
20	**venti** (*vehn*-tee)	
21	**ventuno** (vehn-*toon*-oh)	
22	**venti due** (*vehn*-tee *doo*-ay)	

30	**trenta** (*trayn*-tah)
40	**quaranta** (kwah-*rahn*-tah)
50	**cinquanta** (cheen-*kwan*-tah)
60	**sessanta** (sehs-*sahn*-tah)
70	**settanta** (seht-*tahn*-tah)
80	**ottanta** (oht-*tahn*-tah)
90	**novanta** (noh-*vahn*-tah)
100	**cento** (*chen*-toh)
1,000	**mille** (*mee*-lay)
5,000	**cinque milla** (*cheen*-kway *mee*-lah)
10,000	**dieci milla** (dee-*ay*-chee *mee*-lah)

2 A Glossary of Architectural Terms

Ambone   A pulpit, either serpentine or simple in form, erected in an Italian church.

Apse   The half-rounded extension behind the main altar of a church; Christian tradition dictates that it be placed at the eastern end of an Italian church, the side closest to Jerusalem.

Atrium   A courtyard, open to the sky, in an ancient Roman house; the term also applies to the courtyard nearest the entrance of an early Christian church.

Baldacchino (also ciborium)   A columned stone canopy, usually placed above the altar of a church; spelled in English *baldachin* or *baldaquin*.

Baptistry   A separate building or a separate area in a church where the rite of baptism is held.

Basilica   Any rectangular public building, usually divided into three aisles by rows of columns. In ancient Rome, this architectural form was frequently used for places of public assembly and law courts; later, Roman Christians adapted the form for many of their early churches.

Caldarium   The steam room of a Roman bath.

Campanile   A bell tower, often detached, of a church.

Capital   The top of a column, often carved and usually categorized into one of three orders: Doric, Ionic, or Corinthian.

Castrum   A carefully planned Roman military camp, whose rectangular form, straight streets, and systems of fortified gates quickly became standardized throughout the Empire; modern cities that began as Roman camps and still more or less maintain their original forms include Chester (England), Barcelona (Spain), and such Italian cities as Lucca, Aosta, Como, Brescia, Florence, and Ancona.

Cavea   The curved row of seats in a classical theater; the most prevalent shape was that of a semicircle.

Cella   The sanctuary, or most sacred interior section, of a Roman pagan temple.

Chancel   Section of a church containing the altar.

Cornice   The decorative flange defining the uppermost part of a classical or neoclassical facade.

Cortile   Courtyard or cloisters ringed with a gallery of arches or lintels set atop columns.

Crypt   A church's main burial place, usually below the choir.

Cupola   A dome.

Duomo   Cathedral.

Forum   The main square and principal gathering place of any Roman town, usually adorned with the city's most important temples and civic buildings.

Grotesques   Carved and painted faces, deliberately ugly, used by everyone from the Etruscans to the architects of the Renaissance; they're especially amusing when set into fountains.

Hypogeium   Subterranean burial chambers, usually of pre-Christian origins.

Loggia   Roofed balcony or gallery.

Lozenge   An elongated four-sided figure that, along with stripes, was one of the distinctive signs of the architecture of Pisa.

Narthex   The anteroom, or enclosed porch, of a Christian church.

Nave   The largest and longest section of a church, usually devoted to sheltering or seating worshipers and often divided by aisles.

Palazzo   A palace or other important building.

Piano Nobile   The main floor of a palazzo (sometimes the second floor).

Pietra Dura   Richly ornate assemblage of semiprecious stones mounted on a flat decorative surface, perfected during the 1600s in Florence.

Pieve   A parish church.

Portico   A porch, usually crafted from wood or stone.

Pulvin   A four-sided stone that serves as a substitute for the capital of a column, often decoratively carved, sometimes into biblical scenes.

Putti   Plaster cherubs whose chubby forms often decorate the interiors of baroque chapels and churches.

Stucco   Colored plaster composed of sand, powdered marble, water, and lime, either molded into statuary or applied in a thin concrete-like layer to the exterior of a building.

Telamone   Structural column carved into a standing male form; female versions are called *caryatids*.

Thermae   Roman baths.

Transenna   Stone (usually marble) screen separating the altar area from the rest of an early Christian church.

Travertine   The stone from which ancient and Renaissance Rome was built, it's known for its hardness, light coloring, and tendency to be pitted or flecked with black.

Tympanum   The half-rounded space above the portal of a church, whose semicircular space usually showcases a sculpture.

3 Italian Menu Terms

Abbacchio   Roast haunch or shoulder of lamb baked and served in a casserole and sometimes flavored with anchovies.

Agnolotti   A crescent-shaped pasta shell stuffed with a mix of chopped meat, spices, vegetables, and cheese; when prepared in rectangular versions, the same combination of ingredients is identified as ravioli.

Amaretti   Crunchy, sweet almond-flavored macaroons.

Anguilla alla veneziana   Eel cooked in a sauce made from tuna and lemon.

Antipasti   Succulent tidbits served at the beginning of a meal (before the pasta), whose ingredients might include slices of cured meats, seafood (especially shellfish), and cooked and seasoned vegetables.

Aragosta   Lobster.

Arrosto   Roasted meat.

Baccalà   Dried and salted codfish.

Bagna cauda   Hot and well-seasoned sauce, heavily flavored with anchovies, designed for dipping raw vegetables; literally translated as "hot bath."

Bistecca alla fiorentina   Florentine-style steaks, coated before grilling with olive oil, pepper, lemon juice, salt, and parsley.

Bocconcini   Veal layered with ham and cheese, and then fried.

Bollito misto   Assorted boiled meats served on a single platter.

Braciola   Pork chop.

Bresaola   Air-dried spiced beef.

Bruschetta   Toasted bread, heavily slathered with olive oil and garlic and often topped with tomatoes.

Bucatini   Coarsely textured hollow spaghetti.

Busecca alla Milanese   Tripe (beef stomach) flavored with herbs and vegetables.

Cacciucco ali livornese   Seafood stew.

Calzone   Pizza dough rolled with the chef's choice of sausage, tomatoes, cheese, and so on and then baked into a kind of savory turnover.

Cannelloni   Tubular dough stuffed with meat, cheese, or vegetables and then baked in a creamy white sauce.

Cappellacci alla ferrarese   Pasta stuffed with pumpkin.

Cappelletti   Small ravioli ("little hats") stuffed with meat or cheese.

Carciofi   Artichokes.

Carpaccio   Thin slices of raw cured beef, sometimes in a piquant sauce.

Cassatta alla siciliana   A richly caloric dessert that combines layers of sponge cake, sweetened ricotta cheese, and candied fruit, bound together with chocolate buttercream icing.

Cervello al burro nero   Brains in black-butter sauce.

Cima alla genovese   Baked filet of veal rolled into a tube-shaped package containing eggs, mushrooms, and sausage.

Coppa   Cured morsels of pork filet encased in sausage skins, served in slices.

Costoletta alla milanese   Veal cutlet dredged in bread crumbs, fried, and sometimes flavored with cheese.

Cozze   Mussels.

Fagioli   White beans.

Fave   Fava beans.

Fegato alla veneziana   Thinly sliced calves' liver fried with salt, pepper, and onions.

Foccacia   Ideally, concocted from potato-based dough left to rise slowly for several hours and then garnished with tomato sauce, garlic, basil, salt, and pepper and drizzled with olive oil; similar to a deep-dish pizza most popular in the deep south, especially Bari.

Fontina   Rich cows'-milk cheese.

Frittata   Italian omelette.

Fritto misto   A deep-fried medley of whatever small fish, shellfish, and squid are available in the marketplace that day.

Fusilli   Spiral-shaped pasta.

Gelato (produzione propria)   Ice cream (homemade).

Gnocchi   Dumplings usually made from potatoes (*gnocchi alla patate*) or from semolina (*gnocchi alla romana*), often stuffed with combinations of cheese, spinach, vegetables, or whatever combinations strike the chef's fancy.

Gorgonzola   One of the most famous blue-veined cheeses of Europe—strong, creamy, and aromatic.

Granita   Flavored ice, usually with lemon or coffee.

Insalata di frutti di mare   Seafood salad (usually including shrimp and squid) garnished with pickles, lemon, olives, and spices.

Involtini   Thinly sliced beef, veal, or pork, rolled, stuffed, and fried.

Minestrone   A rich and savory vegetable soup usually sprinkled with grated parmigiano and studded with noodles.

Mortadella   Mild pork sausage, fashioned into large cylinders and served sliced; the original lunchmeat bologna (because its most famous center of production is Bologna).

Mozzarella   A nonfermented cheese, made from the fresh milk of a buffalo (or, if unavailable, from a cow), boiled, and then kneaded into a rounded ball, served fresh.

Mozzarella con pomodori (also "caprese")   Fresh tomatoes with fresh mozzarella, basil, pepper, and olive oil.

Nervetti   A northern Italian antipasto made from chewy pieces of calves' foot or shin.

Osso buco   Beef or veal knuckle slowly braised until the cartilage is tender and then served with a highly flavored sauce.

Pancetta   Herb-flavored pork belly, rolled into a cylinder and sliced—the Italian bacon.

Panettone   Sweet yellow-colored bread baked in the form of a brioche.

Panna   Heavy cream.

Pansotti   Pasta stuffed with greens, herbs, and cheeses, usually served with a walnut sauce.

Pappardelle alle lepre   Pasta with rabbit sauce.

Parmigiano   Parmesan, a hard and salty yellow cheese usually grated over pastas and soups but also eaten alone; also known as *granna*. The best is *parmigiano reggiano*.

Peperoni   Green, yellow, or red sweet peppers (not to be confused with pepperoni).

Pesci al cartoccio   Fish baked in a parchment envelope with onions, parsley, and herbs.

Pesto   A flavorful green sauce made from basil leaves, cheese, garlic, marjoram, and (if available) pine nuts.

Piccata al marsala   Thin escalope of veal braised in a pungent sauce flavored with marsala wine.

Piselli al prosciutto   Peas with strips of ham.

Pizza   Specific varieties include *capricciosa* (its ingredients can vary widely, depending on the chef's culinary vision and the ingredients at hand), *margherita* (with tomato sauce, cheese, fresh basil, and memories of the first queen of Italy, Marguerite di Savoia, in whose honor it was first made by a Neapolitan chef), *napoletana* (with ham, capers, tomatoes, oregano, cheese, and the distinctive taste of anchovies), *quatro stagione* (translated as "four seasons" because of the array of fresh vegetables in it; it also contains ham and bacon), and *siciliana* (with black olives, capers, and cheese).

Pizzaiola   A process in which something (usually a beefsteak) is covered in a tomato-and-oregano sauce.

Polenta   Thick porridge or mush made from cornmeal flour.

Polenta de uccelli   Assorted small birds roasted on a spit and served with polenta.

Polenta e coniglio   Rabbit stew served with polenta.

Pollo alla cacciatore   Chicken with tomatoes and mushrooms cooked in wine.

Pollo alla diavola   Highly spiced grilled chicken.

Ragù   Meat sauce.

Ricotta   A soft bland cheese made from cow's or sheep's milk.

Risotto   Italian rice.

Risotto alla milanese   Rice with saffron and wine.

Salsa verde   "Green sauce," made from capers, anchovies, lemon juice and/or vinegar, and parsley.

Saltimbocca   Veal scallop layered with prosciutto and sage; its name literally translates as "jump in your mouth," a reference to its tart and savory flavor.

Salvia   Sage.

Scaloppina alla Valdostana   Escalope of veal stuffed with cheese and ham.

Scaloppine   Thin slices of veal coated in flour and sautéed in butter.

Semifreddo   A frozen dessert; usually ice cream with sponge cake.

Seppia   Cuttlefish (a kind of squid); its black ink is used for flavoring in certain sauces for pasta and also in risotto dishes.

Sogliola   Sole.

Spaghetti   A long, round, thin pasta, variously served: *alla bolognese* (with ground meat, mushrooms, peppers, and so on), *alla carbonara* (with bacon, black pepper, and eggs), *al pomodoro* (with tomato sauce), *al sugo/ragù* (with meat sauce), and *alle vongole* (with clam sauce).

Spiedini   Pieces of meat grilled on a skewer over an open flame.

Strangolaprete   Small nuggets of pasta, usually served with sauce; the name is literally translated as "priest-choker."

Stufato   Beef braised in white wine with vegetables.

Tagliatelle   Flat egg noodles.

Tonno   Tuna.

Tortelli   Pasta dumplings stuffed with ricotta and greens.

Tortellini   Rings of dough stuffed with minced and seasoned meat, and served either in soups or as a full-fledged pasta covered with sauce.

Trenette   Thin noodles served with pesto sauce and potatoes.

Trippe alla fiorentina   Beef tripe (stomach).

Vermicelli   Very thin spaghetti.

Vitello tonnato   Cold sliced veal covered with tuna-fish sauce.

Zabaglione/zabaione   Egg yolks whipped into the consistency of a custard, flavored with marsala, and served warm as a dessert.

Zampone   Pig's trotter stuffed with spicy seasoned port, boiled and sliced.

Zuccotto   A liqueur-soaked sponge cake, molded into a dome and layered with chocolate, nuts, and whipped cream.

Zuppa inglese   Sponge cake soaked in custard.

Index

See also Accommodations and Restaurant indexes, below.

Doctors, 56
Dominici, 212
Domitian's Stadium (Hippodrome), 176
Domus Augustana, 175–176
Domus Aurea (Golden House of Nero), 139, 162
Drugstores, 56
Duomo (Palestrina), 228
Duomo (Viterbo), 236

E. Fiore, 207
Easter Sunday (Pasqua), 33
Economy Book and Video Center, 203
Ecstasy of St. Teresa, 8
Egyptian-Gregorian Museum (the Vatican), 132
Egyptian obelisk, 157–158
Elderhostel, 36
Electricity, 56
Emanuele, Vittorio, Monument, 46, 143, 179
Embassies and consulates, 56
Emergencies, 57
Emporio Armani, 204
English Home, 206
Enjoy Rome, 46
Enoteca Fratelli Roffi Isabelli, 223
Entry requirements, 28
Escorted tours, 42
Ethnological Museum (the Vatican), 132
Etruscan culture and antiquities, 17, 238–240
    Etruscan-Gregorian Museum (the Vatican), 132
    historical sights, 234–235
    Museo Nazionale di Villa Giulia (National Etruscan Museum), 159

Etruscan-Gregorian Museum (the Vatican), 132
Etruscan Necropolis (Tarquinia), 235
Eurailpasses, 37, 39–41
Euro, 29–30
Europass, 40
Ex Ante, 206
Expedia, 39

Fabrics, 201
Farnese, 210–211
Farnese Gardens (Orti Farnesiani), 176
Fascist architecture, 26, 27
Fashions (clothing), 200, 204
    lingerie, 208–209
Fava, 209
Federico Buccellati, 207
Fendi Italia, 208
Ferragamo, 212
Festivals and special events, 32–33
Fiction, 251
Fiumicino (Leonardo da Vinci International Airport), 44
    accommodations near, 87–88
Flavian Palace, 175
Flea markets, 10, 210
Florentine Church (Chiesa di San Giovanni dei Fiorentini), 188
Flower market, 210
Flying Wheels Travel, 35
Fonclea, 218
Fontana Candida, 231
Fontana dei Draghi (Villa d'Este), 225
Fontana dei Quattro Fiumi, 151
Fontana dei Trevi, 154, 156, 180, 182
Fontana delle Api, 156
Fontana delle Tararughe, 9

Fontana dell'Organo Idraulico (Villa d'Este), 225
Fontana dell Ovato (Villa d'Este), 225
Fontana del Moro, 151
Fontana del Tritone, 10, 47, 156
Fontana di Nettuno, 151
Food. See also Markets
    shopping for, 201, 205–206
Fori Imperiali (Imperial Forums), 142–143
Fornari & Fornari, 212
Foro Italico, 214
Foro Romano (Roman Forum), 140, 170, 172–174
Fortuna Primigenia (Palestrina), 228
Forum (Ostia), 233
Forum of Augustus, 142, 177
Forum of Julius Caesar, 143, 178–179
Forum of Nerva, 142, 177
Forum of Trajan, 143, 178
Fountain of Neptune (Fontana di Nettuno), 151
Fountain of the Bees (Fontana delle Api), 156
Fountain of the Dragons (Villa d'Este), 225
Fountain of the Four Rivers (Fontana dei Quattro Fiumi), 151
Fountain of the Hydraulic Organ (Fontana dell'Organo Idraulico) (Villa d'Este), 225
Fountain of the Moor (Fontana del Moro), 151
Fountain of the Triton (Fontana del Tritone), 10, 47, 156

ACCOMMODATIONS

Restaurants

FROMMER'S® COMPLETE TRAVEL GUIDES

Alaska
Amsterdam
Argentina & Chile
Arizona
Atlanta
Australia
Austria
Bahamas
Barcelona, Madrid & Seville
Beijing
Belgium, Holland & Luxembourg
Bermuda
Boston
British Columbia & the Canadian Rockies
Budapest & the Best of Hungary
California
Canada
Cancún, Cozumel & the Yucatán
Cape Cod, Nantucket & Martha's Vineyard
Caribbean
Caribbean Cruises & Ports of Call
Caribbean Ports of Call
Carolinas & Georgia
Chicago
China
Colorado
Costa Rica
Denmark
Denver, Boulder & Colorado Springs
England
Europe
European Cruises & Ports of Call
Florida
France
Germany
Great Britain
Greece
Greek Islands
Hawaii
Hong Kong
Honolulu, Waikiki & Oahu
Ireland
Israel
Italy
Jamaica
Japan
Las Vegas
London
Los Angeles
Maryland & Delaware
Maui
Mexico
Montana & Wyoming
Montréal & Québec City
Munich & the Bavarian Alps
Nashville & Memphis
Nepal
New England
New Mexico
New Orleans
New York City
New Zealand
Nova Scotia, New Brunswick & Prince Edward Island
Oregon
Paris
Philadelphia & the Amish Country
Portugal
Prague & the Best of the Czech Republic
Provence & the Riviera
Puerto Rico
Rome
San Antonio & Austin
San Diego
San Francisco
Santa Fe, Taos & Albuquerque
Scandinavia
Scotland
Seattle & Portland
Shanghai
Singapore & Malaysia
South Africa
South America
Southeast Asia
South Florida
South Pacific
Spain
Sweden
Switzerland
Texas
Thailand
Tokyo
Toronto
Tuscany & Umbria
USA
Utah
Vancouver & Victoria
Vermont, New Hampshire & Maine
Vienna & the Danube Valley
Virgin Islands
Virginia
Walt Disney World & Orlando
Washington, D.C.
Washington State

FROMMER'S® DOLLAR-A-DAY GUIDES

Australia from $50 a Day
California from $70 a Day
Caribbean from $70 a Day
England from $70 a Day
Europe from $70 a Day
Florida from $70 a Day
Hawaii from $80 a Day
Ireland from $60 a Day
Italy from $70 a Day
London from $85 a Day
New York from $90 a Day
Paris from $80 a Day
San Francisco from $70 a Day
Washington, D.C., from $70 a Day

FROMMER'S® PORTABLE GUIDES

Acapulco, Ixtapa & Zihuatanejo
Alaska Cruises & Ports of Call
Amsterdam
Aruba
Australia's Great Barrier Reef
Bahamas
Baja & Los Cabos
Berlin
Big Island of Hawaii
Boston
California Wine Country
Cancún
Charleston & Savannah
Chicago
Disneyland
Dublin
Florence
Frankfurt
Hong Kong
Houston
Las Vegas
London
Los Angeles
Maine Coast
Maui
Miami
New Orleans
New York City
Paris
Phoenix & Scottsdale
Portland
Puerto Rico
Puerto Vallarta, Manzanillo & Guadalajara
San Diego
San Francisco
Seattle
Sydney
Tampa & St. Petersburg
Vancouver
Venice
Virgin Islands
Washington, D.C.

FROMMER'S® NATIONAL PARK GUIDES

Family Vacations in the National Parks
Grand Canyon
National Parks of the American West
Rocky Mountain
Yellowstone & Grand Teton
Yosemite & Sequoia/ Kings Canyon
Zion & Bryce Canyon

FROMMER'S® MEMORABLE WALKS

Chicago	New York	San Francisco
London	Paris	

FROMMER'S® GREAT OUTDOOR GUIDES

Arizona & New Mexico	Northern California	Vermont & New Hampshire
New England	Southern New England	

SUZY GERSHMAN'S BORN TO SHOP GUIDES

Born to Shop: France	Born to Shop: Italy	Born to Shop: New York
Born to Shop: Hong Kong, Shanghai & Beijing	Born to Shop: London	Born to Shop: Paris

FROMMER'S® IRREVERENT GUIDES

Amsterdam	Los Angeles	San Francisco
Boston	Manhattan	Seattle & Portland
Chicago	New Orleans	Vancouver
Las Vegas	Paris	Walt Disney World
London	Rome	Washington, D.C.

FROMMER'S® BEST-LOVED DRIVING TOURS

Britain	Germany	New England
California	Ireland	Scotland
Florida	Italy	Spain
France		

HANGING OUT™ GUIDES

Hanging Out in England	Hanging Out in France	Hanging Out in Italy
Hanging Out in Europe	Hanging Out in Ireland	Hanging Out in Spain

THE UNOFFICIAL GUIDES®

Bed & Breakfasts and Country Inns in:	Florida with Kids	New Orleans
California	Golf Vacations in the Eastern U.S.	New York City
New England	The Great Smokey & Blue Ridge Mountains	Paris
Northwest	Inside Disney	San Francisco
Rockies	Hawaii	Skiing in the West
Southeast	Las Vegas	Southeast with Kids
Beyond Disney	London	Walt Disney World
Branson, Missouri	Mid-Atlantic with Kids	Walt Disney World for Grown-ups
California with Kids	Mini Las Vegas	Walt Disney World for Kids
Chicago	Mini-Mickey	Washington, D.C.
Cruises	New England & New York with Kids	World's Best Diving Vacations
Disneyland		

SPECIAL-INTEREST TITLES

Frommer's Adventure Guide to Australia & New Zealand
Frommer's Adventure Guide to Central America
Frommer's Adventure Guide to India & Pakistan
Frommer's Adventure Guide to South America
Frommer's Adventure Guide to Southeast Asia
Frommer's Adventure Guide to Southern Africa
Frommer's Britain's Best Bed & Breakfasts and Country Inns
Frommer's France's Best Bed & Breakfasts and Country Inns
Frommer's Italy's Best Bed & Breakfasts and Country Inns
Frommer's Caribbean Hideaways

Frommer's Exploring America by RV
Frommer's Gay & Lesbian Europe
Frommer's The Moon
Frommer's New York City with Kids
Frommer's Road Atlas Britain
Frommer's Road Atlas Europe
Frommer's Washington, D.C., with Kids
Frommer's What the Airlines Never Tell You
Israel Past & Present
The New York Times' Guide to Unforgettable Weekends
Places Rated Almanac
Retirement Places Rated

Let Us Hear From You!

Dear Frommer's Reader,

You are our greatest resource in keeping our guides relevant, timely, and lively. We'd love to hear from you about your travel experiences—good or bad. Want to recommend a great restaurant or a hotel off the beaten path—or register a complaint? Any thoughts on how to improve the guide itself?

Please use this page to share your thoughts with me and mail it to the address below. Or if you like, send a FAX or e-mail me at frommersfeedback@hungryminds.com. And so that we can thank you—and keep you up on the latest developments in travel—we invite you to sign up for a free daily Frommer's e-mail travel update. Just write your e-mail address on the back of this page. Also, if you'd like to take a moment to answer a few questions about yourself to help us improve our guides, please complete the following quick survey. (We'll keep that information confidential.)

Thanks for your insights.

Yours sincerely,

Michael Spring

Michael Spring, *Publisher*

Name (Optional) _____

Address _____

_____

City _____ **State** _____ **ZIP** _____

Name of Frommer's Travel Guide _____

Comments _____

_____

_____

_____

_____

_____

_____

_____

_____

Age: ( )18-24; ( )25-39; ( )40-49; ( )50-55; ( )Over 55

Income: ( )Under $25,000; ( )$25,000-$50,000; ( )$50,000-$100,000; ( )Over $100,000

I am: ( )Single, never married; ( )Married, with children; ( )Married, without children; ( )Divorced; ( )Widowed

Number of people in my household: ( )1; ( )2; ( )3; ( )4; ( )5 or more

Number of people in my household under 18: ( )1; ( )2; ( )3; ( )4; ( )5 or more

I am ( )a student; ( )employed full-time; ( )employed part-time; ( )not employed at this time; ( )retired; ( )other

I took ( )0; ( )1; ( )2; ( )3; ( )4 or more leisure trips in the past 12 months

My last vacation was ( )a weekend; ( )1 week; ( )2 weeks; ( )3 or more weeks

My last vacation was to ( )the U.S.; ( )Canada; ( )Mexico; ( )Europe; ( )Asia; ( )South America; ( )Central America; ( )the Caribbean; ( )Africa; ( )Middle East; ( )Australia/New Zealand

( )I would; ( )would not buy a Frommer's Travel Guide for business travel

I access the Internet ( )at home; ( )at work; ( )both; ( )I do not use the Internet

I used the Internet to do research for my last trip. ( )Yes; ( )No

I used the Internet to book accommodations or air travel on my last trip. ( )Yes; ( )No

My favorite travel site is ( )frommers.com; ( )travelocity.com; ( )expedia.com;

other_____

I use Frommer's Travel Guides ( )always; ( )sometimes; ( )seldom

I usually buy ( )1; ( )2; ( )more than 2 guides when I travel

Other guides I use include _____

What's the most important thing we could do to improve Frommer's Travel Guides?

_____

_____

_____

_____

Yes, please send me a daily e-mail travel update. My e-mail address is

_____

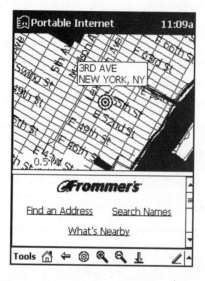